Painting the Mediterranean Phoenician

Worlds of the Ancient Near East and Mediterranean

Series editor: Diana V. Edelman, University of Oslo

Worlds of the Ancient Near East and Ancient Mediterranean brings alive the texts, archaeology and history of the cultures of the regions around the Mediterranean Sea and eastward to ancient Iran and Iraq, from the Neolithic through the Roman periods (ca 10,000 BCE–393 CE). Studies of one or more aspects of a single culture or of a subject across cultures in the regions outlined will form the foundation of this series, in which interdisciplinary approaches are encouraged. Studies can be based on texts, on material remains, or a combination of the two, where appropriate. In the case of a project that focuses on either the memory or the reception history of a place, person, myth, practice, or idea that arose or existed within the prescribed time, chapters that trace ongoing relevance to the present are welcome. The volumes are meant to be accessible to a wide audience interested in how the inhabitants of these parts of the world lived or how they understood their own pasts, presents, and futures, as well as how current scholars are understanding and recreating their pasts or their future aspirations.

Published titles

A History of Biblical Israel:
The Fate of the Tribes and Kingdoms from Merenptah to Bar Kochba
Axel Knauf and Philippe Guillaume

Ancient Cookware from the Levant: An Ethnoarchaeological Perspective
Gloria London

Josiah: From Improbable Stories to Inventive Historiography
Lowell K. Handy

Leadership, Social Memory and Judean Discourse in the 5th–2nd Centuries BCE
Edited by Diana V. Edelman and Ehud Ben Zvi

New Light on Canaanite-Phoenician Pottery
Dalit Regev

Forthcoming titles

Burial Practices in Ancient Israel and the Neighboring Cultures (c. 1500–330 BCE)
Jürg Hutzli and Stefan Münger

Recovering Women's Rituals in the Ancient Near East
Julye Bidmead

Painting the Mediterranean Phoenician

On Canaanite-Phoenician Trade-nets

Dalit Regev

equinox

SHEFFIELD UK BRISTOL CT

Published by Equinox Publishing Ltd.
UK: Office 415, The Workstation, 15 Paternoster Row, Sheffield, South Yorkshire S1 2BX
USA: ISD, 70 Enterprise Drive, Bristol, CT 06010

www.equinoxpub.com

First published 2021

British Library Cataloguing-in-Publication Data

A catalogue record for this book is available from the British Library.

ISBN-13 978 1 78179 825 6 (hardback)
978 1 78179 827 0 (ePDF)

Library of Congress Cataloging-in-Publication Data

Names: Regev, Dalit, 1959- author.
Title: Painting the Mediterranean Phoenician: on Canaanite-Phoenician trade-nets / Dalit Regev.
Description: Sheffield, South Yorkshire ; Bristol, CT: Equinox Publishing Ltd, 2021. | Series: Worlds of the ancient Near East and Mediterranean | Includes bibliographical references and index. | Summary: "This book focuses on the Canaanite-Phoenician economic systems that predominated in and determined Mediterranean history. Phoenician trade networks were sophisticated and elaborate operations that required a highly developed society and institutions in order to spread and be maintained. By tracking the manufacture, use, and shipment routes of Phoenician products, primarily those traded in amphorae and bottles but also fine-ware and their associated assemblages, a new map of Mediterranean connectivity and interrelations emerges, whose routes, operations and cultural affiliation lasted a long time. The Phoenician trade-nets are presented geographically, with special attention paid to the traceable product networks involving wine, salted fish, or perfumed oils"-- Provided by publisher.
Identifiers: LCCN 2020000613 (print) | LCCN 2020000614 (ebook) | ISBN 9781781798256 (hardback) | ISBN 9781781798270 (ebook)
Subjects: LCSH: Phoenicia--Commerce--History--To 1500. | Mediterranean Region--Commerce--History--To 1500. | Pottery, Phoenician.
Classification: LCC HF370 .R54 2020 (print) | LCC HF370 (ebook) | DDC 382.09394/4--dc23
LC record available at https://lccn.loc.gov/2020000613
LC ebook record available at https://lccn.loc.gov/2020000614

Maps by Don Shewan

Edited and typeset by Witchwood Production House Ltd, Sheffield

Contents

List of Maps

Abbreviations

Ad Rom.	Augustine, *Expositio of Epistulae ad Romanos*
Aen.	Virgil, Aeneid
AJ	Josephus, *Antiquitates Judaicae*
Anab.	Arrian, *Anabasis*
Arist. *Pol.*	Aristotle, *Politica*
Cic. Verr.	Cicero, *In Verrem*
CIS	*Corpus Inscriptionum Semiticarum*
CT	Cuneiform texts from Babylonian tablets in the British Museum (London 1896 ff.)
Diod. Sic.	Diodorus Siculus, *Bibliotheca historica*
EA	The el-Amarna Letters
FrGH	Felix Jacoby, *Die Fragmente der griechischen Historiker (Fragments of the Greek Historians)*
Hdt.	Herodotus, *The Histories*
IG	*Inscriptiones Graecae*
Il.	Homer, *Iliad*
Justin, *Apol.*	Justin Martyr, *Apologia*
KAH	O. Schroeder, *Keilschrifttexte aus Assur historischen Inhalts*, Zweites Heft. Wissenschaftliche Vëroffentlichung der Deutschen Orient-Gesellschaft, 37. Leipzig, 1922.
KAI	Herbert Donner and Wolfgang Roellig, *Kanaanäische und Aramäische Inschriften*. 2nd. rev. and enlarged ed. Wiesbaden: Harrassowitz, 2002.
KTU	Keilalphabetische Texte aus Ugarit
Mir. ausc.	*De mirabilibus auscultationibus*

Nin A	RINAP: Royal Inscriptions of the Neo-Assyrian Period: Nineveh A. Erle Leichty, *The Royal Inscriptions of Esarhaddon, King of Assyria (680–669 BC)*. The Royal Inscriptions of the Neo-Assyrian Period, 4. Winona Lake, IN: Eisenbrauns, 2011.
Od.	Homer, *Odyssey*
P.Cair.Zen.	*Zenon Papyri, Catalogue général des antiquités égyptiennes du Musée du Caire*
P.Col.	*Columbia Papyri*
P.Ebers	*Papyrus Ebers*
P.Heid.	*Veröffentlichungen aus der Heidelberger Papyrussammlung*
P.Lond.	Greek Papyri in the British Museum, London
P.Mich.Zen	*Michigan Papyri*. I. *Zenon Papyri*
P.Vindob.	*Papyrus Vindobonensis Graecus*
Pl. *Resp.*	Plato, *Respublica*
Plin. *HN*	Pliny, *Naturalis historia*
Plut.	Plutarch
Vit. Tim.	*Vitae Parallelae: Timoleon*
Vit. Sol.	*Vitae Parallelae: Solon*
Vit. Alex.	*Vitae Parallelae: Alexander*
PRU	*Le Palais Royal d'Ugarit*
RS	The Ras-Samara texts (*Ugaritica* V, 1968)
Strab.	Strabo, *Geography/Geographica*
Theophr. *Hist. pl.*	Theophrastus, *Historia plantarum*
Thuc.	Thucydides
Urk 4	Kurt Sethe and Wolfgang Helck, *Urkunden der 18. Dynastie*. Urkunden des ägyptischen Altertums, 4. Leipzig: J. C. Hinrichs, 1905–09.
Xen.	Xenophon
An.	*Anabasis*
Hell.	*Hellenica*

Preface

This book is the second monograph of my studies of Phoenician culture, following *New Light on Canaanite-Phoenician Pottery*, published earlier this year. The two books were initially conceived as a single manuscript covering pottery and trade, but following the sound advice of the editor and the publisher, it was decided to separate the text into two books, with cross-references between them.

The pottery book focused on certain groups more than on others, and, similarly, this study is not intended to provide comprehensive coverage of all the Canaanite-Phoenician trade networks. Its aim rather is to present an interpretative scheme and to suggest a blueprint for the mechanism behind them. This will be accomplished by focusing on the merchandise contained in pottery vessels, as these are the easiest to track.

As it is, such a study represents a huge endeavor. The publications released in this burgeoning field are ever growing in number, and many, especially from Spain, Portugal, Italy, and North Africa, are not easily available, having limited distribution and accessibility. It is mainly through the generous help of many colleagues and the wonderful libraries of DAI Madrid, UCL Library of the Archaeology Institute, the Royal Botanic Gardens Kew, and Casa de Velasquez in Madrid that I was able to access many of these publications.

In order to maintain a focus and not stray from the main issue, there are many important subjects touched on only briefly in this study. Issues from maritime routes and wind patterns, fish spawning, farming and migration, coins and inscriptions to deities and the *Tophet* are all addressed in a rich corpus of research, publications, and debates. I am making no claim to present all available studies and opinions on such matters.

The completed manuscript of this book was delivered to Equinox Publishing in September 2019; I have been able to include some, but only a partial amount, of research published between that date and September 2020.

Dalit Regev
Jerusalem, September 23, 2020

Introduction

Regardless of who ruled the waves, the Mediterranean maintained a basic commercial unity, as argued by the French historian Ferdinand Braudel. Yet this same inner sea was indisputably divided into regions, stimulating the foundations of enduring exchange networks (Abulafia 2005: 67–8; Broodbank 2013). Much of the research related to Canaanite-Phoenicians has revolved around seafaring, harbors, shipbuilding, and other marine aspects (Raban 1997, 2000, 2009; Marriner 2009; Brody 2002: 76). Unlike in other ancient societies, Phoenician wealth was not acquired by means of political and military power but rather relied on commercial shipment and cultural mediation among all parts of the Mediterranean and even beyond. Phoenician traders also sailed the Atlantic and Indian Oceans and, according to Herodotus (4.42), even circumnavigated Africa around 600 BCE. Maritime enterprise, therefore, was central to Phoenician existence.

While long-distance sailing routes in the Mediterranean operated mainly during the spring and summer months, usually from March to October, short-sailing routes, like those between Cyprus, the Eastern Aegean, southern Asia Minor, and the Levant, operated year-round (Morley 2007: 28; Lowe 2016: 215–16). These known sea-trade patterns, dictated by the environment, induced long periods of Phoenician stopovers in what were, initially, foreign lands. These stoppage periods were long enough to allow inland investigation of these new regions and the establishment of personal, cultural, and institutional connections between the indigenous population and the Phoenician traders. The spread of Phoenician trade and influence was, therefore, a matter of *longue durée*, a developing ongoing affair, and hence a durable phenomenon.

Nothing perhaps summarizes better the influence of Phoenician economy and culture in the Mediterranean than what was said years ago by Sherratt and Sherratt:

> In 1000 BC most of the Mediterranean was effectively prehistoric; by 500 BC it formed a series of well differentiated zones within a world system. The transformation did not take place by passive diffusion of "civilization," but by active intervention and response. Local maritime exchange cycles and routes of long-distance trade were already in existence, and the centers of futures growth were already evident; but what articulated them into a single interacting system was the input of capital from the East. Large

> sailing vessels, and the economic organization which made them possible, drew together the fortune of communities throughout the Mediterranean. This maritime expertise and capital concentration came initially from Phoenicia, and Phoenician vessels were probably the largest ships plying Mediterranean routes until the later Seventh century. Phoenicia was also characterized by other features of advanced urban economies: the use of silver as a medium of exchange, slavery and the labor-intensive manufacture of textiles and perfumes. The Phoenician trading diaspora created contacts with societies at very different levels of social and economic organization; temples and sanctuaries formed important meeting points between the different economic system of Phoenician and indigenous groups. (Sherratt and Sherratt 1993: 374–5, fig.1a–d).

Thus, by the 7th century BCE at the latest, a complex structure of Phoenician presence in the Mediterranean created commercial networks based on the common language, religion, and origin of the Phoenicians and operated as long as these bonds were strong and alive, occasionally breaking down due to regional political changes. Phoenician trade contacts with polities and trade ports outside the Levant started in the Bronze Age, but permanent Phoenician settlements were created later, in the 10th century BCE, in Cyprus, Iberia, and Carthage. However, this shift from trade contact to permanent residency was not linear. Both phenomena coexisted during the Iron Age, as demonstrated by evidence of individual finds from Cilicia, the Gulf of Alexandretta, Neo-Assyrian palaces and fortresses, as well as Greek and Italian sites (Aubet 1993: 57–62).

It has been argued that the driving force behind the Canaanite-Phoenician expansion to the west in the 8th–7th centuries BCE is the Assyrian demand for metals, mainly silver, and the heavy taxation imposed on the Phoenician cities by the Assyrians, who controlled Phoenicia from the mid-9th to late 7th centuries BCE (Beitzel 2010: 51; Fales 2017: 236). This view entails the assumption that the wealth accumulated by the Canaanite-Phoenicians around the Mediterranean was brought to the east and kept in their city-states. However, some part of this wealth was sent eastwards as tributes and taxes, first to Assyria, then to Babylon and Persia. Furthermore, this point of view neglects two main points. The first is the fact that Canaanite-Phoenician trade had already reached the central Mediterranean on one side and Mesopotamia on the other by the Late Bronze Age. The Iron Age trade followed routes established long before. It is therefore not a new venture and associated expansion but, rather, a continuous trade that slowly evolved and entailed more and more areas to the west. It was a process initiated by the Canaanite-Phoenicians themselves rather than a reaction to an outside pressure or demand (Niemeyer 2006; Fales 2017: 272).

Notwithstanding this, the second overlooked point is the magnitude of the Assyrian pressure, destruction, and control over the Canaanite-Phoenician cities and their revenues, as reflected in the Assyrian texts (Fales 2017). Throughout the Assyrian period, the kings of the Canaanite-Phoenician cities were forced to pay tribute to Assyria in precious metals, luxury items including dyed cloths, and timber. The latter was the main product transferred eastward, as indicated in the Assyrian texts, but which has left no traces in the archaeological record. In addition, starting in the time of Tiglath-pileser III (745–727 BCE), the Assyrians positioned tax-collectors on the quays of the Phoenician harbors to take their pick of the imported merchandise before it even reached local Phoenician hands. This, of course, bred resentment, and we hear again and again of how Phoenicians refused to allow the Assyrian tax-collectors to take goods off the boats, and the retaliation of the Assyrian kings against the Phoenician kings on such occasions (Luukko 2012: letter 12; Grayson and Novotny 2012: 4, 33–4; Fales 2017).

Such Assyrian oppression could not have resulted in goodwill on the part of the Phoenician city-states and would not have encouraged long-distance adventurous and perilous endeavors. The Assyrian oppression stimulated the Phoenician city-states to look for a solution that would both allow them to pay tribute to Assyria and thus retain, to some extent at least, their cities and territory, and also to trade freely and accumulate wealth away from Assyrian hands and use it for their own objectives. This solution meant walking a thin line between local hegemony and being subject to the foreign power. The strategy used by the Phoenician kings was the dispersion of wealth, hiding a significant quantity of their trade revenues by offshoring the profits to their new posts in North Africa, Iberia, and the Central Mediterranean. These offshore tax havens were probably manned by members of the royal families and their court.

The entire enterprise was no doubt coordinated by the Phoenician courts: when their kings were dethroned and their city-states conquered in the 6th century BCE (a process that started between 586 and 573 BCE when Nebuchadnezzar II of Babylon besieged Tyre, and ended with the Persian conquest in 539 BCE by Cyrus the Great), the entire Mediterranean trade suffered a depression. Phoenician trade activity was to be partly renewed only in the late 6th–early 5th centuries when Carthage, the Phoenician center in the west, took control over the western trade network. Trade was still also conducted institutionally from the ancient Levantine centers, but by the city councils and on a smaller scale, mainly in the eastern Mediterranean. The cooperation between the eastern and western Canaanite-Phoenician populations continued into the Hellenistic and Roman period, culturally and commercially. The Phoenician diaspora network was stable and operating from the early 1st millennium BCE onward, as will be described in Chapter 2.

Although Phoenician traders are often assumed to have had political control over the ports of trade to which they exported, the reality was more complex and dynamic. In fact, Phoenician trade also occurred in ports where such control was far less visible. Phoenicians traded at all three types of ports of trade identified by Luke, which have been differentiated by the identity of those who held the port's political control (Luke 2003: 1–10). Luke Type A, where control was placed in the hands of the local authority, was probably represented in the Phoenician activity at Pithecusae, in the Red Sea, ports in the Persian Gulf, and India, as well as the Phoenician enclave at Naukratis. Al Mina may also fall into this category. Here, Phoenician imports were restricted to trading with the local elite. Phoenicians also traded with Luke Type B: free ports controlled by traders of various origins, such as Delos and Corinth. Finally, Phoenician traders were also active in Luke Type C ports which they themselves had founded, like Carthage, Kition, Kommos, and Iberian and North African ports.

Phoenician presence around the Mediterranean is revealed by Phoenician finds. This should not be understood as a simplistic equation between pots and people. The term "Phoenician finds" here in its broadest sense means a corpus of finds associated with Phoenician culture or trade and found in Phoenician trading posts. This is not limited to pottery but includes Aegyptiaca, sometimes also Sardinian swords, and Cypriot and Greek pottery. The importance of corpora of finds typical to Phoenician sites is emphasized in contrast to a single find, in the quest to understand the nature of Phoenician culture and way of life (Niemeier 2005: 9). The ethnic identity attached to these objects is multifaceted, carrying traceable and often ceremonial importance. Phoenician objects are agents of social contacts that reveal some of the untraceable Phoenician activities in the communities at their ports of trade (Steadman and Ross 2010).

Examples of corpora of objects from Phoenician ports of trade of all three types described above are examined in this book. These examples and the enhanced data perceptible from corpora will be used to demonstrate and establish the existence, complexity, and span of Phoenician trade-nets. The data gathered from Phoenician corpora also indicate that the Canaanite-Phoenicians acted as the initiators of extensive economic and conceptual changes that came about in the Mediterranean, starting in the 2nd millennium BCE. Nonetheless, it should be stressed that, although Phoenician corpora are similar at various nodes along their trade-nets, each Mediterranean society recontextualized foreign cultural forms into its social and religious discourse in a different manner (Maran 2011: 65*). Thus, although the source of influence may have been the same, it triggered distinctive local forms that differed from the foreign culture that had stimulated these forms. Canaanite-Phoenician corpora in the West, therefore, include, in addition to certain Canaanite-Phoenician pottery forms and goods, certain groups of imported goods from Egypt, Cyprus, and Greece. It also includes local forms produced as a result of interaction between Canaanite-Phoenician agents and local cultures.

Phoenician presence around the Mediterranean is visible not only through the items carried by the commercial networks; there are also architectural elements like temples, tombs, and harbor constructions, as well as cult-related objects like masks, figurines, and burial *cippi*. In addition, abundant epigraphical evidence exists about stelae, architectural elements, and vessels. Much of this relates to the general presence of Phoenicians around the Mediterranean but not necessarily to Phoenician commercial networks. Finally, shipwrecks with Phoenician finds provide crucial evidence in tracing Phoenician trade routes. In this study I will endeavor to present examples drawn from as many of these types of material remains as possible from a large number of sites around the Mediterranean and the Near East.

Considerable space is given in this book to Greek finds in Mediterranean sites, reinterpreting these objects within a Canaanite-Phoenician framework. The underlying rationale behind this is that the present book sets out to challenge the Classical paradigm of a Mediterranean small Greek world. It proposes a different narrative—a chronicle that paints the Mediterranean Phoenician.

—1—

The Canaanite-Phoenician Continuum

Many names for the Phoenician territory and people are used in research: Canaan/Canaanites, Phoenicia/Phoenicians, Proto-Phoenicians, Punes, Tyrians, and Sidonians. The various definitions and interpretations of these names reflect the variegated and complex identity of the ancient group of people we call Phoenicians. Although almost every book dealing with some aspect of Phoenician culture addresses their origin, name, and identity, no definitive answers have as yet been arrived at (Broodbank 2013: 484–5), and even the very existence of the Phoenicians as an entity has been debated (Quinn 2017; Frendo 2018a). It is worthwhile, therefore, to present the evidence supporting the actual existence of the Canaanite-Phoenician entity.

I. The Names and Territory of the Phoenician People

At the heart of the various terms used to refer to Phoenicians lies a correlation between the terms "Canaanites" and "Phoenicians," which emphasizes the continuity of an influential Levantine culture and its enduring impact on the Greek world, the Mediterranean, and beyond. The composite concept, "Canaanite-Phoenician," allows phases in Phoenician history to be placed along a single continuous line of development, with the different names that outsiders had for this group, as well as the labels they used themselves, positioned relationally and chronologically (Aubet 2001: 11–12; Frendo 2018b).

In earlier scholarship, it was commonly believed that the Phoenicians had been a new cultural component that had appeared in the northern Levant as a defined entity during the late 12th–early 11th centuries BCE. This century remains well known as a period of turmoil, a breaking point in Near Eastern history when the great powers fell, some permanently (Hatti as one unit, although it continued in several Syro-Hittite kingdoms) and some temporarily (Egypt). The former understanding had been that outside, smaller, ethnic-political groups, like the Israelites, Phoenicians, and Philistines, had entered the power vacuum resulting from the fall of the great powers (Albright 1949: 109; Culican 1966; Röllig 1995: 348). Currently, the consensus is that the Phoenicians were not immigrants to the coast at the end of the Late Bronze Age but, rather, one group of indigenous Canaanites (Bikai 1990: 67–75; Morris 1992b; Aubet 1993; Herzog 1997; Garbini 2003: 18).

Recent research in ancient DNA shows a strong connection between Phoenician populations and indigenous Canaanites in the Late Bronze Age (Haber *et al.* 2017a; Agranat-Tamir *et al.* 2020). Indeed, only a small fraction of Phoenician ancestry appears to come from external sources outside the "Canaanite gene pool." These studies also show striking continuity in the ancestry of local populations from the Late Bronze Age until the present day, suggesting that population movement, which is known to be prevalent in the Levant, had limited influence on the ancestry of local populations.

The debate on the Canaanite-Phoenician continuum, which is now starting to be addressed by ancient DNA studies too, is reflected in the names by which Canaanite-Phoenicians have been identified. In research of the Bronze Age, the Phoenicians are identified as Canaanites; in research of the Iron Age they are referred to as Phoenicians; while in the research of the Persian/Classical period, they are identified as Phoenicians and Carthaginians. Later, during the Hellenistic period and beyond, they appear as Sidonians, Tyrians, Arwadians, and Beirutians, as in the Greek, Phoenician, Aramaean, and bilingual inscriptions around the Mediterranean. These labels were used by both insiders and outsiders in the Hellenistic period (Gibson 1982; Krings 1995: 19–30, 57–63; Masson and Sznycer 1992; Rey-Coquais 2000; La'da 2002). The Carthaginians also called themselves Canaanites in inscriptions of the Hellenistic and Roman periods.

The term *Poenus* is the Roman equivalent of the Greek term "Phoenician" and was applied by Roman authors to all Phoenicians, those of the west in Carthage and those of the east in the Levant. It was only in the 1st century CE that the term *Poeni* came to be restricted to the Carthaginians, i.e. the Phoenicians of the western Mediterranean. Thus, both *poeni* ("Punes") and Carthaginians are synonymous with Phoenicians. Modern scholars have artificially separated the former two from the latter, both geographically and chronologically, creating unnecessary confusion (Lund 1988: 46: Frendo 1993; Aubet 2001: 12–13).

Consequently, although the ethnic labels appearing in literary sources seem to vary—namely, Canaanites, Phoenicians, Punes/Carthaginians—these ethnic labels, in fact, mark one ethnic group calling itself Canaanite. From an internal Canaanite-Phoenician point of view, there was no change in the name of the group. Although it evolved over time, as all groups do, the continuity and endurance of Canaanite-Phoenicians for millennia is demonstrated by their material culture, language, religion, and trade networks. We now know that Phoenicians considered themselves to be Canaanites and applied this designation to themselves. They were one indigenous segment of Bronze Age Canaanite culture which, unlike some other segments, managed to endure and maintain its identity at least until the late Roman period (Katzenstein 1991: 187–91; Herzog 1997: 36; Keel and Uehlinger 1998; Lehmann 2001: 66, 89–90).

II. Canaan and Phoenicia

The Origin and Meaning of the Terms "Canaan" and "Canaanites"

The earliest reference to Canaan as a geographical area occurs in the texts from Ebla dated ca. 2500–2250 BCE, while the first mention of Canaanites, the inhabitants of Canaan, is found in the Mari letters of the 18th century BCE. Other occurrences of either term are in tablets from Alalakh in the 15th century BCE, in the annals of Amenhotep II from the late 15th century BCE, in the Amarna letters from the 14th century BCE, in Ugaritic texts from the 13th century BCE, as well as in other Egyptian and Hittite texts of the Late Bronze period (Paraskevaidou 1991: 526; Nibbi 1991: 169–78; Lipiński 1992: 87; Krings 1995: 39–63; Koehler *et al.* 1994–2000: כנען; Aubet 2001: 9–11).

Two views have been proposed concerning the origin and meaning of the term "Canaan." The first is that it was a geographical indicator. The Bible describes Canaan in geographical terms: the land of Canaan, a coastal region inhabited by Canaanites (Josh 5:1; Zeph 2:5). The evidence revealed from reliefs, papyri, and stelae shows that Canaan included the entire eastern coast of the Mediterranean, as well as the Egyptian Delta and its coast in some periods (Na'aman 1994, 1999). In the opinion of most, it was the people who gave their name to the region and not vice versa, as some have claimed. In either case, according to this understanding, Canaan was the homeland of the Canaanites.

The second view sees the term "Canaan" as an indicator of a specific type of urban, commercial settlement in the Levant in the 2nd millennium BCE (Na'aman 1982: 131–2). Canaan was indeed characterized by a political organization based on city-states before the Iron I period. The city-state organization contrasted with the contemporaneous organization of the major polities surrounding Canaan as territorial states and empires, Egypt, Hatti, and Mesopotamia, and differentiated Canaan from its neighbors. Yet, as seen above, the name "Canaan(ite)" is well attested in epigraphic sources from the mid-late 3rd and early 2nd millennium BCE, where it does not describe a political system but, rather, a geographical area and its inhabitants. If Canaan had been used as a commercial-political descriptive label at one time, it would have to have been quite early. Already by the 2nd millennium BCE, and probably even earlier, the name was being used as a geographical label (Smith 1986: 41, 45).

Another much-debated issue relates to the geographical extent of the territory of Phoenicia in the homeland in the eastern Mediterranean. In earlier scholarship, the extent was limited to modern-day Lebanon and sometimes extended south to include the northern coast of Israel at Akko. However, Phoenicia is now considered to be synonymous with the term "Levant," encompassing the entire coast of the eastern Mediterranean and some adjacent hinterland, the area reaching from Alexandretta Bay (or perhaps even from Tarsus) in the north to Rhinokorura (El-'Arish) at the border of Egypt in the south. Thus, Canaan and Phoenicia overlap territorially to a large degree (Lipiński 1992: 349–50, fig. 269).

That being said, the Levant is not one homogeneous area. The northern part stretches from Alexandretta Bay (currently in Turkey) to Rass Chekka (in northern Lebanon); the central Levant stretches from there to Rass Naqura (the current border between Lebanon and Israel); and the southern Levant from Rass Naqura to the Nile Delta. These are only the coastlines; the eastern borders of these areas are not as recognizable, but an extended account comprise Syria, Jordan, and for some periods also Egypt and Cyprus. Each of these areas was also divided into sub-regions (Fales 2017: 184–6, fig. 1; Núñez

2018: 118–19, fig. 1). The general lines of historical developments and events were usually common to all its parts, as were religious and cultural beliefs and cult. There was a difference, however, between the three geographical parts of the Levant that were under Canaanite-Phoenician cultural dominance. Not all the Canaanite-Phoenician cities along the Levantine coast always used an identical style, nor did they produce the same products or engage in the same agricultural or industrial activities. In addition, differences arose from regional interaction with neighbors in a specific zone and the different treatment of these areas by various imperial regimes. These differences were often reflected in subtle variances in the material culture.

These two very different views of the conceptualization of "Canaan" demonstrate the problematic nature of this term, the parameters and contents of which are debated. In this book, "Canaan"is used as a geographical term, covering modern Syria, Lebanon, Israel, Jordan, and probably also, at some point, the Egyptian Delta. The northern, southern, and western boundaries of the term are more or less clear, but its eastern boundary is harder to determine. While the Bible limits Canaan geographically to the western side of the Jordan River, DNA studies have shown that, during the Iron Age, the same population group inhabited both the western and the eastern side of the Jordan River, including the Rift Valley and the Jordanian Highlands (Haber *et al.* 2017b). For this reason, Jordan is included within the boundaries of Canaan in this study, although it may have been designated an independent geographical or socio-political region or sub-region by outsiders, contemporaneous with the Phoenicians. In Egyptian texts of the New Kingdom, for example, it is part of the land of the Shasu ("wanderers," perhaps) which extended into Syria (Papyrus Anastasi VI) (Ward 1972; Levy 2009). This is the land of Arab tribes that apparently participated in the Canaanite-Phoenician trade network going east to Arabia and India.

The Origin and Meaning of the Term "Phoenicia/Phoenician"

The origin and meaning of the term "Phoenician" have been widely investigated. The term "Phoenician" as a group marker is better known from 1st-millennium-BCE Greek sources, but the etymological origin of the word is much earlier, in ancient Egyptian hieroglyphs, where the term *fnhw* (plural) is an ethnic marker. Egyptologists have equated the Middle Egyptian word *fnhw* (Fenkhou) with "Syrians" or "Syrian people." The term is written with the classifier for a foreign people with a god of their own. *Fnhw* is the Egyptian word for either a carpenter or a shipbuilder, the Phoenician occupation that became their ethnic label.[1] It has been suggested that the occupational term came to be applied more generally in Egyptian usage to the homeland from where these shipbuilding carpenters originated and the people who inhabited it more generally: Phoenicia/Phoenicians. Phonetically, *fnhw* may correlate with Phoenicians (Green 1983; Ahrens 2015: 353–4; Ercolani 2015: 4).

The first known appearance of the Egyptian term *fnhw* to refer to people from Syria-Palestine dates from the 5th Dynasty (ca. 2400 BCE) in the Old Kingdom period. It presumably continued in use in the Middle Kingdom (ca. 2050–1710 BCE), in the Story of Sinuhe (B 219–21) from the 20th century BCE, and turns up again in text from the 18th Dynasty (ca. 1550–1292 BCE) (*Urk* 4.25.12) (Lipiński 1992: 170, 348; Green 1983: 39–43; Weinstein 1981: 6). It then resurfaces as an archaism to designate the land of Phoenicia or Canaan in a trilingual decree for Ptolemy IV (reigned 221–204 BCE) written in Greek (as Phoenician), Egyptian (as *fnhw*) and Demotic (as Kherou) (Bonadies and Marti 2019: 21).

In the Egyptian sources of the Hellenistic period, *fnhw* territory is described as starting at the eastern Delta border and stretching along the Levantine coast and inland between the Orontes and the Euphrates. The inclusion of coastal and inland geographical territory in the term *fnhw* correlates with the subdivision of this larger land unit into two administrative districts by the Ptolemies: coastal Phoenicia and Koile-Phoenicia. The territorial evidence alone, therefore, seems to support the ongoing connection between Phoenicia and *fnhw* territories and between Phoenicians and *fnhw* people. In addition, ritual texts from the Ptolemaic temple at Edfu correlate the terms Phoenicia and *fnhw* and show clearly that for the Egyptians, at least from the mid-2nd to the late 1st millennia BCE, Phoenicia and the Phoenicians were known as *Fenkhu* (Wilson and Gilbert 2007: 261). The likelihood of an Egyptian origin of the term "Phoenicia" or "Phoenicians" is in line with a coherent Egyptian-Canaanite connection commencing in the Old Kingdom period of the Early Bronze Age.

Classicists, on the other hand, have attributed the first use of the term "Phoenician" to the ancient Greeks. Its exact meaning and derivation, though, remain a matter of considerable debate. Most of these scholars rely exclusively on Greek sources in their work. Their etymological interpretations are often forced and unconvincing, however. Four explanations will be discussed.

Two proposals trace the origin of the name to Greek *phoenix*, meaning "red." The first links it with the alleged color of the famous Phoenician dyed cloth (Harden 1962: 21–2; Moscati 1968: 3; Van den Broek 1972; Nibbi 1991; Paraskevaidou 1991; Krings 1995: 1; Markoe 2000b: 10; Aubet 2001: 6–7; Knapp 2001: 30). This suggestion, however, seems to ignore the fact that the color of the highly prized Phoenician dyed cloth was Tyrian purple, not red. A recent, comprehensive reading of Linear B texts has demonstrated that *phoenix*, i.e. *po-ni-ki-jo* = "red," was only one of four red color options used to describe red cloth. Furthermore, this particular red color was extracted from flowers in Crete, not from murex shells along the northern Levantine coast. *Po-ni-ki-jo*, therefore, is not an ethnic marker, nor a geographical indication (Nosch 2004: 36; Bourogiannis 2018: 45). Another known source of the color red was dye made from the eggs of the cochineal bug, which lived in certain oak trees in the Levant (Edelman 1991). Thus, according to new evidence, the color *phoenix* had nothing to do with the Phoenician production of dye from murex shells.

The second derivation from the color red links "Phoenician" with the legendary bird known as the Phoenix, with two proposed scenarios of origin. One explanation appeals once more to the Mycenaean Linear B term *po-ni-ke*, arguing it refers to "the Phoenician bird," or, alternatively, an aromatic herb or flavor or even red decorations. The other explanation sees the prototype of the Phoenix bird of myth to be the Egyptian *bnw* bird, which was associated with Ra and Osiris and represented the rebirth of the sun. The *bnw* was the great heron, of the genus Ardea. Probably pronounced *boine* in Egyptian, when assimilated into Greek, the initial "b" allegedly was replaced with "f," while the suffix *-ik*/*-ix* was added as the typical Greek way of expressing an ethnic name, yielding Greek *foi`nix*. Coincidentally, the suffix *-k* was also used in Greek to denote animals in general and birds in particular (Faulkner 1962: 82; Van den Broek 1972: 14–32, 51–66; Lloyd 1975: 317; Paraskevaidou 1991: 526; Wilson 1997: 316–17; Aubet 2001: 9; Pinch 2002: 117–18).

The proposed connection between the Phoenix bird and the Phoenicians is tenuous. Nevertheless, it is intriguing to note that, on so-called "Philistine" pottery that was produced in the late 12th to early 11th centuries BCE, which I have identified instead as Phoenician pottery (Regev 2020), the bird featured as a prominent motif and possible symbol. There may have been a meaningful connection between them, even if it is not possible to establish whether the stylized bird on the pottery is specifically a heron or a Phoenix.

A third proposed derivation for the term "Phoenician" is as an occupational category, with two variants. Many have understood it to designate a type of merchant engaged in trade by sea in the eastern Mediterranean which included foreign seafarers of different nations from the Levant and Cyprus. Some believe it was used to describe people instead engaged in piracy or itinerant craftsmanship (Sherratt and Sherratt 1991: 386; Morris 1992b: 103–4, 130).

Advocates of a final proposal have suggested that the term "Phoenician" was a literary trope coined by Homer to shed light on a certain aspect of Greek identity in the period of its formation from the 8th–6th centuries BCE. According to this view, "Phoenicians" were neither historic nor ethnographic entities but representations by the Greeks of what was both different and foreign, used to provide social and economic inspiration for their own identity (Winter 1995: 255–6, 259, 263; Hall 2002: 117–18).

Whether Homer's Phoenicians were a real people or an invented derogatory literary trope is irrelevant to their existence as an ethnic group. There is no doubt that Phoenicians were present and active as a major impetus in Mediterranean trade and culture prior to the period of the Homeric poems, as indicated in the Phoenician inscriptions that began to appear around the Mediterranean around 1100 BCE (Krings 1995: 19–30; Braudel 2002: 199, 206–7; Pisano and Travaglini 2003).

The attempt to derive the origin of the term "Phoenicia/Phoenician" from the Greek language rests upon two faulty assumptions. The first is that Greek sources provide the earliest evidence of the appearance of the term. The second is that Greek sources contain the most reliable information about Phoenician origins. Egyptian *fnhw* was in use centuries before the Mycenaean Linear B term *po-ni-ke*. *Po-ni-ke* likely derived from the Phoenician language, not from Greek or Egyptian. Several Semitic loan words have been identified in Mycenaean, especially items involved in trade (Ventris and Chadwick 1956: 91, 135–6; Van den Broek 1972: 64, 66). Perhaps it was the term used by Phoenician traders to distinguish the shade of red produced from Cretan flowers from three other shades of red among the cloth they transported and sold along their trade routes in the Late Bronze Age. If so, it tells us nothing about their own identity or place of origin.

Of the hypotheses discussed above, the suggestion that the name "Phoenician" comes from Egyptian roots seems the more likely one, based on the etymological analysis and the historical probability. Yet the question as to how and by whom this name was forwarded to the Greeks remains an enigma. It seems unlikely they learned it from the Phoenicians themselves, considering Phoenician sources never use this name as a self-descriptor. Logic points instead, then, to a direct connection between the Egyptians and the Greeks. However, the evidence presented in this study all serves to demonstrate how Egyptian objects were traded in the Mediterranean by Phoenicians; the Egyptians did not trade or travel in the Mediterranean Sea. Thus, the only remaining option would seem to be that Greek sea-traders picked it up directly while visiting Egyptian ports of trade.

Finally, it is apropos here to illustrate how old myths die hard, especially the late Greek one relating to Phoenician origins quoted by Classical authors. Ancient Greek and Latin traditions insist that the Phoenicians immigrated to the Levant from the Red Sea, probably during the Persian period, perhaps from the islands of Tilos and Arados in the Persian Gulf (Hdt. 1.1; 7.89; Strab. 1.2.35; 16.27; Plin. *HN* 4.36; Justin *Apol.* 18.3.2–4). Only one ancient source from the 5th century CE, Book 40 of the *Dionysiaca* of Nonnus of Panopolis, states that the Phoenicians were an indigenous Levantine people.

It is far more likely that Phoenicians colonized Tilos and Arados during the Persian period than that they originated from there, as Pliny claimed. The fact that, in the 5th century BCE, Dionysius of Miletus (*FrGH* 687.F4) called the Red Sea the Phoenician Sea indicates that the Phoenicians controlled the sea routes there in his day, not that this was the Phoenician homeland (Grainger 1991: 194; Macadam 1993: 337).

Greek authors often confused locations and peoples in the ancient East. Herodotus erroneously referred to Sennacherib as King of the Arabs and the Assyrians (2.141). For Greek and Latin authors, Arabia and Mesopotamia were not geographical units with known boundaries until the Roman period. For Herodotus (3.88), Arabia was the area between Syria and Egypt and a vague, non-ethnic label that indicated a desert with shepherds. Not only the land, but also the identity of its people remained obscure as late as the Roman period, as demonstrated by the ethnos *Arabes* in tax lists from Egypt. Only much later, at the beginning of the late 1st century BCE, did Roman historians like Diodorus (Diod. Sic. 3.43–5), Strabo (16.1.12; 16.4.2), and Pliny (*HN* 5.20; 6.31) start labeling the Arabian Peninsula as a distinct geographical unit (Donner 1986; Hanson 1992: 136–40; Briant 2002, 382–384).

III. Literary Evidence for the Canaanite-Phoenician Continuum

Literary evidence for continuity is found in texts dated to the Iron Age and later, where reference is made to Canaan and Canaanites. The literary evidence available for the Canaanite-Phoenician continuum includes data on population, as well as cities and other centers that survived through the Bronze Age and the Iron Age as one unit in terms of language, religion, and culture. This evidence mainly sheds light on the names used to describe the autochthonous people in the Levant during this time, but it may also provide information on the continuity of trade items in this area. Not all the literary sources are equally valuable as origins for concrete, accurate information. Greek and Latin sources are considered historical literature and, therefore, solid, while other sources, like the Bible, are considered religious literature that is not obligated to convey historical events accurately. The body of evidence present in the Greek and Latin sources is also much wider and covers a longer span of time than other literary corpora. It is therefore considered here at some length, although this evidence is the most remote, geographically and linguistically, from the Canaanite-Phoenicians about whom they write. A large volume of scholarship has been dedicated to the study of literary references to the Canaanites and the Phoenicians in ancient texts (see, for example, Lipiński 1991; Winter 1995; Rainey 1996; Cohen 2002; Fales 2017). This short review deals only with markers for Canaanite-Phoenician continuity.

The Bible

The Hebrew Bible/Old Testament mentions Tyrians, Sidonians, and Canaanites, but not Phoenicians. The people and the city of Tyre are found primarily in Ezekiel 26–28 and Isaiah 23 but also appear in some psalms, in Kings, and in other books of the Bible. Altogether, they are mentioned 42 times. Sidon and its inhabitants are mentioned mainly in Ezekiel 27–28, Isaiah 23, and Jeremiah 25. They appear 36 times in the Bible and are included among the sons of Canaan in Genesis 10:19 and are called Canaanites of the coastal region in Numbers 13:29 and Joshua 5:1. Canaanites are mentioned 70 times in the Bible. In Isaiah 23:8, Job 40:30, and Proverbs 31:24, they are merchants. There are also references to Phoenician place names, such as Arwad (Ezek 27: 8, 11; Gen 10: 18; 1 Chr 1:16), Sarepta (Tsarfat) (1 Kgs 17:9–10; Obad 20), and Byblos (Gebal) (Josh 13:5; Ezek 27:9; 1 Kgs 5:32). None of these references post-dates the Persian period. We can learn from these poetico-religious texts that the Canaanite-Phoenicians were well known to the Israelites, mainly in the contexts of trade and religion (Krings 1995: 2, 64–72; Koehler *et al.* 1994–2000: כנעני). The names "Sidonians" and "Canaanites" are interchangeable, and the first is included in the second.

Compared to the Phoenicians and their various names, Greece and the Greeks are mentioned only six times in the Hebrew Bible, Aram and Aramaeans over 130 times, Assyria and Assyrians over 150 times, Babylon and Babylonians close to 300 times, and Egypt and Egyptians (not including place and king names) over 700 times. Egypt, Babylon, Assyria, and Aram are mentioned mainly in contexts of war and conflict. By contrast, the Canaanite-Phoenicians appear in contexts of trade, skilled craftsmen, and royal intermarriages.

In the New Testament, the terms "Syro-Phoenician" and "Canaanite" are equated, demonstrating the ongoing Canaanite-Phoenician continuum in the Early Roman period. Both the gospels of Mark and Matthew contain the story of Jesus' meeting a gentile woman in Tyre, who asks him to cast the demon out of her young daughter. In Mark she is described as "a gentile, a Syro-Phoenician by birth" (7:26), whereas in Matthew she is called a "Canaanite" (15:22), and Jesus encounters her while visiting the district of Tyre and Sidon. Even if the terms used in Mark and Matthew to convey the origin of this non-Jewish woman are geographical, as was common in Roman times, and not ethnic labels, the interchange of Syro-Phoenician and Canaanite demonstrates a clear correlation existed between Canaan and Phoenicia in the mind of writers and their audiences in the 1st century CE.

The Assyrian Record

The Assyrian record includes official royal documents, letters, and administrative documents, where Canaanite-Phoenician territory, cities, and trade has been documented from the early 11th to the 6th centuries BCE. The period of Tiglath-pileser I (1114–1076) is considered by the Assyriologist Mario Fales as the end of the Late Bronze in Assyria, and a text from this period that mentions the coastal cities that paid tribute to the Assyrian king (A.0.87.3, 16–25) is in line with similar, later, lists of the 9th–7th centuries BCE. The sole difference between the lists is the importance of the cities; while Byblos was the first and most important in the earlier inscriptions, Tyre and Sidon were most important and first in the later lists. According to Fales, these texts point to the continuity of the relations between Assyria and the Canaanite-Phoenician city-states, as well as the continuity of the inhabitants of these cities (Grayson 1991: 37; Fales 2017: 218).

A designation of the early 11th century as Late Bronze Age is contested, as most Levantine chronologies consider this time as Iron I. However, whether we consider the period as Late Bronze or Iron Age, this phase is positioned between the Late Bronze Age and the pinnacle of the Iron Age, thus adding another layer to the Canaanite-Phoenician continuum.

Greek, Latin, and Later Authors

Greek and Latin texts refer to a limited range of issues when it comes to Phoenicians. Their history, religion, and society are briefly and indirectly mentioned, if commented on at all. The two main subjects mentioned are their trade activity and their origin. Based on the limited data, there is an ongoing debate in classical historiography about how the Greeks and Romans perceived the Phoenicians. Was it a realistic and accurate view or a biased and hostile one, as seems more convincing by the evidence (Mackie 1996: 6–10; Liverani 1998).

The Homeric poems refer to Phoenicians and Sidonians synonymously (*Od.* 13.272–87; 15.415–26; *Il.* 23.743–5). This same equation is found in later inscriptions from Delos and Athens. The image of the Phoenicians in the Homeric poems is detailed and defined: they are depicted as merchants and slave-dealers, travelers, skilled and shrewd people, and often as dishonest people (*Il.* 6.289–90; 23.743–4; *Od.* 4.614–19; 13.271–86; 14.285–300; 15.425) (Bohak 2008: 107–9, 123–8). In a similar vein, later Greek and Roman historical, literary, philosophical, and juristic texts refer to the Phoenicians using the same two terms: Phoenicians and Sidonians (Krings 1995: 73–83; Winter 1995: 247–71; Isaac 2004). This is likely due to the canonical status of Homer in Greek education and Greco-Roman literary tradition (Cancik 2003; Finkelberg 2003).

Homer's equating of Phoenicians and Sidonians is part of a larger trend reflected in texts dating from the Iron I period to the Early Roman period. Synonymy between Canaanites, Phoenicians, and Sidonians is also found on the stele of Tiglath-pileser I (1114–1076 BC, KAH II.68), in Josephus (*AJ* 11–12), and in the New Testament in Matthew 11:21–22, 15:21–22; Mark 3:8, 7:24–26, 31; Luke 4:26, 6:17, 10:13–14; AA 12:20, 21:3, 7; 27:3. It reflects Sidon's prominence as a commercial center in each of these periods.

Of all the foreigners mentioned in the *Iliad* and the *Odyssey*, only the Phoenicians are described in an ambiguous manner, although the Homeric epics are generally untouched with explicit bias against non-Greeks. The "Phoenician" is portrayed both with positive and negative qualities, creating a persona of a skilled and shrewd merchant and traveler who should be simultaneously respected and suspected (Drews 1973: 5; Morris and Papadopoulos 1998: 257; Hall 2002: 117–18).

The subsequent Greek view of the Phoenicians was certainly unfavorable. In Plato's *Republic* (435e–436a), Socrates characterized the Phoenicians and the Egyptians as lovers of money, as opposed to the Greeks, who were lovers of knowledge. This accords well with the general Greek contempt for traders, moneylenders, and bankers in literature. Nonetheless, the ancient Greeks and Romans also recognized the Phoenician contributions to human culture. They translated Phoenician writings into Greek and Latin and incorporated Phoenician and Punic terms into Greek and Latin technical texts. Based on the Homeric description of Phoenician artifacts, it has even been claimed that the Archaic Greeks admired and recognized their cultural debt to the East (Coleman 1997: 186, 193).

In other Greco-Roman literature, Tyrians usually appear as the agents that spread Phoenician culture around the Mediterranean. They are associated with navigation, the foundation of colonies, and the exploitation of silver, copper, and iron mines. The Tyrians were also known in antiquity for their deity Milqart and for a certain degree of confrontation with Greeks and Romans beginning in the 5th century BCE (Muhly 1970; Wathelet 1983; Krings 1995: 2–3; Winter 1995; Aubet 2001: 9, 31–60, 119–26).

By the Hellenistic period, the Tyrians' reputation as colonists, navigators, traders, and fearless warriors was well established, particularly among the Greeks, who conducted several battles against them in the late 6th–5th centuries BCE (Lancel 1995: 448). The people of the Hellenistic period were aware that the mighty Carthaginians were, in fact, Tyrians. Although Alexander destroyed Tyre at the end of the Persian period, it was soon rebuilt and gained political autonomy in the 2nd century BCE, just like other cities along the Phoenician coast. In fact, Tyre kept its strong position and image throughout most of the Hellenistic period.

Not only were the Tyrians commercial and political rivals of the Greeks, but, starting in the 3rd century BCE, they also became bitter rivals of the Romans. During a large part of the Hellenistic period, continuous wars and acts of hostility were waged between the Carthaginians (i.e. western Tyrian-Phoenicians) and the Romans. While the battle between these two giants for control over the Mediterranean continued until the fall of Carthage in 146 BCE, Greeks and other peoples living in this geopolitical zone were probably not eager to be caught between the two forces or be associated with one party out of fear of retaliation from the other.

During the entire 1st millennium BCE, the political situation and fate of Sidon and Tyre differed from one another. They were not destroyed by the same imperial forces at the same time. This may indicate that, along their history, Tyre and Sidon practiced different political and economic interests which affected their activity and public image (Regev forthcoming). It would account for the prominence of Sidon in Homer, when Sidon would have been the more powerful of the two, and the prominence of Tyre in the Hellenistic period, when Sidon had become eclipsed.

Nevertheless, a reversal of the fortunes and reputation of the two is evident once more during the Punic Wars (264–146 BCE). Carthage and, by extension, Tyre, became the direct enemy of Rome. As a result, individual or group association with Tyre was no longer desired and certainly would not have brought social or economic benefits. Admitting to Tyrian identity before the Greek authorities might have resulted in an accusation of being a potential collaborator with Rome's enemies. No doubt the association with Tyre/Carthage was also an obstruction to such people's trade with the growing Roman superpower. This would definitely increase after the destruction of Carthage in 146 BCE.

To be considered a Sidonian was another matter completely. On a few occasions, people living in the eastern Levantine cities of Marisa, Shechem, and perhaps also Yamnia, presented themselves to the Greek authorities as Sidonians. This differentiation between "good" and "bad" Phoenicians identified the Sidonians as fit for cooperation, although perhaps not for assimilation. Favors—economic or otherwise—were conferred in the Hellenistic world on those who tried or seemed to try to assimilate into the Greek way of life, not to those who differentiated themselves from it. Making a choice of aligning oneself with either the Tyrians or the Sidonians had, therefore, a significant and differentiating connotation during the Hellenistic period (Regev forthcoming).

For the Greeks, "Phoenician" was a general term that included all Levantines, whether they wrote in Phoenician or Aramaic script. For ancient Greek and Latin authors, the Carthaginians, also known as Punes, were Phoenicians, identical to their brothers from the Levant (Lund 1988: 46; Röllig 1992: 93). Such external evidence is certainly a further indication of the strong connections between all Phoenicians and their unshakable ethnic identity, at least until the Roman period. This ancient view contrasts with modern claims for the so-called Hellenization of the Phoenicians, assumed to have commenced by the end of the Classical/Persian period. The Phoenicians/Punes did not lose their identity, their solidarity, their culture, or their religion until the Roman period and the rise of Christianity and Islam.

Other literary sources confirm the biblical usage and demonstrate an equating of Phoenicians with Canaanites already in the late Hellenistic period as well as their continuation until the Late Roman/ Byzantine period. Bilingual Phoenician coins of the 2nd century BCE proclaim Beirut to be Laodicia, the metropolis of Phoenicia in Greek and the mother of Canaan in Phoenician script (Macadam 1993: 344). Then, in Punic inscriptions of the Roman and Late Roman periods, Punes refer to themselves as "Canaanites," and the early Church Father Augustinus of Hippo (*Expositio ad Rom.* 13) states that the Punic North Africans of his day, in the 5th century CE, still called themselves Canaanites.

Augustinus was the bishop of Hippo, which is Annaba, a former Phoenician port city about 300 km east of Carthage by land. Hippo/Annaba is therefore a likely place for the endurance of Canaanite identity and the continuous use of their language in its later west Mediterranean version or versions. The endurance of the language is evident in 3rd- and 4th-century-CE funerary inscriptions from Lepcis Magna, Sabratha, and in the Christian catacombs at Sirte in Libya. The Punic name of Sirte was Macomades, *maqom hadash* (Plin. *HN* 5.3), meaning "a new place," similar to the better-known Phoenician place names based on the phrase *Krt Hadeshet*, i.e. "new city," hence Carthage, Cartagena, etc. The inscriptions were written in Greek, Latin, and Punic. Even when written in Latin, however, the language is identified as Neo-Punic or Latino-Punic (Punic written in Latin), which indicates Canaanite/ Phoenician/Punic was still used in everyday life. With it, Canaanite identity endured (Jongeling and Kerr 2005: 1–9; Jongeling 2008: 13–40, 44–53; Kerr 2010, 211–16, 2018: 399–400).

A much later testimony comes, again, from Sirte. The Muslim Iberian geographer El-Bekri wrote in 1068 CE that the people of Sirte speak a language that is not Berber, Arabic, Persian, or Coptic, which is unknown to anyone but them. He then describes them as fierce merchants of dishonored character who make commercial decisions as a community. The city Sirte is described as surrounded by a wall and has a mosque, a hammam, and markets. It has three gates, including one that leads to the sea. They have palm trees, orchards, and sweet water wells. They have the best goat meat and would not eat any other meat (El-Bekri 1911–13: 18–19, 2003: 177–8).[2]

This text does not necessarily indicate that the people of Sirte were descendants of the earlier Phoenician community in this area, and certainly not that they have a self-identity as Canaanites. However, the combination of unknown language, the former Phoenician history of the local population, their occupation as merchants, and the description of the city with orchards and gardens (similar to Carthage) all hint at a continuous Canaanite-Phoenician identity at Sirte, at least until the 11th century CE.

The Phoenicians likely had their own ideological or religious reasons for calling themselves by the collective name "Canaanites," rather than using the name applied to them from outside: that is, "Phoenicians." The duality in which outsiders on the one hand, and members of the group on the other, designate the same group is not restricted to the Phoenicians. The Jews, for example, have called themselves in private and formal inscriptions and texts by the collective name "the people of Israel," from biblical times until the present. Other nations, however, seldom designated them in this way instead referring to them as "Jews" (i.e. "Judaeans"). It is not that Jews do not identify themselves with the ethnic label "Jews"; rather, they find it more appropriate to refer to themselves—in writing—as "the people of Israel," as is done in the Hebrew Bible, the Talmud, and the prayer book. It is highly unlikely that the correlation between Phoenicians and Canaanites was new in the Roman period and it is unlikely to represent a Phoenician-Christian desire for archaic biblical affiliation.

Evidently, the term "Canaanite" had been used continuously to describe the inhabitants of the Levant, though it may well be that the Canaanites of the Iron age did not occupy the exact same regions as the Canaanites of the Hellenistic and Roman periods. It seems that, in earlier times, the term "Canaanite" was more fluid and general, whereas during the Hellenistic and Roman periods it became more specific, describing mainly or exclusively the Phoenicians. Evidently, at least until the Roman period, the terms "Canaanite" and "Phoenician" described the same old Canaanite-Phoenician people.

IV. Cultural Evidence for the Continuity from Canaanite People to Phoenician People

A fundamental question is whether the *onomastica*, deities and their iconography, and script of the Phoenician towns reflect a direct continuity of Canaanite culture in the Levant from the Bronze to the Iron Age and later. If so, it would demonstrate that the Phoenicians were directly related to the autochthonous Canaanite inhabitants of the Levant and could not have been immigrants who arrived as a result of the political upheavals in the 12th century BCE, according to the now discredited theory (Åström 1992; Caubet 1992).

A large number of studies have provided arguments to support the view that the Phoenicians were the direct successors of the Bronze Age Canaanites (Harden 1962: 22; Moscati 1968: 4–5; Smith 1986: 99–100; London 1989: 45–51; Lipiński 1992: 87, 348–51; Morris 1992b: 125; Millard 2000: 77; Knapp 2001: 30; Braudel 2002: 96, 183, 185, 209; Frendo 2018b). The studies do not differentiate between the two cultures during the Iron Age I. There are great similarities in pottery, architecture, metal vessels, figurines, and religious symbols from the Late Bronze Age into the Iron Age.

Archaeological research in the Levant has demonstrated that the Canaanite culture of Byblos and Ugarit neither ceased nor changed during the last centuries of the 2nd millennium BCE, despite the destruction of both metropolises. The evidence is so compelling that the Canaanite polity of the 3rd–2nd millennia BCE has been identified as the "Paleo-Phoenician" period, followed by the archaic, classical, post-classical, and neo-classical Phoenician periods in the 1st millennium BCE (Gübel 2000: 185).

Evidence of this continuity also has been found in the traces of Hittite and Hurrian culture at Ugarit in the Late Bronze Age. When the city fell at the end of the 13th century BCE, these cultural influences were not extinguished. Examples of Hurrian names and Hittite cremation practices are found in subsequent Phoenician culture. The Phoenician cities that lay within the borders of 2nd-millennium Canaan adopted Ugaritic culture and continued its heritage (Craigie 1983; Röllig 1992: 94).

Already by the end of the 2nd millennium BCE, Phoenician culture was an amalgam of the Canaanite, Hittite, Mesopotamian, and Egyptian cultures, consolidated into the known Phoenician style that traveled throughout the Mediterranean in the 1st millennium BCE.

Examples of Phoenician cultural continuity are multifaceted: some rely on material evidence and some on epigraphic materials or religious symbols. One example is found at Phoenician Sarepta, where continuity in settlement is evident through 11 unbroken occupational strata from the Late Bronze Age into the Iron Age. Twenty pottery kilns have been excavated on site, dating from the Late Bronze Age until the Roman period (Kochavi 1992: 14). This continuity speaks for the preservation of local traditions and the cultural messages they entail. Other examples of continuity of material culture, especially of pottery, has been discussed in detail (Regev 2020).

Evidence of religious continuity is found, for example, in the iconographic presentation of Milqart, the protecting deity of Tyre. Although early representations are not certain, the conventional image of Milqart is a composition of Egyptian and Hittite symbolism, depicted as a male with loincloth and dome-shaped hat, a fenestrated ax on his left shoulder and what may be an ankh or a lotus flower in the right hand (Bonnet 2007). The fact that his image did not change from the Bronze Age to the Hellenistic period shows how deeply rooted his worship was in Phoenician culture at this site. Throughout 2000 years of political, social, and cultural changes, the city's main god remained one and the same. Milqart is not the only Canaanite-Phoenician deity whose worship and iconography remained the same for very long periods. The same happened with Baal, and particularly with the worship of Ashtart (Gübel 2000: 192; Van der Toorn, Becking, and Van Der Horst 1999: 109–14, 132–9, 563–5; Lipiński 1995: 79–90, 105–8, 115–16, 168–9, 243–64, 274–6, 306–9, 360–3).

It was not only the worship of deities that remained intact. Religious imagery that had originated much earlier in Canaanite and Phoenician culture also continued in use. Three examples include the lion of Ashtart, the bull, associated in texts with both Baal and El, and the smiting-god, associated by scholars with both Reshef and Baal. Phoenicians took these images with them all over the Mediterranean (Brody 1998: 18, 29–30, 56, 94; Keel and Uehlinger 1998: 22, 29, 37–9, 103, 118, 173; Wasmuth and Ögüt 2010: 569; Collins 2008: 174; Dothan and Regev 2011).

Epigraphic evidence points to both continuity and change. Despite a few onomastic elements that changed, Phoenician *onomastica* continued in an unbroken trajectory. In fact, the Phoenician script can be traced back directly to the Proto-Canaanite script of the 16th–14th centuries BCE (Röllig 1995: 348).

These are only a few examples of the scholarly data collected from many sub-fields of Phoenician culture. The ceramic evidence documents a recognizable Phoenician repertoire that spanned two millennia (Regev 2020). It provides yet another confirmation of the longevity of this culture from the Bronze Age to the end of the 1st millennium BCE, at the very least. The Phoenician cultural corpus continues to grow, providing additional proof of the Canaanite-Phoenician continuum.

The correlation between Canaan and Phoenicia is evident in bilingual coins minted in the 2nd century BCE in Beirut, reading in Phoenician script "Laodicea that is in Canaan," and, in the Greek script, "Laodicea that is in Phoenicia." Another correlation between the two names is found in a couple of Greek texts of the Late Roman period. Herodianus Grammaticus (7, 32) in the 2nd century CE and Stephanus of Byzantium (s.v. *Chna*) in the 6th century CE identified *Chna*, Canaan, as the ancient name of Phoenicia. This literary evidence shows not only that the name Canaan was still known in the Hellenistic and the Late Roman/Byzantine period, but also that it was known to overlap with Phoenicia (Drews 1973: 15–16).

Phoenicia preserved its ethnic and political identity throughout the late Roman and Byzantine Empires, until the Islamic conquest. From Pompey to Septimius Severus, Phoenicia belonged administratively to the province of Syria. A separate province, *Syria-Phoenicae*, was created ca. 194/5 CE and subdivided ca. 300 CE into western (*Phoenice*) and eastern (*Augusta Libanensis*) parts. A century later the province was re-divided into a coastal area, which became the province of *Phoenicia Paralia* (or *Maritima*), and the inland province named *Phoenicia Libanensis*. Finally, under the Umayyads all of Phoenicia was incorporated with southern Syria into *Jund Dimashq* (Macadam 1993: 335). The Islamic conquest ended the existence of a Phoenician homeland as well as the Phoenicians as a defined ethnic group with a common religion and language. When Phoenicia became Syria, the Canaanite-Phoenicians became Muslims and Christians, inhabitants of the Levant, North Africa, and the Iberian Peninsula. The fate of both the land and the people was one.

—2—

Trade and Diaspora Networks

How did the Phoenicians trade, carry, and distribute their products, items, and wares? To answer these questions, we need to dwell on the theoretical paradigms of long-distance trade and how such models conform to the Phoenician mode of operation. Theories based on modern global economic and political structures are not suitable for explaining the Phoenician phenomenon (Shipley 1993: 271–3).

Phoenician networks operated for very long periods, during which global circumstances changed. Hence, one encompassing global theory cannot describe the changes and periodic adaptations of the Phoenician trade networks into other global systems. Two broad and flexible frameworks are more suitable for understanding the enduring Phoenician long-distance trade: the network and the diaspora. Phoenicians began to operate elaborate and multiple networks in the Late Bronze Age which, by the Iron Age, became organized and based on diaspora networks.

These networks were initiated by the Phoenician institutions in the metropolises on the eastern Mediterranean coast, whose fortune and power were based on the wealth acquired by trade. The networks were operated by means of a diaspora. Agents were sent to establish trading stations, after which craftsmen and other professionals arrived, followed by an ongoing, steady flow of Phoenician immigrants who intermarried with local communities, producing new generations born far away from the homeland. The continuous operation of these networks clearly points to the fact that not only was Canaanite-Phoenician identity kept strong and vivid in these diasporic nodes of the network, but the connections between Phoenicians in all nodes of the networks were strong as well. Such a strong connection, over such a long time, can only be explained by a Phoenician self-image as one people, of one language, and one religion, albeit with various deities and regional affinities (Álvarez Martí-Aguilar 2018). This is the meaning of a diaspora: when those who live in the homeland and those scattered elsewhere share a single sense of identity, and maintain contact (Cohen 2008: 83; Boozer 2015: 3; Arnaud 2016).

The model of network and diaspora network as the best means to capture the essence of Phoenician trade and expansion in the Mediterranean has been generally accepted, although reservations are often made regarding the identity of the participants in this network, whether Canaanite-Phoenicians or an amalgam of many Mediterranean identities (Sommer 2007; Aranegui, López-Bertran, and Vives-Ferrándiz 2011: 317). Quite a few entities were no doubt involved in parts of the Phoenician networks, mainly on a regional scale, but the argument presented here advances the premise that the large networks of an international scale in the Mediterranean during the 1st millennium BCE are Canaanite-Phoenician by definition. The initiative, regulation, financial investments, control, and the overall coordination of these networks was in the hands of Canaanite-Phoenician officials and institutions. This assertion relies also on written evidence from the archives of Karum Kanesh which illustrate an tight Assyrian state control over a complex diaspora network in northern Syria and Anatolia in the 2nd millennium BCE (Allen 1992: 466–7; Larsen 2015: 150–1). The Canaanite trade circles in the 2nd millennium bordered those of the Assyrian and Babylonian diaspora networks. They learned and embedded this mode of operation into their own systems, which became manifest from the mid-2nd millennium BCE onward.

I. Trade Networks

Not all trade interactions are network-related. Trade is any exchange of goods and services between two parties, while a trade network involves a system that circulates the goods. Trade usually refers to local interactions, while trade network is usually employed to designate international systems. Both terms are used here to describe Canaanite-Phoenician operations, but while trade is used to represent the action, the trade network is used to describe the system.

The network framework has also been suggested as a replacement for the old and insufficient concept of colonialism, when it comes to Mediterranean mobility patterns in general, and in particular to the colonialism-as-foundation approach to Greek presence overseas (Donnellan 2016: 111). However, Greek colonialism was not based on trade, at least until the Hellenistic period, while the Canaanite-Phoenician dispersion was trade-related from its first day. These were not simple exchanges between point A and B but, rather, complicated systems that involved different functionaries from the headquarters to the many sites of production, storage, distribution, and consumption.

Trade and the Ancient Economy

Already in the Bronze Age, human societies were often in need of food and other goods not available in their habitational environment. In the 4th century BCE, both Plato (*Resp.* 2) and Aristotle (*Pol.* 7.6.1327a) stated that it is almost impossible to found a city-state (*polis*) in a place where it will not need imports (for the concept and definitions of *polis*, see Morgan 2003; Hansen and Nielsen 2004). Faced with several strategic options for obtaining supplies from other regions and countries, trade was the more efficient and regular strategy to acquire the necessary goods, in contrast to war and piracy, for example (Morley 2007: 18–19).

The meaning of trade, and whether such a term could be implied in ancient economic systems, is debated in the historiography of the ancient world. The two main debates are those known as the "formalist-substantivist" and the "primitivist-modernist." The differences between the debated models of a "primitivist" and a "substantivist" economy lie primarily in the identification of reciprocity, redistribution, and market exchange (Bedford 2007: 325; Manning 2011: 318; Knappett 2013: 6; de Blois and van der Spek 2019: 156–1). Yet evidence relating to such factors is difficult, if not impossible, to detect within ancient societies. One of the main issues behind the variant definitions is the measure of sophistication assumed for the trading culture, where the presence of professional traders is assumed to indicate a high degree of development in their society. Hence, those who are reluctant to believe in the sophistication of ancient societies, especially non-Greek ones, advocate the view that "primitivist" concepts need to be applied to the economic sector of such societies, especially those in the ancient Near East (Knapp 1993: 332–47; McGeough 2007: 8–37; Morley 2007: 10).

In spite of abundant evidence to the contrary, the "primitivist" concept claims there is no evidence of regional specialization in the ancient Mediterranean. It assumes that food was produced and consumed in the same locality and that only a small number of luxurious elite items were more widely distributed. This may be the case in Greek society, but it definitely was not characteristic of Canaanite-Phoenician society. A good example of the wide distribution of foodstuffs in the Canaanite-Phoenician economy is the industrial production and distribution of amphorae and their contents from the Late Bronze Age and onwards. Wine, in particular, was considered a matter of taste and prestige and was widely traded to all classes of society. In addition, the Canaanite-Phoenicians were famous for various specialized industries which included metal vessels, glass pendants and vessels, ivory items, and dyed cloth industries that fall under the category of "elite items" (Sherratt and Sherratt 1991: 364; King and Stager 2001: 146; Morley 2007: 20, 23).

Anther model used to describe the ancient economy is the "world-system theory," which divides countries (city-states, in terms of the Bronze Age), into core, semi-periphery, and periphery, based on the division of labor and capital (Wallerstein 1974; Allen 1992; Stein 1999). This model, too, assumes the superiority and the inferiority of certain parts of the ancient world, a division that is not valid for the Canaanite-Phoenician diaspora trade-net, which diffused both labor and capital.

However, the definition of trade developed by Nicholas David and Carol Kramer from the discipline of ethnology is broad enough to encompass all aspects of human transactions and so is preferred here. Their definition states that "exchange and trade distribute raw materials and artifacts across space, through a variety of physical and institutional mechanisms, and, as items move, information moves with them" (David and Kramer 2001: 360). Their working assumption is that both models, as well as mechanisms associated with trade and exchange, coexisted in developed societies like that of the Phoenicians. Anywhere and anytime, some circles of society may operate in a narrow, "primitivist," and "substantivist" manner, while other circles of the same society operate in a broad, "formalist" manner. Evidence for such a model of multiple exchange patterns was observed in the Ugaritic texts of the Late Bronze Age, which show involvement of the palace, its elite agents, and the temple in various trade and exchange mechanisms. This does not mean that ancient economies operated by the same mechanisms as modern economies or that the same fundamental moral and values were embedded in both ancient and modern economies (McGeough 2007: 337, 339–41).

In addition to the definition of trade proposed David and Kramer, I find complexity theory to be a useful tool to help conceptualize the Phoenician trade network over time. It perceives the economy, including networks, as a dynamic multisystem with different and contemporaneous systems working side by side. This ever-changing system is balanced ad hoc in different locations and different times. Although it denies an organizing source and understands the economy to be self-organized, which I believe is unlikely in ancient societies, this theory encompasses and best describes both the mechanism and character of the Phoenician trade-net, which is a multivariate system (McGeough 2007: 31–5, 351, fig. 9.1; Broodbank 2013: 20).

With its network-based model, complexity theory assumes the necessity of social union and connection between any two nodes in a given network. My approach to networks and their operation is similar; indeed, it will be suggested below that diaspora connections were the social bond that integrated Phoenician economic activities. However, while I accept the idea that networks provide the social framework for economic interaction, I dispute the larger principle within complexity theory that denies that one source can be the point of origin and authority within a given network, as will be demonstrated below by the example of the Mesopotamian diaspora network.

Phoenician Trade

An integral part of the definition of trade being used in this monograph is the "given" that overseas trade demands structures provided by institutions. In antiquity, the "state" would have supervised and regulated trade institutions, whether the originating polity was a city-state, a territorial state, or an empire. In the case of Phoenician states, the supervising institution would have been the palace, ruled by a king with absolute power within (although under Assyrian, then Babylonian, and then Persian demand and command), at least until the 6th century BCE. Control of the Phoenicians kings over seaborne expeditions, boats, and seamen is clear from the biblical evidence (1 Kgs 5:23; 9:26–28) and an Assyrian cuneiform tablet dated to 676 BCE (Parpola and Watanabe 1988: 5, i 1–3). Royal control of trade stations is also evident, for example in KAI 31, dated to the 8th century BCE from Cyprus, where a governor declares he is serving King Hiram, and an inscription on a 4th-century-BCE sarcophagus from Kition with a similar claim (Guzzo Amadasi and Karageorghis 1977: F6).

A council of elders and *suffets* also operated in the Phoenician cities. It may have represented the most powerful merchant families. Until the 6th century, this council only advised the king but did not make decisions. Such counselors are mentioned in the Amarna archive in the 14th century BCE (*EA* 138; 149), and a council of elders is mentioned in a 7th-century-BCE Assyrian text (Parpola and Watanabe 1988: 5, col. 3, l. 7). Thereafter, however, the power of the council and *suffets* seems to have grown and equaled that of the king from the 6th–3rd centuries BCE. Official trading partnerships (*marzihu* societies), the existence of which is mentioned in texts and inscriptions starting with the Late Bronze Age texts of Ugarit (RS 60), through the 11th-century story of Wenamun, to the Hellenistic and Roman period, like KAI 159, *IG* 2.2.141, and KAI 58, also played a role in overseas trade (Krahmalkov 2000: 175–6; Markoe 2000b: 26–8; Aubet 2001: 145–7; Pardee 2002: 220; Sass 2002; Morley 2007: 14, 77–8). After Alexander the Great, starting the 3rd century BCE, the Phoenician cities of the Levant were no longer ruled by kings, a change marked by a new era-counting and a different governmental system. The Zenon papyri indicate an *archon* in Sidon (P.Mich.Zen. 3), but this change does not suggest any lesser Phoenician institutional control over the old trade networks. Rather, Sidon was now controlled by an assembly, as was Carthage, until the Roman period. Evidence for this is found in a text from Puteoli in Naples Bay (*IG* 14.830) dating to the 2nd century CE which clearly reveals the authority of the assembly of the homeland, Sidon, over this trade station (Teixidor 1980; Ameling 1990: 192–3).

The operation of large-scale trade demanded, and spread, literacy. The Phoenician alphabet was forwarded to the Greeks and Etruscans through trade contracts and agreements. Large-scale, long-distance trade also required a system of payment, weights and measures, and legal procedures, which the state established and supervised. In the ancient Near East, from the late 4th and 3rd millennia BCE and onwards, at Uruk and Mesopotamia respectively, payment took the form of established values and equivalencies for commodities. The usual standard employed was based on silver equivalencies before the introduction of coinage, and metal coins were still weighed to establish their actual value once their use became widespread (Dercksen 2016; Krispijn 2016). A developed state was needed to initiate large-scale trade, which, in turn, led to the further development of state institutions that promoted procedures and systems. Already during the Late Bronze Age, the combination of palace and temple with industry and trade was typical of Levantine towns but not of towns in the Aegean sphere. This infrastructure remained the same during the 10th–8th centuries BCE, when Eastern supremacy in craftsmanship and trade over Greece is evident from archaeological remains (Sherratt and Sherratt 1991: 365; Morris 1992a: xiv; David and Kramer 2001: 360; Morley 2007: 77).

Due to a lack of written documentation about Phoenician statehood, it often has been argued that it never existed. It is more commonly assumed that Phoenician merchants operated as private agents and not on behalf of their city-state or in accordance with its interests and goals. As a result, the magnitude of Phoenician culture, its society, economy, and influence, has been substantially downplayed. It is argued more fully below in the subsection on diaspora networks that the Phoenician state, both the palace and temple, was the initiator and supervisor of Phoenician trade, while private and/or semi-private agents participated as financiers and operators of remote trading posts (Morley 2007: 73–6).

Texts from Ugarit indicate that the individual families involved in economic activity, as well as in international diplomatic activity, were members of the elite who cooperated closely with the palace. The same texts show that this activity was handled mainly by two families with palace connections and that involvement in international trade was very restricted, even among the elite. Moreover, trading activity not only was supervised by the palace but also required royal permission: in particular, for large-scale trade in the ports. In one text, merchants are described as working in the service of the king, i.e. as being employed by the king, acting as "business agents" on his behalf (McGeough 2007: 183–4, 204–7). Such business agents cannot be understood as private entrepreneurs who initiated long-distance trade or its networks; the palace initiated and operated all aspects of trade via its authorized agents. The texts from Ugarit and elsewhere personify the term "palace" and illustrate some aspects of the operational modes of the palace; they give no indication of the existence of any other authority beyond the palace. Temples were considered an extension of the palace, as can be seen in the texts and the archaeological records (Pardee 2000: 219; Teba, Theodossopoulos, and Crow 2016).

Canaanite-Phoenician overseas trade used several mechanisms to reduce the enormous risks involved in such operations. These included investors and financiers, described below, as well as associations of traders. Such associations were involved in financing and operating trade and insuring the individual merchant or lender from severe losses in the case of a shipwreck. While in Greek and

Roman societies, such organizations seem to have been uncommon, various inscriptions reveal that in Phoenician society such organizations were common (Morley 2007: 75). Particularly when located in a foreign land, Phoenician merchants often created a formal association or assembly, called a *mrzh* in Phoenician, which strengthened the affiliations within their trade diaspora and reinforced them with religious elements.

As we can see, Phoenician trade was a sophisticated operation which involved institutions, an advanced system of payment, and a social and religious organization that was unique to Phoenician society. In this nation of traders, all aspects of life were incorporated and embedded into commercial life and trade.

What is a Network and How Does It Work?

There are quite a few definitions of network, manifested in different ways, from the mathematical and statistical analysis of clusters and network theory to stories of social networks, which examine the structure of connections between social groups. This study is focused on the economic structure of the Phoenician production and distribution of goods. Although a story is told here, too, it is based on finds from many dots within this economic structure, which makes it a network (Wasserman and Faust 1994; Knappett 2013; Leidwanger *et al.* 2014).

Since trade networks in antiquity dealt with the actual transporting of goods from one point to another, models of road networking are relevant for our discussion. There are two possible modes of operation for road networks: a "dendritic road system" and a "reticulated network." In the first, "tree-like," system, all the roads/branches are connected to the network at one end only, like branches on a tree. In a reticulated network, each end is connected to at least two other ends, forming an irregular or diamond-like structure (Bekker-Nielsen 1993: 180–2).

The Phoenician trade network was dendritic in nature during the Bronze Age and early Iron Age, originating from Phoenicia, but it became reticulated in two of its prominent aspects over time, once production centers became diffused (see Map 3). The network for perfumed oils, the manufacture of which was outsourced to several islands in the east Mediterranean, was reticulated, as was the salted fish network, the amphorae for which were sourced mainly in northwestern Africa and southern Iberia, and the fish mainly in western Iberia and the Balearic Islands. The wine network, however, seems to have been structured dendritically throughout the ages. The Phoenician wine, perfumed oils, and salted fish networks had different volumes of traffic and operated over different ranges and timespans. None operated as a regional economy alone or solely under one political power.

An underlying issue to be addressed when dealing with any globalized economic system or network is whether or not it was organized under the auspices of an official authority. If so, does the existence of such a coordinated, unified network necessarily point to an empire orchestrating the transport of goods? Where the massive movements of armies and associated groups (from craftsmen to technicians) are concerned, the shipping of goods has a different nature from pure trade. So, for example, the need of Roman armies for food, utilities, weapons, and cloth was immense during the Roman expansion in the Mediterranean from the 3rd–1st centuries BCE but reduced substantially after that. An opposite trend is reflected in western Europe, where Roman expansion grew from the 1st–3rd centuries CE and, with it, the shipping of goods. This situation is clearly reflected in the volume of Roman trade all over the Mediterranean (Fulford 1992: 295–300).

The Phoenicians, however, did not send armies, nor did they occupy garrisons or collect taxes outside their city-states; they did not ship supplies to feed and arm their people; and their trade in general was not intended for internal consumption. Hence, the trade patterns of Phoenician goods were completely different from the Roman patterns of supply. The Phoenicians used trade routes, while the Romans used military-supply routes. Even though imperialistic Rome and the Phoenician trade networks provide the only two known examples of commercial activity within or across the united Mediterranean sphere, they are not comparable. There is no way, and no need, to compare Phoenician trade connections during the Late Bronze Age with Mycenaean trade connections in this or in subsequent periods. Greek literature from Homer onwards portrays traders in a negative light. It is unlikely they would have held this opinion had they been engaged extensively in international trade themselves.

As stated in the definition of trade developed by David and Kramer and adopted in this monograph, the transfer of information is a part of any trade, whether or not it is conducted in a network. Trade in general, and long-distance trade in particular, requires premeditated information about routes, weather conditions, ports, market towns, and the value of the merchandise for the end-users. Whatever form the Phoenician network took, it was first and foremost transporting data about supply and demand to all its members. The potential profit and power that existed in the rapid transport of information to members of the same network exceeded any perceived personal benefit of withholding such information internally, especially if the others were family, friends, countrymen, or business partners, as was the case with the Phoenician diaspora. It is feasible that the huge success of Phoenician traders and their reputation was due in part to the data network operated by Phoenicians around the entire Mediterranean. Thus, if we wish to characterize the entire Phoenician phenomenon in one phrase that both explains and gives the framework for the various processes and manifestations of their operation, that phrase should be "the Phoenician trade diaspora network," which is discussed below.

Phoenician Networks: Distribution and Organization

Phoenician seaborne trade departed from organized ports and arrived at such ports, or sometimes at anchorages used by fisherman or natural uninhabited coves, before organized ports had been developed. The monitoring of all imported and exported goods by formal "state institutions" was easily accomplished at seaports. In order to disembark goods at any port, one needed permission from the port authorities; this was as true in the Bronze Age as it is today. Such operational methods dictate to a large degree the institutional character of long-distance trade.

Not only do long-distance Phoenician sea routes point to a complex institutionalized trading system, but they also highlight the complexity of Phoenician trade and the elaborate networks they operated, which involved the cooperation of many nodes. This was not just point-to-point trade, moving finished goods from point A to point B. These were networks that combined the production of containers with the processing of products and the packing of the finished product in containers that were shipped to a distribution center before being transported further to markets. The vast distribution of Phoenician products-in-a-package seems to point to an operation handled by a single operating body like a court/temple or city authority, which used many individuals as agents along the net.

There is an important precedent for state involvement in trade in the earlier, better-documented Late Bronze Age which continued in place in the Iron Age: the exchange of craftsmen between royal courts as goods. The role of craftsmen in the royal gift-exchange system supports the supposition that Phoenician craftsmen operated along similar lines within the framework of a state-controlled system rather than on their own initiative. This gift-exchange model between royal families in the Mediterranean is well known from early times and continued to function without changes until the Hellenistic period. However, it does not explain the large volume of Phoenician trade around the Mediterranean. What does explain is an organized trade system, also demonstrated by the occasional use of official stamped seals on pottery containers used for oil, wine, and other products. In addition, pottery groups distributed by Phoenicians were remarkably standardized in terms of shape, fabric, firing, and surface treatment. The combination of marks and standardization reflects an industry regulated by governmental control (Foxhall 1998: 300; Gates 2001: 141).

Most of the administrative and economic systems of the East remained unchanged until the Hellenistic period. These systems were reused repeatedly by each new ruler, and there is no reason to believe that the operation of Phoenician trade was different in this respect (Briant 1990). The Phoenician economic network seems to have been the most successful at those times when Phoenicians enjoyed some measure of autonomy as cooperating allies with neighboring polities or as vassals of the "superpower" of the day. Pottery evidence points to three major periods in which the Phoenician network operated at full capacity over a millennium and a half, with two relatively short breaks.

The first period of peak performance was during the Late Bronze Age, mainly during the 14th and 13th centuries BCE. It was followed by a period of reduced volume in trade in the 12th and 11th centuries BCE, the era in which the Bronze Age order of the international palace system ended. The second peak ran from the 10th century BCE until the Babylonian conquest of the Levant at the end of the 7th–early 6th centuries BCE, a period of about 400 years. During this period, long-distance trade was constantly increasing (Bedford 2007: 309).

A break then occurred from the early 6th to the late 6th or early 5th century BCE, a period of ca. 50–100 years. The 6th century BCE is still not fully understood or accounted for in Levantine history and archaeology. The break in the Phoenician network in this period may be explained by the political turmoil in the Levant during the ascendancy of the Neo-Babylonian Empire and, under its successor, the Achaemenid Empire, the mandatory employment of Phoenician boats in the Persian navy during the conquests of Egypt (Wallinga 2005: 136–48).

This break can also be seen at the other end of the Mediterranean, at the Iberian site of Huelva. It provides evidence of an economic crisis, a decline in the production of silver, and the disappearance of Greek pottery from the end of the 6th to the mid-5th century BCE (Cunliffe 1993: 68–9). If we accept that, until this period, Greek trade to the West was in Phoenician hands, then the disappearance of Greek pottery in Iberia during a break in the Phoenician network makes perfect sense. This does not imply that Greek trade was non-existent during the 6th century BCE, only that it was focused on other routes.

Archaeological evidence has shown that Emborio in Milos was a major harbor in the Cycladic Islands during the 6th century BCE, en route from Greece to Crete and North Africa. The site was destroyed at the end of 6th century, like other Archaic sites, perhaps as a result of the Persian conquest of Egypt and Cyrenaica in 525 BCE. This would have broken the Greek trade line to North Africa (Dickinson 1994:

236; Catling 2005:, 74). The Phoenician misfortunes of the 6th century may have given space to a rise or expansion in Greek trade in this period. When Phoenician commerce was re-established, then Greek trade reduced. Consequently, by the 5th century BCE, Phoenician–Greek relations became much more competitive and resulted in various conflicts, especially in the West, although occasional collaborations with the Greeks against the Persians, for example, took place in Egypt (Cunliffe 1993: 71).

There ensued a period of less than ideal performance during the Persian period, which spanned about 200 years, from the late 6th–late 4th centuries BCE. However, during this time, the Phoenician trade in products made in the East appears to have been limited to the eastern Mediterranean, as attested by the banded pottery group. This period was a time of considerable turmoil for the Phoenicians. During the 5th century BCE, Phoenician boats were turned into naval vessels and the Phoenicians were forced to fight for the Persians against the Greeks, which severely curtailed their ability to engage in trade. Hundreds of boats and many of their skilled people were lost during maritime battles on behalf of the Persians at Salamis and near the shores of Asia Minor. In the 4th century BCE, the Phoenicians joined forces with the Egyptians and the Greeks against the Persians, again at the cost of their trade interests. The Persians inflicted heavy retribution; they burnt Sidon and massacred its citizens in 348/7 BCE (Diod. Sic. 16.43–51) (Dandamayev 1989: 208–13, 231, 308–9; Betlyon 2004: 471–2). It is small wonder, then, that Phoenician trade during this period was much reduced in comparison to earlier times.

Another break occurred from Alexander's conquest and the destruction of Tyre and Gaza in 332 BCE until the late 3rd century BCE, a period of ca. 100–130 years. This period covers the era of the Diadochoi and the Ptolemaic-Seleucid period, a time when control over the Levant was divided into two. At this time, trade could not pass between Syria, Asia Minor, the Phoenician northern city-states of Tyre, Sidon, Arwad and Beirut, on the one hand, and Egypt and the Phoenician southern city-states of Ashkelon and Akko on the other. Some argue that, during the 3rd century BCE, Ptolemaic control over the Levantine littoral stretched all the way to the Eleutheros river south of Arados, so that the Ptolemaic kingdom included Tyre and Sidon (Mueller 2006: 51). However, two factors indicate that this claim should be rejected. The first, already stated, is the clear break in commerce between the northern and southern Levantine littoral during the 3rd century BCE. The second is that, unlike Akko, none of these major cities in the North was renamed or refounded with a Ptolemaic dynastic toponym (Kashtan 1988).

The Ptolemaic kingdom also controlled Cyprus, now disconnected from northern Phoenicia. The visible decline in copper production in this period, which ceased to be a commodity traded internationally but one only marketed locally in northwest Cyprus, probably resulted from the break between Phoenicia and Cyprus during this time (Alcock 1993b: 198). Trade surged again after 200 BCE and the beginning of Seleucid control over the entire Levantine coast. It is, therefore, reasonable to assume that the enmity between the Ptolemies and Seleucids caused a break in Phoenician trade in the early Hellenistic period. Moreover, this break shows that, at least by the second half of the 1st millennium BCE, the Phoenician network could not function without the continuous connection between all of Levantine ports, Cyprus, and Asia Minor.

The final period of peak performance began in the late 3rd century BCE and extended until the Islamic conquest of the southern Levant in the 7th century CE. A period of particularly intense activity began ca. 150 BCE, when the Phoenician city-states regained autonomy and began regular distribution of Eastern Sigillata A (ESA) pottery. This activity continued throughout the Roman period, covering a period of ca. 850 years. The Levantine littoral was reunified under the Seleucid Empire in 200 BCE, and Asia Minor fell into Roman hands in 146 BCE. About the same time, the Levantine coast was freed from Greek rule, and Phoenician trade reopened in the Mediterranean. In spite of the turmoil of the late Seleucid period, most of the Phoenician cities managed to maintain their stability; several towns even achieved autonomy. The exception was Beirut, which was destroyed in 145 BCE.

The cardinal change in administrative and economic systems that started with the Roman conquest of the East must have affected Phoenician autonomy and trade as well. When "Hellenization" reached Phoenicia and the Levant together with the Roman legions, the Phoenician economic network which had probably been "state"-run—meaning administered through formal, central, governmental organizations—might have been taken over by Phoenician merchants. In spite of the destruction of Carthage in 146 BCE, the unification of the Mediterranean under Roman rule under Augustus paved the way for Phoenician trade once again. Phoenician products were now shipped throughout the Mediterranean, beginning with ESA and other Terra Sigillata products, with Phoenician wine in Phoenician amphorae being added as an additional commodity from the Early Roman period until the Islamic conquest of the Mediterranean.

The Phoenician network had several posts scattered around the Mediterranean. Some served as production centers, which may have exchanged skilled craftsmen. Others served as ports-of-call and distribution centers, depending on the changing political conditions affecting the homeland. Not all these posts operated at the same time. Some were operating for very long periods; some served for a short time. But, whoever operated them, the Phoenician networks were a major factor in and influence on the Mediterranean economy during large parts of the first millennium BCE and first millennium CE.

II. Diaspora Networks

Two early models have been used to characterize Phoenician presence in the Mediterranean during the 1st millennium BCE. The first is "maritime colonization," which is self-explanatory. This understanding has been espoused even by some scholars who have accepted the idea of the diaspora trade-net as the most likely explanation of Mediterranean trade and who argue for the existence of an "eastern" trade diaspora in the Aegean during the Bronze Age. The second model is the "charter group," which entails the idea of a geographically transplanted elite in underpopulated territories supported from the outside. The latter model seems to be the more popular of the two in terms of interpreting Phoenician presence in the Mediterranean, especially in the West, although it is not usually articulated in so many words (Sherratt and Sherratt 1991: 355–6; Kessler 2008: 142).

The widespread dispersal of Phoenician material culture beginning in the Bronze Age, but mainly during the Archaic and Classical periods, reflects neither a colonial power nor a capitalist control over the Mediterranean, though in certain times and certain locations it was the latter, too. It is rather a diaspora network, a mode of commercial communication over long distance that Tilly included in the "trust network" model, which existed from Uruk in the early 3rd millennium to modern time (Tilly 2005: 65–9, 2010: 271–5). It has been debated whether the Phoenician presence around the Mediterranean was only a trade diaspora or if it also included agricultural activity that required territorial expansion.

This activity has been interpreted as very similar to Greek presence overseas, and other similarities have been proposed between the two communities in Sicily, Sardinia, and Spain (Hodos 2009: 230–5). Nonetheless, while for the Greek communities overseas agriculture and territorial extensions were ends in themselves, for the Phoenician communities these were means to enlarge and develop their trade. For this reason, the Phoenician presence around the Mediterranean is a trade diaspora, and the Greek presence is not.

Definitions of "Diaspora"

The word *diaspora*, meaning in Greek "scattering," is used in the *Septuagint* to describe the exiled Jews in Babylonia. In this sense, the word has a negative connotation, describing people forced out of their homeland, mainly the Jews (Freyne 2002: 2). In modern scholarship, the word has been used in a broader way and often has been related to the migration of ethnic groups that maintain their unique culture away from their homeland.

In 1971, the anthropologist Abner Cohen introduced a new term, "the trade diaspora," to designate a physically dispersed but highly interrelated community. In order to qualify as a diaspora, the social interrelationships of the group need to be reflected in religious and/or ethnic origin, with affinity to a metropolis, and a dispersal larger than a few nodes. A diaspora by definition is, therefore, a network of dispersed nodes united by a common religion, ethnic origin, and usually a language, where each node on the net is consciously interrelated to the others. The trust relations that exist between the parties of a diaspora can and often will be extended to include commercial relations, thus forming a trade network or a trade diaspora (Cohen 1971: 267; Curtin 1984: 1, 5–10; Holladay 2001: 141, 2004: 425–6).

Depending on the circumstances in the host land and the degree of urbanization and institutionalism in which they may be engaged, trade diaspora networks may become political entities, even strong ones. The balance of power between traders and hosts has always been asymmetrical and dependent on the strength of the host society. When the host is strong, the traders are restricted in their activities and their ability to express their political affiliation; when it is weak, the traders become a dominant group whose own agenda rules political and commercial life. Both cases are known from Canaanite-Phoenician history; for example, Delos or Naukratis under a strong host and Carthage under a weak host. Time also plays a major role in this balance; in general, the later the period, the stronger the host.

Explicit textual evidence for the Phoenician trade diaspora network and its political aspects is missing. The existing archaeological data cannot fill much of this void either, except for a few public inscriptions that mention associations of merchants but not necessarily ones connected to other Phoenician associations and locations. Nevertheless, when the private and public Phoenician inscriptions scattered in numerous Mediterranean locations are combined with other types of material artifacts, the existence of a vast and widespread Phoenician diaspora becomes clear. Numerous Phoenician settlements were established at river mouths and on islands close to shore, unrelated to settlements of local populations (Pritchard 1971: 18–19; Wachsmann *et al.* 2009). This allowed the development of a trade diaspora network free of host interests and restrictions, in which diaspora nodes could interact and trade with each other. The difference in the pattern of settlement is that the Canaanite-Phoenicians did not conquer land and settle immediately in existing cities or found new cities; instead, they negotiated with locals and set up a presence for purposes of trade, probably with a regular turnover in personnel stationed at the post.

The Dispersal of Phoenicians

While most of the discussion below refers to a trade diaspora, Phoenicians were also forced out of their homeland by the Assyrians. In the 7th century BCE, Assurbanipal deported part of the population from Tyre and Akko, consequently forming a Phoenician diaspora in Assyria, probably at Nineveh (Fales 2017: 246). Although we do not have other written evidence about deportation, the recurrent penalties and destruction forced on the Phoenicians by the Assyrians, evident in Assyrian texts, suggest that additional deportations occurred. Furthermore, other former inhabitants of Phoenician cities that escaped Assyrian annihilation had to flee from home and probably found refuge in other Phoenician cities, either in the southern Levant or in other parts of the Mediterranean. A similar process occurred in the kingdom of Israel, which Sargon II of Assyria destroyed in 720 BCE. The mass deportation of population from Israel was followed by large numbers of immigrants who moved south to the kingdom of Judah, which shows a large increase in population and a number of new settlements mainly around Jerusalem in the late 8th and 7th centuries BCE (Na'aman 2007).

Thus, the Phoenician diaspora was composed not only of merchants and people occupying other functions of trade and cultural life needed in a Phoenician trade port, but also of refugees from the homeland. It is reasonable to assume that this process occurred not only during the Assyrian conquest but also during the Babylonian, Persian, and even the early Hellenistic periods as well, i.e. during the entire period between the mid-9th and the end of the 4th centuries BCE.

Phoenician presence around the Mediterranean can be tied to various circumstances. The Canaanite texts from Ugarit that date to the 14th century BCE show that foreigners in Ugarit were always either merchants or specialized craftsmen from Ur, Cyprus, and Egypt (KTU 4.102, RS 17.130, and RS 88.2158). This evidence indicates that, by the Late Bronze Age at the latest, a diaspora comprised of merchants and artisans was a phenomenon known by Canaanite-Phoenicians. It is, therefore, reasonable to assume that, by the same period, a Canaanite-Phoenician diaspora would have been located in other trade centers, particularly in Egypt, Cyprus, and Crete (McGrail 1991: 87; McGeough 2007: 362–3).

Phoenician diasporas, although mainly composed of merchants in the early stages, also would have included people who could carry out the various functions needed for both maritime trade and cultural life. These would have included sailors, settlers, poets, philosophers, and even priests. The most important group of immigrants arriving at overseas Phoenician trading posts would have been artisans and craftsmen. They undoubtedly played a major part in transforming Phoenician posts that originally had been involved mainly in mining into centers that manufactured Phoenician artifacts and products.

Master craftsmen developed and supervised the production of pottery, metal, and ivory objects, and the industries of perfumed oils, dyed cloth, and salted fish which were probably manufactured by the indigenous populations and perhaps also by slaves. Master craftsmen also established and operated shipyards for the repair of Phoenician boats away from the homeland. Once well established, with enough well-trained local workers, such centers were united into a synchronized trade network, where each center was accountable for its specific part of the network. This could be either the production of a container (for instance a bottle, a juglet, or an *aryballos* for oil), one or more aspects of the manufacture of a specific product (such as extracting scent from certain flowers needed for the perfumed oils industry), or the operation of distribution centers for the finished products.

Sophisticated industries controlled by a palace economy were not unique to the Phoenicians, although the latter operated these on a much larger scale. Archives from Mari from the early 2nd millennium BCE and from Thebes, Knossos, and Pylos from the late 2nd millennium BCE reveal sophisticated networks for the production and distribution of luxury textiles, organized and operated by the state (palace). These industrial networks collected wool from many locations into the palace, which then redistributed the wool to many master craftsmen, who specialized in either a single phase of the textile production or in a specific type of textile. The palace was also engaged in the shipment of the finished products from one craftsman to another in a synchronized chain of manufacture, and in the provision of food supplies to the craftsmen in order to ensure their concentration on the desired product. Although these industries operated on a regional scale, their operation required a single, dominant authority to synchronize all the activities and shipments within the nodes comprising the network (Killen 1994: 68).

The infrastructure, therefore, for a state-controlled, sophisticated network had already been created in the Bronze Age. The mechanisms of operation, attested in the archives above, were also a known phenomenon during this time and were most probably used by the Canaanites as well in their wine industry during the Late Bronze Age. Based on their experience with a regionally synchronized industry for the sourcing, production, and packaging of wine which was subsequently exported by international trade networks across half the Mediterranean, it is highly likely that the Canaanite-Phoenicians had the knowledge and ability to establish new trade networks outside of Phoenicia proper, based on the same state-organized model.

Claims are often made about the spontaneous arrival of individual craftsmen at locations outside their homeland which led to the non-official manufacture and ad hoc distribution of their products. However, there is vast evidence of the transfer and institutional utilization of craftsmen in the palace economy of the Near East until the 1st millennium BCE (see below). Phoenician craftsmen were sent by one or more Phoenician palaces to found new industrial zones which were planned as future nodes on Phoenician trade-nets.

The Phoenician Diaspora

According to Ana Delgado and Meritxell Ferrer, "The Phoenician diaspora, headed by the metropolis of Tyre, was a colonial undertaking mainly of a commercial nature, and involved the creation of numerous enclaves along the Mediterranean coastline (from Cyprus to Gibraltar) and in Atlantic territories (including Gadir, Lixus or Abul)" (Delgado and Ferrer 2007: 20). Even if this trade diaspora was not quite colonial in terms of the Greco-Roman enterprises and those of Europe in the 16th–20th centuries, it was, indeed, of commercial nature, led by Canaanite-Phoenician city-states which initiated numerous nodes along the Mediterranean. By the 6th century BCE, the Phoenician diaspora was no longer headed mainly by Tyre; the gravity center of this trade diaspora shifted to Carthage, producing a two-headed body.

Traces and evidence of the unity between Phoenician bases, including Carthage, and Phoenicians cities in the Levantine homeland are multiple. As reported by Herodotus (3.19), during the takeover of the Mediterranean area by the Persian King Cambyses, his fleet, made up mainly of Phoenicians, refused to attack Carthage. They explained their disobedience as being due to the fact that the Carthaginians were their sons. This explanation was accepted by the king as a valid reason for insubordination. Herodotus explained the relations between Tyre and Carthage using the typical Greek mode of describing the relations between a mother-city and a colony and the treaty binding them. Such a political-legal conception might have been characteristic of the Phoenician world as well, but later evidence might suggest otherwise (Asheri, Lloyd, and Corcella 2007: 419).

Diodorus (Diod. Sic. 20.14.1–2) mentions that, when the Carthaginians became wealthy, they stopped sending a tenth of their revenue to Tyre and sent smaller amounts instead. When they found themselves in danger, they interpreted their loss as a sign of divine wrath and tried to mend all the wrongs they had done to upset their god, which included sending a large amount of tribute to the god's temple at Tyre. Had the relations between Tyre and Carthage been of a legal character, the tribute sent to Tyre would have been regarded as a civilian matter related to the city's authorities, perhaps the palace, not an issue that involved the god or gods. It needs to be recognized, however, that all treaties were witnessed and concluded in the presence of the gods of both parties, who were to enforce the curses laid out should the treaty be broken. In this case, had such a formal agreement existed, the failure to pay the full amount of tribute or tithe would have been an infraction of the stipulations of the agreement. Nonetheless, if the relations between the two cities were socio-religious in nature and the tenth of revenues was sent to the temple, not the secular authorities, then it clearly would have been a matter involving the god of Tyre and Carthage, Milqart—not Heracles, or Cronus, as Diodorus (Diod. Sic. 20.14.1–6) calls him.

A later example of the close bond between Carthage and Tyre is provided by the inclusion of Tyre as part of the Carthaginian trading network mentioned in the second treaty between Rome and Carthage in 344 BCE (Polybius 3.24). It is obvious that, at least as late as the 4th century BCE, Tyre and Carthage were closely related and considered themselves one people (Bresson 2005: 102).

The same relations that were based on and demonstrated devotion and love also characterized the Jewish Diaspora. Both private people and communities sent a tithe to the temple in Jerusalem as tribute until its destruction in 70 CE. The Jewish concept was based on the premise that one who considered himself a Jew should send an annual tribute of half a shekel to the Temple in Jerusalem, according to Jewish law (Exod 30:13), but it was up to the individual to decide whether to exceed this amount. In Nehemiah 10:33–24, the amount was to be a third of a shekel. The Jewish communities of the Diaspora gathered the individual donations and sent them together to the Temple in Jerusalem. Based on the little evidence available, it is quite likely that the same pattern characterized the relations between the Carthaginians and the Temple of Tyre. By extension, the same relations probably existed between various Phoenician trading posts around the Mediterranean and the temples in the cities of origin of their founders, mainly Tyre and Sidon.

The Dispersal of Artisans

One of the earliest features of Phoenician presence in the Mediterranean was artisans and craftsmen, who were renowned throughout the Mediterranean. As indicated by textual evidence, the emergence at the end of the 9th century BCE of new techniques in gold jewelry, metalworking, and ivory carving in Crete and Greece was the result of the arrival of Phoenician craftsmen, who established Phoenician-style overseas workshops (Burkert 1997: 21–4).

Carlo Zaccagnini discusses three main patterns of mobility for craftsmen in the Bronze and Iron Ages. The first is illustrated by the archives of the city of Mari from the 18th century BCE, where artisans were bound permanently as slaves to the palace bureaucracy and regular moves of skilled workers were carefully organized. According to the Mari archives, specialized personnel were assigned to peripheral units for longer or shorter terms of service, after which they would be sent back to their original working places. These moves were intended to maximize the exploitation of the craftsmen's professional capabilities (Sasson 1968: 46–54; Zaccagnini 1983: 247–9; Burkert 1997: 24).

A second mobility pattern presented by Zaccagnini was characteristic of the Late Bronze period, when craftsmen were still tightly bound to the palace organization but no longer as slaves. Specialized craftsmen and their relations with kings are well recorded in the archives of this period. In one case, the king of Ugarit asked the Egyptian king to send him Egyptian craftsmen and was refused (RS 88.2158). In another, artisans of various origins were shipped across the Mediterranean, as a Linear B tablet from Pylos has shown. These were female weavers explicitly, and other Mycenaean texts of this period refer to women weaving for the goddess Potnia in her sanctuaries (Rougemont 2008). It seems that these women were not artisans alone or perhaps at all but rather, or in addition, priestesses or specialists involved in ceremonial and religious activity.

The skilled workers who were sent from one court to another were viewed as prestige goods which were transmitted formally through the mechanism of gift-exchange. One of the models for Late Bronze Age production proposes a series of palace-dependent workshops whose artisans moved from one court to another under royal instruction, a model that may explain the archaeological evidence. Documents from Ugarit and Boğazköy (Hattusa) mention potters affiliated with temples and palaces. The pattern of craftsmen treated as precious goods in the Achaemenid court, exchanged as gifts between kings, is also reported by Herodotus (3.1; 3.125–37) to have been in use during the Persian period, reflecting a long tradition of this practice in the history of the ancient Near East (Zaccagnini 1983: 250, 255–7; Gates 2001: 144; Michailidou and Voutsa 2005; Feldman 2006: 8; Stampolidis and Kotsonas 2006: 346; McGeough 2007: 262; Rougemont 2008).

The third pattern, observed from the 3rd millennium until the middle of the 1st millennium BCE, was characterized by the deportation of craftsmen from their homeland by occupying forces, who viewed artisans as booty of war. After the fall of the palace organizations ca. 1200 BCE, however, the status of specialized craftsmen may have undergone radical changes. Specialists migrated in search of work opportunities, as testified by the *Odyssey* (17.382–6). The emergence of free artisans moving from one client to another might be reflected in this passage from Homer describing qualified artisans who moved on their own initiative looking for suitable jobs. This would be a subsequent modification of the third pattern, then, or would constitute a fourth pattern that needs to stand alone.

Evidence to support the fourth pattern might be provided by the tools and scrap bronze found among the wreckage of the Cape Gelidonya ship, a Canaanite ship according to its construction techniques and the personal effects of its crew, which may have carried on board wandering craftsmen ca. 1200 BCE (Emanuel 2019: 424–5). However, these tools could also have been part of the ship's carpenter's kit or could have belonged to a craftsman sent by a Phoenician palace, one of those that had not yet been eliminated in the wave of destruction that took place ca. 1200 BCE. In any case, the wanderings of craftsmen in search of work may have represented only a temporary stage of unemployment and a blip in the larger history of institutional control and exchange of such artisans, not a permanent and institutionalized condition. A change in the latter direction only occurred in the pre-classical Near East (Zaccagnini 1983: 258–9).

More direct evidence regarding the status of Phoenician craftsmen comes from Ugarit (14th–13th centuries BCE) and stories in the Hebrew Bible that seem to be set in the 12th–10th centuries BCE. Craftsmen were defined at Ugarit as *bns mlk*, "royal personnel," including some cataloged as shipbuilders. This royal or palatial status may have remained the same for specialized craftsmen in the Phoenician city-states during the 1st millennium BCE as well (Linder 2003: 148). In the Hebrew Bible, Bezalel of the tribe of Judah, Oholiab of the tribe of Dan, and Hiram, a bronzesmith from Tyre, are named as craftsmen who operated in a relatively free manner (Exod 31:1–6; 35:30–35; 1 Kgs 7:13–47). In contrast, the Phoenician stonecutters and woodcutters who were slaves of King Hiram of Tyre are said to have received grain and oil in return for dispatching wood to King Solomon (1 Kgs 5:15–25), which would reflect the first or second pattern known in the centralized palace organization of the 2nd millennium BCE.

Phoenician (i.e. Tyrians and Sidonians) carpenters and sailors were sent to Nineveh in the early 7th century BCE to build and launch Sennacherib's fleet against Elam (Grayson and Novotny 2014: 82), but it is unknown whether they cooperated willingly or were forced to by the Assyrian king or his Tyrian or Sidonian vassal kings. The fact that the Achaemenid administration provided foreign craftsmen with wages does not necessarily imply that they worked of their own free will. These wages could have gone to the craftsmen's owners and not into the craftsmen's pockets; wages at Persepolis, where texts mention Phoenicians having worked as artisans in Pasargadae and Persepolis in the 6th century BCE (Edelman 2016: 248, 274), were given to groups and not to individuals. Whatever their legal status may have been, specialist craftsmen and other skilled specialists and providers of services to the palace had a distinguished status in the palace hierarchy (Van de Mieroop 2005: 130; Bedford 2007: 325).

It seems that in the 1st millennium BCE, two or even three patterns coincided simultaneously in the Levant: craftsmen as a commodity, craftsmen as booty, and, perhaps a new phenomenon, craftsmen as free agents. Craftsmen were more often controlled by the palace than traveled on their own initiative. The degree of control available to the palace over craftsmen located away from the homeland depended on how long the palace arm was and how much influence it had over the authorities overseas. Regarding the Phoenicians, it is very likely that their arm was long enough to ensure continuous control over the palace craftsmen, at least until the Persian period. Nonetheless, this does not contradict the occasional existence of free Phoenician craftsmen who established themselves in foreign lands under their own initiative (Burkert 1997: 24–5).

In light of the shipment and movement of Phoenician craftsmen around the Mediterranean, which began in the 10th century BCE at the latest, we must acknowledge that the Phoenician diaspora contained more than merchants and seamen. Immigrant Phoenician metalwork masters had already introduced new techniques and images to Greece in the 9th century BCE, and, by the time we find the first operating Phoenician commercial network in the east Aegean in the 7th century BCE, there had probably been more than just a few skillful Phoenician craftsmen who had worked in this area for centuries. These craftsmen, their descendants, and recent arrivals of artisans from Phoenicia played a major role in the industrial Phoenician networks that operated on a large scale around the Mediterranean (Coldstream 2003: 358; Lipiński 2004: 147–88).

The Operation of the Diaspora Trade Network in Different Periods and Locations

In the absence of legal documents or an archive providing direct evidence from the Phoenicians themselves, correlations for the actual operation of the Phoenician diaspora can be drawn from other trade diasporas known to have operated from as early as the 2nd millennium BCE in Mesopotamia to as late as the 20th century in America. There is a perpetual and ubiquitous quality to most trade diasporas, which have as shared characteristics a common ethnic origin, religion, and language (Curtin 1984; Holladay 2004: 426). Below, notable traits that can be associated with two of these networks will be examined in more depth: the Old Assyrian trade diaspora and the medieval Jewish trade diaspora.

A major component of any long-distance trade was the investors or financiers, who initially were institutions and, later, private people who either owned the boats and goods or provided loans to the traders. Investors and financiers operated in the 2nd millennium BCE in the Old Assyrian trade diaspora in Anatolia as well as in the 2nd millennium CE in the Jewish trade diaspora. This steady component of long-distance trade, especially when it involved risky trade by sea, indicates that the method of operation of long-distance trade and trade networks did not change in antiquity and was organized more or less in the same way from the 2nd millennium BCE to the mid-2nd millennium CE. In addition to both examples that will be discussed below, the Egyptian Muziris papyrus (P.Vindob. G 40822) which dates to the 2nd century CE provides valuable information about loans and financing for trade with southern India. Without going into detail, it should be noted that the Muziris papyrus not only provides another chronological link in the chain of evidence about the mechanisms of trade but also data about trade networks and the various functions of the people who operated such a network (Young 2001: 47–8, 55–7; Morley 2007: 42).

The Mesopotamian Trade Diaspora

During the Middle and Late Bronze Age, Assur constructed a trade diaspora in Anatolia. Its texts, found at Karum Kanesh (Kültepe), reveal elaborate systems of accounting, investment, and partnership structures. These structures formed a commercial organization the complex details of which can likely provide a working parallel for Phoenician trade among Mediterranean cities during the 1st millennium BCE (Burkert 1997: 21; Larsen 2015). Analogous to the Canaanite-Phoenician trade-net, four characteristics of the Old Assyrian trade diaspora network are noteworthy.

The first is solidarity based on ethnic identity, language, and religion. Like later-period Jewish merchants who operated a trade diaspora, the Old Assyrian merchants kept their ethnic identity, language, and religion, through which they were able to persist for many generations (Stein 1999: 48; Larsen 2015: 149–50). There is no reason to assume that the Canaanite-Phoenician trade diaspora was any different; like other diasporas of all periods, the Canaanite-Phoenician diaspora would also have relied on ethnic identity and a common language and religion as the bonds that unified its members as one people.

The second characteristic is the distribution centers. An issue obvious from the Mesopotamian texts is that many of the goods traded between the Assyrian post of Karum Kanesh in Anatolia and Assur did not originate and were not manufactured, or even consumed, at either end of this network; rather, both cities were the transfer stations for many of the goods that had come from elsewhere and were forwarded to other locations (Kochavi 1992: 8; Lamberg-Karlovsky 1996: 166–7). In this sense, Karum Kanesh constituted a distribution center in the Assyrian trade network, regardless of the diaspora status of its Assyrian merchants. Similarly, major Phoenician nodes on the trade diaspora route functioned mainly as distribution centers involved in the shipping and forwarding of goods that had been manufactured elsewhere, sometimes very far away.

The third characteristic is the introduction of native religion, rituals, and social organization at the new host location. Along with commercial concepts, including the use of weights and measures and of pieces of silver as money, the Mesopotamian trade diaspora introduced its religion, myths, rituals, and legal social practices like oath-taking and written agreements into Anatolia. The Mesopotamian–Anatolian commercial contacts and the processes entailed in it were comparable to the Phoenician–Greek contacts during the Late Geometric and Archaic periods, where Phoenicians were the sophisticated party and the Greeks the less commercialized periphery (Curtin 1984: 64–6, 73; Larsen 1987: 54; Allen 1992: 467–8; Hudson 1992: 136; Burkert 1997: 24; Holladay 2001: 137, 141). The fact that the Phoenicians introduced the alphabet to the Mediterranean world is widely accepted; their contribution to Mediterranean—i.e. mainly Greek and Etruscan—religion, rituals, and social organization was no less substantial but has been much less acknowledged. Nonetheless, just as in the Mesopotamian example, the Phoenicians were likely responsible for initiating major changes in many aspects of life and beliefs in regions where they established a trade diaspora.

The final characteristic of note is that only a few elite families were allowed to participate in the trade. Involvement in the Old Assyrian long-distance trade network which included Karum Kanesh was restricted to a few elite families that traded on behalf of Assur with the palaces of Anatolia (Larsen 2015: 152). The same type of restricted-access system is visible in the texts of Canaanite Ugarit in the 14th century BCE. Most likely, then, the Phoenician merchants mentioned in various texts from the Late Bronze, Iron Age, and Classical periods were also the members of but a few elite families who were enfranchised by the palace to trade on its behalf. The fact that they were specific individuals does not make them entrepreneurs or private agents. Rather, it indicates that some aspects of the palace economic activity were entrusted to selected individuals who acted as authorized institutional agents.

The Jewish Trade Diaspora

The best comparison for the Phoenician trade diaspora in terms of routes covering the Mediterranean basin and for which documentation is available is the Jewish trade diaspora reflected in the Cairo Geniza documents of the 10th–16th centuries CE. A careful examination of these documents has demonstrated the existence of a trade diaspora spread between Egypt, Israel, Lebanon, Syria, and, especially, Tunisia and Sicily. Many Jewish merchants active in Tunisia had immigrated there from Spain, Morocco, and Libya; the documents reveal the direct and indirect commercial connections that existed between the

Jewish communities of North Africa and Spain as well as Iraq, Iran, Yemen, Italy, and France (Goitein 1967: 18–22; Gil 2003; Goldberg 2012). Five characteristics of this network will be highlighted.

The first characteristic is distribution centers. The Geniza texts document some of the Jewish regional networks and distribution centers: for example, the trade in thyme that was used as cough medicine. The best thyme plants came from Crete, which was known for its ancient tradition of medicinal herbs. Thyme was exported from Crete to Egypt, and from Egypt was re-exported to India. Evidence for an earlier Jewish involvement in the trade route from India to Alexandria is provided by one Hebrew and two Aramaic graffiti and two Greek jar labels reading *ioudaikon,* i.e. Jewish, that have been found in the port city of Berenike by the Red Sea. The texts all date to the 4th–5th centuries CE. Even earlier epigraphic evidence, however, comes from Edfu, which was located on the road from Berenike to Koptos on the Nile. There, Greek ostraca bearing written dates between 71/72–116 CE mention a Jewish tax (Goitein 1967: 47; Schmitz 2000: 183–9).

The second is the continuity of trade networks, routes, and the use of nodes over long periods of time. The texts show a continuity in Jewish trade lines, trade networks, and distribution centers, at least in part, from the early 1st millennium to the middle of the 2nd millennium CE—1500 years of Jewish trade in the eastern Mediterranean and the East. Not all the routes may have operated simultaneously or with the same volume of goods throughout this period, but the memory, tradition, and ability to conduct trade along the same routes by the same people was maintained. *A fortiori*, the Phoenician trade routes and nets were more likely to have continued for long periods as well, and Phoenician pottery has allowed us to confirm that this was, indeed, the case (Regev 2020). The Geniza provides, therefore, an important comparative source of evidence for the endurance of trade diasporas and trade networks in the Mediterranean for over a millennium. The Phoenicians operated even longer.

The Geniza documents depict a trade diaspora within the Islamic sphere during the Middle Ages. While the Jewish traders operated under different political circumstances than in earlier times, when the Phoenicians were a major force in Mediterranean trade, they used well-established ancient Phoenician routes. After coming to power, the Muslims took over the preceding Phoenician and Punic networks *in toto*. They used the same ports, the same types of sails made from the same materials, and the same sources for boat-building. The earliest naval base used by the Muslims was Acre, old Phoenician Akko. Some time ca. 700–735 CE the naval base was moved to Tyre, another Phoenician metropolis, which then functioned as the chief harbor of the Islamic fleet until 861 CE, when the naval base moved back to Acre. Naval bases were also founded in Alexandria and other Delta cities, where Phoenician presence in earlier times is well known. In the mid-8th century, a naval base was founded at Tarsus, another ancient node on the Mediterranean trade network (Frost and Vari 1981; Kennedy 2007: 330, 335–8).

The third characteristic is the migration of artisans. Another relevant phenomenon reflected in the texts of the Cairo Geniza is testimony concerning the migration of Jewish artisans into Jewish trade centers and their integration into the commercial life there. The immigrant craftsmen crossed long distances at times; for example, many Persian Jews went to Egypt and Tunisia, and Jewish craftsmen from Morocco relocated to Ceylon (Goitein 1967: 49–51).

As mentioned above, Phoenician artisans were transferred en masse to Phoenician trade centers and nodes on the trade diaspora network operated by the Phoenician institutions. Such distant migration was always based on the knowledge and expectation that they could be well received by fellow countrymen, in the 20th century CE, in the Middle Ages, and more so in the late 2nd–1st millennia

BCE. Except for prominent individuals, people do not tend to go into the unknown. Like later Jewish craftsmen, the Phoenician craftsmen were sent by the palace or went to locations where a commercial community of their own people was already established or where they intended to establish such a community. As we see in the Geniza documents, craftsmen did not go to just any node in the Jewish trade diaspora route but to the major trade centers of their time, distribution centers that provided an abundance of opportunities. We should bear this in mind when dealing in the next chapters with any "local" manufacture of goods made in the Phoenician tradition in the various Mediterranean trade centers of all relevant periods.

The fourth concerns the types of cooperation. The operation of the Jewish Diaspora was based on family tradition, trust between people of the same religion, and the use of internal regulation and a jurisdictional system based on religious law. Four kinds of cooperation among Jewish traders appear in the documents. They are based on: a) friendship and informal cooperation; b) partnership and *commenda* (the situation in which one party invests the capital and the other party does the traveling and pursues the activity of acquisition and marketing); c) family partnership; and d) commission and agency. These commercial ties were fortified by matrimonial connections between influential families in various nodes in this trade diaspora network. Apparently, long-distance trade was so hazardous that it was not conducted by individuals but, rather, by partners. Most of the partnerships recorded in the Cairo Geniza were based on internal Jewish community relations. Some partnerships, however, were made with Muslims as well, in spite of the fact that, during disputes, they could not make religious vows at a Jewish court that handled the trade diaspora affairs and were, therefore, not subject to the same measures of domination as the Jewish traders (Goitein 1967: 48–9, 164–86; Gil 2003: 281, 317).

It is reasonable to believe that the Phoenician trade diaspora, although more integrated and institutionalized, operated on the micro level in similar patterns to some of the Jewish trade diaspora, which was not institutionalized. This would include, in particular, the *commenda* partnership, family partnership, and cooperation of agents. Most likely, patterns of cooperation differed over time. While the Phoenician trade diaspora was completely institutionalized, at least until the Persian period, cooperation likely worked through agents of the palace. During the Roman period, however, it presumably worked more through family and community partnerships.

Finally, the fifth characteristic is the merchants' representative, known as *wakil al-tujjar* in Arabic and as *paqid ha-soharim* in Hebrew. He oversaw the representation of foreign merchants who had no partners or family members at their destination in court in matters and legal disputes involving the storage and distribution of their goods and in issues dealing with the Muslim port and tax authorities. This person was a broker holding an ancient position corresponding with the Old Assyrian *tamkaru* and maybe also with the "Inspector of a Merchant Colony" at Ugarit in the Late Bronze Age. The Assyrian trade diaspora system included *tamkaru*, commerce agents who initially represented Ur's temples and court but later on represented the merchants themselves and the *karum*. The *karum* was an institution, a powerful guild of merchants that embraced multiple functions. In addition, the word *karum* came to designate a market town, port of exchange, a trading station, quarters for merchants and sailors, a harbor, and a place where boats moored, and did so in many languages, including Mycenaean texts from the Late Bronze Age. It remained in use with this same meaning until the Roman period (Curtin 1984: 68–70; Kochavi 1992: 13; Bradbury 1996: 57–60; Gil 2003: 314–15; Reed 2003: 46–51; Goldberg 2012: 123–43).

Some of the functions of the *tamkaru* and *karum* were carried out by the person and the position mentioned in the Geniza texts. A somewhat similar position may also have been occupied by Athenian *proxenoi* resident in foreign ports where trade in grain and timber was conducted. It seems quite probable that some structure or body, anything between an institution and a single representative, was a part of most trade diaspora communities. It is reasonable to assume, therefore, especially considering the close commercial contacts the Phoenicians had with the Assyrians, that such a person or institution would also have been part of the elaborated Phoenician trade diaspora and its networks.

The Trade Diaspora: Concluding Remarks

All we know of the Assyrian merchants and their trade diaspora comes from the texts that have survived; nothing is visible in the archaeological finds from the quarter where the Assyrian merchants dwelt. If a documented trade diaspora in the Near East operated in a highly sophisticated and institutional manner about 1000 years earlier and on a smaller scale than the Iron Age Phoenician trade networks, one may assume many similar modes of operation for the undocumented Phoenician trade diaspora. Moreover, if similar characteristics are present in another documented trade diaspora, this time one that worked extensively in the Mediterranean in the early Medieval period but again on a smaller scale, then it is very likely that the undocumented Phoenician trade diaspora operated, to some extent, in a similar way. In any case, it would not have been any less sophisticated than the other two and perhaps more so, due to its geographical and chronological range.

Nonetheless, the Phoenician trade diaspora must have documented its commercial activity in archives in its city and port locations. Unfortunately, they would have been written on perishable materials that have not survived the ravages of time. Nevertheless, limited documentation is provided by the batch-marks that appeared on Phoenician amphorae for thousands of years and Egyptian wall paintings that depict the recording of the goods delivered. In addition, unlike other trade diasporas preceding and following which left no archaeological clues, the Phoenician trade diaspora left traces in some of its locations. Some of its nodes are clearly identifiable through archaeological data, like Huelva in southern Spain. Some are more ambiguous and debated, like Pithecusae (Ischia), while others remain invisible in terms of material cultural remains. To the latter group belong probable Phoenician bases in India and Arabia hinted at in texts (see below).

It should be noted that, although the comparison of the Jewish trade diaspora that operated during the Middle Ages with that of the Phoenicians of earlier times is valid in many ways, there is one major difference between the two. The Jewish trade diaspora operated under a strong imperial force which granted it liberties when it was beneficial to the empire's economy. The Phoenician trade diaspora operated at times under imperial forces, but most of the time, and in many locations, it was the imperial force itself.

Outside the borders of Egyptian, then Assyro-Babylonian, and then Persian domination, the Phoenicians were a cultural, economic, and military force that was usually stronger than local indigenous populations. Yet, despite their supremacy, it is quite unlikely that the Phoenician trade diaspora acted in patterns similar to the British, Portuguese, and Dutch trade empires in Asia during the 16th–18th centuries CE, which enforced militarized trade in their favor and eventually became territorial empires (Curtin 1984: 5). It is difficult to imagine that similar conduct by the Phoenicians would have gone completely unregistered by any of the contemporary witnesses and would have left absolutely no traces in the histories and stories of other groups. The modes of Phoenician operation, therefore, must have been much subtler, even where territorial domination did eventually occur, as in the case of Carthage. I believe it is safe to say that the Phoenician trade diaspora operated in more than one manner in various times and locations. However, based on the current data, I incline toward considering its character to have been more in line with the patterns of the Jewish trade diaspora, revealed in the Geniza documents, than with the European trade empires in Asia during the modern period.

The Jewish trade diaspora also may provide a logical explanation about how the Phoenician trade diaspora continued to endure and operate from the Persian/Classical and Hellenistic periods into the Roman period. One of the reasons for the success of the Jewish trade diaspora was the position of Jews as outsiders. They were not Christians, like the majority living on the northern shores of the Mediterranean, nor were they Muslims, like the inhabitants of the southern shores of the Mediterranean, two rival entities that would not trade directly with each other. The Jews acted as mediators between the two and enabled trade between what otherwise would have remained non-connected nodes.

Likewise, the Phoenicians may have been the only traders able to deliver goods between the eastern Levant and the western Mediterranean in the Classical/Persian period and between the western Mediterranean and the East during the Hellenistic and Roman periods. During these periods the Near East constituted a unit that was politically and religiously different from the Mediterranean: the Persian Empire vs. Greece; the post-Alexandrine Hellenistic kingdoms vs. Persia and eastward (Greek traders were probably unwelcome in the East after Alexander's conquests); and the Roman Empire vs. the East. With their long tradition of trade between these two zones, however, the Phoenicians were able to trade with both. This ability was curtailed once they associated themselves with the imperial power in one zone over the other. This must have been what happened at the time of the Islamic conquest of the Mediterranean, which resulted in the final division of the Phoenician people between Christian and Muslim lands, severing their former ties and unity, in a still unknown process. While the Muslims inherited control of the old Phoenician homeland, the long-established Phoenician trade routes were taken over by the Jews, whose trade diaspora patterns were very similar to those of the earlier Phoenician trade diaspora. As a powerless religious minority, they were able to become the new mediators between the Christian and Muslim political worlds and re-establish trade nodes with resident diaspora communities that reconnected East with West commercially.

—3—

The Early Networks and the Canaanite-Phoenician International Style

In order to better understand the Phoenician trade network that grew into a far-flung commercial empire spanning three geographical zones in the Mediterranean basin and beyond, we need to turn to its earlier beginnings. In this way, we can start to trace the development of both the mechanisms and practices that facilitated its operation and the elements that contributed to the development of a recognizable Phoenician style and corpus. Two early trade networks are presented: the Egypto-Phoenician and the Hittite-Canaanite. The Egypto-Phoenician network was the earliest Canaanite-Phoenician trade network, one that laid many features used in later Phoenician trade-nets and which had a profound impact on later Phoenician styles and corpora. Rather than revolving around a geographical zone, it was based on a unique commercial and cultural bond. The Hittite-Canaanite network also contributed to Canaanite-Phoenician style and religion. The discussion of both these early networks includes a consideration of developing characteristics of Phoenician style and the various elements that typify the Phoenician corpus outside the homeland.

The second part of this chapter revolves around the International Style known from the Late Bronze Age, which is called a Mediterranean *koine* in the Iron Age. This style continued at least to the Hellenistic period. The International Style is not recognized as a Canaanite-Phoenician phenomenon but should be; its components consist of Canaanite-Phoenician elements and other elements traded and circulated by them.

I. The Egypto-Phoenician Network

The Egypto-Phoenician network is the most enduring Mediterranean exchange network, one that left its mark around the Mediterranean from the Bronze Age until the Hellenistic period. The commercial connections between Egypt and the Levant had already begun in the 4th millennium BCE and continued throughout the Old, Middle, and New Kingdoms and into the Late, Greco-Roman, and Byzantine periods. These connections are often defined in terms of the exchange of prestige goods and the maintenance of an inter-social network between Egyptian and Canaanite elites. The first Canaanite-Phoenician hub of this network was Byblos, as indicated by the earliest known reference from the 3rd millennium BCE to large, seagoing vessels in Egyptian texts as Byblos boats. The phrase soon became the idiomatic expression used for any large, seagoing ship (Leonard 1996: 245; King and Stager 2001: 178). Ugarit became a second hub, followed eventually by Tyre and Sidon (Prag 1984; Ben-Tor 1991: 3–4; Bietak 1991; Flammini 2010: 157–8). As a result of the dominance of Canaanites over Egypt in the 2nd Intermediate Period and the increase of Canaanite commercial power in the late 17th–16th centuries BCE, the coastal Canaanite-Phoenician cities and Egypt became business associates.

By the early 2nd millennium BCE, at the time of the 12th Dynasty, Egypt and Byblos were connected both commercially and politically and, soon after, other Levantine cities were involved in similar connections. Excavations conducted in Sidon have shown that, starting in the early 2nd millennium BCE, the city's leading economic relations were with Egypt. This also is the case for Tyre and other Canaanite-Phoenician cities in the Levant. Petrographic analysis has shown that the earliest Canaanite pottery imported to Egypt during the 12th Dynasty (ca. 1991–1803 BCE) arrived from Ugarit and other northern Levantine coastal sites. The pottery consisted mainly of Canaanite amphorae produced in Lebanon and at other Levantine sites. Moreover, Egyptian imitations (or rather local versions) of Canaanite shapes, and not amphorae alone, were already being produced during this period and indicate not only that trade was taking place but also that a Canaanite population may already have been resident in Egypt (Leonard 1996: 237; King and Stager 2001: 179; Betlyon 2004: 455, 466–8; Cohen-Weinberger 2007: 36, 43–4, 142–53; Braun and van den Brink 2008: 643–88; Doumet-Serhal 2008: 57; Kopetzky 2008: 224).

In addition to the known material exchange, Egyptian-Canaanite connections were defined by mutual religious influence. This characteristic is revealed by the adoption of deities and their cults by both sides. During the Hyksos era, ca. the mid-17th to the mid-16th centuries BCE, Baal was syncretized with Seth. Then, during the Second Intermediate Period, the Egyptian god Amon in particular was worshiped in Phoenicia, and Phoenician Ashtart was worshiped in Egypt (Mendleson 1987; Pinch 2002: 108–9, 112; Brandl 2003: 258; Allon 2007).

The special relations between Canaan-Phoenicia and Egypt clearly were based on common interests and the way each empire fulfilled the needs of the other. On the one hand, Egypt did not possess a fleet for long voyages in the Mediterranean, nor in the Red Sea, the Arab Sea, nor the Indian Ocean, and expressed no interest in such enterprises. As a result, Egypt is often not even considered part of the Mediterranean (Bagnall 2005: 339–47; Bresson 2005: 101). Nevertheless, Egypt needed maritime transport for the export and import of materials and goods and, occasionally, a navy to conduct war. Phoenicia, on the other hand, was a coastal Levantine culture with almost no natural resources except wood, a desire for long-distance seafaring, and skilled shipbuilders. Egypt's lack of a means to dispatch cargo dovetailed with Phoenicia's need of a client for its skillful craftsmen and nautical crafts.

In exchange for the use of Phoenician navy boats for war and the enjoyment of wine, olive oil, timber, and raw materials (metals, salt, and glass) that were harvested in various Mediterranean and Eastern locations and traded to Egypt by the Phoenician commercial fleet, the Egyptians provided the Canaanite-Phoenicians with vessels made from alabaster and faience, scarabs, papyri, linen, and ivory. Egypt already had instituted its commercial ties with Levantine coastal cities by the Bronze Age; Phoenician wine amphorae have been excavated in Middle Bronze Age occupational layers in Egyptian sites (Bietak 1991: 44–5, fig. 11.9).

Olive oil was imported from the Levant, and timber was the main raw material originating from the Phoenician region and traded internationally from the Bronze Age onwards, as evident not only from Egyptian texts but also from the Assyrian Nimrud letters of the 7th century BCE (K3500, K4444, K10235) (Saggs 1955: 127–8; Sasson 1966: 130; Moscati 1968: 84; Knapp 1993: 336; Markoe 2000a: 148–50, 156–8; Horden and Purcell 2000: 425–6; McGeough 2007: 168; Kopetzky 2008: 223). Phoenician trade in timber is already evident from the famous story of the Egyptian merchant Wenamun of the 11th century BCE, who was sent to Byblos to buy timber for a sacred barque of Amun.

Raw materials were also important elements of Phoenician-sourced products in demand by their Egyptian trade partners. The Phoenicians were organizing the locals to mine metal at sites throughout the Mediterranean as well as to undertake metal refinement and the production of metal goods. There also is evidence that Phoenicians oversaw salt production; trade in salt by official agents is recorded in texts from Ugarit. Phoenician boats landing in Egypt in the 5th century BCE included salt as cargo. Glass was another product imported by Egypt from Phoenicia (Meiggs 1982: 358–9; Yardeni 1994: 67–78; Serpico 1999: 267–72; Serpico and White 2000b: 398–401; Bourriau 2001: 113–46; Serpico *et al.* 2003: 365–75; Leprohon 2004).

In Egyptian depictions from the Late Bronze Age, two traded goods were especially associated with Canaanites: wine and copper. A painting in the Tomb of Khaemweset (Theban Tomb 261) displays the manufacture and export of wine in Canaanite amphorae to Egypt, while in other Egyptian art of the Late Bronze Age, the copper trade was associated with Canaanites. A mold for casting copper was found at Ugarit, which indicates that some Canaanites also knew how to create finished products from the metal. In fact, it was quite typical of Canaanite-Phoenician trade from its beginning to import raw materials and process and redistribute them for further treatment to yield finished products (Bass 1991: 73; Leonard 1996: 244).

The bulk of the products and materials secured from the Egyptians were not used by Phoenicians themselves but became items plied along their international trade routes. Alabaster vases, faience objects, and scarabs were imported from Egypt but also were produced in Egyptian, Egypto-Phoenician, and Phoenician style in Phoenician workshops. However, ivory obtained in Egypt from Africa and Egyptian linen were two types of essential raw materials for important Phoenician industries. Ivory was carved by Phoenician master craftsmen and Egyptian linen was dyed in Phoenician workshops and fashioned into luxury clothing (Barnett 1982: 43–55; Gübel 2000: 212; Markoe 2000b: 146–50).

The Operators of the Egypto-Phoenician Network

Interpretation of the precise nature of this early network is, nonetheless, debated. The textual and pictorial evidence demonstrates that, by the 3rd millennium BCE, the Egyptians were part of a long-distance Levantine trade network. There is no evidence of any sort that Egyptians sailed their own boats beyond the Nile into the open sea or that they served as crews on Levantine boats. From the earliest stages of the Egypto-Phoenician commercial contacts in the 4th millennium BCE, it was the Canaanite-Phoenicians who sailed to Egypt by boat to deliver timber in exchange for Egyptian goods and not the Egyptians who sailed north along the Levantine coast to collect the wood to take back home. This pattern characterized the Egypto-Phoenician commercial contacts throughout the ages (Curtin 1984: 71; Kochavi 1992; Bradbury 1996: 49–56).

Discussing the foundation of Alexandria in the Hellenistic period, Strabo claimed that the earliest kings of the Egyptians had been content with what they had, had not wanted foreign imports at all, and had been prejudiced against all who sailed the seas (17.1.6). Even if Strabo had misunderstood the motives underlying the failure of the Egyptians to found a harbor on the Mediterranean coast, his explanation reflects the recognition of a deficit in Egyptian seafaring, marine activity, or maritime trade.

Despite the compelling evidence, scholars continue to interpret the presence of Egyptian items abroad as a sign of direct trade connections that had been operating between Egypt and Greece, Egypt and Cyprus, Egypt and the Etruscans in Italy, or other places where these items have turned up. The bulk of the Aegyptiaca that came to be distributed around the Mediterranean was shipped by the Canaanite-Phoenicians, who clearly were not the only mediators who carried goods of foreign origin to various locations. As far as Egyptian products were concerned, however, the Canaanite-Phoenicians had an exclusive and comprehensive monopoly over the distribution of and trade in papyri, linen, ivory, scarabs, and palm wine (Kourayos 2005: 114; Mazarakis Ainian 2005: 98; Wilson and Gilbert 2007: 260–3).

Evidence of the Phoenician monopoly over the papyri market is provided by the fact that Greeks could only obtain these Egyptian products via the Phoenician port of Byblos. The Greek word for papyrus is *byblos* (whence originated the word "Bible," i.e. *biblia*, the Greek word for books) and was in use by the time of Homer (*Od*. 21.391). Other evidence reveals the existence of direct Phoenician commercial ties with Egypt through a variety of objects obtained there. Ivory and elephant tusks were given by the Phoenician rulers to the late Assyrian emperors as part of their tribute. Scarabs of both Egyptian and Phoenician origin have been found only in locations known to have been Phoenician trading posts or where other Phoenician artifacts have been found as well, indicating their direct or indirect origin from Phoenician trade. Palm wine, an Egyptian product, is described by Herodotus (2.86; 3.20–2) and Diodorus (Diod. Sic. 1.91) as "Phoenician" wine. Alabaster urns, often bearing Egyptian cartouches, have been found in tombs as far away from Egypt as Spain, Carthage, and the royal cemetery of Nubia from the 8th–7th centuries BCE (Dunham 1950: 30–2, Tomb Ku.4, fig. 11c.560, 562; Boardman *et al.* 1982: 39; Nibbi 1985: 95–7; Dils 1993: 109; Aubet 1996: 495, 498, 500, 503, 2001: 223, 331–3, fig. 50; Krzyszkowska and Morkot 2000: 326; Murray 2000a: 618–21).

In all cases, including Nubia, other Phoenician finds accompanied those of ultimately Egyptian origin. In Spain and Carthage, Phoenician red-slipped pottery appeared alongside Egyptian and Egyptianized artifacts. In Nubia, the alabaster urns were accompanied by Phoenician amphorae and faience bowls, decorated in the same style typical of Phoenician metal bowls. Such metal bowls are considered among the most characteristic items of Phoenician craftsmanship and trade and have been found between Spain, Iran, northern Italy, and Nubia (Dunham 1950: 81–3, 93–4, figs. 28c.1158, 1160; 31e.667; pl. 64.b; Markoe 1985: 38–9, 341; Almagro Gorbea 2004: fig. 18).

Early Canaanite-Phoenician Distribution of Aegyptiaca: The Case of Crete

The Middle Bronze Age marks the beginning of the period when Phoenicians became regular mediators of Egyptian culture. Already before then, however, Phoenician traders had been distributing Egyptian-oriented small objects. One of the first locations for these objects was Crete, which makes it a good example for demonstrating early Canaanite-Phoenician trade in Aegyptiaca. In the early 2nd millennium, scarabs were known in Crete and Byblos, where they were important enough to be locally imitated. As is clear from various Phoenician temple contexts in Phoenicia and Cyprus, the Phoenicians adopted the Egyptian belief in the scarab's protective power. By the late 18th to early 17th centuries BCE, pseudo-Egyptian scarabs were already being manufactured in Canaan, mixing Egyptian and Levantine motifs. These hybrid scarabs were used as funerary amulets in Canaan, reflecting the adoption of an Egyptian funerary custom into Canaanite culture. This adopted custom was then taken back to Egypt by Canaanite settlers at Tell el-Dab'a, where a dynasty of Canaanite origin ruled over northern Egypt during the Second Intermediate Period (ca. 1700–1550 BCE) as the 14th–17th Dynasties.

Canaanite Byblos probably functioned as the first Levantine agent conveying Egyptian culture and goods to Crete and the main distribution center for both Canaanite and Egyptian goods during the first half of the 2nd millennium BCE. Scarabs were one of the Aegyptiaca items they introduced to other cultures they encountered as they expanded their trade networks. Over time, scarabs became a sacred image of fertility, child protection, and afterlife throughout the Mediterranean (Hölbl 1986: 198, 200). Thus, Byblos launched a tradition of trade in scarabs that moved beyond Egypt and Canaan-Phoenicia proper, which was continued by maritime merchants from other Phoenician cities in succeeding centuries as new markets opened up.

The scarabs found in Minoan Crete have been interpreted as secondary imports that accompanied the main goods exchanged via small-scale trade between Egypt and Crete by a palace-authorized agent. Their importance has been underestimated, however. Scarabs were used as amulets in royal and temple cults and had a strong funerary association. They therefore represent religio-cultural influence and likely were valued for their importance in this sphere. They were not just small trinkets that could be traded on as objects of curiosity in other commercial markets. This claim is strengthened by the fact that Crete became a center for the production of local imitations of Egyptian scarabs. The same material, steatite, and manufacturing techniques were used as in Egypt.

Genuine Egyptian scarabs have been found in Crete exclusively in Minoan burials from the Pre-palatial and Proto-palatial periods (ca. 2600–2000 BCE). They have been uncovered at Lebena, Archanes, Tholos B at Platanos, Gournes, Trapeza Cave, Poros, and Hagia Triada. In contrast, the earliest scarab to have been found in Greece is a rare and unique lapis lazuli scarab, dated at the latest to the 17th century BCE. This item may have arrived in Mycenae indirectly, along with other Aegyptiaca and Egyptianized finds from Crete. The use of Minoan motifs on Cretan imitations of scarabs reveals a lower degree of affinity with Egyptian culture. Local versions were made in imitation of the original Egyptian and Canaanite

Egyptianized scarabs that had arrived in Crete. The original scarabs had not been introduced to Crete directly from Egypt but, rather, via mediators, in this case most probably by Canaanite-Phoenicians, first of Byblos and later of Ugarit and other Canaanite-Phoenician cities (Kochavi 1992: 10; Ben-Tor 2006: 77–8, 80–1, 84).

During the Late Bronze Age, Ugarit took over the role of the main Canaanite-Phoenician distribution center. After its destruction, the role of agents and distributors of Egyptian goods and culture was taken over by other Phoenician city-states, perhaps Sidon and Tyre, starting in the Iron Age I. Other distribution centers of the Egypto-Canaanite-Phoenician trade-net included Ashkelon, beginning in the Middle Bronze Age, Tell Keisan and/or Tell Abu Hawam in the Late Bronze Age, and Akko from the Iron Age onwards (Artzy 2006a; Caubet and Yon 2006; Cohen-Weinberger 2007: 145).

II. The Hittite Canaanite-Phoenician Network

By the end of the Middle Bronze II period, trade had become such a major factor and force in international politics that it was probably the desire to control trade routes that spurred the growth of the Hittite Empire (Maeir 2000: 42). The Late Bronze Age was a period of joint trade ventures, which connected the entire area from Egypt to Hatti. The fact that the Hittites took over part of the Levant, including Canaan-Phoenicia as well as probably Hazor and its hinterland, including the Jordan Valley, underscores this assumption. Control of the Levantine corridor was fought over by the Hittites and Egyptians during this period, with the boundary between the two shifting over time. Nevertheless, the northern coastal area above the Carmel Mountains and northern Galilee tended to be part of the Hittite sphere during the entire period. By controlling these Canaanite lands, the Hittites won control of both maritime trade via Byblos and Ugarit and overland trade routes via Hazor and the Jordan Valley. Hittite and Egyptian literary evidence from this period clearly indicates there was no direct contact between these two empires until the 14th century BCE. Even then, it was based on royal personal connections and gift-exchange which was eventually to become formalized in a parity treaty that was sealed by the marriage of a daughter of Hattusili III to Ramesses II in either 1259 or 1246 BCE, not by trade (Bryce 2006: 10; Genz 2011: 317–20). Subsequently, as some trade moved from Egypt to Anatolia—for example, amulets—it must have been managed and organized by middlemen, i.e. the Canaanite-Phoenicians as agents of the Hittite and the Egyptian Empires.

The close connections between the Hittite kingdom and Canaanite city-states is demonstrated in RS 94.2406, a letter written in Ugaritic and dated to the end of the 13th century BCE. It mentions the voyage of a queen of Ugarit by sea and land. The person in question is perhaps Queen Eḫli-Nikkal, a Hittite princess who was to become the wife of the last king of Ugarit, Ammurapi. The letter is thought to have been written after Ammurapi had rejected her as wife and sent her back home. This event demonstrates that the King of Ugarit considered himself equal in stature to the Hittite king, not a king of lesser power (Sauvage and Pardee 2015).

The distribution of private names observed in the Amarna archive of the 14th century BCE and other contemporaneous onomastics from Canaan demonstrate the extension of the Hittite Empire southwards into Canaan. Semitic names predominate in the southern Levant along the coast up to the

Carmel and Akko, but names of northern influence—Hurrian, Anatolian, and Indo-Aryan—are found at Akko, Gath Carmel (Jatt), and along the Jezreel Valley, as well as in Hazor, which shows mixed influence (Hess 2006). Northern names are also typical in the Jordan Valley. At Ta'anach, half the names are Semitic and a quarter are Hurrian, with additional northern names. Megiddo is mixed, too. In Shechem and Jerusalem, most of the names are Semitic, but some are northern. The occurrence of names is an indication of the presence of individuals of Hittite origin in major political and trade centers in the Levant. These individuals may not have been traders, as there is no hint of such activity in the textual evidence of the period. Rather, they were ambassadors of the Hittite court, as reflected also in the distribution of Hittite figurines of precious metals dated to the Late Bronze Age. These small amulets are personal objects of high-level Hittite delegates. When found in context, these figurines comes from temples in the political centers of Alalakh, Nuzi, and Assur and were also found at el-Amarna and Ugarit (Genz 2017).

A major component of Hittite-Canaanite trade in the southern Levant during the 2nd millennium BCE involved traffic in smelted bars of metal and artifacts made of metal from the Faynan copper mines in western Arabia and the copper mines at Timna. In this proposed interpretation of the Hittite metal trade, the Canaanite-Phoenicians oversaw the extraction and smelting at both Timna and Faynan and transported the resulting bars to Anatolia. Other Hittite-controlled routes operated along the Danube and involved the mines in the Carpathian Mountains, while another was an Anatolian-Greek cooperative venture that moved copper from mines in Attica to Hatti (Stos-Gale and Gale 1982). Local agents operated the routes in those areas. It seems that the Hittites oversaw control of an elaborate network for exploiting metals stretching south, northwest, and southwest of Hatti, but more study is required to understand the extent and the details of their ventures.

The Arabian–Jordan Valley–Canaan Trade Route

The organization and trade of metals along the inland Arabian–Levantine–Syrian–Anatolian branch was conducted by the Canaanite-Phoenicians. The copper mines at Timna were worked by locals in the Late Bronze period and at Faynan in the Iron Age. The older view that the Timna mines had been operated by the Egyptians during this period has been revised in newer studies. The famous Hathor temple has been reinterpreted as a temple for Ashtart. Evidently, a trade route operated from the copper mines at Faynan in western Arabia and from those in the southern Aravah at Timna to move smelted ore to Phoenicia and, ultimately, to Hatti. Two-handled small jars of Hittite shape, which have been found in the Levant, are markers along this route. Their distribution reveals the posts and branches of the Near Eastern traffic in metal (Ben-Yosef 2012; Levy, Ben-Yosef, and Najjar 2018).

Small jars are rare and not part of the local Levantine pottery corpus of the Middle Bronze Age IIC–Late Bronze Age I periods. Their form is more common in central and southeastern Anatolia during the last phase of the Middle Bronze Age and the beginning of the Late Bronze Age and may have originated in this area. Examples from this period have been found at Boğazköy (Hattusa), Gordion, Yanarlar, Arslantepe, Tarsus, and Kinet (Regev 2020: 166–72). The use of this form changed over time. The earliest evidence of its use as a large ceremonial drinking vessel shared by multiple participants comes from Anatolian sites and central Aegean island sites characterized by a number of Anatolian features in the late 3rd millennium BCE. The jar remained in use until the 2nd millennium BCE. From the second half of the 2nd millennium BCE, a smaller version appeared in tombs, indicating its use in funerary rituals (Rutter 2008: 465–7, figs. 1, 2, 8). Similar forms also have been found in Syria from the 3rd millennium to the early 1st millennium BCE and in Cyprus from the Proto-Geometric period (late 12th to early 11th centuries BCE).

The site of Jatt, near Haifa, has yielded imported items that suggest it was on a trade route that had begun already in the Late Bronze Age I period and continued in use into the Iron I period. Examples of Anatolian-inspired small jars have been excavated from layers dating between the Middle Bronze Age IIC and the Late Bronze Age I period. In the Iron I period, metal objects made of ores originating in Transjordan have been unearthed on site (Artzy 2006b: 95–7). The finds from Jatt seem to point to the existence of an ancient trade route that ran along the Jordan Valley and the ridge of Transjordan, carrying perfumes, spices, and metal ores from Arabia to Syria and Anatolia. The Transjordan–Syria–Anatolia route crossed the main east–west route from Beth-Shean to Megiddo to several sites on the Levantine coast, especially those around the Carmel Ridge in northern Israel (Holladay 2001: 146–7; Artzy 2006a: 51).

According to several models, Beth-Shean and Megiddo functioned as distribution centers along this trade route, and the goods transported there also were shipped to sites in their vicinity, like Samaria and Shechem (Leonard 1987: 265; Artzy 1994: fig. 11, 2006a: fig. 5; Sugerman 2009). Based on the presence of Hittite seals, burials, and T-shaped houses, Megiddo in particular has been identified as a Hittite distribution center, where a Hittite diaspora controlling and shipping Hittite goods lived and worked alongside an Egyptian trade diaspora (Holladay 2001: 152–3). Goods reaching both sites would have been transported along a route that branched off from the main route that continued north to Hazor and beyond. This westward branch would have run along the edge of the Beth-Shean and Jezreel Valleys to the coast.

The distribution of these Middle Bronze Age IIC–Late Bronze Age I small jars may indicate that, even in this early period, the Transjordan–Anatolia and Beth-Shean Levantine coastal route was already being utilized as a main east–west trade route for caravans and traders importing goods from Arabia. This route is usually believed to have begun operating in the last phase of the Late Bronze Age II and has been associated with the domestication of camels (Artzy 1994: 131–7, 139). However, this study verifies that the trade route had begun as early as the Middle Bronze Age II, during the Hyksos period. The route appears to have represented a cooperative venture among the Hittite, Egyptian, Arabian, and south Levantine long-distance trade-nets.

One or more branches off the larger route appear to have sent goods into the central highlands. Vessels similar to the above-mentioned Hittite-inspired small jars have been found in tombs at Samaria, Shechem, Jerusalem, Beth-Shemesh, and Lachish. Judging by the large quantities of imported finds from Samaria and Shechem in both the Middle Bronze Age IIC and Late Bronze Age I periods and in the Iron Age I, one of these sites might have been an additional distribution center on a subsidiary route. It is possible that goods were shipped to the central Samarian highlands from Megiddo or Beth-Shean using an established overland route that crossed the Jezreel Valley and ran into the highlands. Alternatively, however, traders and goods could have crossed the Jordan Valley, probably at Jericho, where such urn-inspired vessels have been found, and moved west along one of the small river valleys, probably through the Tirza (Far'ah) Valley and crossing Tell el-Far'ah, before continuing south to Jerusalem, Beth Shemesh, and Lachish or, more often, north, via Samaria or Shechem to Megiddo and the coast.

Small jars of the early Hittite form found in Transjordan in Phase V at Abu al-Kharaz, about 15 km south of Beth-Shean, support the existence of this route as early as the late 16th–mid-15th century BCE (Late Bronze Age I period) (Fischer 1999: fig. 10.1). Additional support comes from a cave in the Baq'ah Valley dated to the 15th century BCE (McGovern 1986: figs. 37.11–13, 38). The Baq'ah Valley north of Amman is on the road connecting Jericho with inland Jordan and Jordan (via Bardala) with Samaria and Jatt.

The finds from Tell Abu al-Kharaz are especially interesting, not only because they are early (16th–15th centuries BCE), but also because of the coexistence of the Hittite-inspired form along with a coastal form known from Middle Bronze Age Byblos (Fischer 1999: fig. 10.1, 3) at the site. Moreover, both vessel types have been found beside Chocolate-on-White Ware (CoW), which petrographic analysis has indicated to have originated from inland southeastern Lebanon near Mount Hermon. The first place of manufacture might have been at Rashiah el-Fukhar in the mountains, from which a short and easy route provided access to Dan and Hazor. The ware was produced subsequently both in Lebanon and the central Jordan Valley. By the time both small jar forms appear in Kharaz Phase V, CoW ware was produced only in the Jordan Valley (Fischer 2006: 154–6).

Another Canaanite-Phoenician pottery type found at Tell Abu al-Kharaz that dates to the Middle Bronze Age III period strengthens the evidence of Lebanese-produced pottery (in this case probably from the area just north of Beirut) in western Arabia and the early trade connections between the two regions (Fischer 2008: 88, fig. 2). This type was somewhat similar to CoW bichrome ware and has been found alongside sherds of CoW in what seems to be an industrial area with a furnace for metal. The Canaanite-Phoenician pottery in question was close in shape and decoration both to the Middle Bronze or Late Bronze Age I Hittite two-handled small jars and the Middle Bronze Age I and Late Bronze Age I Canaanite two-handled small jars from Byblos and the Canaanite-Phoenician coast. Similar vessels have been found at Pella in Tomb 62, dated to the Middle Bronze Age IIC, and at Megiddo X and Dan XII, both of which are dated to the Middle Bronze Age IIA (Fischer 2008: 89–90). Evidence for the continuity of the route connecting the Canaanite-Phoenician coast with Transjordan during the Iron Age II is provided by two sites. A tomb in Madaba contained a small jar of similar form (Herr 2015: pl. 2.6.10.1) and Tell Jawa, south of Amman, yielded biconical bodied small jars with a long ridged neck and black or brown band decoration in a domestic cultic context (Daviau 1996: fig. 6.3, 2001: 216).

The use of this Jordan Valley route by Phoenicians in the early Iron Age, with possible extensions east into Arabia and India, has recently been suggested by residue analysis performed on Phoenician flasks excavated at Dor, Tell Qasile, and Kinneret. Their contents included cinnamon and perhaps also nutmeg (Namdar *et al.* 2013). The cinnamon tree is native to India, Sri Lanka, Bangladesh, and Myanmar, while nutmeg seeds from the *Myristica fragrans* tree are native to the Banda Islands in the Moluccas of Indonesia but was being grown in ancient Malabar, modern Kerala in southern India. Based on the evidence presented for contacts between Transjordan and the Canaanite-Phoenician coast, it is very likely that not only was the trade route between Arabia and the Levant established early but it might also have been operated by Canaanite-Phoenicians from early times. Support for the operation of this route into the Far East already being in existence in the early Late Bronze period has now been provided by finds of vanilla from an Late Bronze Age I tomb at Megiddo. The type of vanilla originated probably from either east Africa, India, or Indonesia. These finds are much earlier than those from Dor, demonstrating perhaps the existence of this trade route during the period of Hittite domination and Canaanite-Hittite collaboration during the Late Bronze Age I (Bower 2018).

The distribution of the Hittite-inspired and Canaanite-Phoenician two-handled small jars corresponds well with the Arabia–Syria–Anatolia trade route and to roads connecting this route to the Levantine coast. Hittite and Assyrian textual evidence is clear that, during the Late Bronze Age, the Hittite court controlled the trafficking of iron and copper along this route, while during the Iron Age II the Assyrian court controlled trade in these metals over this route. It has commonly been assumed that Hittite and Assyrian traders physically moved the goods (Veldhuijzen 2012: 238). The evidence presented here, however, indicates that Canaanite-Phoenicians likely administered major parts of this operation, at least from Arabia to the Syrian coast. The pottery, mines, and sanctuary uncovered at Timna in the Aravah point to the likelihood that Canaanite-Phoenicians operated and controlled the mining, smelting, and religious activity there. All stages of their activity also involved local desert tribes from Arabia and the Aravah, at least from the Bronze Age onward, not Egyptians, as previously believed (Avner 2014). Anatolian metal trade routes had been in operation even longer, at least from the 3rd millennium BCE, and included circumnavigation of the Black Sea. The Kestel tin mine and the tin smelting village of Göltepe in the Taurus Mountains demonstrate that metallurgical techniques had been developed in Anatolia as early as the 3rd millennium BCE (Zimmermann 2007: 65–75, fig. 4; Yener 2008, 2009).

Research conducted in Transjordan sheds additional light on the Arabian end of this route. Excavations and surveys have revealed a series of mines and furnaces from Tell Abu al-Kharaz in the northern Aravah to Faynan south of the Dead Sea. Faynan was probably the largest and longest-lasting of the west Arabian metal mining and industry sites. Other sites within this corridor include Tell Hammeh and a number of smaller sites. Not all the sites were simultaneously active, and it has been suggested that the smaller ones may have operated seasonally. It seems that, during the 2nd millennium BCE, production at Faynan declined while Timna was operating at high capacity (Weisgerber 2006: 13; Veldhuijzen 2012: 246–7). Mining and smelting commenced at Faynan in the EB I in the mid-4th millennium BCE, by which time Canaanites were already trading its metal bars via Canaan, both overland and by sea, as far as Egypt and the northern Levant. Slag from an EB I metallurgical workshop at Ashkelon has provided evidence of a connection between Faynan and the Canaanite-Phoenician coast. Its composition was similar to slag from Faynan, indicating that previously smelted metal bars had been transported from western Arabia to the Levantine coast as early as the 4th millennium BCE. In addition, petrographic analysis of EB II vessels excavated at Faynan indicated the clay they were made from originated on the Levantine coast (Gophna and Milevski 2003: 223–4).

The trade route for copper seems to have started at Faynan and probably ended somewhere in Anatolia, likely at Hattusa, the Hittite capital, where archives document the presence of metalworking and trade beginning in the 17th century BCE (Souckova-Siegelova 2001). At least one segment and branch of the route seems to have remained in use into the Iron Age, when iron became a sought-after commodity in addition to copper. Analysis of the iron slag from furnaces dating to the late 10th to early 9th centuries BCE at Tell Hammeh in the central Jordan Valley and from Beth-Shemesh in Judah has shown a similar composition and may indicate a direct connection between the two sites. Excavations at Beth-Shemesh have uncovered a Phoenician red-burnished small jar from the Iron Age II. These finds suggest this site's likely location along a branch of a Phoenician administered trade route in the mid-9th century BCE which had been in use already in the Late Bronze I period, as indicated by the discovery of Hittite-inspired two-handled small jars in an Late Bronze Age I tomb on site. It is logical to connect it to a branch that ran from Jericho via Jerusalem to Beth-Shemesh and Lachish and which traded metals, among other commodities.

Excavations at Hazor and Akko have revealed major metallurgic industrial areas that correspond to the route and its branches suggested here. Metalworking at Hazor started in the early Middle Bronze Age II, flourished in the Late Bronze Age I, continued throughout the Late Bronze Age, and then, after a gap in the Iron I, resumed during the Iron Age II (Yahalom-Mack *et al.* 2014: 37–8). Located on the route from the Jordan Valley toward Anatolia, the rise in metallurgical activity at Hazor during the Late Bronze Age I fits exactly with Hatti's takeover of this area and the metal trade at that time (Singer 2006). The presence of a Hittite trade diaspora in the adjoining region between 1800 and 1000 BCE has already been claimed, based on the T-shaped houses and Hittite artifacts abundant at Tell Abu Hawam, Megiddo, and Hazor (Holladay 2001). Also, as already discussed, Hittite presence in Canaan is indicated by the distribution of private names of Hurrian, Anatolian, and Indo-Aryan origin in the Late Bronze Age period at, for example, Akko, Gath Carmel (Jatt), Hazor, Ta'anach, Megiddo and along the Jezreel and Jordan Valleys (Hess 1993, 2006).

Hittite presence at Hazor and Rehov continued at least until the 10th century BCE, as is evident from a cooking pot with Luwian seal impressions from Hazor, probably from Anatolia, and the industrial apiary at Rehov that used Anatolian bees (Ben-Tor, Cohen-Weinberger, and Weeden 2017). A metallurgical industrial area has been uncovered at Akko, which currently shows evidence of use in the Late Bronze Age (13th century BCE) and the Persian period (6th–5th centuries BCE). Although iron slag and other evidence for metalworking is dominant during the Persian period, remains of copper indicate that the local industry was still using this metal at this time. However, it is more than likely that the metallurgical industry continued there from the Late Bronze Age onward, with industrial sites at Akko perhaps shifting in different periods. Future excavations may uncover evidence from the missing centuries. Recent excavation has already demonstrated metallurgical activity on site between the late 8th and mid-2nd centuries BCE (Van Horn 2017). This site is located at the end of the east–west route for metal trade that ran from the Jordan Valley via Beth-Shean and Megiddo to the Canaanite-Phoenician coast.

The two-handled small jars used in the Levant during the Bronze Age and the Iron Age have a restricted distribution that points to both overland international trade routes and to Canaanite-Phoenician culture. No tombs in the vast cemetery at Tell el 'Ajjul (Gaza), for example, which dates to the end of the Middle Bronze Age and the Late Bronze I (1800–1500 BCE±), contained the Hittite form discussed above (Petrie 1931; Gonen 1981; Fischer 2003, 2004). Gaza and most of the southern coast of the Levant were part of another trade route, a nautical route that connected Egypt with the northern part of the Levantine coast. Along this route were several harbors, including Gaza, and the boats using it were not used to ship metals.

The presence of the two-handled small jars of Hittite origin in tombs along the internal trade route is intriguing and raises the question of what these finds represent. The presence of individuals bearing Hurrian, Anatolian, and Indo-Aryan names in the correspondence from Canaanite polities in the Amarna archive indicates the physical presence of people with this background in Canaan. Bearing this in mind, do the jars point to the presence of local Hittite representatives in Canaan at nodes along this internal route who maintained their native burial customs? Or, instead, do they point to the penetration of

Hittite religious influence into Canaan after direct trade contact with Hittites in Anatolia, so that local Canaanites along this route, and perhaps more widely, started using these Hittite vessels for communal drinking rituals in tombs as well as cremating the deceased? It would seem that the burials containing these vessels in the Late Bronze Age I were of Hittites or a mixed, Canaanite-Hittite, population.

The inland route marked by the presence of the Hittite-inspired two-handled small jars was operated by Canaanite-Phoenicians, who sourced and moved metal to be used primarily by the Hittite Empire. They likely controlled only the southern part of the route that ended at Hattusa, the Hittite capital. Based on the abundant bichrome pottery of Hurrian tradition found in cemeteries at Mitanni (Epstein 1966; Artzy 1980; Oates, Oates, and McDonald 1998) and the horse burials also typical of the Hurrian Empire (Silver 2014), it is possible that this site and other Hurrian centers were the main northern trading partners involved in ensuring the delivery of the processed metal bars to their final destination.

The Canaanite-Phoenician connection with Hatti did not end with the fall of the Hittite Empire of the Late Bronze Age. The entities that followed it, the Syro-Hittite states (also known as Neo-Hittite) of the 12th–8th centuries BCE, were using Phoenician script in their inscriptions: for example, at Karatepe and Çineköy (Ceram 1956: 218; Hawkins and Davies 1978; Lanfranchi 2007; Hawkins 2009), along with Luwian and Aramaic. From the 10th century these states were divided into northern and southern spheres, with continuous Hittite domination in the northern sphere and Aramaean domination in the southern sphere. One of the states in the latter group was Palistin: the Philistines, who were mainly Canaanite-Phoenicians and not invaders from the Aegean (Regev 2020: 95–104).

The strong trade connections between the Canaanite-Phoenicians of the Levantine coast and the Syro-Hittites, which included also Canaanite-Phoenician elements, continued uninterrupted at least until the Assyrian and then Babylonian conquests of the late 8th to early 6th centuries BCE. This population construction that began at the latest in the 12th century BCE explains the composition of a Canaanite-Phoenician sphere from Alexandretta Bay through the entire Levant during the Iron Age. Although the spread and control of the Achaemenid Empire changed the regional and international map and affected Mediterranean trade in its entirety, the population stayed the same, despite some Assyrian and Babylonian exiles.

III. The International Style of the Late Bronze Age

During the Late Bronze Age, the eastern Mediterranean, Anatolia, and the Near East were united as one region by several seafaring agents from the Aegean and the Levant. The international trade of this period was diverse, conducted both by palatial economies and their merchant-agents. This palatial trade was characterized by what is known as the International Style, an assemblage of decorative styles, artifacts, and other goods that dominated the elite markets of the entire east Mediterranean, including the Levant, Egypt, Cyprus, the Aegean, and Asia Minor (Knappett *et al.* 2005: 25; Van de Mieroop 2005; Feldman 2006: 1–17). In fact, this so-called International Style was the first of three phases of Phoenician style, which was characterized by its inclusion of elements adopted from its contacts with many cultures via trade.

Perhaps the most pronounced feature of the International Style are the palace wall paintings that have been found in Crete, the Levant, and Egypt from the 15th century BCE onwards. Previously, it had been assumed that Crete had been the source of this practice. However, precedents are now known for this trend in the Levant. Palace wall paintings have been uncovered in Beirut that date to the early 2nd millennium BCE, and other magnificent wall paintings are known from the palaces at Mari, dated between the 21st and 18th centuries BCE. Other examples have surfaced in palace complexes at Alalakh in Turkey, Tell el-Burak in Lebanon, and Kabri in western Galilee in Israel (Bietak 2007; Bertsch 2018). Although these early eastern paintings were not identical to the wall paintings that became fashionable in the Late Bronze Age, they have features that are very similar to those of the later paintings, especially floral and vegetation elements.

Moreover, a text written to the last king of Mari in the Middle Bronze Age period, Zimri-Lim, contains a request from the king of Ugarit that he and his retinue, which would include Cretans (*Keftiu*), be allowed to visit his palace in person (Muller 2005). This single text provides evidence that a king from the Levantine coast likely experienced the Mari palace paintings in person and might well have already introduced them into his own palace in the Middle Bronze period. In such a case, the practice would not have gone out of favor for a time and then reappeared again in the Late Bronze Age but would have been implemented along the coast as early as the Middle Bronze period, continuing as a favored decorative tradition there into the Late Bronze period. The excavations at Ugarit have concentrated on the Late Bronze Age city; almost nothing is known about earlier levels, unfortunately.

The Middle Bronze evidence from Beirut and Mari (and Alalakh, Tell el-Burak, and Kabri) shows clearly that, although wall paintings were popular in Late Bronze palaces in Crete and the Levant, this was not an innovation of that period. Palace wall painting already had been fashionable in the early Middle Bronze Age in Mesopotamia and the Levant. Here, therefore, is a major feature of the International Style that was clearly eastern in origin, which influenced a style adopted in Crete and the Minoan culture.

In addition to the palatial wall paintings, the International Style of the Late Bronze Age is known for several pottery groups. These include the Canaanite Jar, Red Lustrous Wheel-made (RLWm) pottery, Cypriot Milk Bowls, and Minoan and Mycenaean Stirrup Jars (Regev 2020: 162–5). Another characteristic of the Late Bronze Age International Style are Egyptian items, known collectively as Aegyptiaca. Levantine Phoenician sites have yielded large quantities of Egyptian finds in the 12th–4th centuries BCE. The clearest evidence of the integration of Canaanite and Egyptian elements to create the first phase of a distinctive Phoenician style are the ubiquitous scarabs, a typical Egyptian element that began to be manufactured by Phoenicians in the Middle Bronze Age. All the scarabs found in the Cape Gelidonya shipwreck of the 13th century BCE, for example, were produced in Canaan, somewhere between Gaza and Ugarit, and dedicated to Amon-Re.

The International Style of the Late Bronze Age also included other items that have been associated with Greek rather than Canaanite culture. An example is faience beads that were manufactured in the Aegean at Tiryns and Thassos during the Mycenaean palatial period. As a Mycenaean product, faience beads did not survive the fall of the palaces there, and their production in the Aegean terminated around 1200 BCE. Glass beads were another item produced at many locations by the Greeks using Near Eastern techniques (Nightingale 2009; Nikita, Nightingale, and Chenery 2017). Mycenaean faience and glass beads are among the status or trademark objects circulated as part of the International Style of the Late Bronze Age.

An examination of the Aegean finds confirms that the technology for their production and sometimes the raw materials employed in their manufacture were brought to the Aegean from the Near East or Egypt. Glass ingots were part of the cargo on board the boat that sank off the coast of Uluburun during the Late Bronze Age. On the basis of the Canaanite Jars among the cargo and the inventory more generally, scholars have argued that the boat was probably operated by Canaanite-Phoenicians and that it was headed to an Aegean market. Although some examples of imported faience beads have been found at Mycenaean sites as well, the majority of such beads were probably produced locally in the Aegean (Pulak 1997; Bennet 2008: 164; Nightingale 2008: 88–90; Tite 2008: 120). Supporting evidence for the Canaanite-Phoenician origin of the ship, and much of its content, comes from renewed analyses of some of the amphorae and the resin it contained. The amphorae on board the Uluburun belong to group 1 from Amarna, Canaanite amphorae that originate from the coastal Carmel area, between Haifa and Akko (Bourriau 2001; Smith *et al.* 2004; Stern *et al.* 2008: 2191).

Finally, a class of pottery that perhaps should now be considered as belonging to this style are the Hittite-inspired small jars found in tombs along the Hittite-Phoenician metals trade network. These small jars were circulated internationally but not to all parts of the eastern Mediterranean like the other pottery groups that belong to the style. During the Late Bronze Age, these small jars have only been found in Anatolia and the Near East. They did not arrive in Cyprus until the Iron Age (Regev 2020: 166–72).

The political and social situation changed considerably with the fall of the great powers of Hatti, Egypt, and Mycenae and their palace systems. By the 1st millennium BCE, seafaring in the east Mediterranean was handled by specialists, i.e. the Phoenicians. From that time on, the Mediterranean world had a western orientation which did not include the inland areas of the Near East (Van de Mieroop 2005: 140). There is no doubt that the Mediterranean commercial networks were ancient, and it usually is recognized that the Canaanite-Phoenicians were the first to unite the entire Mediterranean in long-distance trade.

IV. The Phoenician *Koine* of the 8th–7th Centuries BCE

Evidence from Pre-palatial Crete shows that contacts initiated by those living in the eastern Mediterranean had begun in the Early Bronze Age and continued unbroken thereafter. Even so, Phoenician trade has been considered a new, pan-Mediterranean trade that emerged only during the Iron Age. The unquestionable Phoenician dominance over Mediterranean trade during the 1st millennium BCE has been viewed by some as a rebirth of the 2nd-millennium "Canaanite 'thalassocracy'" rather than as an unbroken line of Canaanite-Phoenician trade in the Mediterranean (Sasson 1966; Sherratt and Sherratt 1991: 375; Knapp 1993; Dickinson 1994: 234–41; Abulafia 2005: 69; Bresson 2005: 97, 101; Feldman 2006: 195).

The Iron Age Phoenician trade networks included goods that exemplify how the Late Bronze Age international artistic style, a Canaanite-Phoenician creation, developed or evolved directly into the

International Phoenician *koine* of the 8th–7th centuries BCE without a break. During the Iron Age, this *koine* is sometimes known as the "Orientalizing" style which was clearly inspired by Canaanite-Phoenician art and religion. The term "Orientalizing" has also been used to refer to a period of time, the 8th and 7th centuries BCE, when this style became popular in Greece and Italy. The style included artifacts made, distributed, or influenced by Phoenicians. The users of products comprising the Iron Age International *koine* were not much different than the users of the preceding style supported by the palace system. In both cases, we are dealing with elite classes interconnected by the same goal of international relations. In both cases, we are probably also dealing with the same merchant-mediators, Canaanite-Phoenicians, who were trading goods for wealth, their long-lasting specialty (Feldman 2006; Horden and Purcell 2006: 460; Bedford 2007: 309).

This second phase of Phoenician style was composed mainly of Canaanite elements, although it used many Egyptian motifs. Scarabs continued to be a staple, and between the 8th and 4th centuries BCE they often were carved of various materials in a Phoenician style. Other major elements of the Phoenician style of the Iron Age included ivories, decorated metal bowls, and several types of pottery groups—mainly bottles and juglets (Scandone 1984; Boardman 1987; Mendleson 1987; Gübel 1988, 2000; Markoe 2000b: 154–6; Brandl 2003: 258; Cecchini, Mazzoni, and Scigliuzzo 2009; Regev 2020: 139–48).

By the 8th century BCE and the so-called Orientalizing period of the Mediterranean, Phoenician style was so influential that it affected and even changed the artistic style of Syro-Hittite culture. The Hittites, once a mighty kingdom that had influenced Canaanite religion and style, were under Aramaean rule by the 8th century and using Aramaean elements, but they were also using Phoenician elements in their art. These elements were of an Egypto-Phoenician style, i.e. the Phoenician adaptation of Egyptian elements into old Canaanite art and images, of which the 7th-century stela from Tell Defenneh (Tahpanhes) in Egypt is a good example. Made in a new style using new techniques, this Phoenician style influenced both the Near East and the Mediterranean during the Iron Age. The Phoenician influence reached a pinnacle during the 8th–7th centuries BCE but began earlier, during the prior peak of Canaanite artistic influence during the Late Bronze Age (Akurgal 1981: 135–9, figs. 1–13; Wasmuth and Ögüt 2010).

Evidence for the ongoing integration of Egyptian style into Phoenician art and style beyond the 8th–7th centuries BCE comes from the Persian period, when Tyrian coins bore Egyptian symbols. Egyptian-style ceramic sarcophagi that had been used in the Late Bronze Age— for example, at Deir el-Balah—appear in stone versions at Sidon, Arwad, Byblos, Beirut, Gaza, Amathus, Kition, Soli in Cilicia, Malta, Cannita in Sicily, and Cádiz in the 7th century and continue until the 4th century BCE (Frede 2000). Stone anthropoid sarcophagi were also popular in Egypt during this period (Buhl 1959), and a few genuine Egyptian sarcophagi were imported from Egypt for the burial of King Tabnit and his son, Eshmunezer II, in the early 5th century BCE. However, it seems that, due to repeated Egyptian rebellions in the 4th century BCE, the Persian kings were no longer keen on Egyptian-style artifacts, which could have been the cause for the decline and desertion of the manufacture and distribution of Aegyptiaca in Phoenician style. By the end of the 4th century BCE, Egyptian-style crafts were missing not only from Phoenician assemblages around the Mediterranean but also from those in the Phoenician homeland.

The Phoenician style also incorporated some elements from the Greek style, as seen in Greek headdresses used to depict the dead on the royal stone sarcophagi at Sidon and also on sarcophagi found at Kition. Greek style did not affect Phoenician pottery or coins, however, except for a single series issued in Sidon in years 8–14 of King ʻAbdashtart I, probably in commemoration of the Athenian decree honoring him for having provided much-needed grain and exempting Sidonian traders in Athens from certain taxes (Edelman 2016: 253–6). The Attic weight standard was used to mint coins in the 4th century BCE for economic reasons, but this practice was abandoned in 275 BCE (Bey, Reinach, and Chantre 1892: 127–43, 145–18; Betlyon 2004: 466–9; Georgiou 2009: 136–7; Jigoulov 2010: 97–9, Edelman 2016; Lorber 2018: 115–16).

However, during the late 4th century BCE, the political connections between the Phoenician cities and Egypt were tightened due to their mutual rebellion against the Persians. In that period, the Egyptian economy declined because of the heavy load of silver taxes paid to Persia, which triggered the rebellion. Even if Phoenician boats could sail westward during the Persian period, they had no Aegyptiaca to carry abroad. The Egyptians were no longer able to mass-produce objects, and Phoenician production was halted as well. This era seems to be the end of the Egypto-Phoenician network, at least the part of the net that redistributed Egyptian artifacts and distributed Phoenician crafts in Egyptian style (Dandamayev 1989: 297–311).

V. The Phoenician *Koine* of the Hellenistic Period

The Phoenician cities along the Levantine coast became servants of the Persian Empire in the 6th century BCE. The Persians requisitioned their fleets and crews for multiple wars, which reduced their ability to carry out commerce simultaneously. As a result, international Phoenician trade in the Mediterranean basin shifted almost entirely to the initiative of the western Phoenician cities and trading posts during much of the Persian and early Hellenistic periods. Eventually, the cities in the "homeland" returned to their maritime commercial activities but were not able entirely to regain their former prominence. Consequently, the Phoenician *koine* in the Hellenistic period was more restricted than ever, and only after some time into the period did things start to change.

Ancient religious and cultural symbols that ornamented many of the items spread in earlier times in wide geographical international circles now ceased to be produced. This included metal luxury items, carved ivories, decorated shells and ostrich eggs, alabaster vessels, and all the Aegyptiaca (scarabs, amulets, mirrors, and so forth). What remained in international distribution was pottery. The Canaanite-Phoenician jar that reached the central Mediterranean as early as the Late Bronze I period was no longer circulated, although it re-emerged as the dominant jar in the Mediterranean and beyond in the Late Roman period (Regev 2020: 19–53).

The first Phoenician pottery group to be widely distributed in the Hellenistic period was the heavy coarse ware *amphoriskos* that was popular in the eastern Mediterranean and around the Black Sea between the 3rd and 1st centuries BCE (Regev 2020: 145–8). This type, although in a new form, continued the tradition of Canaanite-Phoenician bottles and juglets that were circulated for their content, possibly perfumed oils, during the 9th–6th centuries BCE.

The second widely distributed Phoenician pottery group is the Eastern Sigillata A Red Slip pottery. Following an ancient tradition in the Near East, Red Slip was one of the major markers of Canaanite-Phoenician corpora around the Mediterranean starting in the 11th century BCE. Local versions of this group ware were produced in all the Phoenician cities and trading posts around the Mediterranean. Production almost vanished during the Persian period in Phoenicia and the Levant but continued in Cyprus and Spain. This group re-emerged in mass production using an industrial scale in the Levant in the 3rd century BCE but was distributed westward only in the 2nd century BCE, when the Phoenician cities regained autonomy from the Seleucid regime. The process intensified during the Early Roman period, the peak era for this group's distribution (Regev 2020: 63–92).

—4—

Canaanite-Phoenician Style and Corpus

Until now, discussion has concentrated on items and elements included in the Phoenician corpus. It is now time to investigate the details of those elements that composed the Canaanite-Phoenician corpus. As often is the case when dealing with the Canaanite-Phoenicians, elements that scholars should have incorporated into their artistic and religious symbolism have instead been associated with other cultures on a superficial level. As a result, the layers of borrowed influences from several sources and the complexity of many elements comprising the Canaanite-Phoenician style and corpus have been overlooked. In particular, elements borrowed from Mesopotamian, Syrian, and Egyptian styles but adapted to produce a Canaanite-Phoenician version need to be acknowledged as integral parts of the Canaanite-Phoenician corpus. Some elements of Egyptian origin are acknowledged to constitute Aegyptiaca in Canaanite-Phoenician contexts, but not all of them. Some better- and lesser-known examples of Canaanite-Phoenician elements are described in depth below.

Items that have already been described extensively in other studies will be covered briefly. They include metal objects, glass, faience, and ivory. Similarly, perishable items will be given only brief consideration, because they disintegrated over time, leaving insufficient evidence to describe the trade network they would have been part of: for example, the purple dye industry. Items that are being identified as part of the Canaanite-Phoenician corpus for the first time, however, will be given more space.

I. The Syrian and Aramaean Styles

Glass, ivory, and metal objects decorated in Canaanite-Phoenician style with typical motifs that include influence from Egyptian art are often regarded as either of Eastern, Syrian, or North Syrian style. Classical art historians and archaeologists who encounter such objects in Greek contexts tend to make this attribution. However, there is no "Eastern" style; there is no *koine* style that embraced some or all of the motifs and styles of Near Eastern cultures, not during the Bronze and Iron Ages and not in any other era until the Islamic period. In fact, the only Eastern style that integrated motifs of various eastern cultures was the Phoenician style (Åström 1991: 149–50; Strøm 1992: 47; Gübel 2000; Boardman 2001: 6, 255–6; Coldstream 2003: 358–66, 410–11; Wasmuth and Ögüt 2010: 572–4).

The characteristics of the so-called Syrian style are still unclear, even though the label has been applied widely to objects excavated at sites around the Mediterranean. The differences between Phoenician and Syrian styles are debated, as are their chronologies and the differences, if any, between northern and southern Syrian styles. It also has been claimed that the Syrian style was produced and distributed between the 10th and 8th centuries BCE and then incorporated into the Phoenician style. This last claim is certainly not accurate, as demonstrated by archaeological evidence of Phoenician finds from the 10th–8th centuries BCE, especially from Crete and Iberia, excavated over the past 30 years.

The alleged Syrian style has been differentiated from the Phoenician by a claim that it had less of an appearance of luxury and lacked Egyptian motifs. R. D. Barnett identified the Syrian style as a continuation of the Late Bronze Age Canaanite-Mycenaean tradition in its shapes, elements, and technique. Not all objects made in Phoenician style, however, included Egyptian elements. Canaanite elements, on the other hand, were always present. It seems, then, that at least some of the items that have been associated in the past with the so-called Syrian style were, in fact, Phoenician objects that did not include Egyptian motifs.

The differentiations and identifications offered by Barnett were not based on firm data relating to artistic and archaeological criteria but on historiographic and artistic approaches to the Phoenicians that were current in the 1950s–80s. During that time, there was a concerted effort to tone down or silence evidence of the wide distribution of Phoenician products and the cultural impact of the Phoenicians on ancient Mediterranean culture. What Barnett called the "Late Bronze Canaanite-Mycenaean tradition" is now known as "The Late Bronze International Style," which includes a wider variety of elements than Canaanite and Mycenaean alone, as discussed above (Barnett 1982: 43–55). It should be noted in this context that Barnett listed only one site in Syria proper, Hama, as a center of production of Syrian style manufacture. On the other hand, he included as Syrian the neo-Hittite and Mesopotamian centers of Zinçirli and Carchemish. This fact, when added to the alleged differentiation between Phoenician and Syrian styles, increases the questionable identification of a Syrian style.

Another Near Eastern style that has been observed, a different style altogether from what is called Syrian style, is known as the Aramaean style. Irene Winter has called it the south-Syrian style. This Iron Age style cannot be confused with the Phoenician style; not only are its elements different but they are also later than the elements used in Phoenician art. The Phoenician art of the Iron Age was already composed of different elements that were amalgamated during the Bronze Age and did not include new elements until the 5th–4th centuries BCE.

The Aramaean style is made up of elements closer to ancient Mesopotamian art, a style that is hardly found as far west as the Levant and even less so in the Mediterranean. The Aramaean style is, therefore, another Near Eastern style that was not present at Mediterranean sites visited by Phoenician or other Levantine traders. This contemporaneous style was characteristic of Mesopotamia and eastern Anatolia but was not widely distributed (Winter 1976, 1981: 130; Akurgal 1981: 131–5, pls. 16–17; Gübel 2000: 211–12).

Confusion and misunderstanding related to an alleged Syrian style vs. an Eastern style characterize many of the studies dealing with Orientalia in general, especially Phoenician finds, in the Mediterranean context. A Syrian style never existed. An identifiable Aramaean style existed during the Iron Age but was limited in range to the inland, eastern Levant; only rare examples managed to penetrate to the western Levantine coast. Presumably, then, the oriental style that spread through the Mediterranean from the 10th century BCE onwards was Phoenician. It was a distinctive style composed of Canaanite and often Egyptian elements alongside, in its earliest phase, Mycenaean-produced beads and pottery, and Hittite small jar forms used for cremation. The style had gelled into an amalgam by the Late Bronze Age and used a fossilized imagery until the end of the Persian period.

II. Egypto-Phoenician Corpora

Aegyptiaca

The widest definition of Aegyptiaca is "objects that can be characterized as distinctly Egyptian through their stylistics and the materials from which they were made" (Versluys 2016: 74), an enduring and successful global commodity which began to be distributed in the Old Kingdom (27th century BC) in the Nile Valley, the Mediterranean, and the Near East. It has also been stated that the definition of Egyptian material culture consists at least of pyramids, sphinxes, obelisks, statues, stelae, and sarcophagi (Versluys 2016: 74–85). In this study, however, Aegyptiaca is considered only from the stage when it became part of the global Mediterranean International Style and beyond. In this context, it did not include massive elements like sphinxes and obelisks but mainly objects related to death and the afterworld. It included, however, anthropoid sarcophagi, but only in Canaanite-Phoenician Levantine contexts, mainly in royal and elite burials.

Ceramic anthropoid sarcophagi were used by Canaanite-Phoenicians in the Late Bronze Age at Deir el-Balah in the 13th century BCE, for example (Dothan 2008), while a stone sarcophagus was used to bury King Ahiram of Byblos in the 13th–12th or 10th century BCE. Stone sarcophagi became popular again in the Late Iron Age and Persian period, appearing at many of the Canaanite-Phoenician sites around the Mediterranean, from Cilicia in the north to Gaza in the south and from the Levant in the east to Cádiz in the west. None has been found, however, at Carthage, which is intriguing. It is worth mentioning in this context that anthropoid sarcophagi were not used in Tyre until the 5th and 4th centuries BCE, when one example has been discovered from Tyre proper and another from Shavei Zion nearby. Thus, perhaps the Carthaginians maintained the burial customs and practices used in Tyre at the time of the founding of the settlement in North Africa in the 9th century BCE throughout the

Persian period (Porada 1973; Tusa 1983: 247, fig. 26; Moscati 1988: 292–5; Frede 2000: 40–3; Georgiou 2009; Almagro Gorbea *et al.* 2010).

The term "Aegyptiaca" has been borrowed by archaeologists from the Greek author Hecataeus of Abdera, who wrote a book by that name in the 4th century BCE. *Aegyptiaca* was a history of Egypt which combined stories from Herodotus with Egyptian sources. Excerpts from the book have been preserved in the writings of Diodorus Siculus. In modern scholarship, the term "Aegyptiaca" designates all kinds of objects that originated from ancient Egypt. However, classicists limit "Aegyptiaca" to "imports which reached Greece from Egypt, from the Greek colony at Naukratis in Egypt, and from the Levant, as well as the Egyptianizing pieces made by the Aegean itself" (Skon-Jedele 1994). Some Egyptologists have adopted this narrower definition as well. As a result, those who restrict Aegyptiaca in this way fail to acknowledge that the Phoenicians had been the distributors of Egyptian artifacts around the Mediterranean for centuries before the establishment of the Greek colony at Naukratis, for example.

Aegyptiaca was not shipped and distributed to posts and ports around the Mediterranean by Greeks or Egyptians but by Phoenicians, establishing it as a marker of Phoenician presence. Most Phoenician burials and Phoenician-influenced burials around the Mediterranean include Aegyptiaca alongside Phoenician pottery and other artifacts. Items of Aegyptiaca are also found in Canaanite-Phoenician temples but not as often as in tombs. The temple offerings began in the Late Bronze Age around the 15th century BCE but became particularly prevalent during the first millennium BCE and included contemporary as well as heirloom objects.

The clearest evidence of the integration of Canaanite and Egyptian elements to create the first phase of a distinctive Phoenician style are scarabs, a typical Egyptian element that began to be manufactured by Phoenicians in the Middle Bronze Age. All the scarabs found in the Cape Gelidonya shipwreck of the 13th century BCE, for example, were produced in Canaan, somewhere between Gaza and Ugarit, and dedicated to Amon-Re. Scarabs are the most common and widespread feature of the Canaanite-Phoenician Aegyptiaca, but this group also includes: faience amulets, vessels, and beads; stone vessels; ivory and bone statuettes and plaques; and bronze vessels and mirrors.

The swimming girl is a stylistic element of Egyptian origin dating from the Late Bronze Age in Egypt and Canaan which still appeared in Phoenicia in the Hellenistic period. This element of Aegyptiaca has been reinterpreted as a cultic Canaanite-Phoenician element that was distributed by the Phoenicians in Greece, Cyprus, and Italy. This cultic element, usually made of ivory, bone, or wood, is entwined with the Canaanite duck head (see the section on ivory duck boxes, below), and they often appear together on glyptic depictions of spoons and boxes (Michelau 2015). The swimming girl also appeared on other Egyptian objects, like the silver and gold bowls dating to the 13th–10th centuries BCE found at Tell Basta and Tanis, which indicate the broader use of this element in the Egyptian context (Lilyquist 2012: figs. 44, 46). It seems, then, that the corpus of elements, including Aegyptiaca, that may be repatriated into the Canaanite-Phoenician culture is likely to expand over time.

In the Canaanite-Phoenician context, Aegyptiaca consisted primarily of artifacts but also included architectural elements like sacred pools. An example of such a pool was found in Canaan-Phoenicia as early as the 14th century BCE at Deir el-Balah, while a later example has been found from the 6th century BCE in the sacred precinct of Baal in the Phoenician settlement on the island of Motya off Sicily. A baboon statuette and a scarab, both Egyptian religious symbols, were found in the same sacred area at Motya. The Canaanite-Phoenician origin of the sacred pool was clear to the excavators; however, sacred pools need be added to the list of Canaanite-Phoenician Aegyptiaca.

Another category of Aegyptiaca that is not widely recognized is bronze mirrors. Mirrors first appeared in ancient Egypt in the early 3rd millennium BCE. They represented life and were deposited in tombs to assist with the resurrection of the dead. The mirror is also thought to have represented the soul of the deceased. Mirrors are found in Egypt and Canaan throughout the 3rd–1st millennia BCE. They were carried westward, mainly during the Orientalizing period, but the first appearance of a bronze mirror in the central Mediterranean is dated to the 13th–10th centuries BCE. Bronze mirrors were found at the necropolis of Pantalica near Thapsos, at Lipari, and in Sardinia at Cagliari (Lo Schiavo, MacNamara, and Vagnetti 1985: 28–30). Mirrors became very popular among the Etruscan elite. Beginning in the 8th century but especially between the 6th and 2nd centuries BCE, bronze decorated mirrors were a characteristic product of the Etruscans. Although many of these mirrors were found in tombs, their use was not restricted in Etruscan culture to religious beliefs and afterlife rituals; they also were used in everyday life as grooming objects (Thomson de Grummond 1985; Carpino 2008; van der Meer 2016).

Bronze mirrors have been found in Greece, the Aegean, and Iberia, although they never became as common as they were in Etruscan tombs. Mirrors have been excavated at Greek necropolises in the 5th–4th centuries BCE in the Peloponnese, Corinth, Perachora, and at Greek colonies in the Black Sea area (Payne 1940: 142–3, pl. 46; Touchais *et al.* 1999: 685, fig. 47; Burkhalter and Philippa-Touchais 2003: 745, 836–7, figs. 49, 100; Fedoseev 2007: 987–8). While they are rare at Phoenician sites in Iberia, one was found at the Phoenician site Morro de Mezquitilla east of Málaga and another at Doña Blanca at Cádiz (Schubart and Maass-Lindemann 2017: pl. 122.1).

Aegyptiaca in Phoenician Contexts

The Egypto-Phoenician network has left traces that form a distinctive array of material objects in the archaeological record which are extremely significant for the discernment of Phoenician presence around the Mediterranean. Because of the Phoenicians' role as distributors of Egyptian objects, the latter are found in almost every site around the Mediterranean that had any level of contact with Phoenicians, starting with Phoenician trading posts and ending with temple corpora given in tribute to various deities. The Egyptian objects are rarely the only imported objects at such Mediterranean sites. Often, they are found together with Phoenician-made objects of glass and ivory, Phoenician metal objects, and, many times, alongside Phoenician pottery and inscriptions (Hölbl 1986: 197; Mazarakis Ainian 2005: 87–103).

In addition to Egyptian artifacts and elements, the Phoenician corpus of finds at overseas locations typically includes other elements sourced through trade. They consist of Cypriot pottery and, depending on the specific period, one type of Greek pottery at a time, the main groups being Mycenaean, Euboean, Corinthian, or Attic. During the Iron Age II, the Phoenician corpus sometimes also contained Etruscan objects, as well as an occasional variety of objects originating from other contacts around the Mediterranean: for example, from Sardinia. A good example of nearly the entire range of objects found in a Phoenician trade corpus has been excavated on the island of Despotiko in the Cyclades in the Apollo temple, dating to the 7th–6th centuries BCE (Kourayos 2005: 105–33).

Another good example containing a wide range of the Phoenician corpus, this time from the Late Bronze Age, is the Egyptian fortress built at Buhen in Nubia, on the west bank of the Nile below the Second Cataract. Tombs there contained Mycenaean and Cypriot pottery, a RLWm spindle bottle, a base-ring jar, a stirrup jar, a Mycenaean pilgrim flask, and White Slip ware with a wishbone handle. This mélange of styles reflects the International Style and flavor of the Late Bronze Age in the 13th century BCE (Serpico 1999: 267).

Corpora of the character described here that have been found in many Late Bronze and Iron Age Mediterranean locations have generated much debate concerning their origin and meaning. Nonetheless, quite a few have been identified as Aegyptiaca carried by Phoenician traders along with Phoenician artifacts. To this group belong, for example, finds from the following sites:

- The Aphrodite Temple at Thera, yielding a corpus dated to the 8th–7th centuries BCE. Items include Egyptian faience, amulets and vessels, Levantine Egyptianized scarabs, a Phoenician glass scaraboid, and Rhodian Egyptianized faience vessels. Theran tombs of the same date yielded Egyptian figurines, faience beads, a pyxis, scarabs, an *alabastron*, Phoenician glass beads, Cypriot pottery, and Proto-Corinthian pottery, as well as Euboean, Cretan, Attic, and Boeotian pottery (Skon-Jedele 1994: 1649–62; Hölbl 2006).
- The Aphrodite Temple at Miletus, constituting a corpus from the 7th century BCE. Items include Egyptian bronze objects, scarabs and seals, faience amulets and vessels, and Rhodian Egyptianized faience vessels and amulets (Hölbl 1999: 345–71).
- The Artemis Temple at Ephesus, with a corpus dated to the 8th–6th centuries BCE. Items include Egyptian faience vessels and amulets, scarabs, Phoenician ivories, a decorated tridacna shell and a glass pendant, a Phoenician-style griffin with bronze and gold heads of the type used to decorate cauldrons, and an ivory plaque of a Canaanite-Phoenician naked goddess holding her breasts in her hands (Bühler and Pülz 2008: 167, 172, abb. 143; Hölbl 2008: 209–21; Klebinder-Gauss and Puelz 2008: 203, 207, abb. 179; Klebinder-Gauss 2008: 151, 155, abb. 129; Muss 2008a: 106, 116, abb. 70–71, 2008b: 63–6, abb. 26; Pulsinger 2008: 87–8, 92, abb. 36).
- Tombs from Malta and Gozo from the 8th–6th centuries BCE. Objects include Egyptian faience and bronze amulets, scarabs, and Egyptianized anthropoid sarcophagi. A 6th-century-BCE tomb yielded a papyrus with a Phoenician magic spell and Isis image found inside an amulet. Hundreds of plates with dedications to Ashtart and Tinnit in Phoenician script date from the 4th–1st centuries BCE. The bond between Phoenicians and Egyptian objects is undeniable and revealed here in the clearest manner possible. There is no doubt that all types of Egyptian objects arrived in Malta and Gozo with Phoenician traders who were based there and subsequently died and were buried on these islands (Hölbl 1989; Amadasi Guzzo 2000: 181–6).

There are many other examples of such corpora and there is no doubt that they could only have arrived there with Phoenician traders. The lack of Aegyptiaca does not preclude a recognition of the presence of a Phoenician corpus at the site. Other corpora of mixed Phoenician and Euboean pottery, mainly from tombs, should also be counted among the Phoenician sites with mixed corpora, even though they do not contain Aegyptiaca. Such corpora have been found at Pontecagnano in Campania, Sant'Imbenia, Tharros, and San Giorgio di Portoscuso in Sardinia (Fletcher 2006: 187–8). All these sites are in the western Mediterranean and belonged to the West Phoenician trade networks, where Aegyptiaca were apparently considered expendable. Perhaps their symbolism was unappealing in these cultures that lay a far distance from the Levantine coast and Egypt.

Peregrine Horden and Nicholas Purcell have used these mixed corpora, both with and without Aegyptiaca, as evidence that Mediterranean trade was part of cosmopolitan colonization. Their model maintains that Mediterranean emporia were sites housing merchants and colonists belonging to a mélange of communities of various origins (Horden and Purcell 2000: 396–9). That may have been the case for Greek colonies and emporia in Italy, Sicily, and perhaps also in the Black Sea, between the 7th/6th and 4th/3rd centuries BCE. This model, however, does not work for Canaanite-Phoenician culture or Phoenician bases in the Mediterranean. Nor does it fit the epigraphic and material evidence regarding the role the Phoenicians played as agents of Egyptian culture. Horden and Purcell's model contradicts the nature of Phoenician traders as mediators and carriers of portable art, materials, and food products from various locations to others all over the Mediterranean. Such a mode of operation does not necessarily reflect culture-agents of mixed origins but, rather, a network or networks that connected various communities and origins.

Mixed cargo was one of the strategies used by ancient long-distance merchants to reduce the risks of the voyage; in a mixed cargo something would always be sold. This strategy was typical of Phoenician trade, as already indicated by Homer (see above). It was employed along with another familiar strategy of long-distance trade: the adoption of regular routes with steady customers whose preferences are known. The latter strategy ensures the sale of the shipment and would have reduced some of the risks entailed in sea-trade. The mixed corpora found in Phoenician trading posts and shipwrecks, in addition to the ongoing presence of Phoenician goods in certain locations, shows that the Phoenicians used the two strategies side by side.

Contrary to the argument of Horden and Purcell, these mixed corpora need not reflect international ports or trading posts within a foreign port. A good example to the contrary is Kommos, where an enduring Phoenician presence in the Late Bronze and Iron I Ages cannot be denied. Since the finds are of a mixed nature and include Sardinian pottery, the excavator has interpreted them as evidence of Mycenaean, not Canaanite-Phoenician, trade. However, it is more likely that Phoenician mixed corpora reflect a trade strategy, as can only be expected from such a nation of merchants (Jones and Vaughan 1991: 134–6, 140; Morley 2007: 31).

The best-known cases of mixed corpora from locations beyond the Levantine coast and the Carthaginian littoral are Pithecusae (Ischia), Eleutherna in Crete, and Lefkandi in Euboea. However, even in such clear cases where Phoenicians must have transmitted the artifacts, Phoenician involvement has been interpreted in the most restricted frames possible. At Lefkandi, for example, the mixed corpus of Phoenician and Egyptian finds has been said to have arrived initially with Phoenician traders but by the late 8th century BCE; all Egyptian artifacts present at the site supposedly arrived there through the activity of Greek traders and mercenaries who had established a direct connection with Egypt (Tanner 2003: 125).

Herodotus (2.154) claims that regular contact between Egyptians and Greeks began as a result of the addition of Greek mercenaries to the Egyptian army, which he assigns to the time of Psammetichus, from the third quarter of the 7th century BCE onwards. Moreover, he credits the transmission of Egyptian knowledge regarding religion and cult to the Greeks, to Cadmus of Tyre, and to the Phoenician settlers in Boeotia (2.49). The information found in Herodotus does not contradict the picture described here, which interprets the abundant Egyptian and Egyptianized Phoenician artifacts in Mediterranean sites as evidence of large-scale Phoenician trade. These items were not random souvenirs that might have been collected by Greek mercenaries who arrived in Egypt in the mid-7th century BCE (Harrison 2003: 250–1).

Mixed Egyptian–Phoenician corpora have also raised persistent speculations about a Euboean or Cypriot "thalassocracy," even when this term is not being used literally. Such ideas have nothing to do with historical evidence and everything to do with modern Greek and Cypriot nationalism. Similar corpora, when found in the Levant or Cyprus have too often been interpreted as indications of Greek presence, not to say colonization. However, assemblages of objects of the types described are not typical of Greek presence or of Cypriot trade; rather, they are an indication of Phoenician commercial presence (Sherratt and Sherratt 1991: 375; Morris 1992b: xiv; Luke 2003: 45–60; Hirschfeld 2004: 102; Kroll 2008).

An analogous interpretation has been suggested for the Bronze Age, when alleged Minoan and Mycenaean thalassocracies are thought to have controlled trade between the Aegean, Cyprus, Egypt, and the Levant. Soon after its appearance, Bernard Knapp thoroughly rejected this theory, but it still surfaces in contemporary research. The idea of an Aegean thalassocracy during both the Bronze and Iron Ages should be put to rest now. In spite of the strong evidence for Phoenician commercial supremacy during these periods, the concept of a thalassocracy remains, even though it is simplistic, archaic, and an inapplicable theoretical framework (Knapp 1993: 333–4; Cline 1999: 129–30).

Decorated Ostrich Eggshells and Tridacna

Canaanite-Phoenician artisans engraved both of these types of organic substances in Egyptianizing style. This specific style also has been called Phoenicianizing style and may have undergone changes under the influence of an Aramaean style. During the short period of manufacture of Tridacna shells (ca. 650/30–600/580 BCE), both items appeared in Phoenician posts on their trade-net routes. In Rhodian sanctuaries and Etruscan tombs, as well as at Cyrene and Tocra, ostrich eggshells and tridacna were found alongside Phoenician ivories and other oriental luxury goods (Villing and Schlotzhauer 2006: 178; Naso 2010: 65; Bourogiannis 2013: 169). There is little doubt, then, that both types of objects were part of the Phoenician corpus.

Ostrich Eggshells

Decorated ostrich eggshells represent one of the oldest types of artwork in ancient Egypt. The elite Predynastic cemetery at Hierakonpolis, with its human and animal graves, yielded a substantial quantity of such eggshells. Ostrich eggshells were also abundant in the "pillared hall" of the funerary temple at Hierakonpolis. These finds verify the importance of ostrich eggs in tombs and ritual contexts in Predynastic Egypt from the late 4th millennium BCE. In the Arabian peninsula, such finds spread from prehistoric times to the 18th century BCE (Potts 2001: 185–7).

It seems that the main use of an ostrich eggshell was as a container, due to its ability to hold 1.25 liters of liquid and withstand a pressure of 76 kg. Evidence for this use is documented in the Levant, Arabia, Mesopotamia, North Africa, and the Aegean (Phillips 2000; Potts 2001). Engraved eggshells were also used as liquid containers, as demonstrated in a Middle Bronze Age II unprovenanced item from the

Hecht Museum in Haifa, with bronze harness and neck. The eggs were also documented in Babylonian and Assyrian texts as part of medicinal and magical mixtures (Zuckerman 2011). In widespread burials in Dynastic Egypt, they were used as symbol of rebirth and resurrection (Muir and Friedman 2011).

Starting in the 3rd millennium BCE, decorated ostrich eggshells became common in the Levant, Egypt, and Mesopotamia. In the Middle Bronze Age II they have been found in major Levantine sites like Ashkelon, Jericho, Tell Beit Mirsim, as well as at Tell el-Dab'a in Egypt (Herrmann and Johnston 2018: 442). In addition, they have been found through the late 2nd millennium in Ur, Nuzi, Byblos, Mari, and Ugarit, as well as in many Levantine and Arabian sites (Caubet 1983; Matoïan 2008; Brysbaert 2013: 238–9).

In the Aegean, engraved ostrich eggshells have been found from the mid-2nd millennium BCE (Palaikastro, Crete) to the 5th century BCE (Olynthus). Imported to the Aegean from Egypt via the Levant, they have been found in the centers of Aegean culture, including Tiryns, Knossos, Mycenae, Troy, Samos Heraion, Corinth, and Delphi (Brysbaert 2013) and among the cargo of the Uluburun shipwreck. Finds from Cyprus have been dated between the 15th and 10th centuries BCE (Brysbaert 2013: 239, 252).

In the western Mediterranean, especially in Iberia, decorated ostrich eggshells have been recovered in tombs dated mainly to the 8th–6th centuries BCE (Escacena Carrasco 2008: 18), but there are also 4th-century finds from Granada (Barrachina Sánchez and Adroher 2018). Ostrich eggshells were found in tombs at the Boliche necropolis near Almería in southeastern Spain (8th–6th centuries BCE), along with Phoenician pottery and jewelry, and others were found in 6th–4th-century contexts at Villaricos and Jardín (Martin Ruiz 2007: 233–6, figs. 77–8; Lorrio 2014: 34–5, 109–12). At Cuara on the Guadalquivir, not far from Cádiz, ostrich eggshells were found in an 8th–6th-BCE context, along with scarabs and Phoenician pottery (Escacena Carrasco 2008: fig. 4). At the cemeteries of Puig des Molins (Ibiza) and Tuvixeddu (Sardinia), engraved eggshells were found in 6th–4th-centuries-BCE contexts. These were decorated with a Gorgon head, which was popular in the Phoenician world in the West during this time (Costa and Fernandez 2003). At the Etruscan necropolis of Tarquinia, the ostrich is depicted on vessels, and ostrich eggshells were found in a 7th-century-BCE context, as well as at Montalto di Castro (Palmieri 2003). Some eggshells from Jordan bear Phoenician inscriptions and probably come from a looted Phoenician sanctuary (Gübel 2014: 10–11). Decorated ostrich eggs have also been found in North Africa, like those documented from Phoenician cemeteries in the area of Tangier in northwestern Africa by the Strait of Gibraltar: for example, at Ein Dalhia Kabira (Ponsich 1967: pls. VII: 3, VIII). The Phoenician context, then, is clear, and ostrich eggs can perhaps be considered as Aegyptiaca, and in any case as part of the Canaanite-Phoenician style and religious imagery.

Tridacna

Used as cosmetic containers, decorated tridacna shells are part of the Phoenician corpus (Almagro Gorbea 2004: 11). Dated to the late 7th and early 6th centuries BCE, the shells originate in nature from the Indian Ocean, the Persian Gulf, and the Red Sea. They were processed, polished, engraved, sculptured, and painted on the southern coast of the Levant in southern Phoenicia. Decorated tridacna shells were usually engraved and sometimes also painted, predominantly green. The engraved and sculptured decoration usually featured a siren or the head of a falcon but also of an owl. Other decorations included Egyptian religious motifs like lotus flowers or sphinxes wearing the Egyptian double crown, as well as ankhs, raised arms, and falcons. Genies, rosettes, and trees are also depicted. Finally, some shells portray war images of various types of soldiers in Near Eastern dressing, including horsemen, kneeling archers with their equipment, and chariots.

The entire world of images on the tridacna is a mixture of Aegyptiaca and Phoenician symbols, made in the same technique as the Phoenician ivories. The main decorative element of human-headed birds, sirens, or griffin heads also appears on a particular type of bronze cauldron used in banquets and tombs. These cauldrons are dated to the 9th–7th centuries BCE and have been found from Etruria to Cyprus (Geva 1980; Caubet 2014; Gübel 2014: 7–8).

Engraved and decorated tridacna shells have been recovered from Iran, Babylon, Sumer, Assur, and Nimrud in the East and Shechem, Arad, Ekron, Tell el-Far'ah south, and Amman in the inland Levant. They have also turned up at the Athena temple at Lindos on Rhodes, at the Heraion at Samos (where 15 shells were found), and at Perachora in the eastern Mediterranean. In the central Mediterranean, specimens have been found at Etrurian Vulci as well as at Memphis and Naukratis in Egypt. While in the East they appear in palaces and elite residences, in the West they appear mainly in tombs and sanctuaries, like most of the Aegyptiaca and other Phoenician objects (Reese 1988; Reese and Sease 1993, 2004).

Aegyptiaca: Special Items

There are several artifacts that carried a specific religious and cultural message and which are either Egyptian in origin or have been considered Egyptian. Of the three images examined here, the first two, the monkey/baboon and the phallus, are often not taken into consideration among Phoenician Aegyptiaca. The third, the ivory duck box, is very often considered Egyptian, but is in fact Canaanite in origin.

Monkey Imagery

Baboon and monkey imagery in ancient Egypt represented the deity Thoth as both the lunar deity and as the mediator providing safe passage to the afterlife. Egyptian and Egyptianized baboon and monkey amulets are widespread in Mediterranean contexts. Most of the dozens of types found outside Egypt have meanings connected with fertility and protection. They were used primarily by and for women and children but also by sailors. Although regarded as elite items when found outside Egypt during the Bronze Age, by the Iron Age II/Orientalizing period they had become common in Mediterranean tombs belonging to all classes of society. Baboon and monkey statues and amulets were not just alien, exotic items that appealed to elites, as amulets and other small finds are often considered to be. The religious aspects of this symbol had already been adopted by the culture of Minoan Crete in the Middle Bronze Age II period, which demonstrates the strong influence of the Orient on the Aegean in early times (Hölbl 1986: 200; Dothan and Regev 2011).

As with other items that comprise the Aegyptiaca corpus, baboon and monkey imagery circulated around the Mediterranean through Canaanite-Phoenician trade, starting in the Bronze Age. Unlike other artifacts of their corpus that served as luxury and status symbols, or as symbols common in popular belief and superstition, the baboon indicates the assimilation of the core beliefs, cult, and religion of the Phoenicians themselves.

Connection to the trade of a few types of live monkey by Phoenicians is evident in Assyrian royal texts of the 11th–7th centuries BCE. Tiglath-pileser I (1114–1076 BCE) reported that Tyre and Sidon sent a large monkey (baboon?); and a list of commodities sent to Assurnasirpal (883–859 BCE) from Phoenician cities, which included the usual precious metals, timber, and dyed fabrics, also itemized two types of monkey (Grayson 1991: 42, 218). Monkeys were sent to the Assyrian court by Egyptian rulers as well, but the Canaanite-Phoenicians were trading in monkeys imported from African and Egypt at least from the 11th century BCE. This does not necessarily indicate that they also traded in monkey imagery, but, in combination with the vast distribution of baboon and monkey statues and figurines in Canaan-Phoenicia and in Mediterranean sites with other Canaanite-Phoenician traces, the Assyrian texts support a correlation between Phoenician trade and baboon and monkey imagery. The Egyptian, Mesopotamian, and Mediterranean distribution of this image has been displayed in earlier research, and the following discussion focuses on the Aegean-Greek world (Dothan and Regev 2011; Regev 2013; Dothan and Regev 2016a).

The earliest known Minoan representations of monkeys come from Crete and were made of ivory: an ivory seal from Trapeza-Lasithi has been dated to the Early Minoan II–III (ca. 2200–2000 BCE). Two other ivory monkey figurines from Hagios Charalambos and Archanes have been dated to the Early to Middle (ca. 2600–1570 BCE) and Middle Minoan (ca. 2000–1570 BCE) periods, respectively. While baboons and other monkeys are common in Minoan glyptic art beginning in the Middle Minoan IIIA (ca. 1700–1600 BCE), most of the palace wall paintings are dated to the Late Minoan IA (ca. 1550–1500 BCE). The monkeys in these paintings are usually connected with a rite of passage, like some depictions of Thoth in Egyptian art. They play the role of mediators between the human and divine spheres. In most of the monkey depictions found in Crete, the animals are engaged in ritual and votive activities. By the Late Bronze Age, monkeys had become fundamental elements in Minoan religious iconography. As monkey imagery was rare in mainland Greece, it may have entered the Aegean via Crete (Cline 1991: 29, 39–40; Sakellarakis, Sapouna-Sakellaraki, and Nakou Foundation 1997: 636, figs. 690, 694; Betancourt 2005: pl. 102j; Greenlaw 2005: 72–3, 2006: 66).

Although the Mycenaeans did not adopt the monkey image and it is absent from Mycenaean wall paintings, two imported faience monkey figurines with cartouches of Amenhotep II from the late 15th century BCE have been found at Tiryns and Mycenae in a Late Helladic IIIA context. Parallels for these two small figurines, measuring 5–6 cm long, come from late-18th-Dynasty Amarna. A similar monkey type from Egypt, dated to the late 18th Dynasty, has been considered a luxury item; made of green stone, it was used as an ornament on an ointment bowl. Another parallel from Egypt has cultic connotations; the size of an amulet, it is a bronze statuette with inlays of gold depicting a monkey with his arms raised in what may be prayer to the sun. It also has been dated to the 18th Dynasty. The role of monkey representations in Mycenaean culture is uncertain, but the scarcity of this imagery suggests the two known examples and any other unknown ones arrived in Mycenae as luxury items rather than as objects bearing religious significance (Cline 1991: 29, 32).

After the Minoan period, monkey images disappeared in the Aegean until the Geometric period (ca. 1100–800 BCE), although they continued to be represented in Egyptian art without interruption. The reappearance of monkey representations in the Mediterranean during the Orientalizing period of the 8th–6th centuries BCE is specifically related to cult: all the finds from recorded contexts come from sanctuaries and graves. Squatting monkey figurines and amulets in ivory, faience, and clay have been found in an Aegean context at Sparta, Ithaca, Perachora, and Thebes, among other places.

Good examples come from sanctuaries in Samos and Rhodes as well, islands known for their abundant Phoenician and Egyptian finds during the Archaic period (800–480 BCE). They may have been the locations from which monkey imagery had already been entering Greece during the Geometric period. From Samos, relevant finds include a faience vase in the shape of a squatting monkey holding a large (probably Egyptian) jar between his legs, another squatting faience baboon holding a hand to its mouth, a similar image in clay, and ivory scarabs with baboon hieroglyphs. In addition to the monkey imagery, a large quantity of metal, ivory, and faience figurines, amulets, and scarabs were found at Samos, along with an inscription written in Aramaic from the 9th century BCE. Kamiros and Lindos in Rhodes have also yielded a large number of squatting monkey images made in bronze, faience, and clay. Some are imports from Egypt and Phoenicia and some are Rhodian imitations (Kyrieleis 1986: 189, pl. IIb; Eph'al and Naveh 1989; Langdon 1990: 418; Strøm 1992: 48–9; Greenlaw 2006: 66).

A group of faience vases in the shape of squatting monkeys from the 7th century BCE has been found not only at Thebes in Greece and Rhodes in the Aegean but also at other Mediterranean sites that were either Phoenician (Carthage) or known to have been Phoenician trading posts (for example, Etruria). They have been interpreted as perfume flasks. This vessel type had its origins in Egypt, where it is found in contexts from the 18th Dynasty onwards. Although the Egyptian vases inspired the Mediterranean group, they differ in both manufacturing technique and style. Based on the Egyptianizing style and their distribution, these Mediterranean monkey vessels are to be considered Phoenician art and may have originated from a single workshop, either in Carthage or in Rhodes (Vercoutter 1945: 221, item 581; Rathje 1976; Langdon 1990: 418).

Another group of somewhat ambiguously shaped seated monkey figurines made of bronze originated from Greece and the Aegean. Dated to the first half of the 8th century BCE, the figures sit or squat on a stool. Some are portrayed with elbows on the knees and hands reaching to the face, a pose popular in Carthage, and some have hands on the knees, like the common Egyptian depiction of squatting baboons. All figurines of this type that have been found in a secure context come from sanctuaries: for example, in Olympia, Tegea, Mavriki, Sparta, Kamiros, and perhaps also Eretria. This circumstance connects this group with the other monkeys found in the wider Mediterranean in the Geometric/Orientalizing period.

In the 7th–6th centuries BCE, bronze pendants, which some have taken to represent some sort of ape, appear mainly in tombs in northern Greece. The pendant imagery resembles human members of the ape family more than baboons or monkeys, however, and was a local development in that area. Thus, it is unclear whether or not it is a further development from the preceding figurine tradition.

Monkey imagery was brought to Greece as elsewhere. It was Phoenician, not Egyptian, amulets that served as the immediate models for the Greek and Etruscan images. Based on the distribution of the early groups of figurines in Greece, it has been suggested that Sparta was the location where such figurines were first introduced into the Greek mainland, a location already with attested evidence for Phoenician cult by the 8th century (Langdon 1990: 411–22).

Nonetheless, a similar bronze figurine, identified as a weight, was found at Jatt, a site on the main route from West to East in southern Phoenicia, dated to the 11th century BCE. Lead isotope analyses have revealed that the metal ores used to produce the Jatt hoard originated from northwest Arabia (Faynan) and so cannot be claimed to have originated from a Mediterranean source. It is clear that the metal ores were imported to Canaan-Phoenicia from the East and the bronze vessels and objects, including the squatting monkey, were produced in Phoenicia. The bronze monkey imagery of the same style that was popular in the Orientalizing period Greece was evidently used in Canaan-Phoenicia hundreds of years before it reached the Aegean. Similar bronze squatting monkeys were found also in Megiddo in the 11th century and in Ta'anach, dated to the 12th–10th centuries BCE. The bronze monkey from Jatt may be regarded as the prototype for the later Aegean group, which was not a Greek invention inspired by Canaanite motifs but, rather, a local imitation of Phoenician bronzes (Frick, Friend, and Nashīf 2000: 160–1, 268; Artzy 2006b: 46, 66, 72, 115–20, pl. 19.3).

The Phallus

Another element that needs to be added to the Canaanite-Phoenician corpus is the representation of the phallus. The symbolic use of this organ originated in Egypt but was adopted and incorporated into Canaanite-Phoenician culture, becoming yet one more item used in the Levant and exported westward. According to Herodotus (2.49), it was Cadmus of Tyre and his Phoenician companions who introduced the Egyptian tradition of phallic processions during religious festivals to the Greeks in Boeotia (Harrison 2003: 250–51).

Phallic objects have been found in Egypt beginning in the Old Kingdom (2575–2150 BCE) and continuing through the Roman period, but they were most prevalent during the 18th–20th Dynasties (ca. 1550–1077 BCE). They are usually poorly made from wood or stone and are 11–20 cm long. Often, they are painted red and have a single groove around the head which may have been intended to represent a circumcised penis. When made of faience, however, they often have several grooves at the tip, which is perhaps meant to depict an uncircumcised penis (Pinch 1993: 235–8, pls. 52–3). Depictions of circumcision rituals and circumcised boys appear in Egyptian tomb reliefs beginning in the 23rd century BCE (King 2006: 334). Circumcision was a rite of puberty in Egypt.

Phalli have tended to be found in a limited set of contexts. Many have been found as offerings in temples to Hathor at Deir el-Bahri, Mirgissa, Timna, and Gebel Zeit; one example bore a dedication to Hathor, the goddess responsible for pregnancy and birth as well as crop and animal fertility. Hathor was already being worshiped in Byblos in the 3rd millennium BCE (Tower Hollis 2009); in other Canaanite-Phoenician cities, Hathor is the Egyptian version of Ashtart, who had been assimilated into the Egyptian pantheon during the Hyksos rule over Egypt. In addition to examples made of stone and wood, some phalli made of pottery and of more precious faience and ivory occur in these settings (Rothenberg 1988: 268, pl. 155.9, figs. 30.6, 92.5; Pinch 1993: 235). Phallic objects were used during fertility festivals dedicated to Hathor or the male deities Min and Bes, associated with the goddess (Pinch 1993: 241–5). The other main context for phallic objects in Egypt is royal tombs. Examples were found buried with Amenhotep II (died ca. 1400 BCE) and Thutmose IV (died 1391 BCE), both rulers during the 18th Dynasty, and the tomb of Akenaten at el-Amarna, who belonged to the 19th Dynasty (Martin 1974: 93–4, pl. 54, 398; Pinch 1993: 238).These were made of faience and stone; the faience versions were smaller.

Outside Egypt, phalli have been found in the Levant, Cyprus, mainland Greece, and Crete. Among these is a stone phallus from the Late Bronze Age found at Midea in the Peloponnese, with an incised Linear B sign, the syllabogram *ko* (Demakopoulou, Divari-Valakou, and Walberg 1994: 39, fig. 57; Swiny 2006). A possible early Iron Age example has been uncovered at Tel Miqne-Ekron in Building 359 from Stratum

VIb, dated to the late 12th–early 11th century BCE (Dothan and Regev 2016b). A handmade terracotta object from Gezer Stratum XI, dated to the late 12th–mid-11th century BCE, has been interpreted as a model of a circumcised phallus (Dever and Lance 1986: 115; King 2006: 333). A marble phallus was also found at Eleutherna on Crete, a site known for its Phoenician finds beginning in the 8th century BCE. It probably served as a votive object, and although it was found in a 1st century BCE–1st century CE context, the excavator has suggested it may date to the Archaic period (800–400 BCE) (Stampolidis 2004: 147).

In addition to these isolated examples, phallic pendants are common in sanctuaries, domestic settings, and especially tombs at Phoenician and Punic sites in the western Mediterranean, particularly Carthage and in trading posts in Sardinia and Malta. Many were recovered from the Phoenician necropolis of Puig des Molins on Ibiza, in tombs dating from the mid-7th to mid-6th centuries BCE. They are usually 2–3 cm long, are made of stone, gold, ivory, faience, and glass, and the majority are circumcised. The Phoenicians are known to have practiced circumcision. These pendants are considered Egyptian-inspired votives with an iconographic meaning (Fernández, López Grande, and Mezquida Orti 2009: 29–33, 129–41, 281). In a Hellenistic context, a small glass phallic pendant comes from Tel Anafa, when the site was characterized by Phoenician material culture (Spaer 2001: 186–7).

Ivory Duck Boxes

Among the various ivory items manufactured and distributed by Canaanite-Phoenicians, there is one type that is often considered to be an Egyptian import and which also inspired local imitations in many Mediterranean locations. However, ivory boxes in the shape of a duck are first attested at the end of Middle Bronze Age at Ugarit; by the Late Bronze Age I they are common all over the Levant, and by Late Bronze II–III they are common in the Levant and Cyprus. Only in the Late Bronze III (LH IIIA) did these boxes also appear in tombs on Crete (Knossos) and Rhodes (Ialysos), and at Mycenae and Asine. The use of ivory duck boxes continued until the Iron Age.

The first Egyptian examples of duck boxes are rare, dated no earlier than the 14th century BCE (Late Bronze Age, during the reign of Amenhotep III), and were made of wood, alabaster, and ivory. This type is not Egyptian in origin but rather Levantine—more precisely, originating from Canaan-Phoenicia. A later variation of the duck box, an ivory box shaped like a woman swimmer, also is typical of Levantine workshops. Although later versions of duck boxes with separate wings originate from Egypt, duck boxes are not an Egyptian creation. It is worth noting in this context that fragments of five duck boxes were found in the Uluburun shipwreck, a boat probably of Canaanite-Phoenician origin (Gachet-Bizollon 2007: 51–60, 66–70; Emanuel 2019: 424–5).

III. Other Elements in the Phoenician Corpora

Trade networks—i.e. routes, trade mechanisms, and the goods and products shipped along and by means of them—were a central part of Phoenician existence. The goods that were a regular part of Canaanite-Phoenician trade networks can be considered to be constituent elements of identifiable Phoenician corpora. Since there appear to have been several distinct trade networks in operation simultaneously, the substances that typified each would have varied and included precious materials in their raw state, materials in a semi-processed state, or objects in a finished state, as well as processed agricultural products and special items of particular importance.

Raw materials that have been detected so far in the Phoenician trade networks include metal ingots, ivory, alum, which was used in various industries operated by Phoenicians, and glass, obviously a human artifact but considered a raw material when shipped as ingots. Products of fine art manufactured in Phoenician workshops and decorated in a Phoenician style, which include artifacts made of expensive materials, especially metals, ivory, and glass, comprised another set of items that were created and distributed through these networks.

Phoenician artifacts fall into two main groups. One group consisted of objects produced by Phoenician artisans, mainly decorated metal vessels, especially bowls, and artifacts made of ivory. The other group consisted of Egyptian artifacts, Aegyptiaca, which Phoenicians distributed. Although some of these items were produced by Phoenician craftsmen, such as scarabs and beads, the majority were produced in Egypt. The repertoire included faience amulets and scarabs as well as alabaster vessels with Egyptian cartouches and beads made of various materials but mainly of glass and faience (Burstein 1992: 45).

Phoenician wares are often regarded as "luxury" goods and considered at times to have constituted ancient "bric-a-brac" in its Victorian sense of a collection of *objets d'art* for conspicuous display. This is the case particularly for the ornamental metal, ivory, glass, and faience items. Nevertheless, wine and other foodstuffs can be regarded as luxury goods as well. A division of trade into "essential" versus "luxury" goods is artificial and arbitrary, particularly since the definition of these terms changes over time and from one place to another (Morley 2007: 43). One might say, then, that the Phoenician trade in wine, oils, fish, pottery, Aegyptiaca, metal artifacts, glass items, and ivory carvings should be associated with the social demand for these goods around the Mediterranean and ceremonial, societal needs. The vast distribution of Phoenician goods reflects the immense desire for these goods and their use in various religious, mortuary, and civilian rituals.

Metal Ore and Ingots

Metals had been coveted and traded by the Canaanite-Phoenicians since the Bronze Age. Some have considered metals to have been the prime reason for Phoenician voyages and entrepreneurial activity around the Mediterranean (Nijboer and van der Plicht 2008: 109; Hernández 2013; Wood, Montero-Ruiz, and Martinón-Torres 2019). While copper, tin, gold, and silver were scarce, iron and lead could be found in most Mediterranean regions. Metal production was maintained in the Canaanite-Phoenician states, not only in the Levant but also in Carthage, Cyprus, and other nodes on their trade diaspora network (Artzy 2006b; Gübel 2015; Vonhoff 2015; Zamora López 2015; Kaufman *et al.* 2019: 4075–6).

Phoenicians traded in raw metals and distributed them according to demand. A text from Ugarit (PRU 6.140 = RS 19.92) reveals that, by the Late Bronze Age, metals were already being distributed for industrial production in an organized and synchronized system. At Ugarit, one agent delivered copper for processing by another individual, while the final product was then delivered to a third party (Morley 2007: 24; McGeough 2007: 167–8). This early Canaanite example reveals that an elaborate industry and trade in metal and ingots was already known by the Canaanite-Phoenicians and functioning by the Late Bronze Age. They continued their engagement in similar operations during the 1st millennium BCE.

Tracing trade in metal ores and ingots is quite difficult, due to the more expendable nature of the materials. If ore arrived safely at its destination, it would be processed and reshaped; if lost at sea, it would disintegrate over time and in many instances disappear. Metal ingots are rare finds that are most often recovered from shipwrecks—in particular, Canaanite-Phoenician wrecks, like the ones found at Uluburun and Cape Gelidonya from the Late Bronze Age, and from Iron-Age-period wrecks found at Bajo de la Campana and Mazarrón (Emanuel 2019). Nevertheless, metal trade is also traceable through Phoenician finds connected to known ore mines. As seafarers, in plying their metal trade in the Late Bronze Age the Phoenicians sourced the smelted metal ores from Cyprus and other islands in the central Mediterranean. Such finds are mentioned in the description of geographical networks in this book, but not specifically as part of a metal-oriented network in those contexts. Research on Canaanite-Phoenician metallurgy and metalworking is vast and a field of its own; see, for example, the collected essays of Ávila (2015) and more emerging work. It therefore requires no further deliberation in this context, except to focus attention on some features that highlight less-established connections to Canaanite-Phoenician art and metallurgy.

Metal Items

Phoenician metal vessels have been thoroughly dealt with by Glenn E. Markoe and others and, therefore, are not discussed at length here. It is commonly agreed that metal bowls, ornamented with concentric rows which often depict animals but also depict stories and ritual scenes, were made by Phoenician artisans and imported en masse to Cyprus, Greece, and Etruria and in smaller amounts elsewhere. A few of the bowls bear Phoenician inscriptions. These Phoenician metal bowls follow a Late Bronze Egyptian tradition. Dated to the 9th–7th centuries BCE, the metal bowls are one of the most important of the currently identifiable Phoenician fingerprints, due to their strong association with Phoenician culture and cult (Markoe 1985: 149–56, 2000b, 148; Sherratt and Sherratt 1993: 364; Gübel 2000: 195).

The elements depicted on the metal bowls also appear on ivory works and provide evidence of the "multimedia use" of several motifs of Egypto-Canaanite origin. According to Gübel, the "sacred tree" was originally Mitannian and the "female sphinx" and "ram-headed sphinx" Hittite. Even if he is correct, these motifs became so deeply embedded in Phoenician iconography that they survived long after the motifs had disappeared in their original cultures (Gübel 2000: 195, 199, 209–11, fig. 19). It also should be noted that the metal vessels themselves were not the only thing imported from the Phoenicians by other Mediterranean cultures. Metallurgy and new techniques for iron-working were exported to Euboea in the 10th–9th centuries BCE and Etruria in the 8th century BCE as an integral part of their trading activity.

Cauldrons and Pomegranates

A prime indicator of Canaanite-Phoenician cultic practice is metal cauldrons and their (usually) tripod stands, which were often ornamented with griffin heads but also with other animals and mythical creatures (Muscarella 2013: 725–64; Vonhoff 2015). Tripods and cauldrons are shapes associated with the Canaanite-Phoenician *mrzh* which, alongside the ritual, penetrate the Greek *symposion* and

Etruscan and Iberian banquets. These items were so deeply rooted in Greek art and rituals that, from the Geometric to Roman period, it has become also a Panhellenic religious symbol (Álvarez-Sanchís 2000: 68; Papalexandrou 2008, 2014: 263; Nijboer 2013: 103–5; Sannibale 2014: 100; Gübel 2015: 249).

Although it has been argued that the bronze cauldrons originated in Cyprus, later metallurgic studies have rejected this idea and consider the bronze cauldrons to have been Phoenician in origin (Kiderlen *et al.* 2016, 2017). Earlier studies, based on artistic style, suggested Anatolia as the origin of these bronze cauldrons (Broodbank 2013: 517) or a North Syrian, even Phrygian origin. While it has been debated if the Mediterranean bronze cauldron originated from Urartu, it has been demonstrated that, if any of the Urartian style elements impacted on the items distributed by the Canaanite-Phoenicians, it was only the bull head attachments of a specific style that resembles Urartian bronze cauldrons, like those used in rituals in Urartian temples and tombs. Nonetheless, Oscar Muscarella insists that not a single Urartian bronze object has been found outside the homeland and that neither Urartu nor Phrygia was involved in trade and export to the West. It is categorically a Levantine art and trade (Muscarella 2013: 633, 690–1, 725–64; Batmaz 2015: 214–15).

Cauldrons are part of the Canaanite-Phoenician corpus in Greek sites as early as the Minoan period, when they first appeared in the palaces of Knossos and Archanes in Crete (Matthäus 1988; Hermary 1989: 270; Immerwahr 1989; Whitley 2002: 223). A cauldron from Tiryns was ornamented with pomegranates and birds, images that mark this cultic object as one of undeniably Canaanite style and probably of Levantine origin. A bronze tripod with similar pomegranate pendants, dated to the Late Bronze Age, was found at Ugarit in a house. Inscriptions found inside the building have confirmed it belonged to the high priest. Another similar vessel that dates to the 11th century BCE was found at Amathus (Catling 1964: 201–2, pl. 32a, b, f; Schauer 1985: abb. 31.19).

During the Late Bronze Age, bronze cauldrons were used in the process of perfumed-oil manufacture, which was operated and controlled by the Mycenaean palaces. This fact may indicate that the cauldrons that have been found in sanctuaries of later periods might also have been used for heating scented oils or even manufacturing sacred perfumed oils for the gods. In Greece, bronze bowls and cauldrons have been found primarily in sanctuaries dedicated to Hera, but also to Zeus, Apollo, Artemis, and Athena during the late 8th and early 7th centuries BCE. Bronze cauldron griffin head ornaments, as well as the head of a siren, have been recovered from Delphi and Olympia (Shelmerdine 1985: 46, 54, 58; Strøm 1992: 52–5, Rolley 1999: 465, fig. 4).

At first, bronze cauldrons were made in two parts: a tripod and a large bowl. Sometime during the Geometric period, clay copies started to appear in Greece, especially in tombs at the Athenian Kerameikos. The earliest Greek imitations include two variations: a clay tripod alone and a clay tripod with a large bowl on top as one vessel. These finds indicate that the original bronze versions that had inspired the clay ones likely had been made in two pieces which were only subsequently joined into a single unit in a material that facilitated the ability to create the desired end product.

In the Jatt metal hoard from the 11th century BCE, a bronze tripod was fastened by bronze cords to a bronze bowl, creating a tripod cauldron. It has been suggested that the use of cords in this way indicates the tripod was not originally part of the overall cauldron design. It is more probable, however, that the combination and the efforts invested in bringing the parts together show a stage in the typological development between the free-standing tripod with a bowl inserted on top and the tripod combined with a bowl to form an integral unit. The same hoard includes two examples of another type originating from the Levant and dated between the late 13th and 11th centuries BCE. They illustrate yet another contemporaneous version along the typological line of development, where the bowls were installed and used as one with the tripod. The intended connection of both parts led to a more precise design and execution which allowed the two components to dovetail (Catling 1964: 215–23, pls. 38–9; Artzy 2006b: 46–9, 67–8, figs. 2.13–14).

It seems that in the 13th–11th centuries BCE (the Late Bronze II to Iron Age I), bronze tripods were used with a separate plate, bowl, or cauldron on top, depending on the intended use at the time, and that the top element often was fastened to the legs. Whether the vessel was used as an incense burner, an offering stand, or an installation for heating liquids like oil is of little significance for our examination. All three options would have been used during ceremonies conducted in sanctuaries and during burial rites. The presence of cauldrons in primary deposition at a given location, therefore, provides strong evidence of the practice of religious rituals and customs in that context. At the same time, the adoption of the vessel by other cultures is an indicator of the adoption of religious rituals and customs from the Levant, i.e. from the Canaanite-Phoenician culture.

This fact does not indicate, however, that the rituals and customs in which the cauldrons featured as a necessary element were taken over *in toto* from the Levant when the cauldron and tripod were adopted. It is likely that some details, intentions, meanings, and even major parts of the rituals were omitted or replaced by the Greeks, Etruscans, and other communities influenced by Levantine culture. There were probably multiple changes per *ethnos*, since these communities were not made of uniform components and did not share all the traits of their culture with one another. It is quite obvious that the same idea took different forms in, for example, Tarquinia and Campania, just as there were major differences in the absorption of Levantine ideas in Sparta, Corinth, and Athens. Nonetheless, in two different locations similar assimilation of burial use of cauldron has been found. At Lefkandi, Euboea, in Tomb 79, dated to the mid-9th century BCE, a cremated body was deposited in an undecorated bronze cauldron, accompanied by Phoenician pottery and other artifacts that resemble the corpus of Tomb 1 in Achziv. In Fondo Artiaco Tomb 194 at Kyme in Campania, dated to the late 8th century BCE, the cremated body of an Etruscan warrior was deposited in a silver urn inside two bronze cauldrons, alongside electrum, gold, and silver ornaments inside a box (Crielaard 2018). While the second deceased person is not related to a Phoenician context and both show hybrid burial rites and grave goods, their use of the cauldron for burial echoes the ritual use of cauldrons in the Levant.

Like many other items and symbols introduced into the Mediterranean by the Canaanite-Phoenicians, cauldrons were mostly represented in burial contexts and associated with rites and beliefs of the afterworld. Two deposits, each containing two bronze cauldrons, one on top of the other, were found inside the Canaanite 12th-century-BCE temple of Lachish, while another identical bronze cauldron was found in a late-13th–12th-century-BCE tomb at Tell es-Saidiyeh in the Jordan Valley (Weissbein *et al.* 2020: 11–13). These early Canaanite contexts could be the ritual forerunners of the cauldrons used in the burials at Lefkandi and Kyme, although bronze cauldrons are found as early as the 4th millennium BCE in western Anatolia and in burials of the Maikop culture in the eastern Black Sea (Hansen 2013: 154, 2014, fig. 5). Bronze cauldrons in general were not invented or distributed by Canaanite-Phoenicians, and we have evidence from 8th-century-BCE Assyrian reliefs of types similar to those found in the 4th-millennium-BCE contexts above (Crielaard 2015: 355–8). However, the tripod cauldron with griffin handles and other decorations was a product of Canaanite-Phoenician art and religious contexts, and it is these cauldrons that were distributed within the Mediterranean. Still, as demonstrated in Canaanite Lachish and Tell es-Saidiyeh, and the possible Phoenician burial at Lefkandi, simple, undecorated bronze cauldrons were also used in Canaanite-Phoenician rituals.

By the 9th century BCE, when clay cauldrons were being produced as a single unit, the focus of the ornamentation shifted from the tripod legs to the rim of the bowl. Three head ornaments were attached so that they projected above the rim of the bowl. Typically, they took the shape of either griffins, bulls, or winged "sirens." While the vessel shape remained the same, the surface treatment was done to local taste, painted in Geometric and, later, in Orientalizing style. In Etruria in the 7th century BCE, the cauldrons and stands inspired the production of bucchero black-glazed pottery installations which imitated the original, imported Phoenician metal objects in clay (Payne 1940: 51, 70, 126–30; Markoe 1985: 36–8; Berkin 2003: fig. 8; Aubet 2007).

As mentioned above, the Late Bronze Age cauldron from Tiryns was ornamented with hanging pomegranates and birds. As a decorative motif that has usually been associated with cult, pomegranates are known from Jericho in the Middle Bronze Age and in the Levant and Egypt from the Late Bronze Age. Although this motif also was very popular in Cyprus during the Late Bronze Age, it did not originate there but, rather, in the Levant, where it was associated with sacrifice and with burial (Immerwahr 1989; Dothan and Ben-Shlomo 2007). Bronze vessels in Greek sanctuaries have also been interpreted as having been used in the context of the banquet, a ceremony itself borrowed from the East. When used in such a way, these bronze vessels indicate a profound cultural contact between Greece and the Near East during the Late Geometric period and a common religious milieu in the 8th–7th centuries BCE. Moreover, the importance of such vessels in the cultic life of the Greek sanctuaries may have required their direct importation from sanctuaries in Canaan-Phoenicia. There is no evidence that any of these vessels were imitated or produced locally in Greece. Official acquisitions may have been initiated by the Greek sanctuaries, but it is more likely that they had been organized by a Phoenician network (Strøm 1992: 56–7; Burkert 1997: 21).

Bronze pomegranates decorate an incense stand found in a priest's grave at Tel Nami in southern Phoenicia, dated to the Late Bronze Age (13th century BCE). Bronze stands similar to this one have been found in other Late Bronze Age contexts at Ugarit, Beth-Shean, and in a temple at Megiddo. The same priest's grave at Tel Nami yielded two scepters topped with bronze pomegranates. Similar pomegranate-topped ivory scepters have been found in the Canaanite temple at Lachish, also from the 13th century BCE, and in a Phoenician tomb at Achziv, dated to the 8th century BCE. Another ivory pomegranate with a dove on top, both symbols associated later in the Greek world with Aphrodite, was found in a late 9th–early 8th century BCE context in Jerusalem, inside a pool that also contained fish bones and Phoenician bullae. In the Canaanite-Phoenician context, therefore, pomegranates were associated with divinity, most probably with Ashtart, known to the Greeks as Aphrodite (Artzy 1990; Reich, Shukron, and Lernau 2007: 160–3, fig. 10). These pomegranate-related finds all have cultic associations. Pomegranates continued to appear in a Phoenician burial context as late as the 1st century CE, where they decorate a "Sidonian" glass bottle (Israeli 2003: 134).

Pomegranates are native to Mesopotamia and need cultivation in order to grow in other parts of the eastern Mediterranean. The earliest artistic representations of pomegranates are found there starting in the 4th millennium BCE and were distributed through time south to Iran and the Levant, and from there to Egypt. The pomegranate, both the fruit itself and the symbol, was introduced into the

Mediterranean by the Phoenicians, as indicated by the large quantity of the fruit found in amphorae, kraters, and pithoi aboard the Uluburun ship (Ward 2003).

Pomegranate vases have been found at Minoan Phaistos as early as the 17th century BCE. A clay pomegranate dated to the 14th century BCE was found in Mycenaean Athens, faience pomegranates in tombs dated to 900 BCE at Lefkandi in Euboea, and other pomegranates made of gold, ivory, glass, and bronze have been found in Greece in the Late Helladic and Geometric periods. These objects were imported from Phoenician workshops, as revealed by their Egyptianized style, until they disappeared in the 6th century BCE (Levi 1976: pl. 180f; Immerwahr 1989: 398).

During the Early Iron Age, clay pomegranates in the Levant were red-slipped and often burnished, just like the Phoenician pottery of this time. They often were attached to *kernoi* and other vessels used for libation. Their use on libation objects indicates that pomegranates were associated with cultic ceremonies in Canaanite-Phoenician culture (Borowski 1995).

Various regional versions of clay pomegranates, decorated in the local ceramic tradition, were produced in Greece after their initial introduction in the Geometric period until the 6th century BCE. At the Heraion sanctuary in Samos, red-painted, votive pomegranates were the conventional offering made to the goddess Hera and have been found in large quantities from the Geometric period onward. It seems likely that the popularity of pomegranates, as well as other objects and symbols of Canaanite-Phoenician culture found at Samos, was connected to the early cult of Ashtart at Samos. This may be the first appearance of Ashtart as Hera, or Ashtart may have been the deity worshiped at Samos, despite the assumption that the Heraion must have been dedicated to the Greek deity from its earliest phase (Immerwahr 1989: 405–8, pl. 72b; O'Brien 1999: 146; Schmitt 2013: 219). Bronze cauldrons, with or without pomegranate ornamentation, were cultic objects that originated in Canaanite-Phoenician culture. Often found in sanctuaries, they were used for burning incense or for heating perfumed oils.

Glass

It is believed, based on the testimony of Pliny, Strabo, and Josephus, that blown glass was invented on the Phoenician coast at the beginning of the 1st century CE. During the Roman period, then, glass-making was associated with Phoenician craftsmanship (Kouwatli *et al.* 2008). Nonetheless, ancient glass items made initially using the core technique, and, later, molds, were also products of Phoenician workmanship, made from raw material that had likely been sourced from Egypt, at least during the Late Bronze Age. The cargo of the Uluburun shipwreck included glass ingots that had been packed inside Canaanite-type ceramic vessels. It is believed the ship had collected cargo in Egypt and was sailing north along the Mediterranean coast, possibly en route to Greece, when it sank (Nicholson 2008: 8–9; Jackson and Nicholson 2010).

Glass, however, begins to appear in the archaeological record as early as ca. 3500 BCE in both Mesopotamia and Egypt, with glass vessels appearing first ca. 1500 BCE. It is unclear if both cultures developed the process for making glass independently or if one invented it and the other adopted it. If the latter were the case, however, then the material itself and the knowledge of how to produce it would have been mediated by a third party, because no direct trade was conducted between Mesopotamia and Egypt. The likely candidate would be the Canaanite-Phoenicians, who physically occupied the land bridge between the two geographical regions and their cultures. Thus, it is likely that glass was introduced to Egypt by the Phoenicians and not vice versa, unless the Egyptians had developed the technique independently from the Mesopotamians.

The trade in glass ingots and the production of glass in Egyptian territories was under royal control. The Amarna letters mention that glass was being imported to Egypt from the Levantine coast and perhaps also from Mitanni. Beginning in the Late Bronze Age, the glass industry flourished in both Phoenicia and Egypt, yet glass objects found in Mediterranean and Near Eastern sites of the Bronze and Iron Ages are too often considered to be exclusively Egyptian. Possible later evidence for Phoenician trade of glass ingots comes from 3rd-century-BCE Sanguinaire in western Corsica, where a shipwreck with ca. 550 kg of raw glass was found. Some of this cargo was produced in and imported from Phoenicia, and, based on the find location on a known Phoenician trade route, it may have been shipped by Phoenicians (Nicholson 2008: 9–10; Tite and Shortland 2008: 209; Henderson 2013: 168, 227).

Phoenician glass items include mainly small core-formed juglets/bottles used for perfumed oils or medicines, made of blue glass with zigzag decoration in white and yellow, and small glass pendants depicting men's heads, often made of the same colors as the bottles (Grose 1989: 74–6, 82–3; Angelini, Gratuze, and Artioli 2019: 117–18, fig. 18). Other glass items associated with Phoenician trade are beads, scarabs, and scaraboids (Docter and Sonneveld 2009; Eremin *et al.* 2012; Nijboer *et al.* 2013: 149–50, fig. 7; Hölbl 2019: 317–18). A glass jug from a tomb in Aliseda in inland Iberia is a unique find, dated to the 7th century BCE. Bearing a pseudo-hieroglyphic inscription, this is no doubt a Phoenician form, usually made of pottery or metal, imported from the Levant (Taloni 2015: 141, fig. 22).

Faience

Glass and faience are related materials and crafts. In the royal cities of Egypt during the Late Bronze Age at least, they were made of the same basic raw materials and often produced in proximity. However, faience production predated glass production in Egypt. It was easier to manufacture and less expensive.

In addition to its value as a luxury good and status symbol, faience also bore religious and cultural significance. In Egypt, faience and its blue-green color were associated with the goddess Hathor, especially with her function in the rebirth of the deceased. Faience tiles have been found, therefore, in the Pharaonic pyramids as well as in temples. Faience may have maintained its religious meaning in the Minoan culture as well; large quantities of faience were found in the temple repositories at Knossos (Foster 2008: 178–80; Nicholson 2008).

Faience beads and amulets comprised part of the corpus distributed during the Late Bronze Age International Style. Faience items—from beads to amphorae—continued to appear in later corpora associated with Phoenician trade around the Mediterranean. They were often found in tombs and sanctuaries, which might indicate that faience maintained a religious or cultic association in later periods as well (Rathje 1976; Sagona 1980; Hölbl 1987; Redissi 1992–93).

Ivory

Ivory was another material distributed by Phoenicians, both in the form of raw tusks and as finished products, mostly amulets and furniture inlays (Winter 2009; Naeh 2015). Tusks were also found among the cargo items being transported by the Canaanite-Phoenician boats wrecked off Uluburun in the late 14th century BCE and at Bajo de la Campana in the 7th century BCE, some of the latter exhibiting Phoenician inscriptions (Polzer 2014). Objects carved in ivory have often been attributed to Mesopotamian or Syrian origin and artistic influence, even though animals that grow ivory tusks were not native to either location. The ivory products found in these locations during the Bronze Age would likely have arrived there via Phoenician inland trade. Apparently, then, ivory was one of the goods sourced from India and east Africa by the Phoenicians. In subsequent chapters, ivory items are mentioned as constituting part of the Phoenician assemblage whenever they are found at sites that comprised the geographical networks (Röllig 1992: 95; Sakellarakis 1993: 345n13; Gübel 2000: 212–13; Young 2001).

Analyses made of an 8th-century Phoenician ivory, maybe from Arslan Tash, showed that it was gilded and painted (Reiche *et al.* 2013). The tin-foiled or metal-foiled technique may have been one of a set of Phoenician technologies that influenced Greek and Etruscan art. A late example of metal-foiled pottery has turned up in a Macedonian tomb dating to the 5th–4th centuries BCE (Kotitsa, Adudumalli, and Chiaradia 2002: 164–5). It was an *alabastron* in form, a shape of Egyptian origin that had been carried westward by Phoenicians. Greek and Etruscan craftsmen who were trained in Phoenician techniques produced ivory carvings in the Geometric and Orientalizing periods. As we now know that Phoenician ivory carvers were also using paints and gilding techniques, it was probably forwarded to Greek apprentices as well.

Alum

Alum is a chemical compound, a group of salt minerals of sulfuric acid. Pliny called it *salsugoterrae* (*HN* 35.52) and Dioscorides *stupteria* (*De materia medica* 5.123). It was used mainly in the dying and medicine industries (P.Ebers 63.10), but also in the process of separating and cleaning gold and silver ores, for wine preservation (Plin. *HN* 33.84, 94; 35.190) and as wood fire protection (Hdt. 2.180). Alum was extracted in Egypt from the western desert oases of Dakhla and Kharga. Texts like P.Heid. inv. G5166, although late in date (221/222 CE), indicate that the mining, production, and trade of alum was state-controlled (Kruse 2007: 523–5; Dasen 2011: 70; Adams 2013: 268–71).

Trade in alum in the ancient Near East is well documented. An inscription carved in stone from Memphis, known as *The Annals of Amenemhet II* (1914–1879/6 BCE), recorded about 124 liters of alum imported to Egypt from Sinai at an early stage of the Middle Bronze Age (Marcus 2007: 139). The annals recorded lists of precious materials and products, mainly metals of all kinds and other luxuries, which show that alum was a precious, desirable material that was worth mentioning in the king's annals. By the Late Bronze Age and the Canaanite-Phoenician expansion into the Aegean and central Mediterranean, trade in alum from Mediterranean sources can be expected.

Alum was extracted and produced in the ancient Mediterranean, especially on the small island of Lipari north of Sicily and at Milos in the Cycladic Islands, but also in western Sicily at Sant'Angelo

Muxaro (De Angelis 2003: 26). Lipari is one of three locations in the western Mediterranean where the earliest Phoenician finds, i.e. the Canaanite amphora, have been discovered. The other two locations were connected to metal mines in operation in the Late Bronze period. The longevity of the alum industry at Lipari is indicated by the production of a special type of amphora belonging to the Phoenician tradition there during the Roman period to ship alum (Malfitana 2009: 134). An unusually high variety and quantity of Canaanite-Phoenician finds have turned up at Milos, also known for its alum mines (Borgard 2005; Maran 2011). Although data about alum is slim and studies few, it is quite possible, based on the evidence from Lipari and Milos, that alum was distributed by Phoenicians. It was an essential element in several traditional Phoenician industries, including dyed fabrics and metalworking, so the Phoenicians would have ensured that a steady supply was available by shipping it themselves from identified sources.

The Purple Dye Industry

Purple dyed cloth is one of the symbols of Phoenician trade. Famous for its superior quality and value, it was also known as Royal Purple and Tyrian Purple. The dyed cloth and the murex shells were also associated in Ugaritic texts with ritual use, related to the goddess Astarte (Carannante 2014: 278). Archaeological evidence for the existence of a purple dye industry is first found in the Levant during the Late Bronze Age II–III (ca. mid-14th century BCE) in Ugarit, Sarepta, Akko, Tell Abu Hawam, and in contemporary Egypt at Marsa. Purple dyeing activity is documented at Nuzi in an archive of the 15th century BCE, as well as in the 14th-century-BCE archive of Amarna, in Ugaritic and Hittite documents of the Late Bronze Age, and in Mycenaean administrative documents (Nosch 2004; James *et al.* 2009: 1114; Halayqa and Yonge 2010: 303; Reese 2010). As attested by the continuous quantities of purple dye shells at Levantine sites and by the texts of both Strabo (16.2.23) and Pliny (*HN* 5.12), this industry continued to operate into the late Roman period but ended in the Medieval period and was forgotten (Carannante 2014: 273) The rare purple color was obtained by heating immense quantities of murex snails in a long and tedious process (Plin. *HN* 9.62), but the Canaanite dyeing industry was not restricted to the prestigious purple. Two sites in the Timna Valley, near the mines, show evidence of a dyeing industry that was based on plants, operating from the 13th–10th centuries BCE (Sukenik *et al.* 2017b).

Tyre was known as a place of cloth-dyeing and manufacture as late as the Roman period, and murex shells, purple-stained vessels, and dyeing installations were found at Sarepta from the Late Bronze I to the Roman/Byzantine period (Pritchard 1978: 126–30; Markoe 2000b: 163–4; Young 2001: 194; Reese 2010). Dyeing installations dating to the Hellenistic period have been found at Tel Mor (Ashdod), where rare scarabs and seals of Phoenician origin from the Middle Bronze IIB–C to the Late Bronze Age have also been excavated. Although this evidence does not necessarily indicate the continuity of the dyeing industry or Phoenician culture at Ashdod from the Middle Bronze Age to the Hellenistic period, other neighboring sites along the Levantine coast, like Ashkelon and Akko, show such continuity in their industrial activities. Therefore, the Hellenistic dyeing installations at Ashdod may hint that an ancient industry had been located there as well (Barako 2007: 246; Brandl 2007: 205; Cohen-Weinberger 2007: 145).

Vestiges of purple dye have been found on Phoenician pottery from Shiqmona, located on the Carmel coast, during the Iron Age. The pre-Persian finds have not yet been published from this site, which was excavated in the 1960s, but a popular book describes rich levels from the Middle Bronze Age onwards (Elgavish 1994). The stained pottery used in the dyeing industry on site clearly confirms this industrial activity at Shiqmona in the Iron Age (Sukenik *et al.* 2017a).

While current evidence shows that the dye industry began in the Levant in the Late Bronze Age, earlier evidence for a purple dye industry comes from Middle Minoan II (ca. 1900–1700 BCE) contexts on Crete. The Canaanites may have learned the dyeing process through their Middle Bronze Age trade contacts with Crete, but remains of mollusc-dyed purple cloth, found in the Middle to Late Bronze Age royal tomb at Qatna, occupied between ca. 1740/1640 and 1340 BCE, may suggest that the purple dyeing process was already implemented in the Levant at the same time (Bietak 1991, 1997; Kochavi 1992: 9; Dickinson 1994: 243–4; Brody 2002: 74; Nosch 2004: 32–9, Ben-Tor 2006; James *et al.* 2009; Reese 2010). While in earlier research attention has been focused on Crete (Stieglitz 1994), it now seems that the earliest purple dye industry developed in Cyprus in the late 3rd–early 2nd millennium BCE. Spindle whorls, a tank, and clots of purple material made of murex were found in the industrial area of Pyrgos-Mavroraki. The industrial area had existed during the Early to Middle Bronze Age but was destroyed in the 19th century BCE and preserved untouched. Finds at this site show not only connections with the Near East but also with the Aegean (Carannante 2010). Cyprus, therefore, may be the origin of the purple dye industry that influenced both the Levant and Crete. Another candidate for the earliest evidence of purple dye production from mollusks is now the "House of Dyers" in Aegina. Murex shells were found in an Early Bronze Age context dating to the end of the 3rd millennium BCE (Carannante 2014: 274). Still, the Cypriot evidence is more compelling and is based on stronger evidence than just shells.

By the 1st millennium BCE, dyed cloth of the highest quality was associated with Tyre and Phoenicia; the Phoenicians were famed not only for the production of Royal Purple but also for trading in this precious product. The foundation of the dyed cloth industry in the Iberian Peninsula and North Africa should be associated not only with Phoenicians generally but more specifically with the Phoenician fish products industry. Since most of the sites with installations used for fish-salting also have revealed large quantities of murex shells, it has been argued that the two industries were associated and used the same installations and salt beds. Several sites in northwestern Africa, including Mogador, yield such evidence (Lowe 2004; Trakadas 2015: 27, 33, 54, 59, 73, 79, 89). Hence, the discussion of the Phoenician salted-fish network in Chapter 6 is relevant for the study of the dyed fabrics industry and trade.

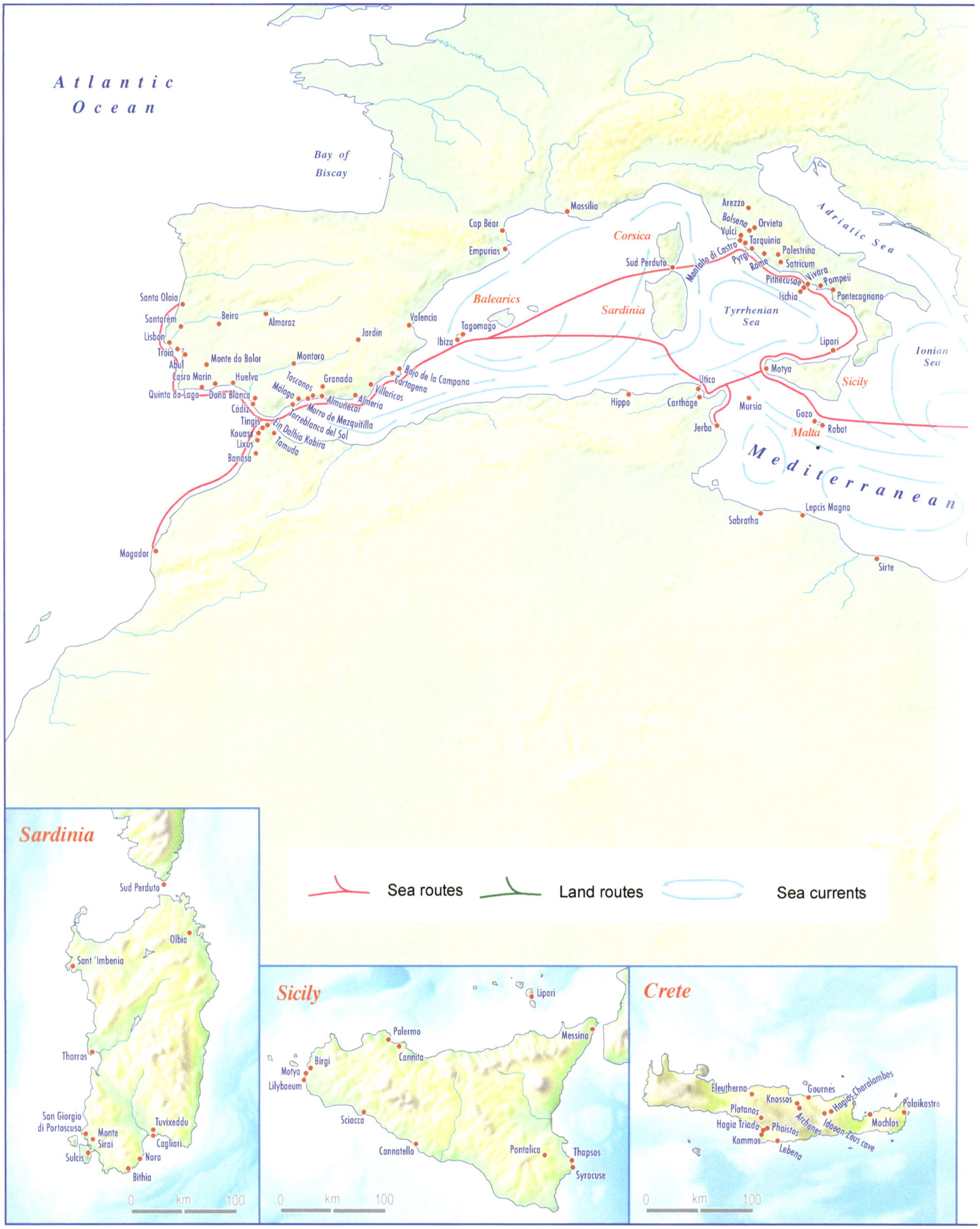

Map 1: Site names mentioned in the text, sea and land routes used by the Canaanite-Phoenician trade networks

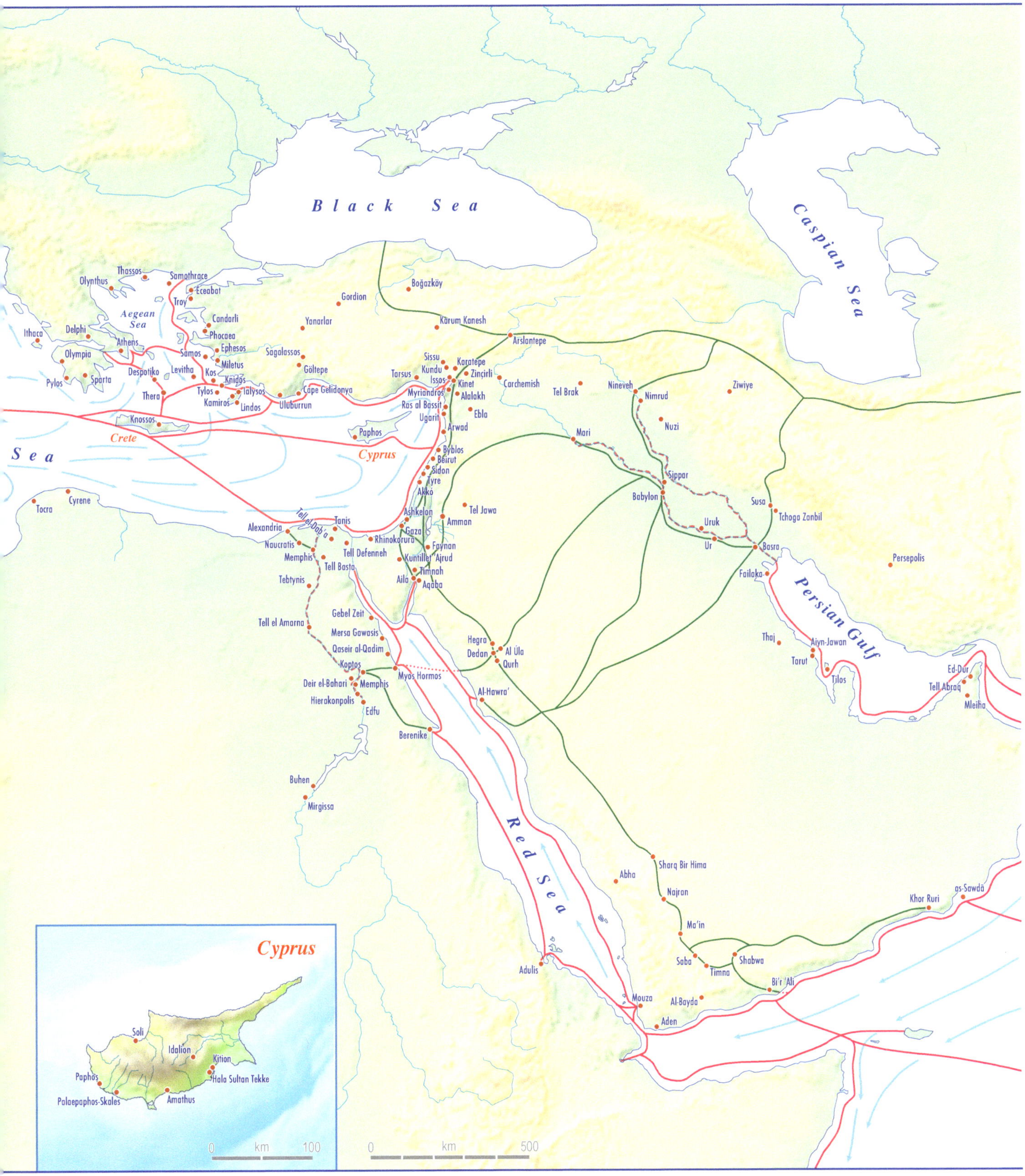

(continued overleaf)

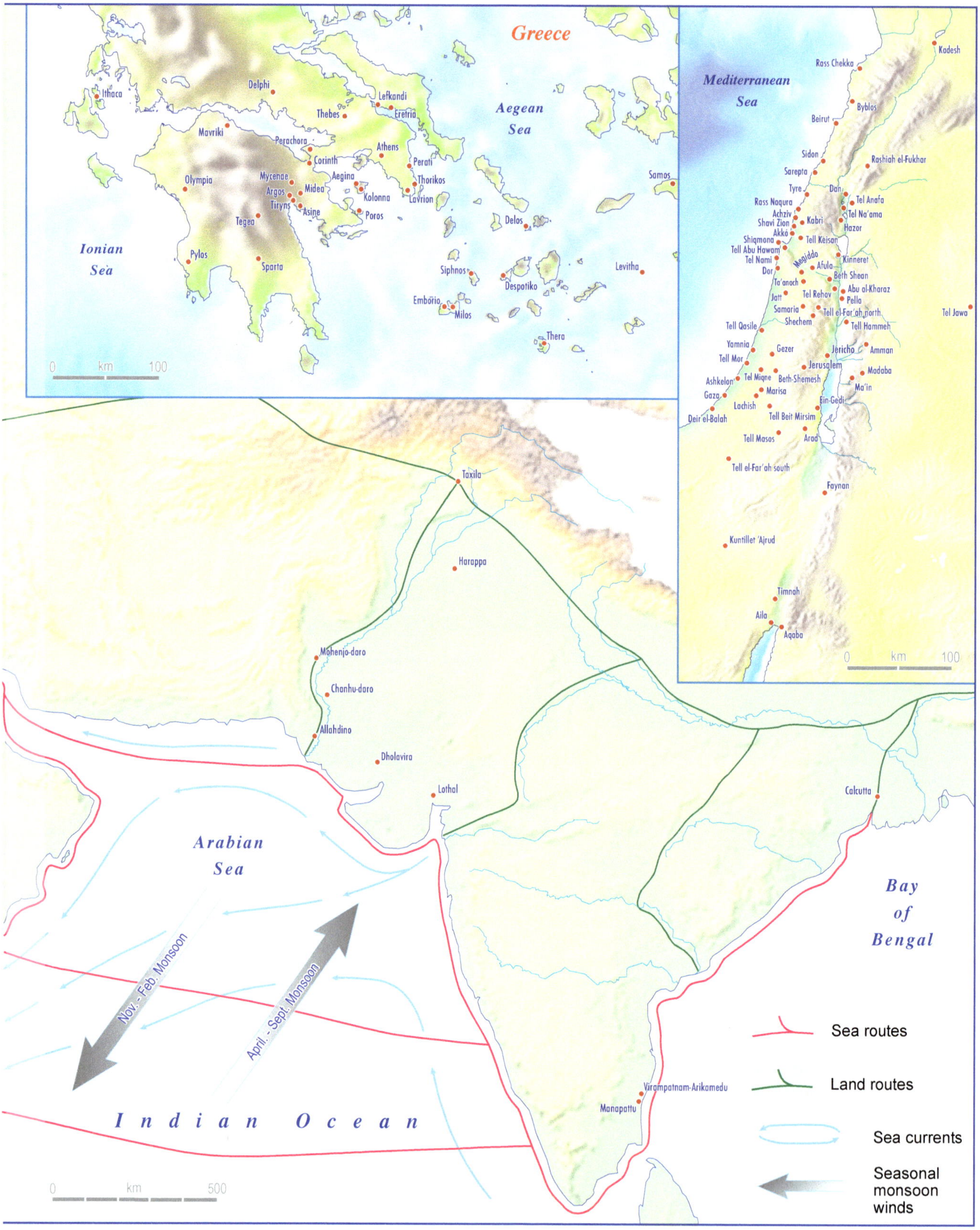
Greece
Aegean Sea
Ionian Sea
Ithaca
Delphi
Lefkandi
Thebes
Eretria
Mavriki
Perachora
Athens
Corinth
Perati
Olympia
Mycenae
Aegina
Thorikos
Argos
Midea
Kolonna
Tiryns
Lavrion
Asine
Poros
Tegea
Samos
Delos
Pylos
Sparta
Siphnos
Despotiko
Levitha
Emborio
Milos
Thera
0 km 100
Mediterranean Sea
Rass Chekka
Kadesh
Byblos
Beirut
Sidon
Rashiah el-Fukhar
Sarepta
Tyre
Dan
Rass Naqura
Tel Anafa
Achziv
Tel Na'ama
Shavi Zion
Kabri
Akkó
Hazor
Shiqmona
Tell Keisan
Tell Abu Hawam
Tel Nami
Megiddo
Kinneret
Afula
Dor
Beth Shean
Ta'anach
Abu al-Kharaz
Tel Rehov
Jatt
Pella
Samaria
Tell el-Far'ah north
Tel Jawa
Shechem
Tell Hammeh
Tell Qasile
Yamnia
Gezer
Jericho
Amman
Tell Mor
Jerusalem
Madaba
Ashkelon
Tel Miqne
Beth-Shemesh
Ma'in
Marisa
Gaza
Ein-Gedi
Lachish
Deir el-Balah
Tell Beit Mirsim
Tell Masos
Arad
Tell el-Far'ah south
Faynan
Kuntillet 'Ajrud
Timnah
Aila
Aqaba
0 km 100
Taxila
Harappa
Mohenjo-daro
Chanhu-daro
Allahdino
Dholavira
Lothal
Calcutta
Arabian Sea
Bay of Bengal
Nov. - Feb. Monsoon
April - Sept. Monsoon
Indian Ocean
Virampatnam-Arikamedu
Manapattu
0 km 500
Sea routes
Land routes
Sea currents
Seasonal monsoon winds

—5—

Phoenician Networks: Geographical Zones and Central Nodes

The Canaanite-Phoenicians were famous for their entrepreneurial seafaring and navigation, which opened and mapped new seaways in the Mediterranean. They also traded on land as far east as Arabia, the Persian Gulf, and probably also India, and as far north as Anatolia, destinations also reached by sea. Textual and material evidence point to four trade routes or spheres of trade where Phoenicians operated. The spheres identified below reflect not only geographical zones but also chronological spheres of Canaanite-Phoenician activity and the gradual progress, though not entirely continuous linear movement, from the eastern to the western Mediterranean.

1. The eastern Mediterranean and the shores of Asia Minor, the Levant, Egypt, the Aegean islands, Crete, Cyprus, Greece, Cilicia and North Syria, and also, to a lesser degree, Lycia and Caria. Canaanite-Phoenician activity here started in the Middle Bronze Age, in the early 2nd millennium BCE.
2. The western Mediterranean and the Atlantic shores of southern Europe and western North Africa, namely Spain, Portugal, the Balearic Islands, and Morocco (Mauritania). Canaanite-Phoenician activity here started at the latest in the 10th century BCE.
3. North Africa and the central Mediterranean islands, namely Carthage and its area, Italy, Sicily, Sardinia, Corsica, and Malta. Canaanite-Phoenician activity here started in the late 2nd millennium BCE.
4. The Near East, Arabia, the Persian Gulf and India. In some parts of this geographical sphere Canaanite-Phoenician activity began in the Middle Bronze Age, in others in the Iron Age in the early 1st millennium BCE.

These spheres were not fixed and rigid through time and tend to change at their borders, depending on time period and point of view. Writing mainly on the Roman period and later and based on

Greco-Roman authors, Arnauld's definitions of three Mediterranean spheres is different. He considers Corsica, Sardinia, Sicily, and the area of Carthage as part of the western Mediterranean and Greece and the Aegean as part of the central Mediterranean (Arnaud 2005: 149–50, 172–3). Based on biblical evidence (Ezek 27:11–24), four concentric geographical areas were defined by Mario Liverani to provide various supplies to Phoenicia during the Iron II Age: from Judea and Israel at the center, producing agricultural products; through north Arabia and Syria, for animals; then from Greece and the Aegean, Anatolia, Mesopotamia, and central Arabia, for slaves, cloths, and metal equipment; and the last circle from the central Mediterranean, south Arabia, and perhaps also Egypt and Africa, for metals, precious stones and ivory (Liverani 1991). Other Phoenician trade spheres of the era before the Persian period have been proposed by Fales, based on Assyrian texts. This comprises five trade circuits: one between Egypt and the Levant; a second links Phoenicia with the eastern Mediterranean (Cyprus, Rhodes, Crete, and Greece); a third links the northern Levant with Anatolia; the fourth links the Levantine shore with Arabia; and the fifth connects the Levant to Mesopotamia and eastward (Fales 2017: 264).

Throughout the ages, three contemporaneous levels of trading spheres existed in the Mediterranean. One level was an overall Mediterranean sphere which operated in times of peace and prosperity, when goods were transferred between major distribution centers throughout the basin. The second level consisted of three of the four large spheres delineated above, the western, central, and eastern Mediterranean, which operated continuously during most time periods, although not always at the same volume. The last level involved smaller regional spheres, which operated on the basis of local connections and considerations, some continuously and some not.

Canaanite-Phoenicians traded at all three levels described, from the entire Mediterranean to the local routes. Phoenician networks were engaged in long-distance trade in all four spheres of the second level, namely the western, central, and eastern Mediterranean and the Near East, although they were less involved in the last one. The organization and production of each Phoenician network operated in a specific sphere, with their products shipped from one distribution center to the distribution centers of other spheres, and from them to the entire area. A good example is the salted-fish network, which manufactured the amphorae on the Atlantic shore of Africa, the fish products on the Atlantic shore of Europe, and used Gaddes as the location where the product was packed and from where the finished merchandise was then distributed. All the manufacturing within and organization of this trade-net took place in the western sphere, but the final product was shipped from its distribution center to distribution centers in other spheres, like the one at Corinth in the western part of the eastern sphere. Likewise, the perfumed-oil and wine networks were organized and manufactured within the eastern sphere and distributed goods westward via one location.

Each of the main three Mediterranean spheres was also home to a few local or smaller trade networks. Some were operated or co-operated by Phoenicians and others by other agents. The smaller routes used by Canaanite-Phoenicians included Phoenicia–Cyprus, Phoenicia–Cyprus–Cilicia, Crete–Rhodes–Kos, Egypt–Phoenicia, Egypt–Cyprus–Phoenicia, Carthage–Sicily–Etruria, Carthage–Sardinia–Corsica, Carthage–Corinth, Lixus–Gades, and Ampurias–Sicily–Morocco, and there were interconnections between the networks. Although it is acknowledged that long-distance routes were produced by assembling route segments (Arnaud 2005: 56), this study deals mainly with the first two levels of the spheres of trade: the Mediterranean overall and the western, central, and eastern Mediterranean spheres along with the Near East.

I. The Eastern Mediterranean Basin

The routes in the eastern Mediterranean basin were by both land and sea. The main land routes went from Mesopotamia to the Levantine coast along the Euphrates and the Gates of the Amanus towards Alexandretta Bay and along the Orontes Valley, and from the Levant to Caria via the Orontes Valley, the Cilician Gates, and from then onwards from Caria to Boğazköy (Hattusa). By sea, the route was roughly circular, connecting the coasts of the Levant, Egypt, Crete, Greece (Peloponnese), the Aegean Islands, Cyprus, and the coasts of Asia Minor. From the Levantine coast, this circular route went in both directions, clockwise and anticlockwise, connecting the Levantine littoral with Greece and the Aegean Islands via southern and western Anatolia and in the opposite direction, connecting the Levant with Crete via Egypt (Sherratt and Sherratt 1991: 357–8; Potts 1993).

This ancient sphere of trade incorporated many short and regional trade routes. One ran along the Levantine and Anatolian coasts, another between the northern Levant and Egypt, and a third between the northern Levant, Cyprus, and Caria. Two connected the Aegean Islands to regions on the Mediterranean coast: one with western Anatolia and the other with Greece. Yet another route originated in Greece and went to Crete via the Aegean, and there was a direct route between Crete and Egypt. These are all known routes; perhaps other routes existed as well. These regional trade routes and the eastern Mediterranean route continued to operate from prehistoric times throughout the Iron Age and later, until modern times (Sherratt and Sherratt 1993: 364).

Starting in the early 2nd millennium BCE, the Phoenician coast, North Syria, and southeastern Anatolia formed a regional economic zone which also included Cyprus and Crete, as indicated in Hittite documents as well as the circulation of Kamares ware (Halayqa and Yonge 2010: 298–9; Soriga 2017: 88). These Canaanite-Phoenician routes in the eastern Mediterranean were later integrated into the long-distance routes to the west, especially the routes that ran from Phoenicia to Egypt and on to Crete and from Phoenicia to Cyprus to Asia Minor to Lefkandi in Euboea, routes that continued on to the west-southern and west-central Mediterranean.

Until the 6th century BCE, control of the eastern Mediterranean sea routes, like most of the Mediterranean sea routes of this period, was in Canaanite-Phoenician hands. "Control" meant the physical operation of long-distance trade routes, not the supervision of regional routes in the hands of Anatolian, Greek, and other traders. The Phoenicians had a monopoly over importing goods from the eastern Mediterranean, especially from Egypt. As long as the East was richer and more developed than the West, their goods were in demand. This situation continued into the 6th century BCE, but to a lesser degree, due to the expansive aspirations of the Persian Empire, which eventually brought down Egypt.

By the 5th century BCE, Egypt was no longer the source of refined art that it had been for the previous 1000 years, and Mesopotamia had been under Persian rule for decades. At the same time, Greece was in its prime, and there was a much lower demand in the Mediterranean for Eastern luxury goods. During this period, the Phoenicians regrouped and strengthened their trading activity in the western Mediterranean around Carthage, while eastern Mediterranean trade activity reduced in volume. During the 5th and 4th centuries BCE, the Phoenician fleet in the East that had not been commandeered to serve as a navy for Persian wars was still operating in the area between the Levantine coast, Cyprus, and Caria. The operation of this trade circuit during this period is confirmed by the distribution of the Banded pottery group (Regev 2020: 105–13).

By the Persian period, Phoenician political control stretched along the entire Levantine littoral and parts of Cyprus. Even so, some Phoenician trade routes declined and others stopped, some forever and some temporarily, once the Persian Empire controlled the Levant and set its sights on controlling Egypt, the Aegean, and Greece as well. Especially in the eastern Mediterranean, the Phoenician fleet was used extensively by the Persians for military activity. As a result, Phoenician trade activity shifted westward during the Persian period. Carthage, which lay outside direct Persian control, now took the lead. Corinth served during this period as a distribution center for the salted-fish network, and an open port and international trade center started to develop on Rhodes during this period, which reached its peak in the Hellenistic period (Hermary 1998; Wallinga 2005: 136–48; Bedford 2007: 309).

The latest evidence of Phoenician activity in the eastern Mediterranean trade sphere to be examined is the distribution of amphorae and Red Slip fine ware. It seems that during the Late Roman/Byzantine period, most of the amphorae imported into the southern Levant from Egypt, the northern Levant, the Aegean, Cyprus, and Cilicia were imitations or versions of the Phoenician-style Gaza/Ashkelon amphorae. During this time, red-slipped pottery belonging to the Phoenician tradition was imported to the southern Levant mainly from Cyprus (Cypriot Red Slip) but also from western Asia Minor (Phocaean Red Slip), from the Carthage area (African Red Slip), and Egypt (Egyptian Red Slip). This evidence not only reinforces the picture of continuous commercial ties between Carthage and the Levantine littoral but demonstrates that the eastern Mediterranean trading sphere operated the same routes from the Bronze Age until the Islamic conquest in the 7th century CE (Sherratt and Sherratt 1993: 364; Kingsley 2004: 102–11). As demonstrated by the Geniza documents, the use of the same routes continued into the Middle Ages, though they were controlled by different agents.

Cyprus as Part of Magna Phoenicia

Located only 50 km west of the Levantine–Phoenician coast, Cyprus is the closest and first stop en route westward and northwestward for any seafarer sailing from the Levant (Demesticha 2009: 397–8). As such, the island was familiar to and frequently visited by the Canaanites from early times. Substantial trade connections between the Levantine city-states and Cyprus are evident in texts and archaeological data starting in the Middle Bronze Age in the early 2nd millennium BCE, although small-scale trade connections precede the Bronze Age (Halayqa and Yonge 2010: 298–9; Soriga 2017: 88; Bretschneider *et al.* 2019: 5).

Documented evidence in RS 94.2475 mentions the king of Alashiya, Kushmeshusha, a name that, though linguistically obscure, may point to a Hittite origin, based on the fact that he addresses the king of Ugarit as "my son" at the time when Ugarit was the subject of Hatti (Malbran-Labat 1999). The period when Cyprus and Ugarit were under Hittite rule is probably the first period when Canaanite-Phoenicians started to manufacture pottery on Cyprus. What may have started as an operation under Hittite command in the Late Bronze Age continued as independent Canaanite-Phoenician manufacture in the 1st millennium BCE. For the Canaanite-Phoenicians, by the 10th–9th centuries BCE, Cyprus was not only a trade destination and trading post but also an industrial zone where they produced their own commodities, as needed. In addition to Phoenician pottery production on the island (discussed below), the purple dye production on Cyprus in the 1st millennium BCE may be associated with the Levantine industry (Reese 2010: 125–6). While current evidence for purple dye production in Cyprus, Crete, the

Aegean, and Italy goes back to the early 2nd millennium BCE (Carannante 2014), the finest fabrics had been produced and distributed since the Late Bronze Age by the Canaanite-Phoenicians, who may have used Cyprus as their factory for this industry. Other Canaanite-Phoenician industrial activities on the island included mining and metal processing (Taloni 2015: 126) and the perfume industry. For the latter, Cyprus's endemic and indigenous flora were used in cosmetic and medicinal products, as well as, in a few cases, sources for blue and yellow paint (Belgiorno 2017). The textual and archaeological data indicate that in all aspects—from temples and burials to residences, industry, and trade ports—Cyprus should be considered part of the greater Canaanite-Phoenician land, part of *Magna Phoenicia*.

There are several Phoenician settlements on Cyprus. The first and best known is Kition, a Bronze Age city that was inhabited by Phoenicians in the early 10th century BCE, perhaps as Qartiḥadašt (KAI 31), and was ruled by Phoenicians until the Hellenistic period, as indicated by its inscriptions and temples for Ashtart and Milqart (Yon and Childs 1997; Demetriou 2001; Hadjisavvas 2007, 2012: 1; Smith 2008). Other Phoenician bases in Cyprus, based on textual evidence and archaeological data, are: inland Idalion, a religious and economic center according to the first known Phoenician administrative archive found there, which dates to the 5th–4th centuries BCE (Amadasi Guzzo 2017); Amathus, with cremation burials dated to the 8th century BCE; Tamassos; Salamis; and Lapethos. The latter two both had Phoenician royal dynasties (Fourrier 2019).

In the past, the stylistic proximity of Cypriot and Phoenician pottery was interpreted in terms of Phoenician–Cypriot exchange at best and, in many cases, in terms of Cypriot influence on Phoenician pottery. However, the relations between these two areas may be better described as the relations between a metropolis and its industrial zone. When examined from this point of view, we can see that, starting in the 14th century BCE, Cyprus had become the location of Canaanite-Phoenician pottery factories. Phoenician pottery factories continued to produce Phoenician pottery on Cyprus until the Late Roman period. During this time, Cypriot workshops produced commissioned imitations of Phoenician forms and types: for example, Bichrome ware, Black-on-Red (BoR), Red Slip and Terra Sigillata. The earliest pottery produced on Cyprus, apparently by Phoenician potters rather than local Cypriot ones, is the RLWm group that was manufactured for the Hittite Empire, according to its criteria and needs. This pottery group was technologically and stylistically foreign to Late Bronze Cyprus, well ahead of its time there. It was at home in the Levant, except for its clay (Regev 2020: 162–5).

Cyprus has several natural deposits of fine clay, especially in its northern regions. From a Phoenician point of view, the northern area of the island would have been ideal for setting up pottery workshops, even though the Phoenicians also are known to have shipped fine clay across the sea. The first Phoenician workshop in northern Cyprus was, therefore, an innovation that required the presence of Phoenician artisans in Cyprus. Phoenician owners might only have supervised later workshops, however, which were scattered over the island. Later on, independent Cypriot workshops produced commissioned pottery for the Phoenicians as well as imitations of these types. Obviously, not all the Cypriot workshops produced Phoenician-related pottery; many of them continued to produce local pottery as well as imitations of Greek or other types of pottery.

Still, in the research milieu of the last generation, where petrographic and instrumental neutron activation analysis (INAA) considerations are assumed to provide the final answer regarding the origin of clay ware, the Cypriot origin of many items of the pottery groups mentioned above has resulted in misleading conclusions. One of the best-known examples is the group known as Cypro-Phoenician pottery, namely the BoR pottery of the Iron Age. Looking only at the clay source of some items and not at their cultural and stylistic background, it is not surprising that not only have such vessels been identified as Cypriot but they have also been assumed to indicate a Cypriot trade and presence in distant locations around the Mediterranean. Such an interpretation would be similar to the clearly unsound view that any outsourced industry nowadays should be identified as foreign: American insurance companies should be recognized as Indian, Israeli fabric industries as Chinese, and so forth. Today, it is obvious that the identity of the investor and the management indicates the identity of the company; it is certainly not indicated by the identity of the labor or the raw material. In the same manner, the use of Cypriot clay and Cypriot workers cannot designate the identity of the "owners" of BoR; the identity of this group is indicated by the people who commissioned its manufacture according to their style and criteria, who probably also owned the workshops, and were the people who distributed this pottery group. These people were Phoenicians.

After the Canaanite-Phoenician objects found on Cyprus in the Late Bronze Age, the earliest pottery of Phoenician origin in Cyprus comes from Kition and the cemetery at Palaepaphos-Skales. Dated to the 11th century BCE, the Phoenician pottery groups include monochrome and bichrome pottery as well as a Phoenician amphora decorated with schematic trees. These and other finds have been considered "Proto-Phoenician" but, in fact, were Phoenician (Karageorghis 2008: 190–2).

A study of trade routes in Cyprus during the Early Roman period has demonstrated the presence of a Phoenician route that operated via Kition, on the eastern side of the island. Imports from the Roman and Greek world were limited to western Cyprus, while those imported from the Levant were found in eastern Cyprus. The existence of different sea routes is reflected in the large quantity of Italian Aretinean Sigillata found at Paphos, while ESA characterized the previously Phoenician site of Kition, indicating its inhabitants had maintained close and continuous connections with the Levantine coast. These archaeological finds from the Roman period confirm that, at least until that period, the Phoenician trade route in the eastern Mediterranean included eastern Cyprus. The route itself endured long after the last of the Phoenicians (Marquié 2002: 294–5).

In addition to its function as the industrial area for Phoenician cities, Cyprus was also a key node and distribution center along the Phoenician trade network, a port-of-call that served most of the Phoenician trade networks westward. The intensive interaction that resulted from the use of Cyprus as an industrial area and its use as a major port had an immense impact on all aspects of the economic, political, and cultural life of Cyprus. Starting in the Late Cypro-Geometric and the Cypro-Archaic periods, the temples and sanctuaries of Cypriot cities were devoted to the Great Goddess, i.e. Ashtart, who was sometimes depicted as Hathor. Cyprus was so important to the Canaanite-Phoenicians that they integrated the island not only into their trade network but also into their own land by founding formal colonies (Sherratt and Sherratt 1993: 365; Hermary 1998: 266, 270; Gunter 2013: 85, 97).

Colonies, in contrast to trade ports and industrial bases, were a rare phenomenon among the Phoenicians. Colonists built temples to their gods and remained connected to the homeland many centuries after their foundation, all while located at a farther distance than the Levant is from Cyprus. It is therefore reasonable to assume close relations between the Phoenicians of the Levant and those of Cyprus, on institutional as well as personal levels. The takeover of Cyprus by the Assyrians in the 7th century BCE may also be related to the island being a Phoenician center of production and trade, an offshore hub far away from the empire's reach, which enabled the Phoenicians to veil some of their operations from their Assyrian oppressors. Nonetheless, Assyrian presence on the island may not have been significant enough to disturb the Phoenician activity there. If Assyrian presence had been significant, we would have witnessed some decline in the Phoenician activity in Cyprus in the 7th century, but such a decline did not occur until the Hellenistic period.

Cilicia and Asia Minor

From the Middle Bronze Age at the latest, trade routes on sea and land connected the Levant and Anatolia, as already discussed. This is indicated by the metallurgic, ceramic, and onomastic evidence from the Late Bronze Age, as well as by bilingual inscriptions in Phoenician and Luwian dating to the 9th–7th centuries BCE and found at Phoenician trading posts: for example, at Zinçirli/Samʾal, Karatepe, Hassan-beyli, and Cebelireis Dağı (KAI 24, 26, 23, and 287, respectively) (Donner and Roellig 2002: 5–8, 70–1; Noonan 2011: 283–7).

Phoenician trade routes to Asia Minor were concentrated between the Amanus Mountains and the Cilician shore, around the Alexandretta Bay, and on Cilicia and the Bolkar Daglari and Ala Daglari Mountains east of the coast, particularly around the estuaries of the Tarsus and Seyhan rivers. Not only is this area where most of the Canaanite-Phoenician traces have been found, but it also was the route of the Hittite princes to Ugarit, as evident from an Ugaritic text (RS 94.2406). While this was probably the case in the Bronze and Iron Ages, in the Persian period the Phoenicians may have gained more access to or more pronounced penetration of western Asia Minor as well, due to their role as the Persian fleet.

During the Middle Bronze Age, trade between Crete and western Asia Minor developed, as demonstrated by the finding of Minoan seals and both Kamares fine ware and domestic vessels at Miletus in the early 2nd millennium BCE. A continuation of Minoan activity in Miletus during the Neo-palatial period (18th–15th centuries BCE) is indicated by Linear A inscriptions, Minoan weights and seals, the use of a sanctuary layout with an altar in an open court and offering tables, and both fine ware and domestic pottery, including stirrup jars. Minoan presence has been observed in other parts of the east Aegean and western Asia Minor as well, mainly at Rhodes, and was followed during the Late Helladic III period by Mycenaean presence. Cretan and Greek interest in Miletus and southwestern Anatolia can be attributed to its proximity to metal mines. Already during the Proto-palatial period, metals had been coveted in Crete, and trade in this commodity had been organized by the palace administration (Niemeier 2005: 3–16, figs. 23, 35–6).

Since the connections between the Cretan palaces and the Canaanite kingdoms are well attested (see Chapter 3), the Canaanite-Phoenicians had no doubt been aware of the operation of this trade route between Crete and Miletus and its prospects. Currently, however, there is no evidence of Canaanite-Phoenician activity in western Anatolia. As Canaanite-Phoenicians were prepared to travel great distances for metals, practically to the end of their known world, something likely prevented their procuring them via Miletus. Their long-time alliance with Crete had perhaps led to an agreed division of accessibility to metal mines, where Crete had taken western Asia Minor and the Phoenicians Cilicia and Cyprus. However, since the Levantine power was superior to the Cretan, there may be some other explanation for the apparent neglect of western Anatolia by Canaanite-Phoenicians in this period.

In the early 2nd millennium BCE, trade routes between Assyria and Anatolia exchanged Anatolian copper, silver, and gold for Assyrian textiles and tin. This activity had been concentrated in Kanesh, where an Assyrian trade diaspora had existed, and in Hattusa in central Anatolia. During this time, Miletus had been the harbor shipping central Anatolian metals westward (Morris 1992b: 146; Niemeier 2005: 4).

The north Aegean island of Samothrace with its mines, however, appears to have been a port-of-call for both the Cretans and the Phoenicians on their sea routes in the early 2nd millennium BCE. Five Minoan clay documents have been found there from this period, and Phoenician activity there has been suggested based on later written sources related to the myth of Kadmos and the *kabiroi* gods (Hellanikos *FrGH* 1.4.F23; Diod. Sic. 5.48; 5.64.4). This may indicate that Phoenicians were sailing off the coast of western Anatolia, even if it does not pinpoint the time period. No Canaanite-Phoenician finds have yet surfaced on Samothrace but may well do so in the future.

Hittite documents and the archaeological finds indicate things changed at the end of the Late Bronze Age and into the early Iron I period, when the Hittite Empire ruled Miletus and the Anatolian western coast. This new political order lasted only some decades, however, before the collapse of the Hittite Empire in ca. 1180 BCE, but while it existed it was beneficial to the Canaanite-Phoenicians. The trade routes to the east Aegean and western Asia Minor were used thereafter by Canaanite-Phoenicians (Niemeier 2005: 20–1). In the 13th–11th centuries BCE, Canaanite-Phoenicians traded for silver from the Taurus Mountains in southern Anatolia and may have used southern Anatolian harbors to ship metals to the Levant, as well as possible shipment overland. Anatolian silver dated to this period has been found at Tell el 'Ajjul, Ashkelon, Keisan, and other Levantine sites (Wood, Montero-Ruiz, and Martinón-Torres 2019). As detailed in Chapter 3, Canaanite-Phoenicians had been cooperating with the Hittite Empire to source copper from the Jordan Valley during the Late Bronze period.

Phoenician presence is well documented in Cilicia and Caria in southern Anatolia, where literary and epigraphic evidence indicate a long Phoenician presence and perhaps even colonization. The epigraphic evidence suggests the settlement was in place by the late 8th century BCE. Several Greek authors report the existence of Phoenician trade bases, especially at and around Alexandretta Bay. Herodotus, writing ca. 440 BCE, claimed the site of Myriandros had been founded by Phoenicians (Hdt. 7.9). He located the bay of Myriandros opposite Phoinike and mentioned another place called Kilix in the same region (4.38). Writing in the first half of the 4th century BCE, Xenophon (*An.* 1.4.6) described Myriandros as a "city on the sea, inhabited by the Phoenicians. This place was an *emporion* and there were many ships at anchor there." Slightly later, in the mid-4th century BCE, Pseudo-Skylax (*Periplus* 102) mentioned Myriandros as a Phoenician harbor. Presence in the region continued for almost a millennium longer. According to Stephanus of Byzantium, who wrote in the 6th century CE, a third town in this area, Aiga, also was a Phoenician settlement. There is good reason, then, to conclude that Phoenicians were indeed living at the foot of Mt. Taurus, having secured access to Alexandretta Bay, and that they operated important nodes on their trade network from there.

Other evidence reveals more aspects of Phoenician involvement in this area. In his annals, King Esarhaddon of Assyria mentioned that, in the year 676 BCE, Sanduri, King of Kundu and Sissu in northeast Cilicia, joined Sidon in an anti-Assyrian coalition (*Nin A* 3.20–38). This evidence reveals that political connections and mutual interests existed between the ruling classes of Phoenicia and Cilicia at that time.

Local Cilician rulers had their inscriptions written in the Phoenician script and language, their adoption of which points not only to a higher level of integration but also to the probable presence of

Phoenicians who were not traders in Cilicia. Those who carved these inscriptions were probably well-educated Phoenician scribes; the script is relatively clear and almost standardized. Such scribes, who were craftsmen (*ummanu*) in their own profession, were "rented" out for special tasks, and a hieroglyphic Luwian inscription mentions a "scribe from Tyre," probably referring to such a craftsman. There must have been a literate public who could read and understand the language. More epigraphic evidence comes from Tarsus, where a Phoenico-Aramaean inscription dated to the end of 8th–7th centuries BCE reads "to Sil-Banit." The proper name is composed of the elements *sl*, meaning "protection," and *bnt*, which is one of the names of the goddess Ishtar, the Akkadian name of Canaanite-Phoenician Ashtart. The two nouns are in construct, yielding the meaning, "the protection of Banit" (Röllig 1992: 101; Abusch 1999; Lemaire 2005: 169–70). Canaanite-Phoenician involvement in Cilicia, therefore, is evident from their influence on the Cilician language and religion as well as from their political and commercial activity.

Greece and the Aegean

Canaanite-Phoenician trade and its trade networks began to operate in Greece and the Aegean in the early 2nd millennium BCE. Near Eastern cultural influence on Greece and the Aegean is undeniable. Commercial connections between the Canaanite-Phoenician cities on the Levantine shore and the Aegean are evident in the Mari texts, where one trade sphere connected Anatolia and the Levant with Crete. During the Late Bronze Age, the same commercial and cultural sphere connected the great powers of Hatti, Egypt, and the smaller kingdoms in their realm with the Minoan culture on Crete and, later, with the Mycenaean culture of the Peloponnese. This entire area was united by the so-called International Style, reflected in palace wall paintings, Canaanite amphorae, Red Lustrous Wheel-made (RLWm) pottery, Mycenaean pottery, and other artifacts.

The identity of the traders who operated this Late Bronze network has been, and still is, debated. The Uluburun shipwreck, which bore elements on board comprising the International Style, suggests strongly, however, that this network was in Canaanite-Phoenician hands. Eurocentric and Hellenocentric approaches have argued in the past in favor of an Aegean or Greek operator for the Late Bronze trade network, and these ideas remain dominant. However, it has long been demonstrated that the skills, the capability for financial investments, the control of metals and exotic materials, and the sophisticated lifestyle that initiated the International Style were all in Eastern hands and all were features of the larger Eastern economic structures. Aegean and Greek cultures had no experience on a similar scale, and their growth during the Late Bronze Age was the result of their interaction with the East. Minoan culture, the earliest Greek entity, took its social and political structure as well as its religious practice from the Levant and the Canaanite-Phoenician cultural amalgam that was created in this period (Bass 1991; Sherratt and Sherratt 1991: 355, 366–8).

Distribution centers along the network operated in the Aegean. The earliest known example was located at Kolonna in Aegina. It was part of a regional network as opposed to the later international trade network. During the Late Bronze Age, Kommos in Crete and Tiryns in the southeastern Peloponnese were also early distribution nodes in the long-distance trade-net (Dickinson 1994: 241–2, 251).

In addition to economic arguments, other evidence reveals the major role of the Canaanite-Phoenicians in the construction of Greek culture. Oriental finds in the early Greek sanctuaries of the late Geometric period in the 8th century BCE may represent Oriental gifts to the Greek gods in the wake of the establishment of cooperation with the local population. The inspiration for the building of these subsequent temples has been explained to have resulted from Phoenician commercial activities. It is thought the temples would also have served as financial institutions. Greek and Etruscan temples flourished and continued to contain an abundance of Phoenician votives during the Archaic period (ca. 700–480 BCE) as well. A less convincing explanation of the Oriental finds in Greek sanctuaries is that they reflect the direct importation of the items by the staff at the Greek sanctuaries, who were heavily influenced by Oriental sanctuaries and religion. At most, this explanation must assume that orders were placed via Phoenician agents and delivered on Phoenician ships. It seems as though those proposing this explanation are assuming that a Greek trading network was in place, which was not the case (Hudson 1992: 136–7, 141–2; Morris 1992a: xvi).

Many of the earlier interpretations of Eastern finds in Greece correlate conceptually with Greece's golden era in the Classical period and the subjective sense of Greek superiority reflected in Greek literature. Notwithstanding, there is no evidence and no infrastructure in place to allow any substantial long-distance Greek trade before the 7th century BCE, certainly not with the far more developed and sophisticated economies of the Levant. The assumption that Greek society, still in its initial stages of development in the 7th–6th centuries BCE, would have been capable of and permitted to found colonies in the heart of the rich and ancient Levantine society is quite ludicrous. Things began to change during the 6th century BCE, when Phoenician commercial activity with Egypt appears to have been constricted by the Neo-Babylonians and Greek merchants were allowed to dwell at the international trading post at Naukratis in Egypt. Even so, there was no Greek foothold in the Levant prior to Alexander and his forceful military takeover of the East.

New finds from a shipwreck south of Levitha island (between Kalymnos and Amorgos), part of the Dodecanese Islands in the Aegean Sea, show without doubt that commerce between the Levantine coast and Greece was very vibrant in the early 3rd century BCE; a cargo of hundreds of amphorae, most of them Phoenician and some Carthaginian, was heading from the Levant to Athens when it sank (Koutsouflakis 2017: 36, figs. 5–6). Such amphorae have not been previously reported anywhere in the Aegean, and their presence provides robust testimony for Phoenician trade during the Hellenistic period in the Mediterranean.

Ports of Trade and Bases for Canaanite-Phoenicians in the Eastern Mediterranean

Crete

The geographical location of Crete made it a perfect node on the trade network going from the coast of Libya northward. Treaties dated to the Hellenistic and Roman periods substantiate this role and undoubtedly reflect older models put in place in the Archaic period. The pottery found on Crete during the Archaic and Classical periods provides confirmation of the island's function as a node on the trade route between Athens, the Peloponnese, and North Africa in these earlier periods. It was a node that did not contribute products of its own to the inventory traded but, rather, functioned as a point of transit trade (Viviers 1999: 228–230; Hadjisavvas and Chaniotis 2012).

Starting in the early 2nd millennium BCE, Crete was the major Aegean base for Canaanite-Phoenician trade. As already discussed in Chapter 3, the local production of imitations of early Middle Kingdom

Egyptian scarabs traded by Canaanite-Phoenicians confirm connections with the Levant. Such items date to the Middle Minoan period (ca. 2100–1500 BCE), the only time period when scarabs were manufactured in Crete (Weingarten 2005; Ben-Tor 2006; Höflmayer 2007). It cannot be emphasized enough that the earliest finds of Levantine origin in Greece and the Aegean were found in Crete and only later in other parts of Greece. These are not occasional finds that may be identified as luxury items but objects of religious significance that were adopted into the Cretan religion and way of life. The Iron Age Phoenician temple at Kommos and the *cippi* found in the cemeteries at Eleutherna and Knossos indicate that not only were Phoenicians trading with Crete but they were also permanent residents (Stampolidis and Kotsonas 2006: 352, 355). The *cippi*, stone funeral memorials, are inscribed in Phoenician language and often display Phoenician symbols, like that of Tinnit or a temple (*naos*). Such tombstones are typical to Phoenician cemeteries and tophets and appear also in Malta, Cyprus, Sicily, Sardinia and North Africa (Karageorghis 1997; D'Andrea 2014a: 37, 50, 83, 88, 2014b; Richey 2019: 229).

The Canaanite-Phoenician–Cretan connection has been widely treated in research. During the Bronze Age, the major sites involved with Canaanite-Phoenician trade were the Minoan palaces of Knossos, Archanes, and Phaistos, as well as the port on the small island of Mochlos off the northeastern coast of Crete and Kommos, in the bay on the central southern coast of the island. These sites yielded Canaanite amphorae and Aegyptiaca, including bronze cauldrons, baboons, and monkey imagery (Cline 1999: 115–22; Phillips 2008).

During the Iron Age/Geometric period, after the fall of the Minoan and Mycenaean palaces, the main sites where Phoenician presence can be observed in Crete are Eleutherna, Kommos, and the sanctuary at the Idaean Cave. Phoenician finds of all types have been recovered from these sites, including Phoenician pottery, Aegyptiaca, and Phoenician inscriptions. The oldest alphabetic inscription found so far in Greece and the Aegean is a Phoenician engraving on a bronze bowl from Knossos dated to the late 10th–early 9th centuries BCE (Coldstream and Catling 1996: 30; Sass 2005: 34–9). More contemporaneous epigraphic evidence comes from a graffito on a Canaanite-Phoenician jar from Kommos (Csapo, Johnston, and Geagan 2000: 108–9). Most of the Phoenician evidence on Crete, including the ivories and bronze bowls and jugs dating to the 9th–7th centuries BCE found at the Idaean Cave, has been interpreted as either the product of migrating Phoenician craftsmen or the result of Cypriot trade. However, the few Phoenician *cippi* found in Knossos and Eleutherna indicate without doubt the presence of Phoenicians residents in Crete in the 8th century BCE at the latest (Kourou and Karetsou 1998; Stampolidis 2004: 238).

Blinded by the celebrated Minoan culture and its magnificent palaces, assumptions are generally made that such an advanced culture had much to offer the Canaanite-Phoenicians; as already pointed out, some even have presumed the existence of a Minoan thalassocracy at this time. However, a comprehensive analysis of the available written and material evidence reveals the astonishing fact that Crete had very little to offer Levantine merchants. Timber was the only product exported from Crete until the Roman period. Even the products of the weaving activity reported in the Mycenaean Linear B texts were consumed locally. Until the Roman conquest in 67/66 BCE, Crete did not produce any merchandise, not even agricultural surpluses, that could have been traded and shipped overseas. A change in Cretan economic patterns occurred only in the Roman period (Chaniotis 1999: 210–12).

However, this picture does not hold true for the Mycenaean period, when Crete was incorporated into the Mycenaean trade network and production of olive oil and wine was introduced to the island.

Mycenaean administrative regulation created agricultural surpluses that were converted to processed products in the form of oil, wine, drugs, and perfumes and shipped in stirrup jars throughout the Mediterranean. Since the Canaanite-Phoenicians had close trade contacts with the Mycenaeans, they may have been the ones who physically shipped these Cretan products to waiting emporia (Ben Shlomo, Nodarou, and Rutter 2011; Hadjisavvas and Chaniotis 2012).

The Canaanite-Phoenician presence on Crete was not restricted to the Late Bronze (Mycenaean Palatial) Age. What were the Canaanite-Phoenicians seeking on their visits to the island? It seems the main reason they stopped at Crete was to replenish fresh water supplies before continuing westward on established Mediterranean sea routes. In addition, since timber was amply available in Crete, ships could have obtained timber for maintenance and repair needs. All the same, these two activities alone would not have produced the significant quantity of Canaanite-Phoenician finds in sanctuaries, tombs, palaces, and habitation levels on Crete from the Bronze Age onwards. I therefore contend that the Cretan products coveted by Canaanite-Phoenicians were plants and herbs, which they required for their perfumed-oil industry. Cretan herbs and flowers had already been utilized in the local perfume industry during the Late Bronze Age, as indicated by Linear B texts from Knossos and other Minoan palaces (Erard-Cerceau 1990; Chaniotis 1999: 207–9). The Canaanite-Phoenician trade-net in perfumed oils extended far beyond Crete over a very long period of time, as described below. Cretan herbs were only one of several elements used by the Canaanite-Phoenicians in the production and bottling of scented oils.

Knossos. This central Cretan site has been widely excavated and published, so it provides excellent data on Phoenician-Cretan relations from the Late Bronze Age into the Iron Age and the Orientalizing period. These relations can be reviewed at Knossos by an examination of burial practices at the site. The changes discernible in Cretan burial rites have frequently been interpreted in terms of Greek influence, but the same discoveries can be understood otherwise, as the following example shows.

Of 120 early Greek tombs excavated in the North Cemetery at Knossos, 16 yielded Canaanite-Phoenician and related finds. Most of the finds in the cemetery were local, as were the finds in these 16 tombs. The Canaanite-Phoenician finds were not isolated to specific tombs, which could have indicated that such tombs contained the remains of foreigners within a local cemetery. Rather, they were found beside local items that also were found in the other tombs. A quarter of the 16 tombs contained cremation burials, between 4 and 14 in each tomb. This form of body treatment became very popular in the Knossos tombs from the mid-9th to late 8th century BCE. Although interpreted as a Greek rite and a sign of Greek community, Canaanite-Phoenicians also used this form of burial. They had likely learned it from the Hittites, with whom they had shared multiple cultural connections during the Late Bronze Age. The fact that the Hittites used both cremation and inhumation simultaneously in the same cemeteries, as the Phoenicians did later, provides evidence of the transfer of this rite from Hittites to the Canaanite-Phoenicians (Bieńkowski 1982; Coldstream and Catling 1996: 674–5; Dayagi-Mendels 2002: 12–15; Singer 2002: 50*–53*; Aubet 2010; Antoniadis 2012).

The same process occurred as early as the Neolithic period, perhaps from Anatolia directly to Greece (Gallis 1983). Cremation was also used in some cemeteries in Greece and Crete in the Iron Age, but then it may have been restricted to upper classes or heroes (Bouzek 1997: 73–6). In Mycenaean Perati, cremations deposited in small jars of Hittite-inspired shape have been dated to the 12th–11th centuries

BCE. Uncovered alongside Aegyptiaca and other foreign items imported from the Near East, these finds and the cremation burials have been interpreted as being introduced to the Aegean sphere from Anatolia via the Levant (Iakovidis 2003: 504, fig. 11). At Eleutherna, a site on Crete with clear Canaanite-Phoenician finds, cremation was used in the 9th–8th centuries BCE (Agelarakis 2016). Cremation was the only burial practice used in Greece during the Proto-Geometric period in the 11th–9th centuries BCE and continued along with inhumation during the 9th and 8th centuries BCE (Alexandridou 2016).

Nonetheless, the thriving practice of cremation in Crete during the Orientalizing period may be connected with Eastern trends rather than with Greek rites. The form of burial alone cannot testify to a particular cultural affiliation of the dead and certainly not to a Greek ethnic identity for the population in Knossos. The Canaanite-Phoenician finds from the tombs in Knossos can be used as evidence, however, that religious and cultural influence from the East was common in the Geometric–Orientalizing period in Crete and likely also in Greece and the Aegean. Just as the practice of cremation in the Knossos tombs may be interpreted in a different way, so other discoveries from Knossos may be open to alternative considerations and interpretations that might be consistent with known cultural practices in the Levant (Coldstream and Catling 1996; Coldstream 1998a, 1998b, 1998c).

Rhodes

The largest of the Dodecanese Islands played an important role in Canaanite-Phoenician trade, not only as a hub on the network but also as a distribution center and production center for perfumed oils and medicines. Most of the evidence concerning Phoenician artifacts and trade appears elsewhere in this study, scattered throughout. However, a few words dedicated to Rhodes are in order here.

Starting in the early 9th century BCE, large quantities of Aegyptiaca, mainly faience amulets and scarabs, have been found in Rhodian burials and sanctuaries, mainly in Ialysos and Kamiros (Hölbl 2019: 307). Finds also have included a Phoenician inscription engraved on a cup and a possible first bilingual Greek-Phoenician inscription on a vessel, both dated to the 7th century BCE. Bilingual Greek–Phoenician inscriptions are still found in Rhodes as late as the late 3rd–2nd centuries BCE, indicating the continuous presence of Phoenicians on the island into the late Hellenistic period, even if these Phoenicians may have arrived there from the Phoenician cities of Cyprus rather than directly from the Levant, as their names suggest (Bourogiannis 2019: 164).

Other Phoenician finds on Rhodes include ivories, metal bowls and other Phoenician paraphernalia, but Rhodes also presents some very unusual Canaanite-Phoenician elements. Chiefly, it is the only place in the Aegean with a substantial amount of Phoenician pottery and local versions of Phoenician pottery, dating to the 8th and 7th centuries BCE. The presence of such pottery in Rhodes is associated with its major role in the Phoenician perfumed oils and medicines trade network (Bourogiannis 2013, 2014; Frère, Garnier, and Elisabeth 2016: 108; Coulié *et al.* 2017). Some of the Phoenician forms found in Rhodes are only typical on this island, such as the bent bottles of the 8th–7th centuries BCE (Regev 2020: 173–80), and the pointed pottery *alabastron* of the Classical and Hellenistic periods (Jacopi 1929; figs.65, 70; Jacopi 1933, fig.43).

Although the early Mediterranean distribution of *alabastra* is of vessels made of stone (alabaster), versions made of pottery and often glazed were produced in the 8th–6th centuries BCE at Assur and Nineveh and distributed to Syria, Jordan, Rhodes, and Etruria. Not only is the distribution of this type associated with Phoenician trade, but also, one example from Tell Jawa is made in a local version of

Phoenician *Black-on-Red*. Similar, Phoenician *alabastra* were found in a tomb at Samos and along the Phoenician coast (Culican 1975: 150; Daviau and Klassen 2014, fig. 6.4). By the 7th–6th centuries BCE, pottery *alabastra* were produced in Carthage (Redissi 2004: 197–203), and some pottery versions started to appear in the Greek corpus in the Proto-Corinthian group and later in Athenian and other groups.

Many of the Greek shapes, however, do not show much similarity to the original *alabastra*. Genuine *alabastra* are narrow and elongated and cannot stand on their base, whether pointed or rounded, as indicated also by their depiction on various objects, from vessels to sarcophagi (Almagro Gorbea *et al.* 2010, fig. 23), whereas many of the Greek shapes called *alabastra* are short and rounded and can stand on their bases (see e.g. Willemsen 2013, fig. 15). The modern association of the Greek types with the name *alabastra* often seems to be the result of their synonymity with an oil flask, due to their use, not as a resonance of their original form made of alabaster. The *alabastron* shape is presumably Egyptian, but its origin may, in fact, be Levantine (Sparks 1996: 59; Pierrat-Bonnefois 2010). It is interesting to see that the Athenian elongated *alabastron*, made between the mid/late 6th to early 4th centuries BCE in one specific workshop in one Geometric style (and not the figurative style most popular at that time in Athens), was distributed outside Athens almost exclusively to Phoenician sites in the central and western Mediterranean (Algrain 2014). This indicates a separate distribution network for the *alabastron*, different from other Athenian pottery of the period—a network that may have been in Phoenician hands.

A direct link between Rhodes and Phoenician culture seems inevitable, then, due to the resemblance of the Rhodian pottery *alabastra* to the original form. In addition, Rhodes has yielded other pointed *alabastra* types made of faience and other glazed material, like those found in tombs in Kamiros, dated to the second half of the 7th century BCE. Some of the glazed pointed bottles found there may have been locally produced to serve the perfume/medicine industry. Residue analyses made on Kamiros Tomb A containers has indicated that local medicinal ointment production took place on Rhodes rather than, or in addition to, perfume production (Coulié *et al.* 2017).

The long tradition of the *alabastron* shape was eventually replaced by various bottle and juglet shapes beginning in the late 6th century BCE, but Rhodes remained the only place that continued production and use of this shape through the Hellenistic period. This legacy seems to indicate the endurance of Phoenician pottery traditions and the continuity of perfume and medicine production on the island.

The exceptional epigraphic and archaeological data suggest ongoing Phoenician residency in Rhodes at least from the early 7th century BCE until the late Hellenistic period (Bourogiannis 2019: 179). The Phoenician community on the island engaged in industrial activity relating to amber and ivory carving and perfume extraction. These activities facilitated or contributed to Rhodes's status in the Hellenistic period as one of the three main harbors in the eastern Mediterranean, along with Alexandria and Delos (Kron 2016: 356).

Euboea

Although considered an isolated import, the earliest Canaanite-Phoenician pottery in Greece was nonetheless found in a tomb in Lefkandi, Euboea (Popham, Sackett, and Themelis 1980: 126). During the golden age of Phoenician long-distance trade around the Mediterranean in the 10th–8th centuries BCE, Euboea was the most prosperous and developed region in Greece. The strait separating Euboea from the Greek mainland provided a sheltered, natural route from north to south and east to west.

Euboea was the main maritime crossroads in the Aegean. The harbor at Lefkandi served Phoenician trade along the main east–west route. Phoenician commercial activity at Lefkandi in the 9th century BCE has been confirmed by the finding of balance weights of a Levantine or Cypriot origin on site. The weights were made using the Levantine standard that prevailed for hundreds of years in the eastern Mediterranean, from the Late Bronze Age to the Iron Age. Found in a cremation tomb that contained other Phoenician finds as well, this tomb may have belonged to a Phoenician trader situated in this important distribution center.

Euboea was also the location where, according to the *Iliad*, the Greek fleet assembled en route to Troy, a testimony that emphasizes Euboea's status as the main sea crossroads. Euboea was the closest shore to Thebes, the city of the mythical figure Kadmos. If there is any reality underlying the Kadmos story, he would have gone from Phoenicia to Thebes through one of the harbors of Euboea (Popham and Lemos 1995; Coldstream 2003: 199; Wiener 2007: 29–31; Kroll 2008: 43–4; Leone 2012).

Metals would have been available through the port of Euboea, which would have added to Phoenician interest in and attraction to this island. Iron might have been exported from Euboea via Lefkandi, which was located close to the silver mines of Lavrion and nearby Thorikos, which apparently was already operating in the Late Bronze Age, although this is still debated (Wood 2019b: 84–6). The other main periods of operation of these mines were during the Archaic (8th–5th centuries BCE) and Classical (5th–4th centuries BCE) periods. Iron, copper, and lead also were mined in Euboea (Stos-Gale and Gale 1982; Skarpelis and Argyraki 2009). From the 2nd millennium BCE onward, Lefkandi was probably involved in one way or another with the silver trade on Euboea. Silver items dating to the 7th–6th centuries BCE from Tel Miqne and Ein-Gedi in the southern Levant contain silver from Lavrion (Wood, Montero-Ruiz, and Martinón-Torres 2019: 21–3, 27). The natural resources from Lavrion and Thorikos and the location of Euboea met the demands of maritime trade in the Mediterranean during the Late Bronze and Iron Ages, demands also met by other Phoenician trade bases in Spain and elsewhere.

Based on the presence or inspiration of Euboean pottery in Greece, Asia Minor, and the Aegean, it has been claimed that Euboea influenced or even colonized parts of these areas. Starting in the second half of the 10th century BCE, Euboean pottery has been found at Tyre, Sidon, Ras al Bassit, Dor, and Tel Rehov, not only open vessels forms but also amphorae and their contents. These few finds have been interpreted by some as evidence of Euboean hegemony in the eastern Mediterranean. In support of this idea, it has been suggested on the basis of biblical texts that Tyre had been so preoccupied with its trade enterprises in Arabia and possibly India that it had lacked any interest in expanding westward. However, distribution maps of Euboean pottery from the 9th–7th centuries BCE show it to have been found specifically in Phoenician trade centers from Tyre in the East to Huelva in the West. In her criticism of the alleged Euboean thalassocracy in the Iron Age/Geometric period, Sarah Morris states, "Euboeans are currently more plausible as apprentices than partners in trade with Eastern and Western non-Greeks" (Morris 1992a: xiv; Sherratt and Sherratt 1993: 365–9, 375; Coldstream 2003: 199; Lemos 2005; Descoeudres 2006: figs.1–3; Wiener 2007: 30n206).

Further evidence of Phoenician influence on Euboean culture is provided by the cemeteries of its two main cities, Eretria and Lefkandi. Bronze cauldrons and Phoenician scarabs have been recovered in the cemeteries at Eretria and the tombs at Lefkandi that date to the 10th–9th centuries BCE. Also found in Eretria is a Phoenician dedication on a bronze horse blinker, dated to the 9th century, although it might have been in secondary use in the 8th, and a Phoenician undeciphered graffito on a cup dated to the

8th century BCE (Kenzelmann Pfyffer, Theurillat, and Verdan 2005: 76–7, 80; Boffa 2013). These tombs have yielded significant quantities of glass and faience beads alongside Egyptian faience amulets and other Aegyptiaca. Nonetheless, because the types of beads from Lefkandi have also been found in tombs at Argos, Tiryns, Athens, Kos, and Knossos, the distribution sphere of these beads in Greece and the Aegean is often thought to provide evidence of an alleged Euboean *koine*. However, a better explanation of the presence of Phoenician scarabs, bronze cauldrons, and Egyptian faience and glass is as a result of Euboea's function as a major crossroads. A mixed corpus of such finds is one of the fingerprints of Phoenician trade around the Mediterranean, as can be observed from the Uluburun shipwreck and later assemblages. Together with Corinth and Attica, Euboea has yielded one of the earliest examples of Greek writing, a fact that may indicate its early connections with the bearers of the alphabet, e.g. the Phoenicians (Röllig 1992: 96; Strøm 1992: 46–7; Coldstream 2003: 199; Lemos 2005: 56; Nightingale 2007: 424).

Lefkandi. The 11th-century-BCE Canaanite-Phoenician pottery that was found in a tomb at Lefkandi may have been an isolated find, but, by the mid-10th century, many other Levantine and Canaanite-Phoenician finds emerge in tombs on site. By the mid-9th century, there are also cremation burials accompanied by Phoenician bichrome jugs, among other finds, from Greece, Cyprus, and the Levant (Popham and Lemos 1995). The finds from this last tomb are very close to assemblages of the late-10th to early-9th-century-BCE tombs in Akhziv and Palaepaphos-Skales and reveal cultural connections in the eastern Mediterranean at this early stage (Crielaard 2018). Keeping in mind that Akhziv in Phoenicia and Palaepaphos in Cyprus were locations where Canaanite-Phoenicians resided, the unifying mediator between these sites is more likely to have been the Canaanite-Phoenicians.

The site of Lefkandi in Euboea appears to have been one of the earliest Greek distribution centers along the Phoenician trade-net, especially during the Orientalizing period. Like other such centers, it may not have served the Phoenicians uniquely but in addition to other groups.

During the Orientalizing period, Phoenician regional routes in the eastern Mediterranean were conducting trade in perfumed oils, mainly via the trade route that connected Samos, Rhodes, Kos, Crete, and perhaps also Cyprus. Their involvement included cultivating, processing, packaging, and distributing perfumed oils and ointments. Lefkandi may have served as a distribution center for Phoenician perfumed oils. The proposed Phoenician regional distribution center in Greece later shifted from Lefkandi to Corinth (Ridgway 1992: 88–9).

Corinth

Situated on both sides of the Isthmus of Corinth, Corinth and Perachora were two sites on the main sea routes from the Aegean to the West and from Attica and Boeotia to the Peloponnese. Consequently, Corinth had been the home of a central port and distribution center throughout the 1st millennium BCE and a major Phoenician trade base. Perachora, facing the Corinthian harbor, seems to have functioned as a sacred site until Corinth's destruction in 146 BCE. It housed temples, sanctuaries, and even a sacred pool, a phenomenon familiar from Bronze Age Egypt which became part of the Phoenician cultural corpus. Most of the Phoenician and Phoenician-related finds in this area come from Perachora. During the 8th–7th centuries BCE, the mixed corpus of finds at this site from Mesopotamia, the Levant, Egypt, Sicily, and more is typical of Phoenician trade. Despite the abundant finds from Perachora, Aegyptiaca is absent in Corinth, but this deficiency has been seen to have resulted from Roman looting (Kilian-Dirlmeier 1985: 227, abb. 10; Skon-Jedele 1994: 191–241; Coldstream 2003: 174–7; Dothan and Brandl 2010: 63–85; Nigro 2015).

At least from the 7th–4th centuries BCE, Corinth's status as a port of trade and a commercial center was unique and different from other Greek towns, whose inhabitants made their living in agriculture. However, many of the inhabitants in Corinth were potters, and the Roman writer Pliny (*HN* 7.198) even credited the invention of the potter's wheel to Corinth. Starting in the early 8th century BCE, Corinthian pottery was exported to Delphi and Ithaca, where the sanctuaries there contained large amounts of it. Later in the 8th century, Corinthian pottery was exported to Sicily and Italy, especially to Pithecusae. By 700 BCE, a potters' quarter had been founded in Corinth, the workshops in which cooperated and shared common installations and manufacture by 650 BCE, producing recognizable fine ware. The latter was in great demand in international markets until the middle of the 6th century BCE. Although it lost its seniority to Attic pottery at that time, it was still produced until the 5th century BCE (Salmon 1984: 81–97, 102–3).

Nevertheless, Corinthian pottery does not indicate Corinthian trade, traders, or ships. Due to the style and distribution of Corinthian pottery, it has long been suggested that it was produced specifically for the export market. The vast distribution of Corinthian pottery also points to the crucial role of merchants in its marketing and exchange, as was the case later with Attic pottery. Although Corinth was a port city engaged in commerce, there is no evidence indicating that Corinth could have operated such an effective and widespread trade network in the Geometric and Archaic periods. Based on the large quantities of Corinthian pottery found in Aegina, and their reputation as seamen, the Aeginaeans have been proposed as the operators of the Corinthian pottery trade network. This may be true for the regional trade network for Greece and the Aegean islands, where Corinthian pottery is usually not very common, except at sacred sites like Delphi and Delos. However, it is not likely to be true for most of the trade in Corinthian pottery, which was exported to the West instead. Sarah Morris and John Papadopoulos have provided a more convincing option that takes into account the wide distribution of the wares in the West. They have proposed that Phoenicians operated the trade in Corinthian pottery and that they lived in Corinth and operated the local pottery industry there (Roebuck 1972: 116–25; Salmon 1984: 106–16; Morris and Papadopoulos 1998: 251–63).

Ancient traditions connect Corinth and Corinthian pottery with the Etruscan kings in Rome and the introduction of special pottery into Etruria. According to the Greek tradition quoted by Pliny (*HN* 35.152), a Corinthian-Bacchidian merchant named Demaratus was expelled from Corinth in the middle of the 7th century BCE, along with all the other Bacchiads. These were the aristocrats who founded the Corinthian polity, fostered its prosperity and growth around the Corinthian Sea, and gained Corinth its commercial standing.

This Greek traditional story is re-examined here in light of the few established facts concerning the special relations Corinth had with Phoenician style and trade. Two points reveal the early influence Phoenician style had on Corinthian pottery. Corinth was the first Greek location where the Orientalizing decorative style appeared on locally produced pottery in the 8th century BCE, during the period of the Bacchiads at Corinth. Secondly, the earliest Corinthian *aryballos* shape was a local version of a Phoenician shape and style. These *aryballoi* may have contained the famous Corinthian iris perfume mentioned by Pliny (*HN* 13.5), and the production of either these containers or the perfume or both probably was initiated and distributed by the Phoenician network of perfumed oils. Moreover, unlike other Corinthian forms exported only until the mid-6th century BCE, the Corinthian *aryballoi* and *alabastra*, both of which had been influenced by Phoenician style, were widely exported and used as gifts in sanctuaries and tombs well into the 5th century BCE. Production of the Corinthian *aryballoi* has also been considered to have taken place in Pithecusae and in Rhodes, two sites with direct connections to Phoenician trade. This point strengthens the Phoenician origin of this form (Roebuck 1972: 106–13; Salmon 1984; Ridgway 1992: 85, 88–92; Luke 2003: 61–2).

In spite of earlier Hellenocentric voices determined to promote the role of Corinthian trade (Coldstream 2003: 186–7), the unequaled rapid growth and spread of Corinthian pottery, especially of *aryballoi*, testify to the pre-existence of a Mediterranean trade network which incorporated the Corinthian product into the commodities it delivered. The find-spots of early Corinthian pottery in Sicily and Etruria show that Corinthian pottery was distributed to sites known to have had pronounced Phoenician activity. Moreover, during the earlier time of abundant Corinthian pottery distribution in the 8th century BCE, the first Corinthian colony at Syracuse had not yet been founded. Thus, there were no available Corinthian distribution centers that could have operated such a trade network. Instead, the trade network that distributed Corinthian pottery and perfumed oils was Phoenician, the most sophisticated trade power in the Mediterranean in the Iron Age/Geometric period.

Corinthian pottery, then, deserves a new title: Corintho-Phoenician pottery, like the earlier Cypro-Phoenician pottery which had been inspired to an equal degree by the Phoenician decorative and formative style. Although many locations where Phoenicians arrived were influenced by their style, very few of them began to manufacture and distribute their own version of Phoenician style in a significant volume, aimed at international markets. Mass production of Phoenician-style pottery occurred only in Cyprus, whose domination by Phoenicians is well known, and in Corinth. The production of Corintho-Phoenician pottery in Corinth tends to indicate that the Phoenician presence in Corinth which began in the 8th century BCE was much more significant than has usually been assumed. It likely involved production by Phoenician potters and distribution by the Phoenician trade-net. The unique connection of Corinth with Phoenician trade was still in place during the 5th century BCE, when Corinth served as a major distribution center for Phoenician salted fish from the West.

Based on this observation, the traditions of Demaratus and the Bacchiads may be interpreted to reflect an early Phoenician presence in Corinth. According to this scenario, the Bacchiads may have been associated with Phoenicians or may even have been Phoenicians themselves, who developed Corinth and included it in their trade diaspora network. There is a conjunction between the political change in Corinth ca. 747 BCE, the rise of the Bacchiad oligarchy, and the emergence of Corinth as a commercial power (Coldstream 2003: 187).

In addition to their maritime activity, the Phoenicians likely founded the pottery industry in Corinth, in the same way they had founded various industries at other bases they had used across the Mediterranean. When all or a part of them were forced out in the middle of the 7th century BCE, they moved westward to Tarquinia in Etruria, a location with large quantities of Phoenician finds, where a Phoenician diaspora had probably already been established. In Etruria, they became part of the elite, as they had been in Corinth. These alleged Bacchiads/Phoenicians also brought with them craftsmen who operated Corinth's pottery industry and started local pottery production in Italy. Given that the sources mention that three craftsmen accompanied Demartus, perhaps only the Phoenicians who were part of the Corinthian elite were expelled, while others of lower status who would have been engaged in pottery production and perhaps also other Phoenicians were not forced out. The latter continued to produce pottery on site and carried on the Phoenician diaspora in Corinth, which operated the distribution center there.

Support for this narrative may be found in the fact that Corinthian pottery in Etruria is very different in its quality and use from all other locations. While in Sicily, southern Italy, and North Africa Corinthian pottery was used as regular table ware, in Etruria it was used as luxury offerings in tombs and was made of a higher quality and sophistication in its shapes and decorations (Salmon 1984: 106). This surprising difference suits the story of the emigration of the Bacchiads to Etruria. The use of luxury vessels in a ceremonial context alongside burial gifts of non-local origin suggests the presence of a different, perhaps Phoenician, population.

A few literary sources point to tight relations between the Corinthian regime, Egypt, and the Levant. According to Aristotle (*Pol.* 1.315B), Psammetichus, nephew and heir of the Corinthian tyrant Periander (late 7th to early 6th century BCE), was named after the Egyptian pharaoh bearing this name. Thucydides (1.13.5) reports that the earliest Greek triremes were built in Corinth and that it was a Corinthian shipbuilder who built four ships for Samos in the 8th century BCE. As shipbuilding in the Mediterranean was a prominent Phoenician occupation, this evidence fortifies the argument in favor of Phoenician residents in Corinth by the 8th century BCE. The art of shipbuilding continued in Corinth during the 7th century BCE, when Corinthian architects were invited by Pharaoh Necho at the end of that century to build a fleet for the Egyptian army (Hdt. 2.159). Herodotus also claims that this same pharaoh sent Phoenician boats to circumnavigate Africa (Hdt. 4.42–3; 2.102.2; 7.96–8).

The commissioning of the fleet from Corinthian shipbuilders took place in the wake of the Neo-Babylonian takeover of the Phoenician fleets in the late 7th century (604/5) BCE, a process that intensified during the Persian period from the 6th century (530s) to the 4th century BCE (Hdt. 3.19.2–3; 5.109.3; 6.6; 6.28.1; 6.31.1; 6.33). Although written in later periods, these three different testimonies from Greek authors depict an unusual amity between Corinth and Egypt and exceptional Corinthian skills in shipbuilding, both of which were traits known to be characteristic of Phoenicians. The conclusion that at least some Corinthians were of Phoenician origin is inevitable (Katzenstein 1979; Tanner 2003: 126; Hirschfeld 2007).

Athens

Currently, the earliest Phoenician finds known from Athens are dated to the 9th century BCE. They include mainly metal and faience jewelry from elite female burials at the Kerameikos, or "Potter's Quarter," and a glass pendant from a well at the Agora. The gold jewelry techniques (granulation, filigree, and the Egyptian and Phoenician inlay) in particular seem to indicate a solid Phoenician influence on local metal artisans. Phoenician finds including Aegyptiaca have turned up in burials in Athens and Attica dated to the 8th–7th centuries BCE, and in an 8th-century context on the Acropolis of Athens. Bronze bowls similar to those found at the Athenian Kerameikos have been found in the sanctuaries of Olympia, Delphi, and the Idaean Zeus Cave. Other bronze bowls have been found at the Heraion sanctuaries in Argos and Perachora (Catling 1964: 215–23; Strøm 1992: 47–9; Coldstream 2003: 55–63; Papadopoulos 2007: 108, fig. 108).

In addition to the cultural ties observed through the adoption of the alphabet and religious symbols in tombs and sanctuaries, evidence confirms that Athens had significant commercial ties with the Phoenicians, mainly during the Late Archaic and Classical periods. Literary evidence (Plut. *Vit. Sol.* 24.4; Diod. Sic. 2.43.3; Aristotle *Pol.* 127.8a7) recalls the efforts of Solon and Themistokles to attract craftsmen, including potters, to immigrate to Athens. Although the names of potters and vase-painters found in Athens in the 6th century BCE so far reveal Egyptian and Lydian/Phrygian immigrants, there is no reason to assume that craftsmen immigrated to Athens only from these locations. Other craftsmen, Phoenicians in particular, were also probably attracted to Athens by the tax benefits offered. The Phoenician craftsmen who would have immigrated to Athens would have become part of the Phoenician community in Athens, which also included merchants and diplomats. When the circumstances were right, these Phoenician craftsmen were in a perfect position to become artisans producing goods for a new node on the network of the Phoenician trade diaspora (Burkert 1997: 23).

During the Persian/Classical period, a trade route operated between Athens and Phoenicia. I have argued that the vast distribution of Attic Black Glaze pottery at this time should be credited to Phoenician distribution (Regev 2020: 118–23). The Mediterranean *Periplus* of Pseudo-Skylax, written in the 4th century BCE (*Periplus* 112), reported that the Phoenicians exchanged Attic pottery, perfume, and Egyptian stone for ivory and animal hides with locals on the Atlantic coast of Africa (Morris 1992b: 127).

A possible argument that could explain the Phoenician agreement to distribute Greek pottery, first Corinthian and then Attic, involves the reopening of the silver mines at Lavrion in southern Attica in the 6th century BCE, which resulted in access to large quantities of extracted silver. Traces of this silver appear in samples dated to the 7th–6th centuries BCE. Smelted silver from the same mines had been shipped via Lefkandi in earlier times (Cunliffe 1993: 69). The steady Phoenician interest in metals is well known. There was a pressing need for silver during the Persian period for the payment of imperial taxes. Carrying Greek pottery along with the Greek silver, therefore, made sense and explains the distribution and popularity of Attic Black Glaze ware at trading posts that were part of the Phoenician silver trade network in the Levant and Near East.

The same scenario may also account for the considerable increase in Greek pottery in Iberia beginning in the middle of the 5th century BCE. Once Greek pottery had been introduced into the Phoenician trade system and distributed in large volumes, it would also have been distributed to additional nodes in the Mediterranean Phoenician trade network, and Iberia was certainly in their network. In fact, the use of silver as a standard of exchange in the Near Eastern economy had already been established in the late 3rd millennium BCE, and interest in the precious metal had grown ever since. Greece may have been producing silver that was already being used in the East in the Late Bronze Age or even earlier, as the mines of Siphnos might indicate. The gold and silver items from Mochlos in northeastern Crete may provide evidence of a date before the Late Bronze Age (Sherratt and Sherratt 1991: 361, 367–8; Cunliffe 1993: 70–1).

Trade between the rest of the Mediterranean, the Levant in particular, and Athens was not restricted to luxury items or wine. During its floruit in the 5th–4th centuries BCE, Athens, with its growing population, needed essential supplies to nourish and maintain its power. Food supplies, especially grain, were increasingly imported by Athens beginning in the 5th century BCE. Although the prime source for grains was the Black Sea area, grain also was imported from Sicily, Italy, Egypt, Cyprus, and Kyrene. Written sources show that most of the people trading with Athens in the 5th–4th centuries BCE were foreigners.

Phoenicians were included among these traders. In the mid-4th century BCE, Xenophon (*Ways and Means* 3.12) wrote that Athens was in need of imported food supplies due to the loss of its maritime supremacy. He encouraged foreign ships to embark at the city's port and suggested that the Athenians attract merchants to settle in Athens by offering them hospitality and honors to sweeten the burden of the *metoikon* (the non-citizens' tax). An Athenian *proxeny* from this same period honors "Strato" (King 'Abdashtart I of Sidon, ca. 365–352 BCE) and his descendants for having supplied grain to the city and grants Sidonian residents and traders in Attica exemptions from the foreigner tax and other civic tax obligations. In this case at least, the Athenians went beyond Xenophon's advice by waiving the foreigner tax to entice Sidonian merchants to settle in Athens. Two Phoenicians from Tyre (*IG* 2.2.342+) were also granted awards and honors by the Athenians for providing grain to the city (Walbank 1985; Finley 1999: 162–4; Reed 2003: 17, 54–61, 126–7; Morley 2007: 56).

If Xenophon's advice was followed in other cases as well, and Athens became a favored port of trade in the second half of the 4th century BCE, this situation can add weight to the suggestion that the popular Attic Black Glaze pottery was shipped as return cargo by foreign merchants, including Sidonians. Not only were traders from Sidon exempt from the obligations of the metic and harbor tax but so were traders from Kition, who were allowed to buy land to build a sanctuary for Aphrodite (Ashtart?). It is reasonable to assume, therefore, that Phoenicians were involved in providing Athens with the supplies that Xenophon indicated were needed and that, while in port, they loaded Attic Black Glaze pottery as cargo to trade with other regions along their sea routes, including North Africa. The presence of Phoenician traders in Athens is, therefore, evident, and so is Phoenician trade in Attic Black Glaze pottery (Reed 2003: 44–5; Wallinga 2005).

II. The Central Mediterranean Islands, Italy, and North Africa

> The Phoenician centers in the west Mediterranean clustered in the triangle formed by western Sicily, southern Sardinia and the Gulf of Tunis, their node at Utica/Carthage. Some of these had now [8th century BCE] acquired the status of formal colonies, but their interest was in trade rather than in the acquisition of territory (Sherratt and Sherratt 1993: 367).

The earliest Phoenician finds from the central Mediterranean known thus far are Late Bronze Age Canaanite amphorae from Vivara, a small island with copper mines north of Sicily. It was a likely location for Phoenician finds in this period, when Phoenician activity was focused on metal exploitation. Vivara was once an active volcano, and, by the late 15th or early 14th century BCE, its harbor had sunk and the island's population had moved to nearby Ischia, where Phoenician activity has been most recognizable during the Orientalizing period. More Canaanite jars have been found in Sicily and Mursia nearby. In addition, a copper statue of the Canaanite-Phoenician smiting god (probably Reshef) was found at sea near Sciacca in southern Sicily and dated to the 12th–11th or even the 13th–12th centuries BCE. This statue has been considered the earliest Phoenician find from Sicily and evidence of Phoenician presence there beginning in the 12th century BCE (Mazar 1965, pl. 17.3; Tusa 1965: 33–4, pl. 17.1; Marazzi and Tusa 2005; Rizio 2005; Vianello 2005: 83).

Sicily, in particular, has yielded a variety of Canaanite and Phoenician artifacts and clearly played a major role in the Phoenician networks going through the central Mediterranean. Archaeological evidence of inland indigenous settlements in Sicily shows how strong the Phoenician–Sicilian connections were and how integrated their fate had become by the Archaic and Classical periods. Excavations have demonstrated that, as long as Phoenicians were settled and operating in Sicily, the indigenous settlements thrived and prospered. However, once the Greek settlers of Sicily defeated the Phoenician settlers there in 480 BCE, leading many of them to leave the island and move to Carthage and other Phoenicians centers, the indigenous inland settlements were abandoned. This event in Sicilian history provides a rare glimpse into the mechanism of the Phoenician mode of operation. It seems to have involved an integrated, peaceful cooperation with indigenous populations, resulting in assimilation and prosperity for all. The Greeks, in contrast, did not adopt this mode of operation (Morris 2003: 49).

Other Late Bronze Age finds in Sicily originate directly or indirectly from the eastern Mediterranean. Tombs in eastern Sicily contain imported and locally imitated Cypriot pottery. Mycenaean pottery that dates between the 15th–14th and 13th centuries BCE has also been found in southern Italy, Sicily, and Sardinia, including stirrup jars produced in Crete and found in Cannatello, Sicily. Although connections during the Bronze Age between Greece, Italy, Sicily, and Sardinia are well documented, these locations also functioned as nodes on the Canaanite-Phoenician long-distance trade route westward. Chemical and physical analyses made on a vast quantity of Mycenaean pottery samples from dozens of sites in Italy, Sicily, and Sardinia have provided surprising results; it seems that most of the Mycenaean pottery in Italy consisted of locally made imitations. In addition to Mycenaean imports, there were imports of Mycenaean imitations from Crete, Rhodes, Cyprus, and the Levant. Furthermore, it would have been odd for Mycenaeans to have distributed imitations of their own pottery made in other locations, particularly pottery made in places known to have had close connections with Phoenicians (Cyprus, Crete, and Rhodes) and, in addition, pottery from the Levant (Phoenicia?) itself (Almagro-Gorbea and Fontes 1997: 351; Alberti 2005; Belardelli *et al.* 2005; Day and Joyner 2005; Jones, Levi, and Bettelli 2005; Nicolis 2005; Vianello 2005).

This evidence, therefore, seems to strengthen the suggestion made above that Mycenaean pottery was distributed by Phoenicians and not by Mycenaean Greeks. In addition, of the Italian locations examined, Sicily, with its marked Phoenician presence, was the place where the earliest imported Mycenaean pottery had already arrived in the Late Helladic I–II period (late 16th–15th centuries BCE). It was discovered at Aegina and was found together with a Canaanite jar produced in Phoenicia. Later, Mycenaean pottery was imported to Sicily from Cyprus. On mainland Italy, imported Mycenaean pottery was quite rare in the Late Helladic I–II periods, and the majority consisted of imitations dating to the Late Helladic III period (Goren, Jones, and Levi 2001; Jones, Levi, and Bettelli 2005: 541). This process shows, that, at least during the Bronze Age, Mediterranean imports entered Italy and the central islands area via a central Phoenician route; they traveled via Cyprus, Crete, and the southern Peloponnese to eastern Sicily, where Thapsos near Syracuse was the main harbor at this time. The contemporaneous Greek sea route, however, followed the Peloponnese and western coast of mainland Greece and then turned westward to southern Italy after stopping at Corfu, following the southern Italian coastline and arriving finally in Sicily (Sherratt and Sherratt 1991: 372; La Rosa 2005, pl. 134e; Militello 2005: 592, pl. 135).

The Greek route does not accommodate the distribution map of Mycenaean pottery described above. Moreover, the presence of Canaanite amphorae in Sicily alongside the earliest Mycenaean pottery in the central Mediterranean shows that the eastern Mediterranean trade was operated by the Phoenicians, who carried goods from locations along their route to the West. This trade entered the central Mediterranean area through the islands, especially via Sicily. It is more likely that Cypriot and Mycenaean pottery found in Sicily, Sardinia, and southern Italy was carried by Phoenician traders than by Greek ones. As established from other Mediterranean locations, from the Late Bronze Age and onwards, a mix of Mediterranean pottery and artifacts is one of the characteristics of Phoenician trade.

Most of the Phoenician finds in this part of the Mediterranean date to the 8th–7th centuries BCE, which was the early Orientalizing period in Italy. They have been excavated primarily in Sicily but also in mainland Etruscan elite contexts. The most famous are the finds from Pithecusae (Ischia) in the Bay of Naples, where rich tombs have yielded luxury goods of elite association, a mixture of Phoenician, Euboean, and other Mediterranean artifacts. The majority of the pottery finds in this site were local, but many of these forms were local versions of Phoenician shapes, including amphorae and plates alongside *aryballoi* and other perfumed-oil containers. While some have claimed Pithecusae was a Greek–Euboean colony, others have recognized the prominent Phoenician presence there. The site has become an example of the Mediterranean cultural *koine* of the Orientalizing period (Buchner 1982: 277–98, Ridgway 1992: 64, 1997: 325; Luke 2003: 63; Morley 2007: 39–43; Donnellan 2016: 126–8).

Without entering into a discussion here about the ethnic and cultural identity of Pithecusae, with its mixed corpus of finds that is typical of Phoenician Mediterranean presence, the site was clearly a point on the Phoenician trade route. The route to the central Mediterranean originated either directly from Phoenicia, certainly during the Late Bronze Age, or from Phoenician posts in Cyprus, Crete, and North Africa. The route first approached Sicily and moved along its shores before continuing north toward the small islands between Sicily and central Italy like Vivara and Ischia. The islands functioned as gates to Etruria, Latium, and Campania, and all three regions have yielded an abundance of Phoenician and Phoenician-inspired artifacts. Moreover, these islands played a major role in the manufacture and distribution of metals (Niemeyer 2001: 89, fig. 5d; Marazzi and Tusa 2005: pls. 142, 148–50).

The central Mediterranean route turned westward from central Italy and included Sardinia and Corsica. Judging by the large quantity of Phoenician finds from the western coast of Sardinia, a second, different route may have connected North Africa directly with Tharros in western Sardinia. From Sardinia, the route led perhaps to Corsica and/or to the Balearic Islands and Spain. These routes explain the Etruscan and Sardinian artifacts that have been found in Spain, usually together with Phoenician or Punic finds. These routes correspond with other sites in Italy that have yielded Phoenician finds. Tombs from the 8th–6th centuries BCE in Etruria, Latium, and Campania contained amber figurines, amulets, and scaraboids that were often found together with ivory and/or faience figurines and amulets of similar types. The ivory artifacts were made by artists trained in ivory carving who had arrived in Italy from the East: either Phoenicians or artisans trained by Phoenicians in Rhodes.

The artistic style of the amber artifacts points not only to a Phoenician influence but also to the presence of Phoenician craftsmen in Italy. Their iconographic representations are clearly Canaanite-Phoenician. The amber figurines and amulets primarily take the shape of monkeys and nude females, but lions, dogs, and cows are found as well. All these symbols are well-known representations of Canaanite-Phoenician deities or a Phoenician adaptation of other oriental deities, especially the nude female that is the traditional representation of Phoenician Ashtart. In addition, evidence for the trade of amber by Phoenicians comes from the shipwreck at Bajo de la Campana in Spain, dated to the late 7th century BCE. The cargo included raw lumps of amber, ivory items, and Phoenician pottery (Polzer and Pinedo 2011).

Stelae with the naked goddess holding her breasts, a pose typical of Ashtart in the ancient Canaanite tradition, were found in Strata IV and III at Motya, a Phoenician city in western Sicily. The strata have been dated from the second half of the 6th century through much of the 5th century BCE. The same strata yielded other stelae of the same type, with a dressed goddess. Many of these stelae depict the full moon or a full and a crescent moon above the deity's head, the same image associated with the Punic-Phoenician deity, Tinnit. The crescent and full moon often appear above the heads of squatting baboon statuettes and figurines representing the Egyptian deity Thoth as well. These amber artifacts from the Iron Age point to the application of Phoenician symbolism and techniques used first on ivory carvings, like those found at Nimrud in Assyria from the 9th–7th centuries BCE, for example, to amber, a new medium. It seems that Kamiros on Rhodes became the main center where both materials were used to produce such pieces of art. From there, the carved ivory and later amber carvings, as well as the technique itself and maybe also the craftsmen, were shipped westward via Cyprus to Satricum and Palestrina in Latium. Since Phoenicians alone are known to have been present at all these nodes, it is logical to assume Phoenicians handled the route (Moscati and Uberti 1981: 57, 212–14, pls. 83–91; Waarsenburg, Docter, and Briese 1992–93: 41, 48–52, 69–71).

Substantial elements of Phoenician culture are visible in Italy in addition to the artifacts found in tombs. The early temple at Tarquinia from the 7th century BCE and the temple at Bolsena from the 6th century BCE both reflect Eastern layouts. These temples were built by Etruscans, but their adoption of Canaanite-Phoenician temple architecture points very clearly to a close connection with the Phoenicians. Another striking religio-cultural connection can be seen in the bilingual Etruscan–Phoenician inscriptions from Pyrgi, a site known to have served subsequently as a Punic trading post. Dated ca. 500 BCE, the inscription commemorated a dedication by the Etruscan king to Ashtart (Etruscan Uni). The equating in Italy of Ashtart with Uni began much earlier, as attested by bronze statuettes from Satricum and the marble statuette from the Cannicella sanctuary of Orvieto. At Satricum in particular, the same representation of Ashtart appeared both in the sanctuary and in a contemporary "amber tomb" (Cunliffe 1993: 71–2; Bonfante 2006: 13; Colonna 2006: 147; Simon 2006: 47, 61).

The Oriental representations of Ashtart and the monkeys and other figurines and artifacts found in the iconographic and epigraphic evidence from Italy indicate a direct connection between Phoenicia and Italy. Hence, there must have been a Phoenician trade route in operation until the 6th century BCE that did not yet include Carthage but, instead, went from Phoenicia via Cyprus, the Aegean Islands, and Crete to Italy. This route was much older than the route going from Carthage to Italy and westward.

Not only was Ashtart represented in Etruscan religion, but also the deity Milqart, who influenced the appearance of Hercle in archaic Etruscan art in Etruria. Despite his Greek-inspired name, Etruscan Hercle was a popular god, not a hero like Greek Herakles. In their Etruscan/Italian shape as Uni and Hercle, both Ashtart and Milqart were quite different in character from their Greek versions as Aphrodite and Herakles (Simon 2006: 58, 61). A direct connection between Etruria and Phoenicia is attested by this synchronization of deities from the 7th century BCE at the latest. Also, the Etruscan banquet was inspired by the Phoenician *mrzh*, and urbanism and Etruscan city-states were influenced by the Canaanite-Phoenician city-state. All these revolutionary changes in Etruscan society took place during the same period as the Orientalizing of art and culture.

Two main material features that appeared during the Orientalizing period (8th–6th centuries BCE) in Etruscan material culture and which served as its markers were the Etruscan amphora and bucchero pottery. Bucchero pottery consists of shapes new to the Etruscan world which were black-slipped and burnished. They were influenced primarily by Phoenician metal vessels and motifs and have been found in both mortuary and sanctuary contexts in the early phases of this pottery group. Bucchero ware also included bowls and plates made in traditional Phoenician shapes but with black slip instead of red slip.

Bucchero pottery became extremely popular in Italy and Carthage and continued to be produced in Italy until the (re)appearance of red-slipped vessels there, i.e. Terra Sigillata, during the Roman period in the 1st century BCE. A striking example of direct Phoenician influence on this group has been provided by the finds from Tomb A.169 in Carthage. This burial from the 7th century BCE contained a Canaanite-Phoenician oil lamp, a red-slipped, mushroom-rim Phoenician jug (Cintas form 65), and a bucchero trefoil-mouth jug which was identical to Phoenician trefoil-mouth jugs (Cintas form 160). The distribution of bucchero pottery is about the same as Etruscan amphorae, which can be seen even at the fringe of their distributional sphere: for example, in southern France (Cintas 1950: pls. 6.65, 12.160; Thuillier 1985: 156–7; Leegaard 2002: 158).

Just like bucchero pottery, the Etruscan amphora (Cintas 268) appeared in the 7th century BCE in tombs and sanctuaries, initially. It has a distinctive shape which resembles the Canaanite amphora of the Middle and Late Bronze Ages. The main difference between the two types is the handles, which are small in the Canaanite type in the Bronze Age but loop-like and high in the subsequent Etruscan type. Although the resemblance between the two types is undeniable, the time gap between these types is puzzling and has not been explained.

The most reasonable source that may have inspired this shape was Carthage, although contemporary Carthaginian transport amphorae were quite different from the Etruscan amphorae. Amphorae from Phoenicia appeared in Carthage in the 8th–7th centuries BCE, but these were clearly not the prototype for the Etruscan amphorae either. Their shape developed over the years and, by the Iron Age II, had become different from their ancestor Canaanite amphorae. As far as we know, Phoenician transport amphorae did not arrive in Italy in the 8th–7th centuries BCE.

What did arrive in Italy from Phoenicia and Carthage during this period, however, were two vessel categories that were close in shape and function to the Etruscan amphorae: ceramic small jars with similar high-loop handles and alabaster urns with small-loop handles. As can be seen in the *tophet* sanctuary at Carthage, these vessels were quite similar and were contemporary with the early Etruscan amphorae. In Italy, the Etruscan amphorae appear mainly in sanctuary and mortuary contexts, which might explain the shape of this amphora. Initially, it is likely the Etruscan amphora was not intended to function as a commercial vessel but as a ceremonial vessel that imitated contemporary Phoenician and Punic urns, which were also ceremonial vessels. It should be noted that the closed shapes of the Middle Bronze Age in the Levant had also been used as burial vessels. Two examples come from Tel Na'ama near Tel Anafa in northern Israel, an area under Canaanite-Phoenician influence from the Bronze Age and onwards, and 'Afula in the lower Galilee, where two Ashtart figurines were found (Cintas 1970: pls. 18.81, 19.92, 95, 21.113; Fajardo and Parcerisa 1983–84: figs. 5, 7, 8B, E; Gal and Covello-Paran 1996: 54, 61–2, figs. 25.6, 32; Greenberg, Kolska-Horwitz, and Lernau 1998: 17, figs. 10, 17.1–2; Aubet 2001: 221, figs. 50, 101.558).

The distribution of Etruscan amphorae in the central Mediterranean reflects the Phoenician trade routes in this area. Etruscan amphorae have been found mainly along the shores of the Tyrrhenian Sea in Sicily, western Italy, and Sardinia but also in North Africa, including Carthage, and in Spain. Beginning in the 7th century BCE, they also started to appear in the Rhône Valley, mainly in the littoral region and among underwater finds off the coast of southern France. Some still bear remains of their contents: resinated wine.

It is, therefore, quite likely that, by the 8th century BCE, the Phoenician route in this area was going from Carthage through Sicily to the western coast of Italy and the small islands nearby. It then turned westward to Sardinia and, from there, to the Balearic Islands and Spain. This route was still active during the 5th century, as indicated by the Etruscan amphorae found in Valencia on the Spanish littoral opposite the Balearic Islands, together with Phoenician and Punic amphorae. In addition, a route going along the northern Mediterranean coast from Etruria to the Rhône Valley was operating from the 8th–6th centuries BCE. This trade route carried Etruscan pottery and bronze vessels along with Attic pottery, and provides another dimension to the theory that Greek pottery was distributed via Phoenician trade lines and trade centers. Moreover, when Etruscan pottery was no longer imported by the littoral area of the Rhône Valley, neither was Greek pottery. In spite of continuous commercial activity in this area evidenced by the presence of Marselliot amphorae and local pottery, imports of Greek origin did not arrive there between ca. 550–350 BCE (Leegaard 2002: 158–64).

The mid-6th century BCE was a time of decline in Phoenician activity in the Mediterranean, and the absence of Etruscan and Greek pottery in locations where such finds had been present before can be related to the downturn in Phoenician commerce during the Persian period. As nothing of Phoenician nor Punic origin has been found in southern France with the Etruscan and Greek goods, it seems reasonable to assume that, in this period, the northern route along the Mediterranean coast from central Italy to southern France was operated by other agents who had loaded their merchandise at a Phoenician distribution center in central Italy, perhaps at Pithecusae. This center probably continued to be operated by Phoenicians, but the agents may have been Etruscans or traders from southern France. Judging by the finds, they were definitely not Greek.

In the Hellenistic period, a ship sank near Lilybaeum, Sicily, in 241 BCE. Due to a lack of significant numbers of amphorae or other solid cargo on board, the ship is believed to have been a warship and not a commercial ship. There were no rocks or reefs at the point of sinking, yet there also were a few Punic shipwrecks in the same location, suggesting perhaps that a naval battle had taken place there (Tusa and Royal 2012). The shipwreck contained a mix of Punic amphorae, types of gray ware known to have been produced at Ampurias in the Iberian Peninsula which were commonly exported to Morocco in that period, three Italian Campana A bowls with Phoenician graffiti, and Pompeian Red dishes.

In addition, included in the published cargo are two bowls that look earlier than the assigned date. One (Frost and Vari 1981: fig. 106f) is a red-slipped hemispherical bowl with bands of the type usually classified as "East Greek" and dated to the Persian period; it is, in fact, of Phoenician origin (Regev 2020: 105–13). The other (Frost and Vari 1981: fig. 106l) is a bowl decorated with "cream slip" on both sides, a surface treatment known to be part of the Phoenician ensemble of the Late Iron Age and early Persian period. As items from several ships may have become mixed over time in the dispersal of their wreckages and by subsequent tides and currents, these finds, though published as part of this boat corpus, may have come from another, earlier Phoenician/Punic boat. This conclusion is supported by the epigraphic finds, as graffiti on a few bowls were dated by William Culican much earlier, to the 6th–3rd centuries and even possibly to the 8th century BCE. This script can be dated to the 2nd century BCE only if read as Punic, but this is not the date of the wreck in any case. These dates do not correspond with the reason given for the ship sinking in a battle nor with its identification as a battleship. Some sort of sea hazard existed at this location, as indicated by earlier boats that also had sunk there. Perhaps this had been a popular spot for pirate activity. Alternatively, some sort of weather conditions might have accumulated around or been particularly active in this area that lay close to the commercial port of ancient Lilybaeum.

William Culican concluded that this corpus of pottery fit best in a central Italian context, but Honor Frost saw this ship as evidence of a Phoenician trade route operating between Etruria and Carthage, even when Rome had a garrison in Etruria at this point during the 3rd century BCE. A similar corpus of pottery typified Ampurias in the 2nd century BCE. The assemblage of finds illustrates a Phoenician trade route that operated between Ampurias, Etruria, and Carthage at least in the 3rd–2nd centuries BCE (Culican and Curtis 1974; Frost and Vari 1981: 16, 143–90, 276).

Support for the existence and endurance of the Phoenician route that went from North Africa to Sicily to western Italy and on to eastern Spain is provided by Athenaeus (5.206–9), who wrote in the Hellenistic period. He mentioned that wood for large ships was available in the 3rd century BCE from Mt. Etna on Sicily. The same location was still providing wood for boats of the Muslim fleet located in Tunis (area of Carthage) during the early Muslim period (7th–9th centuries CE). Phoenician trading posts that exploited nearby forests for timber were also known in southern Spain. Like other Phoenician ports in the Levant and Cilicia, Phoenician sites in Iberia were positioned at the mouths of rivers and streams, which made the mountain forests upstream accessible. In each area, these ports were undoubtedly used for shipbuilding and were tied together into a Phoenician timber trade network that operated continuously from the early 10th century BCE into the Islamic period, until the forests were no longer dense enough in this area to make timber harvesting profitable (Meiggs 1982: 335–9, 345–6, 357–9; Freumann 2009: 169–82).

The shipyards and sources of ship timber seem to be yet another enduring feature in the Mediterranean economy that affected trade routes. These routes were sustained through major political changes as long as the raw materials were still available. Neither the Roman nor the Muslim conquests of the Mediterranean changed these routes, although the timber supply probably became short during periods of turmoil.

Ports of Trade and Bases for Canaanite-Phoenicians in the Central Mediterranean

This vast area includes two main zones. The first encompasses the central Mediterranean islands of Sicily, Sardinia, Malta, Corsica, and Lipari, along with small islands off the Italian shore like Vivara and Ischia. The second zone includes the Mediterranean coasts of North Africa. Although there is plenty of evidence to demonstrate that direct contact took place between the Canaanite-Phoenicians and the Italian mainland population, primarily the Etruscan elite, the sites where such finds were uncovered were not trade centers and thus not detailed below.

As is the case with the Canaanite-Phoenician centers in the western Mediterranean, there is variety within these zones. Each of the islands has his own characteristics and version of Canaanite-Phoenician acculturation. Some are major trading posts, like Motya and Palermo in Sicily, the latter being the major trade center for all the islands, or Tharros, Sulcis, and Cagliari in Sardinia; and some were primarily production sites like Lipari. Others, like Malta, are mainly stations en route to the West. In North Africa, there is a huge difference between Carthage and Utica. Carthage was the capital of a Canaanite-Phoenician state in the central and western Mediterranean and the trade bases in Libya.

North Africa

Continuous Phoenician presence on the Mediterranean coast of North Africa is currently dated to the 9th century BCE, but the trade routes to the central and western Mediterranean show that the connection had already been established in the Late Bronze Age. The two main trade and distribution centers on the Mediterranean North African coast were Carthage and Utica. Further to the east, in Libya, were two other Phoenician trade centers, Sabratha and Lepcis Magna.

Carthage. The largest, most important and renowned Canaanite-Phoenician city outside of the Levant, Carthage was founded in the center of the North African coast, facing the major central Mediterranean islands. It is the only one of their cities that has its own founding myth and the one that was no doubt founded and inhabited by people from Tyre (Álvarez Martí-Aguilar 2018). It is the earliest location where a *tophet* was founded in the 8th century BCE. Other *tophets* were founded between the 8th and 4th centuries BCE, and some were still in use until the 2nd–3rd centuries CE (Xella 2013). The best-known *tophets* are those at Motya in Sicily, Rabat in Malta, and six in Sardinia: Sulcis, Bithia, Tharros, Nora, Cagliari, and Monte Sirai. All of these *tophets* are within reach from Carthage and under its influence and, perhaps, its control. About 30 *tophets* are currently known in North Africa in the area of Carthage and its hinterland, and the phenomenon in general is considered to be of Carthaginian origin rather than an Oriental Phoenician tradition, although the debate over whether *tophets* were related to or originated from Carthage is still ongoing (Bernardini 2013; D'Andrea and Giardino 2013; D'Andrea 2014c).

As this is nonetheless a cultural phenomenon that unifies what is called the "Circle of the Tophet" (Quinn 2013: 30–3), the search for the unifying factor is still an open question. A reasonable answer would be the specific Phoenician population that inhabited these sites, a population that was mainly concentrated in Carthage and Sardinia (or first in Carthage and then in Sardinia), which may have been different from the Phoenician population in other Western sites. Based on what we currently know, the Phoenician city the language and characters of which were different from other Phoenician cities in the Levant in the 1st millennium BCE was Byblos (Peckham 1992: 410–11; Woudhuizen 2007), although there is no evidence of a *tophet* in this site in any period of its long existence.

Like many of the Canaanite-Phoenicians' network bases, Carthage, too, was processing metals. Metal smelting, mainly iron, was conducted in Carthage from the 8th century BCE until its destruction by the Romans in 146 BCE. Other industries produced glass colored by iron slag from imported glass ingots, and pottery (Docter *et al.* 2003; Bechtold 2012; Eremin *et al.* 2012; Kaufman *et al.* 2016).

The authorities in Carthage operated a large proportion of Canaanite-Phoenician trade networks, both independently and jointly, with the Levantine city-states. This is especially true of the salted-fish network, from the 6th century BCE onwards. Nonetheless, there is vast research on Carthage, and many discussions on its pivotal role in the Canaanite-Phoenician trade. The current study tries to paint a picture of the Mediterranean overall and does not focus on Carthage.

Carthage, which maintained a direct connection with Tyre and the Phoenician littoral, was also a major distribution center until it was destroyed in 146 BCE. Having being rebuilt during the Roman period, it continued to serve as a node in the Phoenician trade network, despite a constant reduction in its population from the 1st–4th centuries CE. It was still a large enough city to operate the distribution of red-slipped pottery in the Late Roman period until the 7th century CE. The fact that Carthage has yielded by far the largest percentage of imported Gaza/Ashkelon amphorae anywhere in the Mediterranean demonstrates the ongoing connection between Phoenicia and Carthage (Kingsley 2004: 94–101).

Utica. Located on the coast of central North Africa about 40 km northwest of Carthage, Utica was the first city founded by the Canaanite-Phoenicians in North Africa. According to ancient sources like Pseudo-Aristotle (*Mir. Ausc.* 134), Pliny (*HN* 16.216), and Veleio (Velleius Paterculus 1.2–3), Utica may have already been founded by the late 12th century BCE, although currently this date is not supported by the finds on site. The earliest date provided by ^{14}C analyses points to the end of the 10th century BCE (López Castro *et al.* 2016; Luís Cardoso *et al.* 2016: 314–15).

The name "Utica" derives from the Phoenician word for "old, ancient," which is *'tq* (Hebrew *'atiq*). The city name meant "Old City" versus Carthage, the "New City" (Ghaki 2015: 66). As the "old town," Utica was probably founded first, but Carthage became much more important in the Canaanite-Phoenician trade.

Sabratha and Lepcis Magna. Located on the Mediterranean coast in western Libya, Sabratha and Lepcis Magna were Phoenician ports along the trade route from Carthage eastward. Lepcis Magna was founded in the 7th century BCE and Sabratha was founded probably in the late 6th–early 5th centuries BCE (Brogan and Wilson 2016a, b).

Sicily

By the Late Bronze Age, Sicily was already serving as a major hub for Canaanite-Phoenician activity. With several major Phoenician bases surrounding its western territory and traces of Phoenician imports in its eastern region from the Late Bronze Age to the Classical period, Sicily served as the most important Canaanite-Phoenician base in the central Mediterranean. The existence of a sea route through the Messina straights is evident from Canaanite-Phoenician finds from the Late Bronze to the Archaic period at Thapsos and Lipari, while Phoenician finds of the Archaic period were found at Messina (Zancle) (Bacci 1998, 2005, 2008; Bacci *et al.* 2012) as well as in the area of Syracuse. I observed these Phoenician finds at the Paolo Orsi Syracuse Archaeological Museum in September 2018.

Thapsos. Located on the eastern shore of Sicily near Syracuse, Thapsos was a port city in the Bronze Age (15th century BCE), located en route to the Bay of Naples and its islands. Some of the earliest Canaanite finds in Sicily come from Thapsos, which was the most important Canaanite-Phoenician base on the island during the Late Bronze Age. Evidence of the earliest metallurgic activity in Sicily comes from Thapsos and its area (Giardino 2005: 500; Giumlia-Mair, Albanese Procelli, and Lo Schiavo 2011). Metal workshops in Thapsos and its area manufactured types of swords known as Thapsos-Pertosa forms, dated to the 13th–12th centuries. These swords also were distributed to the small islands north of eastern Sicily, especially to Lipari. Thapsos swords appear alongside Ugaritic and Mycenaean sword forms in Egyptian wall carvings dating to the reign of Ramesses III (ca. 1187–1156 BCE). Such swords were also found on the Uluburun shipwreck and in a Late Bronze Age I context at Beirut (Jung 2018: 274–9). Reinhard Jung interpreted the distribution of the Thapsos swords alongside certain pottery groups as evidence of the eastward migration of a Sea People group, but it points instead to an element of the International Style of the Late Bronze Age that was circulated by the Canaanite-Phoenicians (see Chapter 3 Section III).

Motya. Motya (San Pantaleo) Island is located in a lagoon off the southwestern coast of Sicily. Salt has been and still is produced in this area and along the western coast. This was the most important Phoenician base on Sicily starting in the 8th century BCE. In addition to its function as a major trade center, Motya was an important walled city in the Canaanite-Phoenician world. It contained a sacred compound which included several temples and a sacred pool, the only one of its type in the central and western Mediterranean known so far. Only one other is known outside the Levant and Egypt, and this was located at Perachora (Corinth) (Nigro 2015). Motya also had a *tophet*, perhaps the only one in Sicily. In the 7th century BCE, due to a lack of sufficient space for the city's deceased, a causeway was built from the existing necropolis to a new burial ground located at Birgi, on the shore (Orsingher 2016: 292; Sconzo 2016: 327).

Lilybaeum. Located in the western corner of Sicily, Lilybaeum (Marsala) was a Phoenician city founded by the inhabitants of nearby Motya, after their city was destroyed by Greeks from Syracuse in 397 BCE (Pseudo-Skylax, *Periplus* 13). This was a major Phoenician harbor and trade center in Sicily, which maintained its central position when it became Roman in 241 BCE (Hornblower and Spawforth 1999: 861; Hoyos 2010: 168). Based on burial inscriptions, there may have been a *tophet* here, too (Bisi 1967: 151–4).

Palermo. Palermo was founded by the Phoenicians in the 8th century BCE as a city named Tzitz ("flower bud"). This name is written in Punic script on its early coins. From the 5th century BCE onwards, however, Palermo was called Panormus, as reflected on the later coinage (Jenkins 1971: 27–33, 40–5).

Lipari. The largest of the Aeolic islands northeast of Sicily, Lipari was a metallurgic and industrial center from the Late Bronze Age onwards. Known for its deposits of alum and obsidian, it drew the attention of the Canaanite-Phoenicians in early times.

The Islands between Sicily and the Italian Peninsula

The *Phlegraean Islands*, part of the Neapolitan Archipelago off the shore of Italy in the Bay of Naples, played a key role as a trade base and gateway to inland Italy, mainly to Etruria but also to Latium. Evidence for Canaanite-Phoenician activity was found at Vivara in the Late Bronze I period and at Pithecusae in the 8th–7th centuries BCE.

Pithecusae (Ischia) is the ancient name of the largest island of this group, whose name derives from the Greek word for monkeys; the Romans called the group of islands Aenaria, the Latin term for monkeys (*Inarime* by Virgil, *Aen.* 9.716). There was never any evidence in ancient times or later of monkeys actually living on the island. The name may have something to do with the monkey symbol introduced to this area by the Canaanite-Phoenicians. During the Bronze Age and the Archaic period, at least some of its population had a long history of contacts with Canaanite-Phoenicians, having moved from Vivara to the island around 1400 BCE. Nonetheless, Pithecusae was known primarily for its thriving trading post in the 8th–7th centuries BCE, which has commonly been labeled a Greek *emporium*, despite the overwhelming evidence of Canaanite-Phoenician presence. It has also been noted that the academic reconstruction of Pithecusae as a Greek colony of Euboea predates the latter formation as a *polis* and, therefore, is unlikely (Donnellan 2016: 127–8).

Vivara. This small island was the first base for Canaanite-Phoenician contact in the 16th century BCE Around 1400 BCE, however, a volcanic eruption blew up half of its surface, and its inhabitants moved to the neighboring island of Ischia (Pithecusae) (Rizio 2005).

Sardinia

One of the largest islands of the Mediterranean, Sardinia was en route from the Levant to the Balearic Islands and the Iberian Peninsula, as well as a destination in its own right, due to the copper, silver, and lead mines on the island. Canaanite-Phoenician presence on the island is dated from the 10th or 9th century BCE, but trade bases were founded later, on the southern and western coasts, starting in the 8th century BCE (Webster 1992; Hornblower and Spawforth 1999: 1356; Hoyos 2010: 45–7; Ben-Tor 2018: 294).

Tharros. A harbor in the Bay of Oristano in western Sardinia with easy access to fisheries and salt beds, Tharros was probably the oldest of the Canaanite-Phoenician bases on Sardinia, although archaeometric analyses have only tracked Phoenician pottery dating from the 7th century and later on site so far. Tharros was also a center of Carthaginian metal production, which made it one of the most important Phoenician trading posts in the central Mediterranean (Amadori *et al.* 2016, table 1; Kaufman *et al.* 2019: 4098). There may have been an old Nuragic, indigenous port located there before it became a Phoenician city in the 8th century BCE. Although not the closest to the Etruscan shore, it was the Phoenician port of Tharros that had the closest commercial links between Sardinia and the Etruscans, as well as with Spain; it was the wealthiest and most important distribution center in Sardinia and had a *tophet* as well (Grant 1980: 35; Moscati and Uberti 1985; Zucca 1987; van Dommelen and Finocchi 2008).

Sulcis (Sant Antioco). One of the oldest Phoenician bases in Sardinia, perhaps as old as Tharros, Sulcis was founded in the 8th century BCE. Archaeometric analyses have confirmed this date (Amadori *et al.* 2016, table 1). The site had a *tophet* as well. Situated on a small island (Sant Antioco) in southwest Sardinia, Sulcis, like other Phoenician cities, played a part in Phoenician history in the western Mediterranean and its conflicts with the Romans. Sulcis is situated in a mining area, and metallurgic activity is attested there starting in the 12th–11th centuries BCE. Around the late 8th to late 7th centuries BCE, the Phoenicians of Sulcis founded a sacred site with a temple at nearby Monte Sirai (Piga *et al.* 2008: 144–5). This site had a 4th-century-BCE *tophet*, one of the latest founded, not including North African *tophet*s (Lo Schiavo, Maddin, and Muhly 1985: 27; Bartoloni 1989, 2008; Russell and Knapp 2017, table 2, figs. 2b, 6d).

Nora. This site is famous for yielding the earliest Phoenician inscription found in Sardinia, which is dated to the late 9th–8th centuries BCE (Lipiński 2004: 235–42). Nora was another node on the Phoenician trade route from Carthage to Sardinia and a former Nuragic administrative center (Pilkington 2013: 123–5).

Cagliari (Karalis). This Phoenician harbor at the southern coast of Sardinia was established in the 8th century BCE. In addition to its role as a trade station, it had large salt lagoons. The *tophet* of Cagliari was founded in the 5th century BCE and functioned until the 3rd century BCE, as did the large necropolis of Tuvixeddu (D'Andrea and Giardino 2013: 13).

Malta

The islands Malta and Guzo south of Sicily and north of Libya served as a Canaanite-Phoenician trade base beginning in the 8th century BCE or even in the 10th century. Malta maintained a *tophet* of its own, as well as other Phoenician cemeteries on both islands, until it came under Roman dominion in the late 3rd century BCE. This is one of the rare examples where Phoenician presence was not related to access to local resources but, rather, to its location en route to their established trade routes, supplying safe harbors, food, and water (Sagona 2014).

III. The Western Mediterranean and the Atlantic

Phoenician trade routes and Phoenician cultural traces in the western Mediterranean have been studied at length in the renowned works of Maria Eugenia Aubet, especially the evidence concerning the Iberian Peninsula and its vicinity (Aubet 2001, 2008). It has also been the focus of the research of many other scholars in Spain and Portugal, whose work has often not crossed the language barrier and been made known and available to other scholars whose research is focused on the Phoenicians in the eastern Mediterranean.

Two main routes led from Phoenicia to Spain and the Atlantic Ocean: one was along the southern shores of the Mediterranean via Egypt and North Africa; the other went through the central Mediterranean via the Aegean, Crete, Sicily, Sardinia, and the Balearic Islands. From southern Spain, the route continued to the Atlantic Ocean, on both sides of the straits of Gibraltar, in the area also known as the "Circle of the Straits." Trade routes connecting to this area had begun in the Chalcolithic period and were well established by the time the Phoenicians arrived and used them in their trade network (Teichner and Pons Pujol 2008: 303; Aranegui, López-Bertran, and Vives-Ferrándiz 2011: 299). Later, in the 1st millennium BCE, there were two more Phoenician routes going from Carthage to Spain and the Atlantic Ocean: one along the North African coast to southern Spain and the Atlantic Ocean; the other via Sicily, Sardinia, and the Balearic Islands to eastern Spain and, especially, to the area of Barcelona (Emporias).

Initially, the location of mining in these areas motivated these routes: first and foremost the mines in southern and southwestern Iberia, but also those in southwestern and northern Sardinia. As the finds reveal, the route from Phoenicia westward was directed to these locations. Alum mines were in Lipari, north of Sicily; copper, silver, and lead mines were in western and northern Sardinia; iron, copper, silver, and gold mines were in south and southwestern Iberia, where remains of Phoenician metallurgic activity have been observed (Plin. *HN* 33.66–7, 77–8, 79, 96–7, 106); and iron mining and Phoenician metallurgy was already taking place in Carthage in the 8th century BCE (Lancel and Thuillier 1982; Tylecote 1982; Niemeyer 2001: 83, 85–6, fig. 1; Borgard 2005; Fletcher 2006: 180; Kaufman *et al.* 2016).

Metal mining also seems to have been one of the main reasons behind the Phoenician presence on the Atlantic coast of Iberia, where it was located at specific river mouths carefully chosen with a specific goal in mind. These coastal locations show that the Phoenicians had a thorough acquaintance with both the geography of the area and the indigenous settlements. Based on ^{14}C analyses, Phoenician presence in Spain had already been established in the 10th century BCE. The beginning of a Phoenician trade route to the western Mediterranean can be dated, therefore, from the 13th–10th centuries BCE at the latest, and probably earlier (González de Canales Cerisola, Serrano, and Llompart Gómez 2006; Nijboer and van der Plicht 2008; Nijboer 2008; Docter *et al.* 2008).

Analysis of silver from the southern Levant has demonstrated that it originated from various Mediterranean regions: Iberia, Anatolia, Attica, and perhaps also Sardinia. The silver from Iberia has been dated to the 13th/12th–11th centuries BCE, indicating that direct trade in silver was already being operated by the Canaanite-Phoenicians in the Late Bronze Age. It was not only the silver itself but also new techniques exported from the Levant to Iberia that allowed the processing of silver there (Wood, Montero-Ruiz, and Martinón-Torres 2019).

In western Iberia around Beira Alta and Beira Baixa, areas rich in tin, gold, and other metals, 11th–10th-century radiocarbon dates have come from remains associated with early iron knives made in a Near Eastern tradition and other finds. These areas were accessed directly via the rivers at the mouths of which Phoenician presence has been detected. This evidence shows that Phoenicians were trading with western Iberia for metals no later than the 11th–10th centuries BCE. Evidence of religious and cultural Phoenician presence along the Atlantic Iberian coast has also been found following a massive growth in Phoenician settlements in this area from the 8th century BCE onwards. A sanctuary site was founded at Abul, located between two important and heavily Orientalized indigenous sites (Arruda 2009: 113–23).

Silver, tin and gold, and iron were processed in situ in Iberia at least from the 8th century BCE onwards but not before the Phoenician presence. By the 7th century BCE, Phoenician sites in western Iberia had developed a metallurgic industry, as indicated by furnaces in Santa Olaia, located at the mouth of the Mondego river, a melting pot at Almaraz, and combustion structures at Santarém. It has even been claimed that the Latin word for iron, *ferrum*, originated from the Semitic word for iron, *barzel*, suggesting that initial knowledge of iron arrived from the East, probably with Phoenician technology and use of this metal. A Phoenician tradition from the early first millennium BCE claims that the Phoenician hero Chousor invented iron. Based on the archaeological finds from Iberia, there might be some truth behind this legendary story (Morris 1992b: 86ff.; Lipiński 1992: "Chousor"; Niemeyer 2001: 92–3; Arruda 2009: 126).

Indications of metallurgy were found in all the Phoenician sites in southern Iberia, but metals were the only driving force behind Phoenician interest in Iberia. Other Phoenician interests focused on agricultural products and the marine-based industries in purple dye and salted fish. There is vast evidence for the latter two marine-based industries in many of the Phoenician settlements around the Mediterranean. However, this does not imply that a need for more dyed cloth or salted fish initiated the Phoenician activity at all of these sites. The Phoenicians may have been driven to certain locations in a quest for metals, but, once they had become established at a coastal site, they might have founded additional, specialty industries there for both local consumption and surplus for trade.

Evidence of Phoenician culture is abundant in all the coastal areas of the Iberian Peninsula, including the Atlantic coast, as well as in western North Africa on both the Mediterranean and the Atlantic coasts.

Since their beginning, Phoenician sites in Iberia contained clear Phoenician elements, including pottery, building methods and architecture, temples, and burials, but also local elements, mainly handmade pottery. This admixture represents what seems to be an integration with local population throughout the Phoenician settlement in Iberia. A similar situation can also be observed in other locations that have considerable archaeological data available, like Sicily and Sardinia (Hernández 2013).

The Phoenician Iberian sites also contain elements that illustrate the long route that was sailed from the Levant to Iberia, i.e. finds from many nodes along the way. These finds consist mainly of Aegyptiaca in the form of Egyptian stone vessels, scarabs, and faience artifacts but also pottery and metal objects from Cyprus, Greece, Sicily, Sardinia, and Italy. Unlike similar corpora of mixed culture found in the central Mediterranean, which have often been attributed to Greek commercial or colonial presence, the assemblages found in the Iberian Peninsula were recognized from the beginning to have been Phoenician and to reflect Phoenician presence. Iberian archaeology has not been subjugated to the Hellenocentric-Eurocentric approach to the same degree as Greek, Italian, and often even Levantine archaeology has been for a long period. Nonetheless, we need to examine closely the finds often regarded as evidence of Greek presence and trade in Iberia and the western Mediterranean. It is essential to determine whether Greeks might have had direct access to the West during the Late Bronze and the Iron Age or whether Greek finds arrived there on Canaanite-Phoenician boats.

Mycenaean pottery discovered at inland Montoro in the Córdoba area in Andalusia dates the maritime connection between the eastern Mediterranean and Iberia as early as the 13th–12th centuries BCE. Mycenaean pottery was part of the International Style *koine* that circulated in the Mediterranean in the Late Bronze Age, which also included Canaanite Jars produced by Canaanite-Phoenicians. It is quite possible that Mycenaean pottery arrived in southern Iberia with Phoenicians who traveled westward from the east, collecting goods on their way. Moreover, a Mycenaean text (Jn 829 from Pylos) seems to reveal that the Mycenaean palaces did not have a strong fleet capable of such long-distance runs by sea (Almagro-Gorbea and Fontes 1997: 345; Álvarez-Sanchís 2000: 74; Del Freo 2005).

In addition to Mycenaean pottery, other "Oriental" shapes have been found in Late Bronze contexts in southern and southwestern Iberia. They include "hourglass" stands and hemispherical kraters, the same forms that characterized the later Phoenician presence in Iberia. Also, changes in central Iberia during this time were earlier than or simultaneous with the first Phoenician posts established on the southern Iberian coast. Other finds that have been dated as early as the 12th–10th centuries BCE are burial stelae from Portugal with engraved shields and vehicles of a type also found at Idalion in Cyprus and in the *heraion* at Samos and at Delphi. These items exhibit connections between Iberia and the eastern Mediterranean during the Late Bronze Age. The use of such stelae continued in Portugal and Tartessos until the middle of the 7th century BCE, a time of indisputable Phoenician presence and influence. This continuity can be traced back and interpreted as a mark of early Phoenician cultural impact in Iberia which began in the 12th century BCE (Cunliffe 1993: 56, fig. 2; Almagro-Gorbea and Fontes 1997: 352–6, Álvarez-Sanchís 2000: 74).

Other examples of pottery groups that were first attributed to Greek influence are the Kuass red-slipped pottery and the Gray Burnished Ware. Both groups are typical of the "Circle of the Straits" in two phases, one from the 8th–6th centuries BCE and the other from the 6th–1st centuries BCE, and both are now associated with Phoenician culture (Regev 2020: 78–9, 123–4).

The evidence presented above attests to a Phoenician presence in the western Mediterranean contemporaneous with its existence in Greece, the Aegean, Sicily, and Vivara in the Gulf of Naples. This presence is certainly much earlier than previously believed and stretches back to the Late Bronze Age. Center–periphery models that have emerged from world-systems theories have been used to examine Greek finds from the 6th–4th centuries BCE in Iberia. The examination has demonstrated that, during this time, Greek finds were not the result of Greek trade and initiative but, rather, the result of regional Iberian/Carthaginian trade networks and their interactions with Greeks. Phoenicians initiated and developed Iberian trade, and Greek goods arrived in Iberia via Phoenician trade routes (Cunliffe 1993: 72–7; Cabrera 1998: 191–4).

During the 8th–7th centuries BCE, the Phoenicians used Greek pottery as exotic and luxury goods in a system of gift-exchange with the Tartessian elite. Euboean *skyphoi*, Attic "SOS" amphorae (SOS being a style of decoration consisting of concentric circles and two parallel vertical wavy lines), and Proto-Corinthian *kotylai* were all part of Phoenician trade goods, not a sign of Greek–Iberian trade or Greek acculturation in Iberia. Even in the Archaic period, from the mid-7th to mid-6th centuries BCE, Greek trade entered Iberia via Cádiz in particular and via other Phoenician centers along the southern shore of Andalusia, using the Phoenician trade network with inner Iberia. When the center–periphery model is applied to Iberia, the ports of Massilia and Ampurias emerge as the centers, the eastern Iberian coast the interface, and inland Iberia the periphery. However, during the first half of 6th century BCE, these places did not play an important role in the regional economy, and Catalonia did not play an important role in the Phoenician economic system.

Greek finds from southern Iberia declined during the second half of the 6th century BCE and disappeared completely by the early 5th century BCE. This process happened at the same time as the trade network between Cádiz and the other Phoenician centers in Iberia was changing as a result of developments in the Persian period in the Levant which affected Phoenician trade. The link between Greek and Phoenician trade in this era shows that, at least until the 5th century BCE, Greek goods were carried by Phoenicians and not by the Greeks themselves. Even when Greek Athenian imports were plentiful, they may have resulted from internal Iberian political and economic changes and not from Greek activity. In conclusion, "the idea of the *fundamental role certainly played by the Greeks* should be dismissed, or at least restricted to the territory in the immediate proximity of Emporias" (Cabrera 1998: 203 [emphasis original]; see also Cabrera 1998: 193–8; Cunliffe 1993: 62–77; Álvarez-Sanchís 2000: 71–7).

The center–periphery theory is too narrow to allow any coherent examination of trade in the Mediterranean, a sphere without a center, where events at one end affected trends and events at the other. Since 1993, several scholars have criticized the use of this theory, which was popular during the 1980s and early 1990s, and many have now rejected it. The theory can be seen as a late and sophisticated branch of the old Eurocentric and Hellenocentric approaches that dominated scholarship until the mid-20th century. Center–periphery concepts lost their credibility after the appearance of *The Corrupting Sea* by Peregrine Horden and Nicholas Purcell in 2000, which reintroduced and corresponded with Fernand Braudel's concept of the *longue durée* (Alcock 1993a; Cunliffe 1993: 78; Shipley 1993; Malkin 2005: 2 Maran 2007: 18).

If, indeed, Greek pottery and other Greek finds were carried westward by Phoenicians until the Hellenistic period, then the trade routes from the eastern Mediterranean to Iberia, and probably also to Italy and the central Mediterranean islands, may have been exclusively operated by

Canaanite-Phoenicians. Punic/Phoenician trade was active around the entire Iberian Peninsula until its Roman occupation at the end of the 3rd century BCE, as Punic finds in northwestern Iberia show (González Ruibal 2004).

From around the 6th century BCE and beyond, the east–west route chosen may not have been a direct one. Except for the direct route between Carthage and Tyre, indirect routes were probably used to ship goods from east to west and back. Such routes would have involved traveling via the Aegean islands and Greece and also via Italy and the central Mediterranean islands. Judging by the small quantity of Greek goods that have been excavated in Iberia, it is very likely that such goods had been added en route to other goods originating from Phoenicia as ships sailed westward. Greek and Etruscan pottery arrived at Iberia with the Phoenicians by Phoenician trade routes (Cabrera 1998: 202–4; Martín Ruiz 2018: 292).

As observed in Corinth during the 5th century, it is quite possible that several distribution centers operated along these routes, centers that received goods from various places and sent them onwards. The commercial texts from the Old Assyrian trading colony at Karum Kanesh in the Middle Bronze Age illustrate how distribution centers were an essential part of a trade network. The inhabitants of these centers did not necessarily consume any of the goods they traded. Such centers are recognizable by the vast variety of regional and international items found in them.

Ports of Trade and Bases for Canaanite-Phoenicians in the Western Mediterranean

This sphere of Canaanite-Phoenician activity included the Iberian Peninsula, the Balearic Islands, and the Atlantic northwestern shores of Africa. There was a huge variety within these areas: Atlantic Iberia was very different from southern Iberia and exhibited traits of periphery versus center, while eastern Iberia was not as dominant as its south and had smaller trade centers. Ibiza in the Balearic Islands was a major trade center, and Atlantic African sites were more production centers than trade centers. Unlike sites described in the eastern and some of the central Mediterranean, the western trade centers were all founded and initially inhabited by Canaanite-Phoenicians.

The Iberian Peninsula

The larger part of the Iberic peninsula, surrounded by the Mediterranean and the southeast corner of the Atlantic, was the major contact area with Phoenicians from the east and from Carthage.

There were at least five different zones in this area, with different patterns of trade and production. The most important zone was that of Cádiz and Huelva, west of Gibraltar, while other zones were those of Málaga and Almuñécar, Alicante, the Balearic Islands (mainly Ibiza), and along the Tagus river near the Atlantic Iberian coast. Secondary zones in this area were Emporias (Barcelona) and inland sites along the Guadalquivir in the center of the peninsula.

Huelva. The site of Huelva is situated on the Atlantic coast of southwestern Iberia, outside the straits of Gibraltar and the Mediterranean Basin proper. Considered the earliest site of Phoenician presence in Iberia, Huelva was in an area known for its silver mines and was the port from which silver ingots were exported. It was also associated with the introduction of iron to the Iberian Peninsula (Cabrera 1998: 193; Bruins, Nijboer, and van der Plicht 2011: 211–14; Wood 2019a). Evidence dating from the 9th century BCE included Phoenician building techniques, metallurgic activity, pottery (table ware and amphorae), and ivory (Catalán 2007: 130, fig. 39). Radiocarbon analyses have established Phoenician presence in Huelva as early as the 10th century BCE, where Phoenician finds were uncovered in occupational levels. (González de Canales Cerisola, Serrano, and Llompart Gómez 2006; Nijboer and van der Plicht 2008). However, silver from the Huelva mines had already been processed in the Levant by the 11th century BCE, some of it mixed with silver from Lavrion in Greece, which verifies early commercial connections and probably also some presence of Phoenicians in Huelva (Wood, Montero-Ruiz, and Martinón-Torres 2019: 15) In all aspects of material culture, Huelva has yielded evidence of the earliest adoption of Phoenician techniques and style into Iberian life (Torres Ortiz 2014).

Cádiz. Located along the Atlantic coast of southwest Iberia, west of the straits of Gibraltar, Cádiz, along with the nearby site of Doña Blanca and other sites on the Bay of Cádiz, are the oldest and richest Phoenician sites in Iberia. Sites in the bay include commercial and industrial areas, burials, residential areas, and sanctuaries. Along with Huelva, Cádiz is the main harbor and distribution center for Phoenician commerce in Iberia, especially from the 7th century BCE until the Roman conquest (Higueras-Milena Castellano and Sáez Romero 2018).

During the 9th century BCE, the Phoenician assemblage in this area included Phoenician table ware and amphorae (Catalán 2007: 131, fig. 40). Soon, Cádiz became the major production center for all Phoenician products, from pottery to dyed cloth and fish products. It was the gateway into Phoenician Iberia, and, from the mid-7th to the mid-6th centuries BCE, Greek trade also entered Iberia via Cádiz. Cádiz was so important to the Mediterranean economy that, even when Iberia was conquered by the Romans, it received the special status of *foedus*, an entity with whom Rome had an amicable treaty. The other Iberian cities were subdued and had to pay tribute to Rome (Luaces 2015; Sáez Romero, Luaces, and Moreno 2016: 65–6).

The main distribution center for salted fish and fish sauce for the entire Gibraltar Circle (which includes northwestern Africa and southwestern Iberia) was in Cádiz. All south Iberian fish products were sent to Cádiz, where they were packed in the trademark amphorae produced around that local area. Most of the salteries in Iberia were located in the larger area of Cádiz; they date from the 6th century onwards, but were preceded by an earlier period of local Phoenician operation for domestic use (Muñoz Vicente and De Frutos Reyes 2009: 83). Salted fish was perhaps already being produced in the Cádiz area some time in the 9th or 8th centuries BCE, but it became a prominent aspect of the city's economy in the 6th century BCE (Curtis 2001: 319–20; Zimmerman Munn 2003: 200; Trakadas 2005: 48). Amphora type Mañá C2b, used for fish products, was produced in Cádiz from the 2nd century BCE onward.

In addition to known Phoenician forms and groups, Cádiz produced local red-burnished pottery, known as Kuass ware, which continued to be produced until the 2nd century BCE. Another locally produced pottery group was Gray Slip, with its combination of indigenous and Phoenician traits. It first appeared in the 8th century BCE at Phoenician sites in the Bay of Cádiz. By the 5th–4th centuries BCE, it had spread to indigenous sites in the lower Guadalquivir river, throughout the Iberian Peninsula, and in a few North African Phoenician sites (Regev 2020: 78–9).

Málaga and Almuñécar. Phoenicians populated the area of Málaga Bay, around the mouth of the Guadalhorce river by the end of the 9th century BCE. Remains of metallurgic activity at La Rebanadilla are dated to the 9th century BCE, followed by a residential phase soon after. Twenty shaft tombs which have been dated to the 9th–8th centuries BCE have been excavated in the Laurita Necropolis in the Phoenician settlement at Almuñécar, Granada. The tombs contained a mixed corpus which included large quantities of Phoenician red-slipped pottery and amphorae, many alabaster urns with cartouches of Egyptian pharaohs, painted Phoenician inscriptions, scarabs, ostrich eggs, and two Proto-Corinthian vessels. Málaga Bay continued to serve as an industrial area where amphorae and metal objects were manufactured, and agricultural products were processed throughout the era of Phoenician hegemony. In addition, it was known to be the main distribution center for goods exported to North Africa (Catalán 2007: 107–23; Martín Ruiz 2018).

The Balearic Islands: Ibiza. Founded in the 7th century BCE, with one of the largest and richest cemeteries in the Phoenician west (Puig des Molins), Ibiza is currently the first place in the west Mediterranean to yield evidence of the presence of individuals with eastern Mediterranean and northern African ancestries (Zalloua *et al.* 2018; Olalde and Posth 2020: 5). Located by the main spawning grounds of tuna fish, Ibiza was a major node in the fish-production network. Products from Tagomago were distributed in the central Mediterranean in the 5th century BCE, and production of wine and amphorae for the wine trade began even earlier (Sáez Romero 2017: 243). Ibiza was probably also involved in the purple dye industry; quantities of broken murex shells have been found in several locations on the island (Alfaro Giner and Costa Ribas 2008).

Lisbon, Santarém, and Abul. In the western Iberian Peninsula, two main areas had Phoenician sites. The major area was located in central Portugal along the Tagus river, and included Lisbon and Santarém, as well as the Sado river around Abul. The second area was located on the southern coast and included the site of Casro Marin, not far from Huelva. Unlike the direct connections between the Phoenician sites in Spain and the Levant and Carthage, the sites in Portugal received Phoenician and Phoenicianized artifacts primarily from Cádiz and, to a lesser degree, from the Málaga area. There were hardly any connection with Carthage, and certainly none with the Levant. However, a burial stele from Portugal that dates to the 12th–10th centuries BCE is of a type also known in Cyprus and Samos. It reveals connections between Iberia and the eastern Mediterranean during the Late Bronze Age (Cunliffe 1993: 56, fig. 2; Almagro-Gorbea and Fontes 1997: 352–6).

Lisbon is known for the quality of its salt, produced in many local salteries. The earliest radiocarbon results associated with a Phoenician presence at Santarém date between the late 10th and early 8th century BCE but most probably to the last years of the 9th century BCE. At the inland site of Monte do Bolor (Beja), ^{14}C results indicate a Phoenician presence in the 9th century BCE (Mongo Soares *et al.* 2017). By the 8th century BCE a Phoenician sanctuary was built at Abul, and metal industry, probably Phoenician-oriented, is evident in the area of Tagus and Montego rivers in the 7th century BCE (Arruda 2009: 113–26).

Northwestern Africa: Lixus, Kuass, and Mogador

Beginning in the 8th century BCE, the most important Phoenician base on the Atlantic North African shore was Lixus. Its salt basins made it one of the most important Phoenician centers for fish products. Fish amphorae were produced on site. Lixus was also a center of Carthaginian metal production, which made it one of the most important Phoenician trading posts in the western Mediterranean (Kaufman *et al.* 2019: 4098).

Located between ancient Lixus and Tingis (Tangier), Kuass was the most important production center for pottery on the Phoenician Atlantic coast of North Africa. Kuass ware dominated the table ware market in the predominantly Phoenician Gibraltar Circle, in the Atlantic sites of Morocco and Portugal, and in the southern Iberian Peninsula and North Africa (Niveau de Villedary y Mariñas and Sáez-Romero 2016). Kuass was also an important node in the fish-production network; it had salt basins, installations for fish processing, and kilns for producing fish amphorae (Trakadas 2005: 66–8, 115).

An island close to the shore, Mogador is probably the southernmost Phoenician site in North Africa. Phoenician finds are dated from the 7th to mid-6th centuries BCE, after which the island was probably abandoned. Based on onomastic analysis, it has been claimed that the Phoenician population arrived from Cádiz (Lopez Pardo and Ruiz Cabrero 2006). Mogador's industrial installations and finds indicate it was a center for fish production and metal processing (Trakadas 2005: 54–5).

IV. Phoenicians and the East: Arabia, the Persian Gulf, and India

Even though Phoenicians were renowned for their maritime skills as navigators, shipbuilders, sea-traders, and harbor engineers, their skills in overland trade were quite significant too. Phoenician art was well known in the royal courts of the kings of Assyria, Babylonia, and Persia, and the Phoenicians had probably also reached the Persian Gulf and India (Dayton 1984: 371).

There were several routes from the Mediterranean to the East, and the Canaanite-Phoenicians used some, if not all, of them. The earliest route, so it seems, followed the Fertile Crescent from the northern Levantine littoral around Ugarit via Mesopotamia to the mouth of the Euphrates at the Persian Gulf. There was a northern route going from Ugarit through Alalakh, Carchemish, Nineveh, Ashur, and Nuzi, and a southern route going from Ugarit (also from Byblos) through Mari. Both eventually led to Babylon and Ur (Curtis 2009: 99–102). Mesopotamian economic activity had also proceeded via the Persian Gulf by the end of the 3rd millennium BCE. From the edge of the Persian Gulf, land routes turned southwest along the coast of Arabia and southeast along the Persian coast to the northwestern part of the Indian Peninsula. Another land route used by Canaanite-Phoenicians led from Gaza and Ashkelon in the southern Levant to Aila in the northeastern corner of the Red Sea and then from Aila by sea south along the Arabian Peninsula via Yemen and Oman to India.

The main route, though, from the mouth of the Euphrates river, was by sea, going south to the Gulf of Oman. At the eastern tip of Arabia the route split. One branch went to India. The other circumnavigated Arabia to the port trade-cities of Khor Kuri, Qana, and Aden in southern Arabia, through the Gulf of Aden into the Red Sea, to access the port-cities in western Arabia, Punt, Nubia, and Egypt, the most important of which were Adulis, Berenike, Leuke Kome, and Moys Hormos (Casson 1989: 11; Sherratt and Sherratt 1991: 368; Potts 1993: 423–6; Young 2001: 136–86).

Ashkelon or Gaza was the terminal point of the Arabian incense route. Caravans followed this land route across Arabia, going through, in different periods, Dedan, Tayma, Hegra, and Al-Ula to the trade distribution center of Ma'in; and from there to Ma'rib/Saba (the Sabaean capital), to Qataban (the capital of Timna); and from there to Qana (Young 2001: 90–135, map 3.1; Durand 2019). Evidence from the 1st century BCE indicates that this land route was not handled by one party alone. According to

Strabo (16.4.19) and Diodorus of Sicily (Diod. Sic. 19.94.5), in their day, valuable perfumes and spices, mainly frankincense and myrrh, were moved along this long route from one local people to another until they reached the Nabateans, who delivered them to the Levantine coast. The Nabateans, however, were not active in the spice and perfume trade before the Hellenistic period, and their predecessors were either other Arabian tribes or Canaanite-Phoenician merchants.

The trade route to Arabia was sufficiently profitable in itself that not all ships arriving in southern Arabia would have continued their journey to India. There were two routes from the Red Sea to India, one to northwestern India which followed the northeastern coast and one to southern India which sailed along the southwestern coast of the Red Sea. Frankincense was harvested in Arabia in the autumn, but ships intending to sail to India using the monsoon winds had to leave the area of the Red Sea in June or July. Climatic concerns, therefore, dictated the need for two separate trade routes to Arabia and India. Other routes leading eastward from the Mediterranean originated in Egypt; the pharaohs traded with groups in eastern Africa and Arabia, on both sides of the Red Sea (Young 2001: 27, 34). The following discussion focuses on whether Canaanite-Phoenicians were involved in one, some, or all of these routes. It seems unlikely they would have been involved in all of them simultaneously. The Levant–Arabia–India route was directly operated by Canaanite-Phoenicians, and they likely operated parts of the other two routes described as well.

Literary sources and archaeological remains provide evidence of Phoenician presence along the routes that traveled eastward. Unlike the Phoenician trade and culture observed and studied in the Mediterranean, the eastern sphere of their activity has not been studied in terms of trade activities but only with regard to their fictitious Arabian or Persian origin. Nevertheless, in multi-ethnic Babylon in the 8th–7th centuries BCE, Phoenician presence was not restricted to a few craftsmen (carpenters of the Lebanon, for example), as was the case with other ethnicities. Numerous Phoenicians are mentioned in Babylonian documents, including 30 sailors and 126 residents from Tyre, but the most striking reference is to Hanunu the Phoenician, the chief merchant of the king in a list of high officials at the Babylonian court. Some of the Phoenician population in Babylon was exiled there by the Babylonians but not all of them, as demonstrated by the case of Hanunu. The Phoenician exiles have left traces of their presence in communities in the region of Nippur, with place names that reflect their home metropolises, like Ashkelon, Tyre, Sidon, and Kadesh. However, one document tends to indicate that at least one of these Phoenician settlements, Tyre, may have been founded before the Babylonian deportation of Tyrians. Even if the Tyre mentioned in the Babylonian texts is not actually in Babylonia but, rather, refers to the metropolis of Tyre, the documents provide evidence of significant trade activity between Tyre and Babylon in the 6th century BCE (Dandamayev 2004: 140–5).

Greek presence and involvement in the East have been unjustifiably promoted on the basis of a handful of sherds that could have been imported by other Easterners. This includes Babylonia, where Greek influence was insignificant. However, during the Ptolemaic period, when the annual pattern of the monsoon winds was deciphered by Greeks in the late 2nd or early 1st centuries BCE, the Red Sea trade route toward India was developed and extended. During this period, trade with India became faster and cheaper for Greek merchant ships, although it remained a low priority. Things changed with the Roman conquest of Egypt, however, when, for about a century, Mediterranean–Indian trade flourished. Nonetheless, the monsoon winds had been known to Phoenicians and Arabs much earlier; Phoenicians had used them to trade with India before any other Mediterranean traders and had kept them a secret. In this connection, one should recall the story told by Herodotus (4.42) that, around 600 BCE, the Phoenicians circumnavigated all of Africa, a journey that would have shown them the way to India, if they had not already known it (Casson 1989: 11–12, 283–91).

Arabia and the Persian Gulf

Trade routes between the Near East, Arabia, and the Persian Gulf already existed in the 3rd millennium BCE, but they became established long-distance trade networks by the middle of the 2nd millennium BCE, a time of increased international trade in the Levant. One of these routes originated in India and crossed the Persian Gulf to Dhūfar in southern Oman, where the sea crossing was easy. In Arabia, the route crossed Yemen through Hadhramaut and turned to the eastern side of the Hejaz Mountains along the Red Sea, where plentiful springs provided the caravans with water. The route then ran via Arabia Felix (Yemen), which provided incense, and ended at Gaza and Akko (Dayton 1984: 364–6, 371).

The Canaanite-Phoenicians were involved in the spice trade from Arabia by the early 1st millennium BCE. Their trade route was taken over by, or handed over to, Arabian tribes sometime before the Hellenistic period. This data establishes the probability of Canaanite-Phoenician contacts with Arabia, in spite of the meager material evidence available (Grainger 1991: 187–219; Bedford 2007: 309).

A variety of evidence, including inscriptions, architecture, tombs, pottery, and iconography, demonstrates that the trade agents between the Mediterranean and Arabia and the Persian Gulf were Levantines, whether Phoenicians and/or Arabs. It is unlikely that the Phoenicians, who traveled by sea to the ends of the Mediterranean for metals alone, would have neglected a rich and profitable route closer to their homeland. Arabia could provide the Phoenicians with wood for their boats, incense, and a route that their Arab allies could use to provide aid, as necessary. In addition, the route eastward by land and sea was a well-traveled and established one, less hazardous and, therefore, more profitable for the Phoenician authorities who sponsored and conveyed the trade missions.

Failaka and the Phoenician Connection

Failaka is an island and an important trade node off the shore of modern Kuwait in the northern Persian Gulf. Failaka may have been connected quite early with foreign maritime cultures due to its unique location on an island near the mouth of the Tigris and Euphrates rivers. As early as the Bronze Age, at the end of the 3rd millennium and in the early 2nd millennium BCE, when Failaka was known as part of Dilmun, a large temple was built on the island. Too big to serve the inhabitants of the island alone, this temple probably also served maritime traders in the region, including perhaps, Canaanite-Phoenician seafarers trading in the Gulf area. It indicates the central position of Dilmun/Failaka in the regional trade routes (Calvet 1991; Andersson 2014).

The finds from later occupation layers at Failaka include Aramaic and Greek inscriptions, small quantities of Greek pottery, figurines, and coins. The figurines excavated in the sanctuary dating to the Hellenistic period belonged to two categories: one eastern, consisting of horse-and-riders and nude female figurines, both known Phoenician images, and the other "Greek," consisting of statues of Herakles, i.e. the Greek name and appearance of the Phoenician Milqart. It has been suggested that a small Seleucid garrison had been installed on the island, perhaps early in the 3rd century BCE, the soldiers from which cohabited with the indigenous, Aramaic-speaking population. This interpretation of the finds is not very likely; the Greek presence on the island could have been limited, at best, to Greek sailors who stopped to pay tribute to the gods after a long and safe sea journey.

The finds on this island are similar to those at many other Phoenician sites around the Mediterranean and likely illustrate a standard corpus of artifacts related to Phoenician trade. As such, they would not point to a mixed or otherwise acculturated local population on Failaka. This interpretation is strengthened by the finding of coins from Phoenician Byblos dating to the early 3rd century BCE in the sanctuary on Failaka and a funerary stela dated to the Hellenistic period from the harbor of the island, Qal'at el-Bahrain, bearing the Phoenician name Abidistaras, "Ishtar's servant" (Salles, Calvet, and Beyer 1986: 81, 105; Potts 1990: 195; Salles 1993: 245–8; Puech 1998; Elayi 2009: 220).

Other Sites in Arabia

As demonstrated by the excavations at Tell Abraq on the coastline of the Persian Gulf (United Arab Emirates), trade connections between Arabia and Mesopotamia continued uninterrupted from the 3rd–1st millennia BCE. Starting in the 9th century BCE, camel caravans transported goods from the Persian Gulf to Mesopotamia, as indicated in the Assyrian royal annals (A.0.100.5: 64b–80a, 90–103, 120–7) (Grayson 1991). Archaeological evidence shows that Levantine trade with the Gulf region and beyond increased during the 1st millennium BCE under the Assyrian regime. These trade routes were subsequently taken over by the Persian Empire (Dayton 1984: 363–4; Potts 1993: 436–7; Bedford 2007: 309; Lemaire 2010).

The earliest known item from the Persian Gulf area that might possibly be Phoenician was found in a temple on Bahrain and dated to ca. 1400 BCE. It is a faience face-pendant of Ishtar/Ashtart of a type well known in the area between Hala Sultan Tekke in Cyprus and Tchoga Zanbil in Iran. Although this particular artifact has been identified as Babylonian or Mesopotamian in origin, as well as a local imitation produced in the Gulf area, it also could have originated from Canaanite-Phoenician culture. The distribution map of this object in Cyprus, where Babylonian or Mesopotamian connections have never been observed but Canaanite-Phoenician connections are amply attested, indicates that the object may have originated in the Levant. The artifact was found in Bahrain, ancient Dilmun, a site known since antiquity as sacred. Mesopotamian texts name it as the place from which the Sumerian god Enki originated. It is not surprising, therefore, that a Phoenician votive would be found at a sacred site in Arabia; foreign traders would often dedicate votives to local deities (Lamberg-Karlovsky 1996: 157; Denton 1999: 150–2).

Other evidence of early connections between the Canaanite-Phoenicians and Iran is provided by the ivories found at Ziwiye in northwestern Iran as part of a hoard but which have subsequently been associated with the Mannean fortress that occupied the site in the 8th and 7th centuries BCE (Sheikhi 2014). The ivories exhibit Scythian, Assyrian, Urartian, local Mannean, and Phoenician styles. The main mythological creature attributed to Phoenician origin is the sphinx. The ivories found at nearby Hasanlu, on the other hand, are mainly Assyrian, dating sometime in the 9th century before 800 BCE, when the site was destroyed and an Urartian fortress occupied the acropolis. They include many battle scenes (White Muscarella 1980: 221–2). The widening of styles of and implied sources for the manufacture of goods reaching northwestern Iran after 800 BCE can be related in part to the expansion of the Assyrian Empire westward. It suggests that the submission of the Levant to Assyrian control led to the increase of Canaanite-Phoenician goods flowing eastward to Assyria.

Evidence of trade routes that were used to move goods between the Levant and Arabia exists in the archaeological record at least from the 12th century BCE. Sites in the Beersheva Basin, mainly Tel Masos, were nodes on this route and seem to have been related to the copper trade (Finkelstein 1995: 120–3; Singer-Avitz and Eshel 1999: 46–54; Steen 2010: 177–8). If this is indeed a copper trade route, this operation is no doubt related to the Canaanite-Phoenician Late Bronze Age I operation described in Chapter 3. Later evidence for direct connections between Phoenicians and Arabs is provided by the south Arabian script, which was adapted from the Phoenician script sometime in the 11th–10th centuries BCE (Sass 2005).

A bronze memorial inscription written in Sabaean from Al-Bayda in Yemen describes a Sabaean trading expedition to Dedan in northern Arabia, Gaza, and the towns of Judah. It took place ca. 600 BCE. This inscription is contemporaneous with Sabaean and other south Arabian inscriptions that have been found in the Negev, or even earlier. These inscriptions may confirm the biblical story of the close connections between King Solomon and the Queen of Sheba and could reflect commercial connections between Judah and Sheba that had already begun by the second half of the 10th century BCE. The rise in Levantine–Arabian trade at this time may have been the result of the collapse of the Late Bronze trade centers and systems (Sass 1991: 86–93; Sherratt and Sherratt 1991: 375; Sass 2005: 96–132; Holladay 2006: 316–28; Lemaire 2010: 55–9).

Another 1st-century-BCE bronze inscription, probably from Yemen, reveals that, at the time, Ashtart was worshiped in a temple at Saba as "Athtar Haraman," an unknown aspect of Ashtart or a male version that had probably been worshiped in this area at least from the 7th–1st centuries BCE (Jarus 2019). The planet Venus appears to have been associated with a pan-Semitic deity conceived of as male in some cultures and female in others. The male form of the deity is attested in texts from Ebla ca. 2500 BCE, Ugarit ca. 1300 BCE, Moab in the 9th century BCE, and among Arabs who had contact with Assyria in the 7th century BCE (Heimpel 1982: 13–15).

Ezekiel 27 connects the Arabian trade with both Judahites and Tyrians in what seems to be the same route, if not the same enterprise. In 27:20–22, Tyre's trade in the late 7th century BCE is described, giving specific locations in Arabia: Dedan, Qedar, Saba, and Rama, all known centers and tribal names in Arabia. Dedan is also mentioned in the Al-Bayda inscription. Since the Bible informs us of another long-distance commercial venture that engaged both King Solomon and King Hiram of Tyre, it is very likely that both courts collaborated in sponsoring and manning trade routes by sea and land. If the Al-Bayda inscription is indeed authentic, then the Israelites and Judahites were closer to Phoenicians than previously assumed. The Phoenician inscriptions from Kuntillet 'Ajrud which have been dated to the late 9th–early 8th centuries BCE provide additional testimony to this closeness (Ahituv 2014).

Other south Arabian inscriptions dated to the 8th–7th centuries BCE have been found on temple columns at Ma'in in Yemen, in addition to the ones from as-Sawdā. They are the earliest religious texts found in Yemen and can probably be seen to provide references to a common deity, in spite of the change in gender. The inscriptions from the 8th–7th centuries BCE demonstrate the existence of a direct connection between Phoenicia and Arabia which began at least at this time and probably earlier. The names of the cities of Tyre and Sidon also occur in south Arabic inscriptions at Ma'in as late as the 3rd–2nd centuries BCE, indicating the longevity of the Levantine/Phoenician–Arabic connections (Lipiński 1992: "Astarté", "Arabie"; Breton 1998: 68, fig. 9).

By the Persian period, the Phoenicians acted as trade agents for the Persian Empire. While many of their commercial Mediterranean vessels were commandeered for use in the Persian military fleet—and they were ordered to build additional boats for use in war—some vessels that operated in the Persian Gulf might have continued to engage in trade in this region: a region that delivered goods to ports that were terminal points for overland trade routes to Mesopotamia and the various Achaemenid courts. It is quite likely, therefore, that, during this time at least, some of the contacts between the Levantine coast and the Persian Gulf, perhaps even India, were handled by Phoenicians. The regional trade in spices that moved from Arabia through Judea and Samaria to the Phoenician coast was likely partially in Phoenician hands (Dayton 1984: 363–4; Bedford 2007: 309).

The connection between Persian domination and Phoenician trade activity in Arabia, the Persian Gulf, and perhaps India may be demonstrated by the fact that Phoenician activity came to a halt at the end of the Persian period. Phoenician trade activity along the route that ran from Phoenicia via Arabia to the Persian Gulf quite plausibly operated from the Bronze Age through the Persian period, while, later, this route was handled by Arabian tribes. As reported by Eratosthenes in the 3rd century BCE (Strab. 16.767–9), Ptolemy II reopened and completed the canal between the Nile and the Red Sea that had partly been dug by Darius I and Necho II before him. Ptolemy II established ports of trade like Berenike-Troglodytica on the shores of the Red Sea and took control of the trade route to the Persian Gulf and India (Strab. 17.804) (Dayton 1984: 367; Mueller 2006: 203; Whitewright 2007). Nonetheless, even if the Greek Ptolemies controlled this trade route beginning in the 3rd century BCE, this does not mean that the Phoenician part in this trade was completely extinct in the Hellenistic period or afterwards.

By the Hellenistic period, Canaanite-Phoenician overland trade activity had been operated by Nabataeans and probably other Arabian tribes as well. These land routes were part of the Canaanite-Phoenician trade networks from much earlier periods, and the Arab tribes were part of these networks which joined the perfume and spice production centers in Arabia with the Phoenician cities on the Mediterranean coast. This network remained in operation, and the cooperation between Canaanite-Phoenicians and Arab tribes also continued, as shown by coins from Byblos and Arados dating to the 4th century BCE which have been found at the salt mine near ancient Gerrha in the Arabian Peninsula. The mine had been actively worked since the 7th century BCE. Knowing Phoenician interest in mines of all kinds and their shipment of salt to Egypt, mentioned in a 5th-century text from Memphis, the coins might imply a Phoenician presence at these mines (Lombard 1988: 124; Grainger 1991: 187–219; Figueras 2000: 67–9; Young 2001: 90–1; Elayi 2009: 221). The 5th-century text corresponds well with other historical and textual evidence that indicates the existence of a Canaanite-Phoenician trading post in Memphis by the 7th century BCE (Hdt. 2.112; KAI 50) which remained active down to and throughout the Hellenistic period (CIS 1.97; KAI 48). Coins of Alexander the Great minted in Byblos and dated to 285 BCE were also found at Failaka (Kuwait), further demonstrating Phoenician connections to Arabia and the Persian Gulf during the Hellenistic period (Elayi 2009: 220–1).

Although Nabataeans and other Arabian tribes operated the trade with southern Arabia in frankincense and myrrh, they were not involved in trade with India or its goods. Arrian (*Anab.* 2.25.4) and Quintus Curtius Rufus (*Histories of Alexander the Great* 4.6.30) describe a force of Arab mercenaries in the Persian army that fought to defend Gaza against Alexander and the Greek army. This story reflects Arab economic interests in Gaza, which was the terminal port of the incense road controlled at least partially by Arab tribes (Figueras 2000: 67; Young 2001: 91–2).

Greek and Latin authors had knowledge of some distant recollection of Phoenico-Arabic connections but transformed it into a legend about the origin of the Phoenicians. One story was told by Herodotus (1.1) in the middle of 5th century BCE and repeated by later authors (Dionysius of Miletus *FrGH* 687.F4; Androsthenes of Thasos 711.F2; Justin, *Apol.* 18.3.1–5). It described the origin of the Phoenicians from the Persian Gulf. This story should be dismissed as unreliable, the result of ignorance or confusion about anything concerning the East.

At the beginning of the Roman period, Strabo told another story about Phoenician connections with the Persian Gulf. He described the existence of Phoenician colonies at Tilos and Arados and their temples on these islands in the Persian Gulf (Strab. 1.35; 3.16; 16.3, 4). Even though misinterpretations are clearly involved here as well, this story might be based on a tradition that knew of a direct and continuous connection between Phoenicia and Arabia at least from the 8th–1st centuries BCE. In fact, these stories maintain the impression of an ancient reality in which Phoenicians traded with, and may also have had trading posts in, the Persian Gulf. Since Yemen is on the coast of Arabia, facing the Arab Sea which was connected by trade to the Persian Gulf, which in turn was connected to trade with India, it is reasonable to assume that Strabo's story also implies the existence of an ancient connection between Phoenicia and India (Lipiński 1992: "Arabie"; Lamberg-Karlovsky 1996: 155–6; Asheri, Lloyd, and Corcella 2007: 75).

Some of the earliest finds relevant to the Phoenician–Arabian trade route are red-slipped and black-slipped pottery that has been excavated in Arabia. Both types often have been treated as local pottery, but the Edomite pottery of the 9th–8th centuries BCE that inspired Arabian black-on-red painted pottery also had its roots in direct Phoenician influence. A few sherds of possible Phoenician pottery from the 9th–8th centuries BCE have been found in Oman, which might indicate an early direct connection between Phoenicia and Arabia. If this is the case, then the first presence of Canaanite-Phoenicians in Arabia and the Persian Gulf took place in the same period and for the same reasons as their presence at other metal mines in Cyprus, the Iberian Peninsula, and the central Mediterranean islands, from the Late Bronze Age onwards (Dayton 1984: 370–1).

Locally made red-slipped incurved rim bowls, carinated bowls, and plates of the Hellenistic period have been found in inland and coastal Arabia at Thaj, Tarut, Ayn-Jawan, and on the island of Failika at Qal'at el-Bahrain, where they were classified as "Arabian Red-Washed ware." Lise Hannestad, who coined the term, believed that this group was inspired by Greek pottery, but other archaeological studies of Arabian culture have firmly claimed that red-slipped pottery in Arabia was local and not influenced by Greek culture. The so-called "Arabian Red- and Black-Washed wares" ceased to appear by the end of the 3rd century BCE, a time when red-slipped pottery had not yet appeared in Greece. Greek influence on Arabian Black Slip also has been rejected; influence from the Punjab in India has been suggested instead (Hannestad 1984: 71–2; Potts 1990: 39, 106; Boucharlat and Mouton 1993: 287; Salles 1993: 241–48).

However, it is more likely that this ware was an Arabian imitation of pottery produced in the early 1st millennium BCE that had been taken to the Hejaz by Levantine copper exploiters, probably Phoenicians. They introduced their specialties in copper mining and smelting to sites in Arabia, the Hejaz, and later the Oman peninsula, where copper deposits were located, as well as timber forests and frankincense. These sites had been used continuously from the Iron Age to the Hellenistic period, when the imported material consisted mainly of amphorae, and the finds were similar in nature to Iron Age finds. Occupational levels at sites in Oman have been dated by ^{14}C from the late 2nd millennium

BCE until the last third of the 1st millennium BCE. Mesopotamian texts from the late 4th millennium BCE name Dilmun, the island of Bahrain in the Persian Gulf, as a source of copper (Dayton 1984: 370–1; Boucharlat 1991; Boucharlat and Lombard 1991; Lamberg-Karlovsky 1996: 154, 158).

The population of the Arabian–Persian Gulf, where such "Arabian Red-Washed ware" was found, may not have been the same as the population in western and central Arabia in the 3rd–2nd centuries BCE but, rather, an ethnic mixture from India, Iran, Babylon, and Syria. Bearing this in mind, some have labeled the pottery "Hellenistic" rather than "Arabian," although the most typical shapes of the Hellenistic pottery corpus, like *laginoi*, mold-made bowls, and kraters, were absent in this area. This pottery group, therefore, does not qualify as Hellenistic culturally, only chronologically, and should be interpreted instead as local imitations of Levantine production (Salles 1993: 242–4, 255).

So, what did the local pottery look like in Bahrain during the Hellenistic period? There were three basic Phoenician bowl shapes: the open flat plate (often considered a "fish plate" during Hellenistic period), the hemispherical incurved rim bowl, and the carinated bowl. All three shapes were new in Arabia and the Persian Gulf in the Hellenistic period and usually appear with white, yellow, brown, green, and blue glazed surfaces. The glazed ware tradition in this part of the Near East goes back to the Iron Age and was in continuous use from the 9th–8th centuries BCE until the beginning of the Hellenistic period. It was used subsequently as well in Parthian and later Islamic pottery styles. Glazed ware composed about 50% of the pottery corpora in Arabia and the Persian Gulf during the Hellenistic and Roman periods. This group was a combination of the three Phoenician shapes and the ancient local tradition of a glazed surface treatment (Potts 1990: 167–8; Tite and Shortland 2008: 149).

The "Arabian Red- and Black-Washed wares" of the Hellenistic period in Arabia point to Phoenician cultural influence, although maybe not a first-hand one. Although a constant combination of the three shapes together in red slip appeared from the Bronze Age in Canaanite-Phoenician culture, the hemispherical bowl was new in this period to Greek culture as well. As evident from the local imitations of red-slipped bowls, the inhabitants of Arabia and the Persian Gulf were aware of the popular vessel shapes of the Hellenistic period: that is, the three-bowl assembly. During this period, the shapes and style were probably introduced into Arabia by Arab merchants who operated camel caravans through the desert and could not carry the heavy pottery.

Nonetheless, due to the long connections of Mesopotamian and Canaanite-Phoenician cultures with Arabia, it is possible that Arabian people were aware of the religious connotation of this pottery group as a *mrzh/symposion* set when it was produced in shiny red slip. Judging by their lack of interest in Eastern Sigillata A (ESA) and related pottery, the people of Arabia and the Persian Gulf may have deliberately refrained from using the original Phoenician product or making very close copies of it.

It is quite clear that no real effort was ever made to export ESA or other Phoenician pottery to Arabia. The land route from Phoenicia to Arabia might have been too long for fragile vessels. This would have been the case whether the route led north via Syria and Babylonia or whether it led south through the southern Levant and the Red Sea. Nevertheless, since ESA had reached more distant locations by sea and by land, the reason for its absence in Arabia must have been a lack of demand, not the hardships of the road. The people of Arabia may not have been open to imports and foreign cultural influences during the Hellenistic period.

There is no sign of profound Greek influence on Arab material culture either during the Hellenistic period. There is no reason to assume there had been Greek connections instead of Phoenician involvement in the eastern network from the Levantine coast to India via Arabia and the Persian Gulf. There is an almost total absence of Greek finds and Greek influence in Arabia and the Persian Gulf during the Hellenistic period (Boucharlat and Mouton 1993: 289). Even so, red-slipped pottery has been be uncovered in small amounts in Arabia in the Hellenistic and Early Roman periods at sites where no material evidence of Greek presence could be found. It seems that ESA or other Hellenistic Sigillata groups did not reach Arabia and the Persian Gulf in any significant quantities. Imitations of ESA hemispherical bowls have been found at Qal'at el-Bahrain in the late 3rd century BCE, as well as Karranah and Failaka on the same island. These groups, though originating in earlier Canaanite tradition, were locally imitated to some extent both in inland and coastal Arabia (Potts 1990: 111).

Excavations at Berenike-Troglodytica, located on the Egyptian coast of the Red Sea, have uncovered mainly local Egyptian pottery but also some imported items. The latter consisted primarily of Terra Sigillata of all types: A, B, Cypriot, Italian, and African Red Slip, dated between the 1st and early 5th centuries CE. Similar finds characterize Qaseir al-Qadim, another port on the Red Sea route north of Berenike. The pottery from Berenike has been used to support the existence of the trade route that operated from Alexandria via Koptos to Berenike. The route is well attested in papyri from the Roman period which describe the trade route from India. This route, however, was established much earlier than the Roman era; its main ports were used by the pharaohs of ancient Egypt and their trade allies, the Canaanite-Phoenicians (Hayes 1996: 147–3).

Arretine Terra Sigillata has been recovered at Timna in south Arabia on the trade route to India. This find, together with ESA, Eastern Sigillata B from the southern shores of Asia Minor, and some glass, were the only imported vessels found at the site. The somewhat surprising finds have been explained as a sudden expansion of the "cultural horizons" of the local inhabitants toward the sophisticated flair of the Hellenistic culture. Red-slipped pottery of forms similar to Terra Sigillata, however, had been familiar in Arabia centuries before the appearance of Terra Sigillata, due to connections with the Levant, not with Hellenism (Comfort 1958: 199–201).

Trade in Cypriot Sigillata, on the other hand, seems to have been well organized. Cypriot Sigillata has been found at Aqaba and Qaseir al-Qadim by the Red Sea, and imitations of it with feet made of astragali have been excavated at Failaka and at Ed-Dur in the United Arab Emirates in the late Hellenistic–Early Roman period. The distribution of this Sigillata overlaps to a large extent with Cypriot pottery in the Late Bronze Age, Iron Age, and the Late Roman period. Since the production and distribution of Cypriot pottery in all these periods was entwined with Phoenician pottery, it seems only reasonable to assume that here, too, from the late 1st century BCE to the early 1st century CE, Phoenicians were involved in the production and distribution of some Cypriot pottery groups, including red-slipped pottery (Lund 1997: 207–11).

In conclusion, the fact that ESA shapes were locally produced in Arabia and the Persian Gulf only shows how familiar they appeared to be to the local population, despite the lack of versions in the Hellenistic period. It demonstrates the antiquity of the red-slipped tradition there, in both shapes and surface treatment. The character of the finds in Arabia and the Persian Gulf during the Hellenistic period also reflects echoes of cultures transported by agents who had no real interest in these cultures; it was the Arab merchants who carried the idea of red slip eastward but probably did not carry ESA itself. Eastern Sigillata A only reached those portal trade centers that ships, perhaps Phoenician ones, could access. It should be stressed that Greeks and Romans never dominated Arabia and the Persian Gulf, either by force or by trade, and their cultural influence there was minimal to non-existent (Salles 2002).

The situation described in Arabia and the Persian Gulf not only points to an ancient Phoenician trade route but also emphasizes the Phoenician character of the three-bowl corpus that has mistakenly been interpreted as evidence of Greek influence on the East. Because these areas did not experience first-hand contact with the Greeks or Romans, they obviously could not have been influenced by their culture, whatever its material components. The red-slipped tradition had been known in this area from much earlier times, when Phoenician presence had been much more evident, and it was transmitted again in some form by Arab merchants in the Hellenistic and Roman periods.

It should be mentioned in this context that inland Arab–Nabataean sites in the Levant manufactured ESA imitations and original painted fine ware locally. That happened only in the Early Roman period, however, when ESA had become so popular that it appears to have lost its identification as *mrzh/ symposion* ware (Negev 1974, 1986). The same situation took place in Arabia, the Persian Gulf, and India, where local ESA imitations have been found alongside local decorated ware in the late Hellenistic and Early Roman periods.

While imports from the north, i.e. Parthia, Babylonia, and Mesopotamia are commonly acknowledged to have entered Arabia and influenced its material culture, Canaan-Phoenicia can be added as another major source of foreign influence. The original Phoenician vessels whose shapes were eventually adopted locally probably arrived from the north or the west with Arabian camel caravans. Even Failaka, with its temples and Greek inscriptions in the Hellenistic period, may not represent a notable Greek influence. The Arabian Peninsula lay outside the boundaries of the Seleucid Empire which ruled the traditional Phoenician core cities on the Levantine coast. As a result, it never was Hellenized, and its culture was first and foremost Arabian. The fall of the Achaemenid Empire brought an end to foreign domination in Arabia and the Persian Gulf for several centuries, and the Gulf area maintained its autonomy until the 2nd century CE (Potts 1990: 21–2, 167–8, 351).

India

The earliest evidence of a connection between the Indus Valley and Mesopotamia comes from a long-barrel carnelian bead, 11 cm long, of a type common at Harappan sites (Mohenjo-daro, Harappa, Chanhu-daro, Dholavira, Allahdino, and Lothal). Found in the mid-3rd millennium at the royal cemetery in Ur and in the late 3rd millennium at a temple at Ebla (ca. 2200–2100 BCE), these beads indicate the existence of direct trade between the Indus, Mesopotamia, and Syria. More examples of these carnelian beads come from 3rd millennium BCE contexts at Susa, Mari, and Tel Brak, which were also involved in Canaanite-Mesopotamian trade. The beads are often found along with lapis lazuli and gold beads produced in Mesopotamia, some made in Indian techniques (Peyronel 2015). The combination of imported and locally made precious beads in royal and sacred contexts emphasizes the importance and value of these beads and the efforts invested in their importation and production. The quantities of these beads over a vast geographical spread and over centuries in time point to ongoing trade between the Indus Valley and western Asia in the period from 2500–2200 BCE.

The earliest evidence of a connection between the Indus Valley and the Persian Gulf comes from Tell Abraq (ancient Magan) in Arabia on the Persian Gulf. Weights and pottery from the Indus Valley that date to the late 3rd millennium BCE have been found there. Since trade connections between Tell Abraq and Mesopotamia were well established during this period, this evidence demonstrates one route by which trade moved between Mesopotamia and India in the late 3rd millennium BCE (Potts 1993: 423–7). It seems a maritime leg might have offloaded goods at Magan, and from there they were sent overland to Mesopotamia and on to Syria. Since the Levant, Mesopotamia, and Syria were well connected during the 3rd millennium BCE, the Levantine Canaanites may have been involved in some way in this very early trade route to India.

Evidence for direct connections between the Levant and India may be attested in the Iron Age. A residue analysis made on Phoenician juglets from Dor shows the presence of cinnamon from India and perhaps also nutmeg from Sri Lanka (Namdar *et al.* 2013; Gilboa and Namdar 2015). The first known occurrence of vanilla in the Levant, found at Megiddo and mentioned above in Chapter 3, supports this connection as well (Bower 2018). Despite what seems to be persuasive evidence, however, the origin of both cinnamon and nutmeg from India has been contested. It has been claimed that, in the 3000 years that have passed from the date the flasks were filled to the time of their analysis, the samples have likely been contaminated. In addition, the presence of one chemical cannot point to the presence of a single plant species; the results could point to other plants like myrrh or the Mediterranean storax, *Liquidambar orientalis*, commonly known as oriental sweetgum, which is common in Syria. Another proposed option is *Cassia abbreviata Oliv.*, a bush common in east Africa from Somalia to South Africa (Manniche 1989: 88–9; Haw 2017). It cannot be concluded at this stage if the cinnamon detected in the Levantine Phoenician juglets and flasks is indeed from India, but it is at least possible.

Until recently, academic discussion of trade with the Far East, including India and Sri Lanka, had focused on the Roman period and later, due to the data available in Roman texts. However, Indian excavations and studies have verified a long tradition of trade and elaborate trade networks between India and the West and India and Southeast Asia that had begun to operate in the early 1st millennium BCE (Pavan and Schenk 2012; Seland 2014, 2016; Tripati 2017).

As demonstrated by the author of the *Periplus of the Erythraean Sea*, who was probably an Egyptian who wrote in *koine* Greek in the 1st century CE, a long-distance trade network was already highly developed and operating by this time between Egypt, Arabia, and India. Based also on Strabo's testimony (15.4), the sea route to India was well known before the time of the *Periplus*. The extent and complex nature of this network can be seen, for example, in the Muziris papyrus (P.Vindob. G 40822), which has been dated to the 2nd century CE. This network consisted of ports-of-trade, administrative centers, and production centers and was supervised by various polities in Arabia and India. This highly developed system had likely been formed prior to the Early Roman period, because systems that are so well coordinated and smooth-running develop over time, and, as demonstrated above, there is early evidence of trade between these areas. The system described in the *Periplus* was characteristic of other areas, primarily those around the Mediterranean Basin associated with Phoenician trade activity and its patterns of collaboration with local states, kingdoms, or elite groups. The case of Italy in the Iron Age/Archaic period is a comparable example (Casson 1989: 21–7; Smith 1998: 34–5; Young 2001: 6, 18, 47–8, 55–7; Morley 2007: 42; Seland 2007: 212, 217).

Herodotus (1.111) says it was the Phoenicians who introduced cinnamon, which was native to Ceylon and southern India, to the Greeks. Several towns in southern India from Taxila in Pakistan to modern Calcutta have yielded Achaemenid architecture, which suggests there had been Achaemenid control over the region in the Persian period. Thus, it is possible that the Persian fleet that consisted of Phoenician ships manned by Phoenicians had been present in India during this period and might have conducted commercial business on behalf of Phoenician cities as well. In the early Hellenistic period, Arrian (*Anab.* 6.22.4) wrote about Phoenicians who had followed Alexander's army to India and collected the resin of bdellium. Bdellium is a type of incense made from the sap of a tree that grows in northeastern India. The author of the *Periplus* mentions (37.12.20) that this resin was also being exported to the West in the 1st century CE. It is clear from Arrian that in his lifetime, the 4th century BCE, bdellium was unknown to the Greeks and all other groups comprising Alexander's army, except for the Phoenicians. Phoenician knowledge of Indian scented materials might have developed quite early, therefore, from their confirmed trade with some parts of India during the Iron Age II, but probably even earlier (Dayton 1984: 367, 369, 371; Casson 1989: 11, 185).

Arretine Sigillata pottery has been found at Virampatnam-Arikamedu in southeastern India, where local glass, metal, ivory, and shell workshops also were found, and perhaps a fabric-dyeing industry as well. Arikamedu has been identified with ancient Podukê, a major port mentioned by the author of the *Periplus* (60.20.6a) as well as by Ptolemy (*Geography* 7.1.14). Tamil literature describes the quality wine brought to India by westerners (*yavanas*, i.e. Greeks?), and the *Periplus* (49, 56) confirms that Mediterranean wines were exported to India.

Indeed, large quantities of Mediterranean amphorae that date from the late 2nd century BCE to the 1st century CE have been found in all the excavations conducted at Arikamedu (Podukê). Wine amphorae from Kos made up over 50%, but other types of amphorae included imitation Koan wine from Pompeii, Rhodes, and Knidos, perhaps because they included salt and could have arrived in India in good condition, or because Koan wine was considered medicinal. In addition to wine, olive oil and fish sauce also arrived in Arikamedu, but in small quantities, probably for consumption by the foreign traders resident in this port-city. Oil arrived from Istria and then from Spain, and fish sauce was also imported from Spain. "Punic-type" olive oil amphorae that were produced in Tunisia and other North African sites in the 3rd–6th centuries CE arrived at Arikamedu. Both Spain and North Africa were known bases of Phoenician industry. The oil and fish sauce shipments from Spain to Arikamedu at least might have been in Phoenician hands. Still, we cannot rule out the possibility that all trade activity at Arikamedu was conducted by local merchants and not by foreigners, even though the trade involved goods produced in the Mediterranean (Casson 1989: 228–9; Young 2001: 31–2; Will 2004: 433–9).

Arikamedu was a coastal trading settlement that shared three factors with Phoenician bases in the Mediterranean. These were its location at the mouth of a river, its workshops, and its function as the main port for both a local network operated in the Bengal Bay and Sri Lanka and an international network connected to Arabia and the West. However, not only have Western imports been found in India, but Arikamedian and other Indian pottery dating to the mid-1st century BCE to the mid-1st century CE has been found at Berenike by the Red Sea, an important station on the trade route from India to the West via Alexandria. Eastern Sigillata A or Arretine Sigillata also has been found in Sri Lanka, as well as Hellenistic mold-made bowls or imitations of this type. Excavations in Sri Lanka also yielded a Late Egyptian scarab from the 8th to mid-4th centuries BCE and glass. Several sites in Sri Lanka have revealed connections with the Mediterranean under the Ptolemies, perhaps through India (Begley 1983; Begley and Tomber 1999; Tomber and Begley 2000; Bouzek 2000).

The trade route between the Persian Gulf and India did not cease in the Early Roman period; the Sassanian Empire rebuilt ports and trading posts in the 3rd century CE along the Persian Gulf and southern India and traded as far as China. Inscriptions indicate that a Christian community using the Persian language was living in south India between the late 6th and 9th centuries CE. These Christians were part of the Persian Church, which dominated Persia, the Gulf area, Bahrain, Oman, and south India. The church was based at the as yet unlocated Rew-Ardashir, which was populated by Christians deported from Syria by the Sassanian king in the middle of the 3rd century CE. Muslims also used the route from Arabia via the Persian Gulf to India. They connected this trade route with former Phoenician trading posts in the Mediterranean. Recent evidence of such continuity has surfaced at Manapattu, 20 km south of Arikamedu, where Mediterranean finds have been uncovered that date from the 10th–17th centuries CE (Gropp 1991; Will 2004: 439).

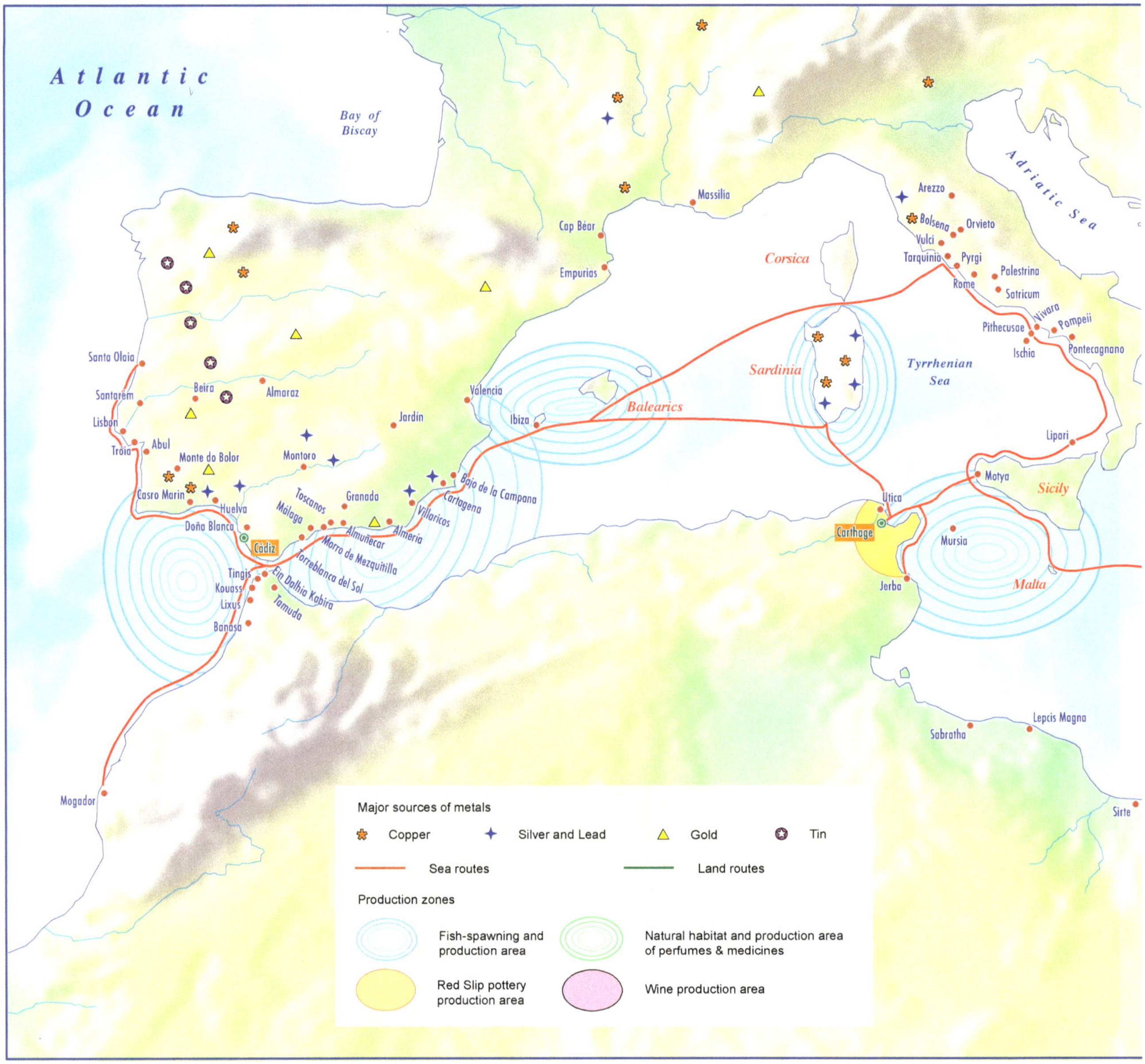

Map 2: Production areas of the Canaanite-Phoenician networks of wine, pottery, perfumes-medicines, and fish products

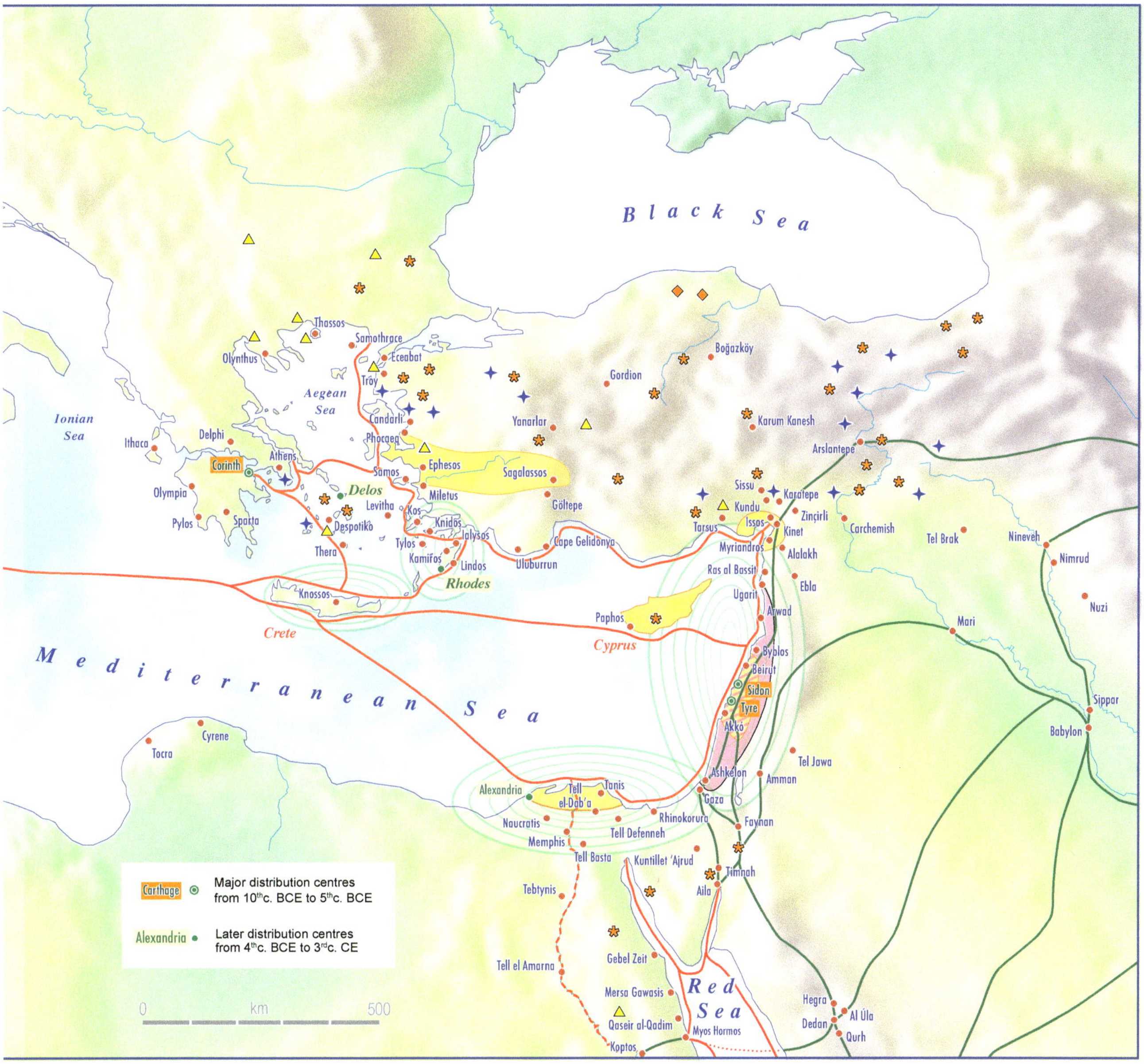
Black Sea
Ionian Sea
Aegean Sea
Mediterranean Sea
Red Sea
Crete
Cyprus
Rhodes
Delos
Thassos
Samothrace
Olynthus
Eceabat
Troy
Candarli
Phocaea
Ephesos
Samos
Miletus
Sagalassos
Gölteppe
Yanarlar
Gordion
Boğazköy
Karum Kanesh
Arslantepe
Sissu
Karatepe
Zincirli
Kundu
Tarsus
Issos
Kinet
Carchemish
Tel Brak
Nineveh
Nimrud
Nuzi
Mari
Sippar
Babylon
Myriandros
Alalakh
Ras al Bassit
Ebla
Ugarit
Arwad
Byblos
Beirut
Sidon
Tyre
Akko
Tel Jawa
Ashkelon
Amman
Gaza
Faynan
Timnah
Aila
Paphos
Cape Gelidonya
Uluburrun
Lindos
Ialysos
Kamiros
Tylos
Knidos
Kos
Levitha
Despotiko
Thera
Knossos
Athens
Corinth
Delphi
Ithaca
Olympia
Pylos
Sparta
Cyrene
Tocra
Alexandria
Tell el-Dab'a
Tanis
Naucratis
Memphis
Tell Basta
Tell Defenneh
Rhinokorura
Kuntillet 'Ajrud
Tebtynis
Tell el Amarna
Gebel Zeit
Mersa Gawasis
Qaseir al-Qadim
Myos Hormos
Koptos
Hegra
Dedan
Al Ula
Qurh
Carthage
Major distribution centres from 10th c. BCE to 5th c. BCE
Alexandria
Later distribution centres from 4th c. BCE to 3rd c. CE
0 km 500

—6—

Phoenician Industrial Networks

Phoenician industrial networks are coordinated trade networks that were primarily controlled by the palace and temple of the main city-states. As a result, much of the traded merchandise was state-controlled; the state financed, organized, shipped, taxed, and enriched its capital. In the 2nd millennium BCE, these cities were mainly Byblos and Ugarit, and in the 1st millennium BCE mainly Tyre and Sidon, and, later, Carthage. Each of these cities controlled other, smaller cities which operated as key production and distribution centers. Due to the lack of written data, we do not know exactly which of the major city-states controlled which of the smaller cities, when, or for how long. Hence, though prominent, we can assume that these five cities were not the only ones that organized and controlled the Canaanite-Phoenician trade networks.

At the heart of state control and organization is the systematic use of capital invested to create wealth; this was the case in the Canaanite-Phoenician trade networks. The question is still debated whether this was a semi-capitalistic system that involved private ownership and investment or a state operation which also integrated members of the royal family and the nobility (Moore and Lewis 2000; Scott 2019).

The textual and archaeological data indicate five distinct categories of Canaanite-Phoenician product:

a. Raw materials that were processed to initial stages: metal bars, glass bars, and wood logs.
b. Industrial products: dyed fabrics and cloth.
c. Ornamented artifacts: metal objects, ivories, tridacna shells, ostrich eggs, and jewelry.
d. Ritual and religious objects: scarabs, figurines, amulets, masks, and bronze mirrors.
e. Agricultural products: wine, oil, processed fish, and perfumed oils and medicines.

This chapter deals primarily with agricultural products but includes Terra Sigillata ware, a form of decorated, highly burnished pottery used in banqueting. Many perishable agricultural products have been lost to historical and archaeological research. When remains like olive pits, grains, seeds, and even the bones of animals and fish are found, they often are no longer in or associated with their original containers and thus tell us little about their precise origin and the route by which they arrived at the site where they were brought to light.

Fortunately, not all organic products are untraceable in the archaeological record. Amphorae that had contained wine, salted fish, and various types of vegetable oil are commonly found during excavation. Residue analysis can sometimes determine what the final contents of a jar or container had been. Research into vegetable oils has not yet sufficiently progressed to be able to distinguish between separate classes of oils. Perfumed oils and medicines that were contained in bottles, juglets, and jugs, are also only partly identifiable by trace analysis and botanic examination (Manniche 1989; Serpico *et al.* 2003). Given the wide range of plants used in the perfume and medicine industries, the botanical evidence presented in this chapter is elementary and uneven; in order to cover the issue adequately, specialist botanical knowledge is required. The evidence I have used revolves around Canaanite-Phoenician trade, but I am aware of the restrictions of my comprehension of the issue.

Even if we cannot identify the exact composition of the products, we can identify their packaging and the use of standardized, recognizable Canaanite-Phoenician commodities. In particular, the use of Phoenician products in rituals points to a cultural-religious Mediterranean *koine* during the times when Phoenician wine, perfumes, and medicines were in high demand. Their growing consumption seems to point to a much more fundamental influence of Phoenician culture and religion on rituals and the way of life in evolving Mediterranean societies during the 1st millennium BCE, especially Greece and Italy, during the Orientalizing and Classical periods (Foxhall 1998: 300, 306–7). The use of Phoenician wine may be associated with the introduction of the *mrzh* and religious beliefs in these regions by Phoenicians, where the rising elites emulated them, creating the local tradition known as the *symposion* (Regev 2020: 56–61).

Large-scale Phoenician trade involved industrial activity that resulted in a large variety of products for long-distance global operations; nevertheless, the discussion presented here is selective and focuses on specific items of the Phoenician trade network. It does not include the trade in timber and metals, two perishable commodities that appear to have composed the major volume of Phoenician commercial traffic. Trade in both commodities is mentioned in the remaining chapters dealing with trade-nets when relevant to the specific area under discussion. Both timber and metals are difficult to track in archaeological records, although advancing techniques in chemical analysis of metal composition are permitting an identification of ore sources. The scant historical record of their trade has been exhausted until new texts come to light (Krings 1995: 73–83, 247–81, 354–61, 426–39; Pare 2000; Aubet 2001: 70–143; Kassianidou and Papasavvas 2012).

Trade in the valuable products of famous Phoenician craftsmanship in metal, ivory, and glass is not discussed either. Such items, although providing valuable information about chronological and cultural contexts, do not indicate nor demand the existence of an orchestrated trade network that includes the manufacture, assemblage, and distribution of the product. By definition, such luxury items do not indicate any commercial contacts and might have resulted from casual visits or gift-exchange. Moreover, luxury items of these types, especially those made of metal and ivory, might have been produced at least in part by itinerant or emigrant Phoenician craftsmen. All the same, the distribution of

Phoenician luxury items follows the trade network routes, and they appear at the same sites associated with Canaanite-Phoenicians.

Instead, the evidence presented here relates to large-scale operations that involved industrial activity initiated and organized for long-distance trade in a global pattern. The trade networks examined are those that focused predominantly on wine, salted fish, perfumed oils, and Terra Sigillata fine-ware pottery. Trade in these products demanded elaborate coordination, trading to distant locations, and was, by its nature, a long-lasting phenomenon. Each of these networks reveals another angle of Canaanite-Phoenician history and shines a different light on various aspects of their cultural and economic connections with neighboring peoples and others further away.

Among the most durable Canaanite-Phoenician trade networks was that of wine, which existed from the Middle Bronze Age until the Late Roman period, coordinated by the Levantine Phoenician cities. From what we know, the Canaanite-Phoenician perfumed-oils and medicines network operated from the Iron Age until late Hellenistic period and included production and packaging activities in several locations in the east Aegean. The Canaanite-Phoenician salted-fish network was the most short-lived of the three, lasting from the 6th or 5th century until the 1st century BCE, after which it was taken over and continued by the Romans until the 5th–6th centuries CE. This network revolved around production areas located mainly in the western Mediterranean and along the Atlantic coasts of North Africa and the Iberian Peninsula. Finally, the Terra Sigillata network manufactured and distributed pottery from the 3rd century BCE in the Levant until its end in the 7th century CE, when production centers moved to North Africa.

Another known large-scale industrial activity operated by the Phoenicians, at least during the 1st millennium BCE, was the production of dyed cloth and fabrics. This Phoenician commodity is well known from textual evidence and from the excavation of red-dyeing vats and heaps of murex shells found in Phoenician sites all over the Mediterranean. However, unlike the other industrial products discussed here, dyed textiles were not transported in durable packaging, unlike wine, fish, and oils, which are usually traceable in clay amphorae. As a result, the destinations of textiles cannot be physically traced nor found in excavations on land or at sea. For this reason, dyed textiles, though part of an elaborate network of long-distance trade, are not dealt with here. Any description of a network must include the distribution of consumers and, currently, this is impossible in the case of textiles. Nevertheless, since the dyeing process itself and the installations needed for it were similar to those used for salted fish, it is commonly assumed that the two industries were related: dyeing took place in the same Phoenician fish-processing factories after the fishing season ended. The locations of dyeing installations can be used, therefore, as indicators for the location of the salted-fish industry. It should be noted, however, that, in many cases, the heaps of murex shells that have been found might indicate a dietary habit rather than industrial activity (Lowe 2004: 46–7).

The wine and pottery trade networks were coordinated from the homeland. The perfumed-oils and medicines network was coordinated from the homeland as well, but it required diaspora bases in several other locations where the perfumed oils were actually produced. The salted-fish network was coordinated entirely by diaspora bases in the western and central Mediterranean. These four networks were organized and based on market demand and the location of the raw commodities involved, i.e. where the best flowers grew or best fish lived. Since the routes were determined by access to the raw materials needed in each case, they had little overlap. Nonetheless, based on shipwreck evidence in the

Roman period, the cargo carried by merchant ships was seldom limited to one type of product alone; most of the ships found carrying amphorae filled with fish products were also carrying amphorae containing wine and oil (Lowe 2016: 229–30). Network overlap, therefore, occurred primarily in certain distribution centers and on board merchant ships but not in the production centers.

I. Pottery: Terra Sigillata

The first to be described is the pottery network. Although Terra Sigillata is not the most enduring trade network of the Canaanite-Phoenicians, it is a product that follows an earlier tradition of red-slipped pottery, described in *New Light on Canaanite-Phoenician Pottery* (Regev 2020: 63–92), and it carried the most significant religious and cultural message of any of the other trade networks.

Terra Sigillata ware is a pottery group that is part of an ongoing, Phoenician, red-slipped pottery tradition. It became prized as luxury table ware and thus was manufactured and traded as a commodity in its own right. The trade networks for wine and scented oils dealt with various products that were packaged in ceramic containers manufactured for that purpose. It was the contents that were desired first and foremost, not the containers themselves. In the case of Sigillata ware, however, it was the pottery itself that was sought after.

Initially related to Canaanite-Phoenician *mrzh* ceremonies, there was a steady demand for the precursors of Terra Sigillata in locations where Canaanite-Phoenicians had settled. Once these ceremonies and their associated institutions were adopted by the Greek and Roman cultures and practiced under the term *symposion*, however, the demand and market for the table ware, now produced as Sigillata ware, increased steadily. The ware became a highly sought-after international trade commodity, particularly in the Early Roman period, and continued its peak popularity through the 4th century CE (Regev 2020: 56–61).

Eastern Sigillata A (ESA) ware could be made in many different locations, wherever there were Phoenician potters who had access to a particular kind of clay. Neutron activation analyses and petrographic analyses have confirmed its production from clay of the Taqiya formation, which is very common along the Levantine coast from Alexandretta Bay in the north to Akko Bay in the south. The pottery was probably produced in several places along this coast and probably at other Phoenician locations as well, since we know today that the Phoenicians transported raw clay for pottery manufacture in their boats at least as early as the 5th century BCE. The long-distance transport of clay for manufacturing purposes also occurred in the Roman period. Specific clay suitable for perforated vessels was transported 450 km from western Anatolia to a production facility at Eceabat in northwest Anatolia. The same practice continues today (Yardeni 1994: 70; Tekkök 2004: 102). Thus, ESA could have been manufactured simultaneously in Cyprus, Phoenicia (including sites within modern Israel), and Syria. In time, due to the political and economic circumstances of the Hellenistic and Early Roman periods, ESA manufacture might have moved from certain Phoenician sites to others within these regions.

In addition, the chronology and distribution of other Sigillata groups seems to support the view that there had been one main network for Terra Sigillata production and distribution around the

Mediterranean. The cultural predominance reflected in the spread of Terra Sigillata is attested in particular in Athens. The city, once a cultural center that had dictated pottery fashion, had begun to show a growing tendency in the 2nd century BCE, after the first appearance of ESA there, to imitate imported shapes and styles, especially those from Asia Minor. By the Roman period, all Athenian local pottery was an imitation or local variant of imported shapes. Athens had shifted from a preference for black-slipped pottery during the Classical and Hellenistic periods to red-slipped pottery imitations of Terra Sigillata and other groups in the Early and Late Roman periods (Hayes 2008: 9–10).

If we examine the Mediterranean as a whole during the entire period when Terra Sigillata was manufactured, we see two important trends. The first involves the appearance of various Sigillata wares in locations around the Mediterranean. Eastern products have been found in the West and vice versa. At any given time, from the 2nd century BCE to the 7th century CE, there was at least one center and usually more that produced Terra Sigillata. This fact reflects the existence of an overall Mediterranean trade network that shipped products from every part of the Mediterranean Basin to other parts. The second feature of the Terra Sigillata network was the existence of areal spheres of production. Within these areas, there was constant change and balance between several production centers. The manufacture at the centers within each area did not usually overlap but shifted from one production center to another over time.

The Eastern sphere included the Levantine coast, Cyprus, Egypt, and the coast of Asia Minor. This area was the first to produce Terra Sigillata. The production focus moved from the Levant to Cyprus, then Asia Minor, and eventually also to Egypt. The first production of ESA ware in the northern Levant probably began in the 3rd century BCE and lasted until the 2nd century CE (Regev 2020: 83). In Cyprus, production started in the late 2nd century BCE and continued through the 1st or 2nd centuries CE, while in Egypt Red Slip or Sigillata ware was produced rather late, from the 4th–7th centuries CE. Several production centers in Asia Minor were also active. Their products include: a pottery type previously known as Eastern Sigillata C (ESC) from Çandarli, made from the late 2nd or 1st centuries BCE until the early 4th century CE; Eastern Sigillata B (ESB), previously known as Samian ware, which was made in western Asia Minor from the late 1st century BCE to ca. 200 CE; Sagalassos ware, which was manufactured from the 1st century BCE to the 3rd or 6th centuries CE; and Phoecaean ware, also known as Late Roman C ware, from the 4th–early 7th centuries CE. In the Eastern sphere, Terra Sigillata was produced in massive quantities from the 2nd century BCE to the 2nd century CE but continued to be produced in lesser quantities until the 4th or 5th centuries CE, when Late Roman ware began its massive distribution. It was still produced in smaller amounts in Egypt until the 7th century CE.

These manufactured products were distributed locally within the Eastern sphere. ESA had the widest distribution, including Greece and the Aegean alongside the production areas themselves. The Cypriot and Egyptian Sigillata ware, on the other hand, were restricted primarily to the eastern Mediterranean, excluding Greece (Lund 2002: 185, 189, 204, 2003: 125, 2006: 217–18; Hayes 2008: 1–11, 49, 53, 83–8; Johnson 2008: 73–94).

The Western sphere included Italy, France, and Spain. Production there began in Italy, first at Arezzo in former Etruria, where Phoenician connections had already been established in the 8th–7th centuries BCE and so were centuries old when the manufacture of Sigillata began in the mid-1st century BCE. Later, production included various other locations in Italy. The Italian centers produced Sigillata in large amounts for quite a short period, from the mid-1st century BCE until early in the 1st century CE, although reduced production continued until the 2nd century CE. From the early 1st–4th centuries CE, production centers in Gaul (France) were the prominent centers of Terra Sigillata in the West, and production centers also operated in Iberia from the 1st–5th centuries CE (Madrid Fernandez and Buxeda i Garrigos 2002: 287). The distribution of Terra Sigillata produced in this geographical sphere was mainly in the western Mediterranean, although Arretinian Sigillata was widely distributed in both the eastern and western Mediterranean, except for the Levant. The other Western groups are hardly found in most of the Eastern sites, Athens included.

Terra Sigillata only began to be manufactured in the area of Carthage and North Africa from the 1st–7th centuries CE and is known as African Red Ware. Carthage had been destroyed in 146 BCE but was rebuilt again. It took some time to recover, however. After ESA, this is the largest of the Terra Sigillata groups; the two do not overlap chronologically. African Red Ware took over when ESA was no longer being produced (Hayes 2008: 67–73; Johnson 2008: 41). It did overlap chronologically, however, with the wares produced in Gaul and Iberia in the Western sphere. Unlike those and ESA, however, African Red Ware was distributed over the entire Mediterranean.

The origin of Terra Sigillata ware in factories located at Phoenician facilities along the Levantine coast indicates it was a product made and distributed under Phoenician initiative and organization. While the Romans eventually took over the production and distribution networks, during the Hellenistic period and until their eclipse under the Romans, Phoenicians first developed an Eastern network for this ware and then a Western one in the Early Roman period. Eventually, the two were combined into a single network based at Carthage in North Africa.

II. Wine

In antiquity, "wine was a marker of civilization, an essential component of various kinds of social gatherings, and an enormous range of different varieties and qualities of wine made it possible to convey subtle messages about social standing. The wine trade both responded to and helped to realize the desire for social differentiation" (Morley 2007: 38).

The earliest known wine was made during the 6th millennium BCE in western Iran from wild vines and contained resin from the pistacia tree. The wild vine was native to the Near East and the Mediterranean, but domesticated vines only started to appear in the Jordan Valley and the southern Levant in the 4th millennium BCE. Shortly afterward, they spread to Egypt as well, although manufacture of wine there was apparently in Canaanite-Phoenicians hands (Curtis 2001: 142–3, 184). Cultivars were introduced to the western Mediterranean by the Phoenicians in the 1st millennium BCE.

Since antiquity, wine has had a religious status and a complex social position. In ancient Egypt, wine was associated with Horus, and Papyrus Harris, for example, reports that pharaohs dedicated hundreds of thousands of wine jars to temples. The Egyptian gods themselves were seen as drinkers of wine, and the beverage was consumed in banquets, as it also was by the Sumerians and the Assyrians. In Hatti during the 2nd millennium, most references to wine are from a religious context, such as libations and worship. Minoan and Mycenaean texts in Linear A and B indicate the ceremonial feature of wine in Bronze Age Aegean society, where most of the texts recording wine in the archives of Pylos and Knossos list it with other types of sanctuary offerings.

As late as the Hellenistic period, wine, and Phoenician wine in particular, was mentioned in Ptolemaic temple ritual texts. A text from Edfu mentions Phoenician (*fnhw*) wine as being among the finest wines used by the king. The text also specifies that, when a *fnhw* wine offering is made in the temple, Pharaoh receives dominion over the *fnhw* land. It seems that some magical quality is attributed to the use of Phoenician/*fnhw* wine. The statement may relate to the renewed Egyptian Ptolemaic dominance around 200 BCE over the southern Levant and its Phoenician cities, mainly over Akko Ptolemais. The reuse of the archaizing Egyptian term *fnhw* here may point to an attempt to connect the renewed domination during the Hellenistic period to earlier Egyptian domination over the Levant in the Late Bronze Age (Palmer 1996: 278; Horden and Purcell 2000: 426; Curtis 2001: 143–5, 220, 222; McGovern 2003: 120–5; Wilson and Gilbert 2007: 261).

Modern religions either prohibit or are averse to wine, like Islam and Buddhism, or sanctify wine in rituals, like Christianity and Judaism, in spite of the divine prohibition in Leviticus 10:9. In a similar way, wine was an important commodity in ancient religions and societies. Wine was used not only in cultic and social gatherings but also as medicine in the process of mummification (Hdt. 2.86; Diod. Sic. 1.91) and as an ingredient in perfume. Wine had an important use as a means of purification in temples, mortuary cults, and private cultic activities (Dils 1993: 122; Palmer 1996: 278; Murray 2000a: 620; Curtis 2001: 145, 374).

In antiquity, wine was usually considered a luxury commodity, an aristocratic beverage offered to the gods and consumed by the elite. In pre-Ptolemaic Egypt in particular, wine made of grapes was expensive and, therefore, reserved for the elite and for special occasions. The Hittite records from Boğazköy and the texts of Ugarit indicate that wine in both locales was also the beverage of the elite; ordinary Mycenaeans probably drank wine only on special occasions. Textual and pictorial evidence from the Classical period in Greece demonstrate a similar status and use of wine (Palmer 1996: 269, 284; Murray 2000a: 602; Curtis 2001: 220, 223).

Nonetheless, wine has not always been a privilege of the rich. In certain periods and in certain places, it was considered a basic necessity, like bread, and was provided even to slaves and hard laborers as part of an ordinary diet. In the 340s BCE Pseudo-Demosthenes (35.32, 34) mentioned poor-quality wine and salted fish that was provided to workers in the Black Sea area. So it is evident that, albeit of poor quality, wine was expected by and provided to the lower classes as well (Bresson 2005: 96). A variety of wines of different qualities were used for different purposes, including palm wine and date wine. According to Herodotus (2.86; 3.20–2) and Diodorus (Diod. Sic. 1.91), palm wine was used in Egypt to rinse the intestines during mummification. Both texts used the Greek phrase "Phoenician wine," which is translated in all editions as "palm wine." Wine was made from palms in Egypt, where the dom palm was sacred and its parts were known to have medicinal characteristics (Murray 2000a: 618–21, 2000b: 593; Aubet 2001: 7). Palms do not grow in the northern Levant, so palm wine was probably not produced in Phoenicia. There might have been a Phoenician palm wine industry in Egypt, although we have no evidence of such activity.

Interestingly, the palm, called in Greek *phoenix,* was depicted on Punic stelae and coins, testifying to a special connection between palm trees and Phoenician and Punic religion. The date palm was a particularly Tyrian emblem, evident on coins. It was sacred, and various palms were identified with deities (Frost and Vari 1981: 61; Murray 2000b). A likelier explanation of the connection between "Phoenician" and palm wine, however, seems to be the distribution of Egyptian palm wine in the

Mediterranean by a Phoenician commercial network. Like other Egyptian items that were exclusively distributed by Phoenicians—for example, paper and scarabs—Phoenicians introduced palm wine to the Mediterranean, including the Greek world. Its clients thus naturally considered it "Phoenician wine" and, indeed, Herodotos and Diodorus both used this terminology.

The fact that it was an extremely luxurious wine and a symbol of refinement is evident in Herodotus (3.20–2). He relates that this wine was one of a few carefully chosen gifts from the Persian King Cambyses to the Ethiopian king, whose cooperation was very much needed by the Persians. These gifts, some of which may have also included Phoenician crafts like purple cloth and alabaster boxes, are described as special things that delighted the Persian king but were ridiculed by the Ethiopian king for not being good enough, except for a Phoenician wine amphora, which he found excellent (Asheri, Lloyd, and Corcella 2007: 419).

Phoenician wine was considered to be of superior quality. In one Ugaritic text (KTU 1.22.i.17–20), "wine of happiness, the gem of Lebanon's necklace, dew of the must cultivated by El" is depicted as coming from vines on Mount Lebanon that were grown there by El himself. The wine of Lebanon is described in this context as a nectar made by the gods. The Bible also presents Phoenician wine as the best wine: "the scent thereof shall be as the wine of Lebanon" (Hos 14:7). In *The Learned Banqueters* (1.29b–c), Athenaeus praises "the Bibline wine from holy Phoenicia" in detail and mentions (another?) "Phoenician wine" drunk in the banquet (2.57e). Hesiod, in *Works and Days* (589), also mentions "Bibline wine" which some have identified as a "celebrated Thracian wine." The text seems to have been misunderstood, however, because Hesiod, who lived in Boeotia, indeed drank wine from Phoenician Byblos on special occasions (Braun 1995: 29; Foxhall 1998: 303; Watson 1999: 778, 782; McGovern 2003: 202; Most 2006: 135n36).

Possible evidence regarding the trade and use of Phoenician wine during the Persian period is provided by an Aramaic text recording taxes collected from Ionian (*ywny*) and Phoenician-Sidonian (*sdn*) ships carrying goods to and from Memphis in Egypt in 475 BCE. According to the document, the Phoenician ships carried Sidonian wine, cedar wood, metals, and clay. This Sidonian wine must have been shipped in contemporary Phoenician amphorae, providing us with rare, explicit testimony of amphorae that were the product of Phoenician people. Another text dating to the reign of Darius I (died 486 BCE; *CT* 55.435) records the shipment of a tithe from the governor of Byblos to the Ebabbara temple at Sippar. It included two jars of wine in addition to other valuable goods from Phoenicia in the form of silver, purple wool, and cedar. Although the equating of the source of this tax payment from Gubal with Byblos has been debated, the ensemble of goods described in the text is comprised of traditional Phoenician merchandise, thus making the identification of Gubal with Byblos credible (Zadok 1985; Yardeni 1994: 67, 70; Briant and Descat 1998: 60–2; Stager 2003; Dandamayev 2004: 144).[3] The brief evidence presented above confirms that wine was a famous Phoenician product which was made and traded by Phoenicians at least by the Late Bronze Age, as the Ugaritic text reveals, and as late as the Persian period, as other literary evidence shows.

Trade in Wine

Beginning in the 4th millennium BCE, wine was traded via long-distance routes between Mesopotamia and Iran; later, in the 4th millennium, the Canaanites started to trade in wine too. As early as the Old Kingdom period in Egypt, Byblos became a center for wine export to Abydos, if not other additional

Egyptian ports. During the Late Bronze Age, the ongoing presence of a Phoenician wine trade to Egypt is depicted in a scene in Kenamun's tomb, and two shipwrecks along the coast of southern Anatolia were found carrying large amounts of Canaanite amphorae. Some of the amphorae contained all kinds of agricultural products, but some inevitably contained wine. In the 8th century BCE, two Phoenician trade boats sank west of Ashkelon, probably on their way from the Levant to a southwestern destination. Hundreds of Phoenician amphorae of standardized shape and dimensions have been found on board. They were clearly products of a specialized industry; special-purpose pottery designed for the specific needs of a certain commodity, perhaps wine (Sherratt and Sherratt 1991: 364; Greene 1996: 311, 317; Leonard 1996: 247; Curtis 2001: 142–5, 185–7; King and Stager 2001: 146; Emanuel 2019).

Discussions of trade in antiquity often deal with the question of whether it was organized and operated by institutions, the aristocracy, private dealers, or a combination of these agents sharing various degrees of control. The trade in wine required an elaborate network far beyond the means of private agents. Viticulture required considerable investment to buy land and plant vines, to build expensive wine-making installations, and the financial resources to wait long periods to receive returns on one's investment. In addition, the establishment of a complex and elaborate commercial network was needed to sell the wine, as well as the ability to incur losses if the ships transporting the wine sank at sea or if the wine was unsuccessful in the marketplace. These requirements were clearly beyond the means of subsistence producers (Greene 1996: 316).

In ancient times, such requirements could only have been be met by the monarchy, priesthood, or aristocracy. From earliest times, the wine trade would always have been strictly monitored by governmental bureaucracies at both ends. Particularly significant evidence for palace control over the production, distribution, and sale of goods included in Canaanite-Phoenician trade has been provided by the Ugaritic texts, which date to the Late Bronze Age. That control likely traced back to the initial trade, however. Old Kingdom Egypt has provided evidence of similar palace control over wine production in paintings and in texts and inscriptions on wine amphorae. Support for the institutional character of the wine trade is provided by a depiction of the entire process, including production facilities, processes, and the shipment of the finished product painted in the Tomb of Khaemweset (Theban Tomb 261), dated to the Late Bronze Age, where it was clearly a process supervised by the Egyptian king's palace. It seems that similar control was also employed over wine production in Proto-palatial Aegean culture around 1800 BCE, where the appearance of a wine ideogram in the earliest Linear A texts in Crete shows that wine was collected and monitored by the Minoan palace (James 1986: 14–15, fig. 11; Leonard 1996: 237; Palmer 1996: 284; McGeough 2007: 165–6, 375–6).

The Bronze Age palace societies also imposed restrictions on wine use. It could be consumed regularly by the palace, be used for trade and tax collection, and could serve as a gift to gods and be used in religious festivals. The Ugaritic example reveals that the palace control involved a complex network which included elite members and temple officials. In this case, the palace may not have controlled the economy *per se* but was at the intersection of most of the network's connections (McGovern 2003: 120–5; McGeough 2007: 380).

The centralized control of wine production and distribution by royal or civil authority was an intrinsic and fundamental aspect of the wine trade which continued in Greece in the Classical and Hellenistic periods. Thassos provides evidence in the form of official decrees and the stamps imprinted on vessels that demonstrate the control of the state over the wine industry on the island in the 5th century BCE

(Koehler 1996: 333). The stamped handles on Rhodian amphorae reveal that the same situation obtained on Rhodes during the Hellenistic period. Phoenician trade in wine in the 1st millennium BCE probably maintained the same governmental character it had displayed in the earlier trade in wine. The ability to think ahead and invest in future ventures is, again, a feature of advanced social-economic institutions, like the Phoenician courts and temples of the 1st millennium BCE. Neville Morley claimed "the nature of the ancient city [was] as a center of consumption rather than production" (Morley 2007: 5, 8), an idea he backed up with examples from the Roman Empire and Medieval Europe. The Phoenician cities were certainly centers of production, however, as already revealed in the Ugaritic texts and by the products shipped in amphorae. Although perhaps not all the Phoenician cities produced wine themselves as Ugarit did, the wine industry would have not been possible without palatial organization.

The organized industrial nature of wine trade as part of complex societies with centralized administrations is also demonstrated in Carthage. Evidence for viticulture and a wine trade around Carthage begins only in the 4th century BCE. The belated beginnings of vine cultivation and wine production in North Africa can be explained by a lack of complex societies there until the region developed sufficiently after being made part of the Mediterranean trade system. Phoenician settlements in North Africa had already begun by the 9th century BCE, but it took a very long time for the circumstances to coalesce until wine could be produced there. This has to do with the population, the climate, and the geographical conditions in North Africa which were less favorable for wine production than other environments settled by Phoenicians.

A serious impetus for vine cultivation in North Africa came in the aftermath of the Second Punic War (218–201 BCE) and the migration there of masses of Punic refugees from Sardinia and Sicily. These new immigrants were well acquainted with vine cultivation and received land around Carthage and the island of Jerba. They built villas there and produced regular wine from their grapes and perhaps also sweet wine from raisins, called *passum* (Greene 1996: 317; Fentress 2001: 264–5).

Vines were not introduced to the Iberian Peninsula before the 10th century BCE. Analyses of vegetal substances from archaeological excavations in Iberia related to occupational levels dating to the 8th–6th centuries BCE indicate that vines were introduced from the East and cultivated by the Phoenicians, as were olive trees and other fruits and vegetables. By the 8th century BCE, wine production had started there, as well as in southern France. Ibiza produced not only wine at this early stage but also amphorae for the wine trade (Buxó 2009: 147; López Castro 2019: 590). Thus, not only does the existence of a wine trade indicate a complex society and centralized systems, but, conversely, its absence points to the opposite socio-political situation. The correlation between the presence of a complex society and the wine trade can also be seen in the Aegean. Development of Greek amphorae began only in the Archaic period, in the 8th–7th centuries BCE, the same time that the complex societal system of the *polis* arose there and trade became an essential part of Greek activity around the Mediterranean.

Archaeobotanical evidence has demonstrated that viticulture had been practiced in Greece since the Neolithic period, but trade in wine was a completely different enterprise. It is very likely that, initially, Greek trade in wine during the 8th–7th centuries used the ancient, established Phoenician network to market its wines. Based on the Corinthian pottery found in Phoenician trading posts, it is quite likely that Phoenician networks distributed Greek wine and perhaps other products at least until the end of the 6th century BCE. This process faded slowly at different paces for different Greek cities during the 5th–4th centuries BCE. This was due to increasing confrontations between Greeks and Phoenicians over control of the trade routes and posts. In addition, the reduced ability of Levantine Phoenician cities to carry out commercial trade in the eastern and central Mediterranean because of the commandeering of their ships by the Persians for war purposes was another factor (Koehler 1996: 323; Palmer 1996: 283; Buxó 2009: 158).

The Wine Network

The Production of Wine

Wine was produced in the Levant. Vineyards and wine presses were located in the coastal area as well as on the hills and mountain slopes inland, from northern Syria to southern Israel. During the Bronze Age and the period of Hyksos control over Egypt, vineyards and wine presses were also located in the Nile Delta.

The Production of Packaging (Amphorae)

Wine amphorae were produced in the Levant. Pottery production centers manufactured amphorae in the Levantine littoral from the Bronze Age to the Roman period. Amphorae warehouses were located primarily in the northern Levant between Beirut and Akko but also around Ashkelon. During the Late Roman period, amphora production centered around Ashkelon.

Distribution Centers

The distribution centers of wine amphorae were located in the Levant. The centers changed over time from the Bronze Age to the Late Roman period. They included, in chronological order: Byblos, Ugarit, Tyre and Sidon, Akko, Beirut, and Ashkelon. Some of these centers operated simultaneously.

Distribution Areas

Wine was distributed throughout the entire Mediterranean but not in all locations at all times. During the Middle Bronze Age, wine went to the Levant and Egypt; during Late Bronze, to the Levant, Egypt, Nubia, Cyprus, Greece and the Aegean, and Italy. During the Iron Age, wine was distributed to the Levant, Egypt, Nubia, Cyprus, Greece and the Aegean, Italy, North Africa, and the Iberian Peninsula; during the Persian Period, to the Levant, Egypt, Nubia, Cyprus, and Greece and the Aegean. During the Hellenistic and Early Roman periods, distribution was restricted to the Levant, Egypt, and Cyprus but expanded again dramatically during the Late Roman period to include the Levant, Egypt, Nubia, Cyprus, Greece and the Aegean, Italy, North Africa, the Iberian Peninsula, Gaul, Germany, Britannia, the Black Sea, Arabia and the Persian Gulf, and India.

Organization

All three main elements on which this network was based—the production of the wine, the manufacture of amphorae, and distribution centers for delivering the final packaged product to customers—were concentrated in the eastern Mediterranean and were operated by the local Phoenician population. An efficient shipment system was needed to deliver vast quantities of wine from the wineries inland to the distribution centers along the coast. It is unknown how the wine was transferred to these centers. Perhaps it was in sacks made of animal hides that were emptied upon arrival at the coastal distribution center into waiting, empty amphorae. Or, perhaps the standardized amphorae were shipped empty to the wineries and filled there before being transferred back to the coastal distribution centers filled and ready to ship. Eventually, all the wine was decanted into the standard Phoenician amphorae of the period and stored, before shipment by sea, in warehouses in harbors which served as the distribution centers.

From the Levant the wine amphorae were shipped to other regional distribution centers, which changed from place to place over time. Kommos in Crete was such a center during the Late Bronze Age, Lefkandi in Euboea during the Iron Age, Corinth during the Classical/Persian period, and Rhodes and Delos during the Hellenistic period. In Egypt, the regional distribution centers shifted from Avaris to Memphis to Alexandria, to name the most important. Distribution centers also changed in Cyprus, in North Africa, in Italy and the central Mediterranean islands, in Asia Minor, and elsewhere. From the regional distribution centers around the Mediterranean, the wine amphorae were sent forward to both central markets in the city that served as distribution center and to other local, smaller distribution centers. The Phoenician wine reached some end-users in its original amphora packaging, but not in all cases. Those who would have bought a smaller portion at a local store or market would have had it poured it into a local vessel of some sort.

III. Perfumed Oils and Medicines

The Canaanite-Phoenicians were trading in aromatic and medicinal substances at least from the early 2nd millennium BCE. The long list of precious products, brought from the Canaanite-Phoenician coast to Egypt, is detailed in the *Annals of Amenemhet II* of the late 20th–early 19th centuries BCE. This list includes perfumed oils made of, or consisting also of, cedar, olive, and pine; 271 sacks (about 13,000 liters!) of fragrant stuff (possibly cinnamon or camphor), terebinth resin, and medicinal plants and herbs (Marcus 2007: 141, table 2). Later on, a Phoenician association with trade in perfumed herbs in the Iron Age is mentioned in the Bible (Ezek 27:22), where it is associated with the Arabian kingdom of Saba and other Arabic tribes as traders on behalf of Tyre (Frangie-Joly 2016: 41). Canaanite-Phoenicians not only traded in perfume and medicine ingredients but were also known to have been involved in the production of perfumes. Evidence from the Early Roman period indicates that even the production of the glorious, most coveted, and expensive perfumed oil known in the Hellenistic and Roman periods as Mendesian perfume, because it was produced in Mendes in the eastern Nile Delta, was taken over by the skilled Phoenicians and was produced in the Roman period in Phoenicia itself (Plin. *HN* 13.2.4–8). This evidence may suggest that some of the perfume production in Egypt was already in Phoenician hands in earlier times and continued into the Roman period.

Arrian (*Anab.* 6.22) reported that Phoenician merchants trading in perfume and medicinal herbs accompanied Alexander's army to northwestern India (Gadrosia) in the late 4th century BCE. The Zenon papyri of the mid-3rd century BCE also testify to the Phoenician perfume trade in association with Arabian incense. Literary evidence of the Roman period testifies to the production of perfumes, mainly in Sidon (Plin. *HN* 13.2.12), and of medicines in Beirut (Galen, *De compositione medicamentorum* 12–13). Various perfume and medicine plants are mentioned as products of the Levant (Plin. *HN*

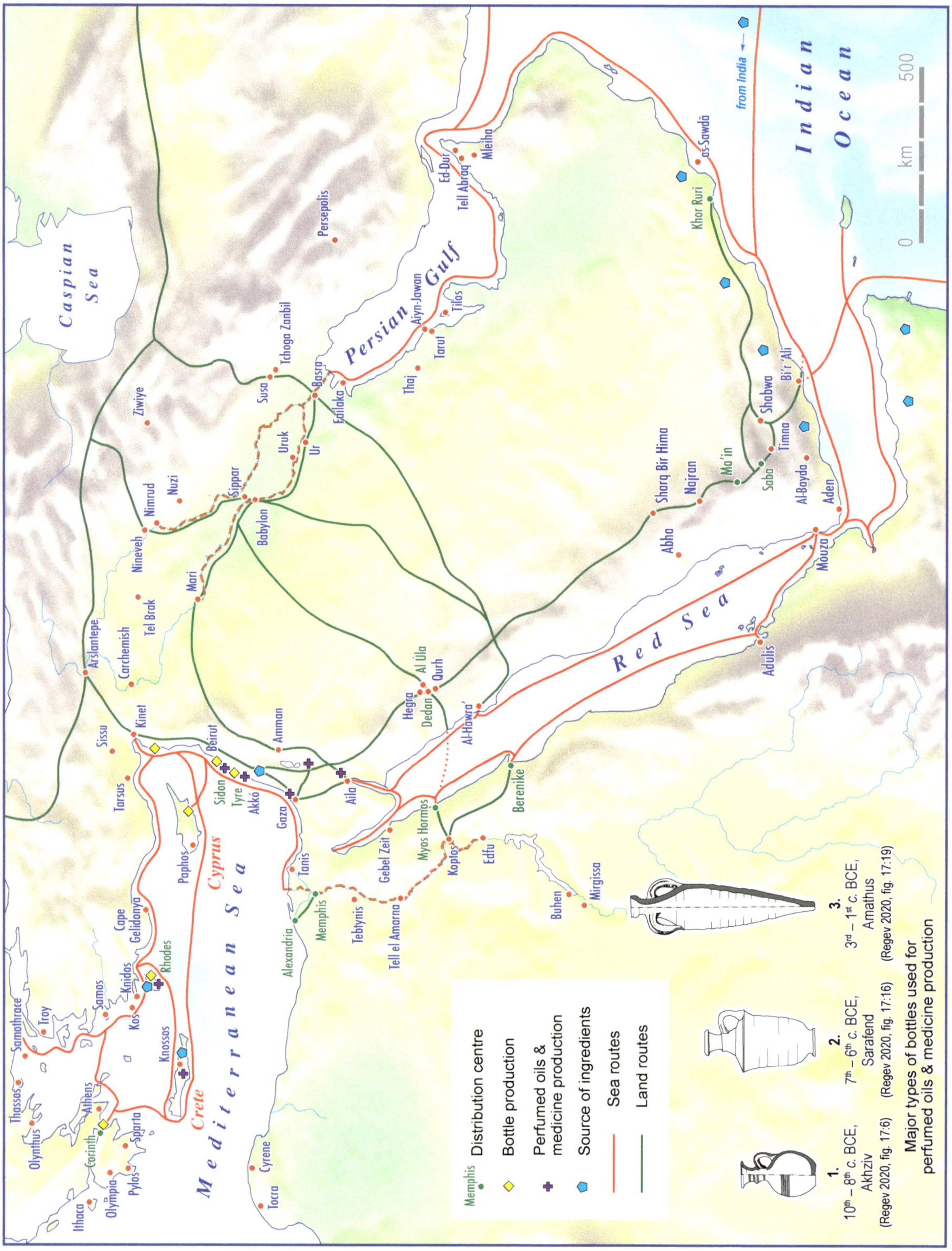

Map 3: The perfumed oils and medicines network

12.50.108; 55.125; 21.69.115). Other evidence of this period reveals that perfume and medicinal plants were cultivated for the perfume and medicine industry at inland northern Phoenicia, including *Acorus calamus* (sweet flag) and resin trees like juniper and cedar (Theophr. *Hist. pl.* 9.7; Plin. *HN* 12.48.104–6). *Acorus calamus* was already mentioned as a perfume plant in Chester Beatty Papyrus VI, a medical papyrus dated to ca. 1300 BCE (Manniche 1989: 74). It is reasonable to assume, then, that the Canaanite-Phoenician perfume and medicine industry thrived at least from the Late Bronze Age and continued through the Iron Age and the Persian and the Hellenistic periods into the Roman period.

Although many of the Greek and Latin authors (for example, Diod. Sic. 5.42.2; Strab. 16.2.18, 20; 16.4.19, 24) focused on Arabia and the wealth obtained there from herbal perfumes, mainly myrrh and frankincense, the Canaanite-Phoenician trade and manufacture of perfume and medicine herbs was not restricted to Arabia. The production area of ingredients for this Canaanite-Phoenician trade network covered a range from Arabia and India, through Egypt and the Levant, to the Dodecanese and Crete. It involved or incorporated several smaller, regional networks and numerous merchants and facilitators, mainly along the way from India and Arabia to the Mediterranean.

Plants were used for spicing food, scenting oils and ointments, and as medicines. As we shall see in the case of saffron and the healing goddess from Thera below, specific plants were associated with specific healing deities, usually with goddesses. Another example, though of an odoriferous plant that was only used as medicine, is the association of *Cynoglossum officinale,* also known as dog's tongue, with the Akkadian goddess Gula (Böck 2014: 129–63). Supernatural and mysterious aspects were a major part of medicine from the very beginning to modern times. Incantations were used as often as plants and considered as or more powerful, as reflected in all ancient texts from Egypt and Mesopotamia (Dafni and Böck 2019: 3). Ashtart, the Canaanite-Phoenician goddess who was protector of kings, sailors, and fertility, might also have had healing qualities; she is depicted holding lotus or water lily flowers. However, in the Canaanite-Phoenician pantheon, the male deities Shadrapha, Eshmun, and Milqart were considered healing deities. None had plants associated with their images (Cornelius 2004: 78, 93–101; Christian 2014; Xella 2019).

The lotus and water lily are often synonymous in archaeology, but true lotus (*Nelumbo nucifera L.*) is of Indian origin and did not arrive in Egypt before the Late Bronze Age, during the 18th Dynasty (1549/1550–1292 BCE), when seeds of the lotus were found at Deir el-Medineh. This workers' village next to Luxor provided rich testimony about everyday life during this period, including the renowned medical ostraca that testify to the presence of physicians and the use of medicines on site (De Vartavan and Amorós 1997: 167; McDowell 1999: 53–7). However, the seeds found at Deir el-Medineh represent a single piece of evidence, which was not repeated until later times; thus, lotus may not have arrived in Egypt until much later, during the Persian period around 500 BCE (Counsell 2008: 204–5).

The water lily (*Nymphaea*) had been used in Egypt since Predynastic times for food and, beginning in the Early Bronze Age, also as perfume and medicine. This is evident from depictions of the plants' harvest and storage in paintings on walls of tombs and by small stone and faience vessels found in temples and elite tombs. According to one of the oldest medical papyri (P.Ebers 209 and 479), dated to 1538 BCE, water lily plants were immersed in wine to yield a medicinal potion. To conserve the water lily scent for perfume, the flowers were pressed and mixed with binding oil. In the Middle Bronze period, the water lily symbolized beauty and pleasure and acquired its religious significance (Counsell 2008: 204–10, Pommerening, Marinova, and Hendrickx 2010).

The pomegranate, a fruit of many medicinal qualities, was associated with Canaanite-Phoenician cult. Some Phoenician metal bowls depict a goddess holding a lotus flower in one hand and a pomegranate in the other (Ackerman 2013). Even so, the fruit cannot be associated with one specific deity. In Egypt during the Late Bronze Age, pomegranates began to be used in the perfume, medicine, and dyeing industries and as a wine additive, in addition to its culinary uses. Canaanite-Phoenicians were engaged in all of these industries. Both the fruit and its cultic symbolism need to be associated with Canaanite-Phoenicians. The Canaanite shipwreck found at Uluburun, dating to the Late Bronze Age, included amphorae containing pomegranates (Bass 1991: 74; Ward 2003). Pomegranate syrup may also have been traded in one or more of the bottles and juglets associated with scented oils.

The earliest recipes for medicines, perfumes, and cosmetic oils and ointments are found in Egyptian texts that were composed in the Late Bronze Age. Treatments for diverse problems, from critical illnesses to facial wrinkles, were based on combinations of plants and plant products like resin, gum, salts, minerals, oils, honey, and beeswax, as well as animal parts. Some of the ingredients were used for their scent or medical quality, some for stabilizing the fragrance, for absorbing the active ingredients, or for solidifying the blend (Manniche 1989). Still, these were predominantly perishable materials, and we must, therefore, rely heavily on the evidence provided by the containers that packaged these substances.

Closed small containers, decorated and plain, made mainly of pottery, glass, and faience, have been found in archaeological contexts from palatial, religious, and elite settings to domestic layers. However, since they are found primarily in burial contexts, bottles, juglets and amphoriskoi are presumed to have contained perfumed oils used to anoint the body of the deceased and to relieve bad odors in tombs during the burial ceremony. By extension, when found in other contexts, the bottles are still assumed to have contained scented oils and ointments used as cosmetics and pleasant-smelling substances.

Some of the bottles clearly contained perfumed oils for these purposes, but not all of them. Many of the substances that produce a pleasant odor are also medicinal, and many of the spices, herbs, and plants used by humankind are medicinal and fragrant as well as flavorful. Judging by the efforts invested in acquiring many of the ingredients used in the production of such oils, it is unlikely the end products would have been used solely for grooming. It is also unlikely that non-elite customers would have invested so much in things that were not essentials. Medicines, however, are a different story; people would pay anything to preserve their lives and those of their loved ones. The distribution of bottles, juglets, and amphoriskoi show that whatever had been contained in them was widespread. It is more likely, then, that their popularity was due to their containing medicines rather than perfumes.

The bottles and juglets used in each period were different, and their shape was also influenced by the main production centers of the era. During the 10th–8th centuries BCE, they were made in the Levant and Cyprus (mainly Black-on-Red juglets); from the 8th–6th centuries BCE in the Aegean islands, mainly around Rhodes (coarse carinated bottles and *alabastra*); and, during the Hellenistic period, manufacture moved back again to the Levant (coarse amphoriskoi).

Residue analyses performed on vessels from Rhodes, Sardinia, and Etruria, all sites with a strong Phoenician presence, have yielded possible evidence for the use of Phoenician bottles and juglets as medicine containers in the 8th–6th centuries BCE. All the types of small containers (*alabastra*, *aryballoi*, *lekythoi*) found in 7th-century Kamiros were manufactured in several locations: Corinth, Athens, Laconia, Rhodes, and Lydia. Nevertheless, all contained the same particular and rare medicinal ointment produced on Rhodes. These facts would seem to validate the hypothesis that some ointment vases were produced in one location and shipped empty to an ointment production plant in another location, where they were subsequently filled (Frère, Garnier, and Elisabeth 2016; Coulié *et al.* 2017). Nonetheless, not all medicines were traded as a liquid remedy in bottles; many of the medicinal materials, like herbs and spices, were traded as dried products, in amphorae and perishable packages.

There was a large variety of both scented oils and medicines. Some were made of fairly common elements in the Mediterranean; for example, *Salvia* species were used primarily to treat lung and throat diseases. These plants are easy to grow and to extract. Some were made of rarer elements: for example, cinnamon, myrrh, and frankincense, brought from Arabia, east Africa, and probably also India. The latter two were very potent antibacterial remedies, imported from afar or complicated to extract. Myrrh resin is extracted from the *Commiphora* species and is one of the oldest, most expensive, and rarest essences that can only be acquired by those with financial means. A 100-year-old examination of herbal materials from ancient Egypt is worth mentioning, in spite of its age. In 1893, Flinders Petrie collected resin from a Late Bronze Age tomb at Tel-Amarna in Egypt which was subsequently identified as myrrh resin at the Kew Gardens Herbarium (Kew Economic Botany: Egyptology Objects, courtesy of Mark Nesbitt). Cinnamon was not used to spice food or beverages in the ancient Mediterranean; it would have been used only in medicine (Haw 2017: 6; Mavrogenis *et al.* 2019: 1532).

The bottles used as containers for medicines and ointments varied in shape and fabric. While most of the bottles that have managed to survive were made of coarse ware and fine painted pottery, others were made of precious materials like glass and faience. In the latter instances, we should assume there was some correlation between the value of the content and value of the container, as evident, for example, from their appearance in the royal Macedonian tombs of queens, princesses, and priestesses that date to the 5th century BCE (Kottaridi 2011: 120, figs. 130–5). Even so, pottery vessels could contain precious contents, as shown by the possible cinnamon remains in the Phoenician flasks dating to the Iron Age (Namdar *et al.* 2013). Most of the evidence for metal bottles used as containers for more precious ointments and medicines has been lost, because metals tended to be melted down and reused. Fragile glass bottles holding these products were quite prone to damage and loss, leaving us primarily with the evidence obtainable from pottery containers.

Scenting Materials and their Dual Function

Scents were sourced from many locations. Myrrh, which grew in Arabia and eastern Africa, but also spices like cinnamon, which grew in India, and perhaps also vanilla, may have been brought from the east. As already noted, residue analysis conducted on Phoenician flasks excavated at Dor, Tell Qasile, and Kinneret from Early Iron Age II occupational layers has identified the contents to have been cinnamon and perhaps also nutmeg, despite the reservations described earlier. Vanilla, or rather one of the *Vanilla planifolia* species (vanilla is native to Mexico) was found in a tomb at Megiddo dating to the Late Bronze I period and would have been exported from other vanillin-containing plants in east Africa or India. Flower extracts were the specialty of some Greek islands. During the Late Bronze Age they were produced mainly in Crete and during the Iron Age until the Early Roman period, mainly in Rhodes (which means "roses"). Distillation of oils from flowers like the rose was already being practiced by the Minoans in the first half of the 2nd millennium BCE (Dickinson 1994: 254; Burkert 1997: 16–17n15).

According to Pausanias, there was a pharmaceutical industry in Chaeronea (Boeotia, Greece) in the 2nd century CE which produced analgesic ointments from lily, rose, narcissus, and iris (Mavrogenis *et al.* 2019: 1531).

One species that belongs to the iris family is *Crocus sativus*, domesticated from its wild progenitor *Crocus cartwrightianus*, commonly known as saffron crocus, from whose stigmas saffron is collected. Although saffron production today is dominated by Iran, genetic analysis has indicated that the origin of this spice, which is the most expensive in the world, is the area of Attica or Crete (Rubio-Moraga *et al.* 2009; Nemati *et al.* 2019). Depictions of saffron flowers gathered by women and monkeys are found on Minoan wall paintings of the early Late Bronze Age (17th century BCE) in Knossos and in Akrotiri, Thera. They are considered botanically accurate pictorial representations of saffron. In the Xeste 3 fresco from Akrotiri, saffron is offered to a healing goddess by a monkey, and the same two elements, saffron and monkeys, are found in the same scene on a wall painting in Knossos (Ferrence and Bendersky 2004; Hood 2005: 62; Rubio-Moraga *et al.* 2009; Wolfson 2018: 45).

Like other spices, saffron, too, was used in the production of both perfume and medicine from early times. According to Susan Ferrence and Gordon Bendersky, "saffron has been used both in ethnomedicine and in experimental studies for the treatment of 90 distinct medical indications" (Ferrence and Bendersky 2004: 211). This is quite unusual, compared to other herbal medicines, even those known as "adaptogenic" plants that protect cell mitochondria (Panossian and Wikman 2009). A prominent medicinal use of saffron in the ancient Mediterranean was to enhance women's fertility, which explains the association of the plant with a female deity in Minoan culture, on a fresco at Akrotiri. In Egypt, Mesopotamia, and Greece more generally, it was associated with healing deities, both male and female. As perfume, Greek and Latin literature (Hikesios, *Athenaeum* 15.689Cd; Plin. *HN* 13.9) states that saffron was one of the most prestigious scents used on festive occasions, as part of a blend, often with rose and myrrh (Brun 2000; Grami 2013; Dewan 2015).

Medicinal Plants and Substances

When dealing with medicinal substances from plants, the most important thing to remember is that we know very little about plant components. "The chemistry of many plants has never been analyzed. It is well known in only a comparatively few cases, usually when a commercially important substance is concerned" (Haw 2017: 8). It is, therefore, very difficult to use chemical analyses to identify the specific plants used as medicines in ancient times. The various chemical compounds found in plants used in ancient remedies can still be harvested from various sources today. An example is camphor, which is a chemical component produced by several separate plants. Moreover, several plants belonging to the same family but available in a limited geographical range can be used to treat the same illness in different parts of the world; an example is Asian and American ginseng.

Another complicating factor is that the same name is commonly applied to plants belonging to unrelated genera. To make things even more complex, herbal medicines are often made from the compounds of several plants, not just one. This is the case today as well as in the past, as we can see in Papyrus Ebers, written in the 16th century BCE, which mentions myrrh and saffron as two of eight herbal ingredients in a potion for a weak eye made of herbs, oil, and animal substances (Ritner 2000: 109). The study of ancient plant medicines is growing, but we have not yet reached the stage where residue analysis of the contents of ancient vessels can identify a plant or a blend of plants with a reasonably high degree of certainty.

However, we are not searching in the dark for infinite plant-substance possibilities. In addition to modern studies of herbal medicines, we have historical sources with descriptions of plants used in medicines. This evidence, however, has its own limitations. As stated by Barbara Böck, "More than one thousand medicinal plant terms are known from Mesopotamian texts. Similarly to other traditional societies and cultures, the terminology for plants was not standardized, with the effect that a plant had more than one name: common alternative designations, names in foreign languages, or special names known only to practitioners" (Böck 2014: 129). This reality gave rise to plant-name indices in ancient Mesopotamia; about 50 such compendia are known today, alongside plant guidebooks called *Lists of Simple Drugs*. Nonetheless, most of the plants in these ancient lists cannot be identified today. This applies to all such ancient texts, no matter what the language or scripts—Akkadian, Egyptian, Greek, or Latin (Gledhill 2002: 1–14; Dafni and Böck 2019).

The oldest Egyptian texts detailing the preparation of medicinal prescriptions date from the early 2nd millennium BCE, and the latest ones from the Roman period. Some medical papyri from the 14th century BCE incorporate incantations translated from Semitic languages, including Phoenician. They mention Amun, an Egyptian deity, together with Ishtar and Eshmun, Canaanite-Phoenician deities. Such texts no doubt reflect Canaanite-Phoenician sources and the transfer of knowledge and medical practices between Canaan and Egypt. Akkadian references to medicines have been recovered from Mesopotamian trading posts in the Hittite Empire that operated during the Late Bronze Age. Other important evidence found in letters of Ramesses II and in Hittite sources shows that medical knowledge also transferred between these two courts and Egyptian physicians. It is more than likely that medicines or medicinal formulas were already being sent from Hatti and the Levantine coast to cure illnesses in Egypt in the Late Bronze Age. This knowledge was then passed down among Egyptian physicians, whose subsequent expertise led to the selection of some to serve as court physicians for the Achaemenid kings (Ritner 2000).

Egyptian texts of all periods reveal that these Hittite and Canaanite connections contributed to the Egyptian pharmacopeia of medicinal herbs. Egyptian drugs were introduced to the Greeks and Romans in later periods and their Egyptian origin is acknowledged in the known Roman and later medical texts, such as the *Periplus of the Erythraean Sea* and Dioscorides' *De materia medica* (Ritner 2000: 113, 116). The use of a pharmacopeia, i.e. a stock of medicinal herbs, is found in Homer and especially in the writings of Hippocrates, most of which date to the 5th–3rd centuries BCE but with some copies as late as the 2nd century CE. This is in fact a corpus of about a dozen-and-a-half medical scripts, partly preserved, the origin of which is attributed to Kos, Knidos, and Alexandria. The influence of Egyptian medicine on Greek medicine is, therefore, well documented and indisputable (Mavrogenis *et al.* 2019: 1532).

The implication of the evidence is that herbal medicines from Anatolia were already known and being used by Canaanite-Phoenicians and Egyptians in the Late Bronze Age, while those that originated in Iran became internationally known and used during the Persian period (6th–4th centuries BCE). From there the road to India is short, and these ancient texts support the supposition that medicinal substances from India, including spices and other ingredients, were traded and used by Canaanite-Phoenicians in the early 1st millennium BCE, if not earlier.

Although the description of medicines in ancient texts are often not very accurate and leave a lot to speculation, they still provide lists of trees, bushes, flowers, barks, and resins used as medicines. Several Classical authors mention clearly that cinnamon originated in Arabia or Ethiopia, but no cinnamon species grew there (Haw 2017: 10). Such evidence may point to another plant that had originated from this area, like the *Cassia abbreviata* mentioned above, but it might point instead to the port of origin for the commodity, as in the case of Cádiz and fish products. In addition, there are ongoing debates over the names of products; is modern cinnamon the same as ancient cinnamon? This debate cannot be resolved, and it seems that only further analyses of ancient residues and the complete charting of the chemical composition of plants can give us verified answers concerning the origin of plant medicines used in antiquity in general and by the Phoenicians in particular.

Oils

Perfumed oils were acknowledged and widely discussed in ancient texts from Mesopotamia, Sumer, Hatti, Egypt, and Ugarit. Oils were mostly used in the anointing of royalty or the priesthood, deceased corpses, and in various rituals of life-cycle passage. The Epic of Gilgamesh from the Middle Bronze Age even states that anointing with fine oil makes a person a "civilized being" (Pennsylvania Tablet OB.2.108) (Vigo 2014). Scented oils were in demand in Near Eastern courts, sanctuaries, and burial grounds before they became common in the gymnasia of the Greco-Roman world. Perhaps the latter use can also be considered an act of civilizing.

Oil was an essential ingredient, whether it was used to create perfume, cosmetics, ointments, or some types of medicines. The types of oil used depended on ancient formulas, the availability of oils, and their cost. In ancient Egypt, the two most popular oils used in the perfume, cosmetic, and medicine industries came from local trees: the *Moringa oleifera* (Ben oil) and *Balanites aegyptiaca*. Many other oils, however, were used as well. A book by Theophrastus entitled *Enquiry into Plants, And Minor Works on Odours and Weather Signs* (*Historia plantarum*), written in the 4th century BCE, indicates that Egyptian *balanos* was the most popular oil in perfume-making because of its glutinous nature and the pleasant smell of its fruit shells (Manniche 1989: 48–59; Blouin 2014: 74).

Some remains of *balanos* oil were identified in 1888 at the Kew Gardens Herbarium from samples taken by Flinders Petrie at his excavations in Egypt. Other samples analyzed at the same facility yielded castor oil seeds from an Egyptian tomb (Cemetery 1600–1699), dated to ca. 3500 BCE and excavated by the Robert Mond expedition in 1937. Olive stones were found at the Saqqara animal necropolis, and in a grave in the cemetery of Hawara, dated to the Greco-Roman period (ca. 1st century BCE). Olive twigs were found in a pyramid at Lahun, dating to the 12th Dynasty in the Middle Bronze Age. These isolated records do not supply evidence of the regular cultivation of oil-producing plants in Egypt to yield a steady supply of oil; nevertheless, they indicate these oils were known and probably used in Pharaonic Egypt (Kew Economic Botany: Egyptology Objects, courtesy of Mark Nesbitt).

Olive oil was produced in large quantities in the Levant and the Aegean, but, based on pollen analysis, olive tree cultivation occurred first in the southern Levant in the 5th millennium BCE. The southern Levant started to produce olive oil about 1000 years before olive tree cultivation was introduced to Crete; ca. 3000 years before cultivation began in Anatolia and Italy in the 2nd millennium BCE; and at least 4000 years before it was cultivated in Iberia, i.e. sometime during the 1st millennium BCE, contemporary with Phoenician presence in the Iberian Peninsula (Langgut *et al.* 2019; López Castro 2019: 590). As the evidence of Canaanite amphorae from Vivara shows, Canaanite-Phoenicians had already arrived in this area in the mid-2nd millennium BCE (Regev 2020: 31), and their arrival may have been accompanied by the introduction of olive tree cultivation and the production of olive oil. There is no doubt that the cultivation and production of olive oil in the Iberian Peninsula was introduced by the Phoenicians.

Other common oils made widely around the Mediterranean were extracted from nuts, almonds, grape seeds, castor seeds, hemp seeds, safflower, and flax. Oils made from the fruit of oil palm and from sesame seeds, however, were not common in most of the Mediterranean. Their production was limited to the eastern Mediterranean, in Egypt, the Levant, Anatolia, the Near East, and northern Africa (Serpico and White 2000b).

During the period that the perfumed-oils and medicines network operated, profits would have been maximized by avoiding as much as possible the costs of shipping the mass amounts of oil needed. Therefore, it is likely that, if possible, the oil needed to manufacture perfumed oils was sourced close to the production centers for the ointments. In the Aegean, for example, the oil may have been produced on Delos (Brun 1999). However, in order to produce more finely scented products, oils with little natural odor might have been shipped to some production centers.

We do not yet know which vegetable oils were actually used by the Canaanite-Phoenician trade network. It is currently impossible to establish which single type of oil or perhaps multiple types were included in the manufacturing process, only that it was vegetable oil. While it cannot be proven, two strong arguments can be presented in favor of the use of palm or sesame oil, in particular. The first is that the odor of these oils is mild and sweet, unlike olive oil, and therefore more suitable for cosmetics and perfumes. The second is that these oils were readily produced and available in the Levant (Bedigian and Harlan 1986). Palm oil is also semi-solid at room temperature, making it especially suitable for ointments. Bitumen, extracted from the Dead Sea, was also used as a base for some known unguents. These oils, then, would have had to have been exported from the Levant to the production centers in Rhodes and Crete used by the Canaanite-Phoenicians.

Camiron Tomb 1 on Rhodes has provided an unusual example of the rare use of animal fat, probably a dairy product, as the base for a medicinal ointment. This ointment also included resin and bile acid; the latter is mentioned in ancient recipes, along with milk, for eye and ear treatment. The absence of vegetable oil in the perfume vases of the Rhodian tomb is unique, compared to all the analyses concerning *alabastra*, *aryballoi*, and *lekythoi* from other regions of the Mediterranean (Coulié *et al.* 2017).

The Scented Oils and Medicines Network

Production

The production of both perfumed oils and medicines involved oils, spices, and flower extracts that were processed using various techniques to create aromas and medicinally infused oils. As in modern perfumery and herbalism, blends of several plants were used to create a certain medicine or fragrance. As texts dated from Late Bronze Age to the Roman period indicate, perfumes and medicines were made by professionals who mastered not only the nature and uses of each ingredient but also the production techniques, which were very complicated and required practice and knowledge (Manniche 1989: 48–59).

Each component of the final product may have had a different origin and required different expertise. The process of extracting essence from fresh flowers, which need to be collected at dawn and to be treated immediately, is not the same as the process required for cinnamon bark, which arrived after lengthy transport by sea and land and required a long process to dissolve its active ingredients in oil or alcohol.

Indeed, many ingredients could be dissolved in oil to create perfumed or medicinal oils and ointments, but others needed alcohol, honey, or water instead to release the active components within the plant. Plants often contain several chemical components that need special treatment in order to extract them. Saponins, for example, a necessary ingredient in ointments, can only be dissolved in water; resins can only be dissolved in alcohol; and many alkaloids cannot be dissolved in water but only in organic solvents, like wine. Not only the plants but also the substances they were soaked in were sometimes considered medicinal. Wine, for example, has been known from ancient times for its medicinal benefits in cholesterol management, which has been confirmed by modern research (Haseeb *et al.* 2019).

The process of alcohol distillation had already been mastered by the 3rd millennium BCE, and the alcohol produced was used in part for medicinal purposes (Schlosser 2011: 1–2). Some plants could be dissolved in wine without recourse to the more potent distilled alcohol, but others required use of the purer liquid. Even today, medicinal plants are combined with alcohol to produce what is now known as "liquor." An example is Sardinian *mirto*, which is made of the berries of the myrtle bush and is a known medicine for pain and fever.

Factories

The production facilities that manufactured the scented oils, ointments, and medicines were located in various places. Two types can be identified: 1) distribution centers that gathered all the necessary raw materials, processed them into finished products, and then facilitated their shipping and distribution to markets; and 2) areas rich in flowers, to which oils had to be shipped so the ether and essence from the fresh flowers could become infused in a suitable suspension. When products included essence from flower blossoms, they had to be created where the flowers grew and were picked fresh.

The first type of production center included Alexandria and Corinth, two major Mediterranean crossroads. In the Hellenistic and Roman periods, Alexandria was known for its perfume production (Plin. *HN* 13.6.26; Athenaeus 15.689a). It was located at the end of one of the routes bringing spices and incense from India and Arabia via the Red Sea and the Nile, and perfumed oils were manufactured there from such substances (Rotroff 1997: 176; Young 2001: 51–4; Morley 2007: 96). To Alexandria we should add the successive capitals of Egypt's Mendesian nome, Mendes (Djedet, Tell el-Ruba) and probably also nearby Thmuis (Tell el Timai), both major ports on the Nile Mendesian branch known for perfume production in the 3rd century BCE (P.Cair.Zen. 1.59089; 2.59292) (Blouin 2014: 81–90; Gentelli and Medhat 2017).

Corinth was well located on the route from the eastern to the western Mediterranean. It served as a major node along the Greek trade routes that moved goods from north to south and from east to west in Greece and the adjoining islands (Thuc. 1.13.5) and also as a major node on the Phoenician trade route from west to east. Corinth was famous for its iris (*Irinum*) perfume (Plin. *HN* 13.5), which was exported in *alabastra* and *aryballoi* from the 8th–6th centuries BCE. These celebrated vessels were mass-produced in the potters' quarter at Corinth in one large factory building that housed many workshops sharing water installations and probably also kilns and a workforce. This industrial operation was no doubt orchestrated by a central institution, although questions have been raised about the identity of its operators. The potters, the artists who painted the vessels in the new Oriental style, and the traders who forwarded the products, may all have been Phoenician, judging by both the style and technique and by the vast distribution of the products, especially to the West. The iris rhizomes used to scent the oil, on the other hand, although grown around Corinth, were also probably imported from as far away as Illyrium and the Epirus Mountains, as was the case during Pliny's time in the Roman period (Plin. *HN* 21.40). The rhizomes needed to be aged for many years before they could be processed (Firmin *et al.* 1998).

The industrial manufacture of the pottery, the recognizable new decoration, the importation of materials for the scented-oil industry, and the large-scale distribution, all illustrate the elaborate nature of the trade network for perfumed-oils. Such a trade network, especially during the early and peak periods of the Corinthian operation in the 8th–7th centuries BCE, was very unlikely to have been operated by anyone but the Phoenicians. This does not mean, however, that every person involved in the stages of production and shipment of this network was Phoenician. However, the creative drive and the coordination of this network was no doubt Phoenician, as were the major potters, painters, perfumers, and traders. Although the export of Corinthian vessels reduced during the 6th century and stopped by the 5th century BCE, the production of perfumed oils continued at the site at least until the Hellenistic period and probably well into the Roman period, as reported by Plutarch (*Vit. Tim.* 14.3) (Salmon 1984: 117–18; Sherratt and Sherratt 1993: 371; Foxhall 1998: 301; Morris and Papadopoulos 1998; Brun 1999: 145).

Another major crossroads during the Hellenistic period was Delos, where a perfume factory in operation in the late 2nd to early 1st century BCE has been found. It is assumed that this factory provided goods for use primarily in the many local cult centers. The need for perfumes in Delos at this time may have been related to the growth of a population of Eastern origin on the island, and their cult. According to inscriptions from Delos, they were mainly Phoenicians. This timing also correlates with the destruction of Corinth in 146 BCE, a fact that may have stimulated the transfer of the perfume industry from there to Delos. In addition, some Arab incense dealers may have been associated with the Delian production of perfume. If so, their involvement would tend to indicate that the type of perfume produced in Delos included spices secured from their trade networks (Rotroff 1997: 176; Brun 1999: 142, 145; Frangie-Joly 2016: 46, 53). Factories that belong to the second type, in areas rich in flowers, were located during the 8th–6th centuries BCE mainly in the Greek islands of Crete, Rhodes, and Kos, and perhaps also in Samos. By the Hellenistic period, they had also been established in Cyprus (Rotroff 1997: 176).

Packaging Production (Bottles)

Bottles and other small containers for scented oils and unguents were made for the Phoenician perfumed and medicinal oils industry in the Levant, Cyprus, and the Aegean. There was also Phoenician bottle production in the central and western Mediterranean from about the mid-8th to the late 6th centuries BCE, but we have no evidence for the production of perfumed and medicinal oils in this area in the 1st millennium BCE by Phoenicians or any others. The bottles used in Phoenician contexts in the western and central Mediterranean are usually associated with burial contexts and are made of coarse ware (Orsingher 2010). The content of these bottles may have been imported from the eastern Mediterranean and poured into them. Pottery production centers in the Levantine littoral for manufacturing bottles and unguentaria operated during the Iron Age and until the Early Roman period, mainly in the northern Levant, between Beirut and Akko. During the Iron Age, primarily in the 10th–8th centuries BCE, Red Slip and Black-on-Red bottles were manufactured in Phoenicia and Cyprus. These new, empty vessels were then shipped by Phoenician traders to Crete and the Dodecanese to be filled with products manufactured there (Sherratt and Sherratt 1993: 365; Coldstream 2008: 170). During the 8th–7th centuries BCE, Rhodes was a major production center for bottles as well as perfumed oils and medicines. This is evident from the unequaled volume of importation and local production of Phoenician pottery, mainly of bottles and juglets (Bourogiannis 2014).

Plain orange bottles that had been manufactured in Phoenicia during the 8th–6th centuries BCE have been found predominantly in eastern Aegean production centers. This shape may have been copied subsequently on Samos and/or Rhodes. About the same time, in the late 8th or early 7th centuries BCE, decorated bottles started to appear in Corinth, first in the same shape as the Phoenician bottles with mushroom-rim and band decoration which were manufactured in the Levant and then in different shapes and decoration: namely, the *alabastra* and *aryballoi* that were used as perfume containers (Sherratt and Sherratt 1993: 370–1).

During the Hellenistic period, Phoenician perfumed oils were distributed in amphoriskoi, which have been found in large quantities in the eastern and central Mediterranean, in lesser quantities from the Black Sea, and in a specific form of unguentaria found only in Phoenicia and Carthage. Both vessel types were manufactured in Phoenicia. Other bottles that were probably related to the Phoenician perfume industry during the Hellenistic period were made in the ESA technique and are typical of Cyprus. These bottles were made of fine orange ware and were red-slipped from lip to mid-body or slightly lower. Such bottles are very rare in the Levant and represent the Phoenician production centers in Cyprus, the same centers perhaps that also produced Phoenician bottles for the perfumed-oil industry of the Iron Age period in the eastern Mediterranean (Hadjisavvas 1999: 602–3, fig. 9).

In addition, as already noted, at least one ingredient used to manufacture perfumed oils during the Late Bronze Age was packed in Canaanite-Phoenician amphorae of the period. *Pistacia terebinthus* resin, and perhaps also bitumen, were shipped in amphorae found aboard the Uluburun shipwreck. Various analyses[4] has demonstrated that, at least in this case, the resin was traded for its own value and did not function as an interior coating for jars containing wine (Stern *et al.* 2008). Terebinth resin has been used also as medicine, due to its anti-inflammatory qualities (Giner-Larza *et al.* 2002). These materials could have been shipped in amphorae during later times as well, at least until the end of the Classical/ Persian period.

Distribution Centers

The centers used for this network were based in the Levant and the eastern Mediterranean. They changed over time; in the Levant, they began at Ugarit and shifted eventually to Tyre and Sidon, Akko, Beyruth, Gaza, and perhaps also Kinet or Issos at Alexandretta Bay. Some of these centers operated simultaneously. In the Aegean, the earliest center was somewhere in Crete, but other centers subsequently operated on Rhodes, Samos, Delos, in Corinth, and on Cyprus, probably at Kition.

The Area of Distribution. Scented oils and unguents were distributed throughout the entire Mediterranean, but not in all locations at all times. These products have been found in Iron Age contexts in the Levant, Cyprus, Greece and the Aegean, Italy, North Africa, and the Iberian Peninsula. During the Persian period, their scope was reduced to the Levant, Cyprus, and Greece and the Aegean, while during the Hellenistic and Early Roman periods, Egypt was added to the distribution network.

Organization

This study deals with Canaanite-Phoenician networks and, therefore, focuses on its production and trade nodes. However, when talking about this Eastern network of perfumes and medicines, we cannot emphasize enough the major role played by Egypt from the Late Bronze Age or even earlier. In light of the special ties between Canaan-Phoenicia and Egypt, as described above, it is quite certain that, among other Aegyptiaca, the Canaanite-Phoenicians also traded Egyptian perfumes and medicines made in Egypt. Like other ancient Near Eastern people, they used Egyptian texts and knowledge to develop their own perfume and medicine production. Bearing in mind the itinerant, specialized craftsmen in the Bronze Age, particularly the occasion when the king of Ugarit asked the Egyptian king to send him Egyptian craftsmen (RS 88.2158), it is very likely that Egyptian masters were involved, willingly or by order, in the Mediterranean Canaanite-Phoenician perfume and medicine industry.

The complicated network for scented oils and medicines required the cooperation of several nodes around the eastern Mediterranean to work efficiently. Beginning in the 2nd millennium BCE, Canaanite-Phoenician trade in spices and incense moved overland from the East, probably via Arab caravans, to the area south of the Dead Sea as well as from Mesopotamia to the central and northern Levant. In the Hellenistic and Early Roman periods, after the Ptolemies opened the canal between the Red Sea and the Mediterranean, via the Nile, spices and incense arrived from the East by sea at Aila. They were then transported overland to the Levantine littoral and to Egypt. Ashkelon and Gaza were major Phoenician cities, and the land route might have ended at one or the other. Literary evidence from the Hellenistic and Roman periods point to Phoenician Gaza as the major hub of trade in perfume (Plut. *Vit. Alex.* 25.6–8; P.Cair.Zen. 1.59009). Then, the cargo would have been shipped by sea from Ashkelon, either directly to the Aegean factories or, more probably, via one of the more central Phoenician cities, like Tyre or Sidon. From there, the spices and incense would have been shipped to various locations for various uses. However, in earlier periods, the spice and incense route may have ended at a more northerly point along the Levantine littoral. This might have been Akko, using the trans-Jordanian route that cut west through the Beth-Shean and Jezreel Valleys to the coast, or a city even further north.

The oil that was needed in large quantities and was available in many locations was probably collected from the vicinity of each factory, although it could have been shipped, as needed, from other locations, especially from the Levant, Asia Minor, and Greece. Bitumen, which was used to waterproof containers, for mummification, as incense, and as medicine, was sourced from the Dead Sea (Nissenbaum 1999; Nissenbaum, Rullkötter, and Yechieli 2002; Pećanac *et al.* 2013). Terebinth (*Pistacia*) resin also was used for sealing containers, but primarily as a preservative and for its aromatic and medicinal qualities. It was extracted primarily from trees in the central Levant in northern Israel during the Late Bronze Age. Any *Pistacia* resin that might have continued in use beyond the Bronze Age to produce medicinal unguents would have been shipped to the factories from the Levant but perhaps also from Greece and Asia Minor (Serpico and White 2000a: 430, 434–6; Giner-Larza *et al.* 2002; Serpico *et al.* 2003: 373).

The factories that produced oils perfumed with flower extracts were located, as far as we know, primarily in the Aegean islands. Fresh flowers were needed to produce the extracts. Each factory, therefore, may have specialized in a specific scent, based on the local flora. It is unknown whether or not flowers were propagated specifically for use in the perfume industry, but, from the quantity of material needed, wild rose petals do not seem a likely option.[5]

A perfume factory in the east Aegean would have sourced oil, flowers, or herbs locally as much as possible. Additional ingredients like wine and honey were probably also secured locally, but other ingredients like spices, incense, *Pistacia* resin, and bitumen needed for a particular product, would have been imported. Such a factory also would have imported the trademark packaging containers from Phoenicia, as well as from Phoenician factories on Cyprus, designed to guarantee the quality of the product for buyers. At some point, however, some factories began to produce their own ointment vessels. This may be the case for Rhodes, Kos, and Crete, where large quantities of Phoenician Red Slip and Black-on-Red bottles were found in contexts from the 10th–8th centuries BCE and, soon afterward, were locally imitated. Some have suggested that, initially, these vessels may have been imported pre-filled with perfumed oils and that, later, local imitations may have been used to repack perfumed oils that had been imported in bulk. The underlying logic in the extra proposed repackaging step is unclear, unless it was to accommodate a larger or smaller volume than would have been available in the original bottles. This cannot be the case if the same-sized vessels were being imitated locally, however. A more plausible alternative would be that, when the volume of local production in Rhodes became significant, the bottles were both imported *and* locally made to keep up with the volume of production (Coldstream 1982: 268–9; Sherratt and Sherratt 1993: 365; Foxhall 1998: 301).

The scented oil or unguent may have been decanted into bottles at the factory, or, like wine, may have been shipped in gross in large containers to a local warehouse and distribution center, where it was decanted into bottles. It is unlikely that the scented extracts or prepared oils were shipped to Phoenicia for bottling, because no foreign packaging has been found there or at least identified as such as of yet, except for the Cretan stirrup jars in the Late Bronze Age. In the periods when Phoenician bottles served as the main official packaging for scented oils, unguents, and medicinal preparations, which was the case in the Iron Age and the Hellenistic period, Phoenician bottles were exported from Phoenicia to the production centers. Each island producing scented oils may have had its own bottling center, or there may have been one or two bottling centers that served the entire east Mediterranean.

In the Hellenistic period in particular, it seems likely that perfumed oils were forwarded in large quantities in any local amphora to regional centers, where they were decanted into the common amphoriskoi made in Phoenicia. The huge quantity and large distribution of Phoenician amphoriskoi found in this period tends to indicate that an organized, central packaging process was being used instead of packaging in each factory. If the packaging indicated the quality of the product at all, then the Phoenician perfumed oils of the Hellenistic period were not of the best quality. Perhaps it was their relative availability that made them so popular. Even so, markets would have demanded a seal of quality to persuade customers, which in this case would have been provided by a recognizable vessel that relied on the Phoenician reputation in the perfume industry.

Based on the uniformity of the pottery used for perfumed oils, it seems likely that the perfume factories organized by the Phoenician network were shipping their products to a central bottling and distribution center. This hypothesis is strengthened by the known Phoenician mode of operation for both wine and salted fish, which involved products and packaging made in different production centers as well. In the case of Phoenician wine, relatively short distances separated the inland wine production centers from the coastal amphora production centers, and it is possible the wine was added to the amphorae at the vineyard rather than in a separate, central place from which all the filled jars were then loaded directly onto boats or shipped to warehouses for loading. Nevertheless, the larger process could have been used in all three industries, even if it required the movement of the products and containers by sea over longer distances for assemblage at a central location, from which the finished products would have been sent to waiting markets.

These assumed bottling and distribution centers for perfumed oils did not remain the same from the Iron Age to the Hellenistic period. In the Iron Age, it seems that one such center operated at Samos or Kos and another may have operated in Cyprus, although the latter may have been only one of the production locations of fine-ware bottles. Starting in the late 7th–6th centuries BCE, the bottling and distribution center transferred westward, perhaps as a result of political disturbances in Phoenicia that shut down the mass production of pottery there for a period of time. In addition, a perceived need might have developed to avoid the control and taxation of the Neo-Babylonian and then Persian imperial domains established in the eastern Aegean.

The bottling and distribution center eventually moved to Corinth. The city's importance as a major industrial and distribution center in the perfumed-oils network is demonstrated not only by the fact that it was known to have produced both the containers and the product, but also by the fact that it was home to several other industries. These included a dyed-fabric industry, the production of roof tiles and architectural ornaments, and the supply of other building materials. All these products were widely exported throughout Greece and dominated the Greek market, fortifying Corinth's position from the 8th–4th centuries BCE as a major center of industry and trade. In addition, literary evidence from the 5th–4th centuries BCE (Thuc. 1.120.2; Xen. *Hell.* 7.2.17–23) indicates that Corinth served as a regional distribution center for other Peloponnesian cities. Thucydides described it as an emporium (1.13.5) from where the Corinthians exported their agricultural products and imported grains and metals. Apparently, the infrastructure required for the operation of a trade network on the regional as well as international level was well established and operating at Corinth. Even during the era of Athens's supremacy in the 5th–4th centuries BCE, Corinth remained one of Greece's major ports and economic centers and served as the major one for the Peloponnese (Salmon 1984: 117–27, 131, 133).

Later in the Persian period, the Mediterranean network for perfumed oils may have ceased operation, like other economic activities that were either shut down or reduced during this period. The Persians commandeered the Phoenician ships and crew for their war needs, which meant commercial operations could not continue as widely and efficiently as before. Perfumed oils were being still produced, but their trade was limited during this time.

Beginning in the Hellenistic period, the Mediterranean was once again open to long-distance trade, and the Phoenician networks were flourishing again. A center for the perfumed-oils industry could have been established again in the eastern Aegean and could have been based in Rhodes or Delos, but also in one of the major cities at Alexandretta Bay, like Kinet or Issos, or even at Kition in Cyprus. Any major harbor city with a big Phoenician community could have operated the final bottling and international shipping.

Textual evidence from the late Hellenistic period reports the arrival of a boat from Egypt in Italy in 73–71 BCE containing cargo of purple cloth from Tyre as well as incense, perfumes, pearls, Greek wines, Asiatic slaves, and perfumers from Delos (Cic. *Verr.* 2.5.254) (Brun 1999: 145–6). The character of the mixed cargo seems typical of Phoenician merchants. The cargo may have been gathered at Alexandria, the main distribution center in the Levant during this period. This text indicates that Phoenician trade was once again active as it had been in previous centuries and also points to the likely presence of Phoenician traders and a Phoenician diaspora in Hellenistic Alexandria. In addition, it demonstrates that perfumes were still being traded by Phoenicians. If the final group mentioned in the list of cargo were indeed related to the perfume industry on Delos, which seems to be the case, the text also bears witness to the trade of perfumed oils produced in Delos by a Phoenician trade network.

IV. Salted Fish and Fish Sauce

In the Canaanite-Phoenician coastal cities, fish was a staple food, as evidenced by some archaeological records. It was also offered in rituals and documented in tombs, either eaten in funerary banquets or offered to the dead (Delgado and Ferrer 2011: 193). Recognition of the role of fish, therefore, in the diet and the identity of Canaanite-Phoenician society is imperative; it is a role that remained important in their settlements across the seas.

Fish were preserved for long-term consumption and trade in Canaan at least from the Late Bronze Age II, as recent finds from Tell Abu Hawam, south of Akko, indicate. Currently, the earliest evidence for fish preservation is found in Giza, Egypt, in tomb reliefs dated to the 3rd millennium BCE. Evidence for fish processing in the Levant in the 2nd and 1st millennia BCE is very rare, but the use of the same butchering techniques depicted in the Egyptian tomb depictions at Tell Abu Hawam, indicated by the analysis of fish remains found on site, indicates there might have been continuity in the eastern Mediterranean fish industry. From the mid-14th to mid-13th centuries BCE, Tell Abu Hawam served as an anchorage for exporting agricultural commodities. Finds from the northern Levant, Egypt, Anatolia, Cyprus, and the Aegean suggest that this site was a node on the international commerce network of the time. Over 60% of the fish remains on site come from two types of luxury fish: grouper, *Epinephelus sp.*, from the Mediterranean and Nile perch, and *Lates niloticus*, from Egypt. These fish in particular, but other types found at Tell Abu Hawam as well, may have been imported to this commercial harbor and not processed on site (Zohar and Artzy 2019).

The earliest written evidence for fish traded by Canaanite-Phoenicians is currently dated to the late 9th–8th centuries BCE. It comes from the City of David in Jerusalem, where a pool full of fish bones and Phoenician bullae has been found (Reich, Shukron, and Lernau 2007: 160–3, fig. 10). In the 7th century BCE during the reign of Assurbanipal (668–631 BCE), a tribute list of goods sent from Arvad to Assyria includes fish among the other luxury goods (Fales 2017: 254). As none of the other items shipped to Assur is new to the list of products traded by the Phoenicians, it is reasonable to assume that Canaanite-Phoenicians had traded fish for a long time prior to the mid-7th century.

Later evidence for fish processing in the Levant may be provided by a unique type of amphora with an elongated shape, a narrow mouth, and one handle, found in the area of Samaria (Stern and Magen

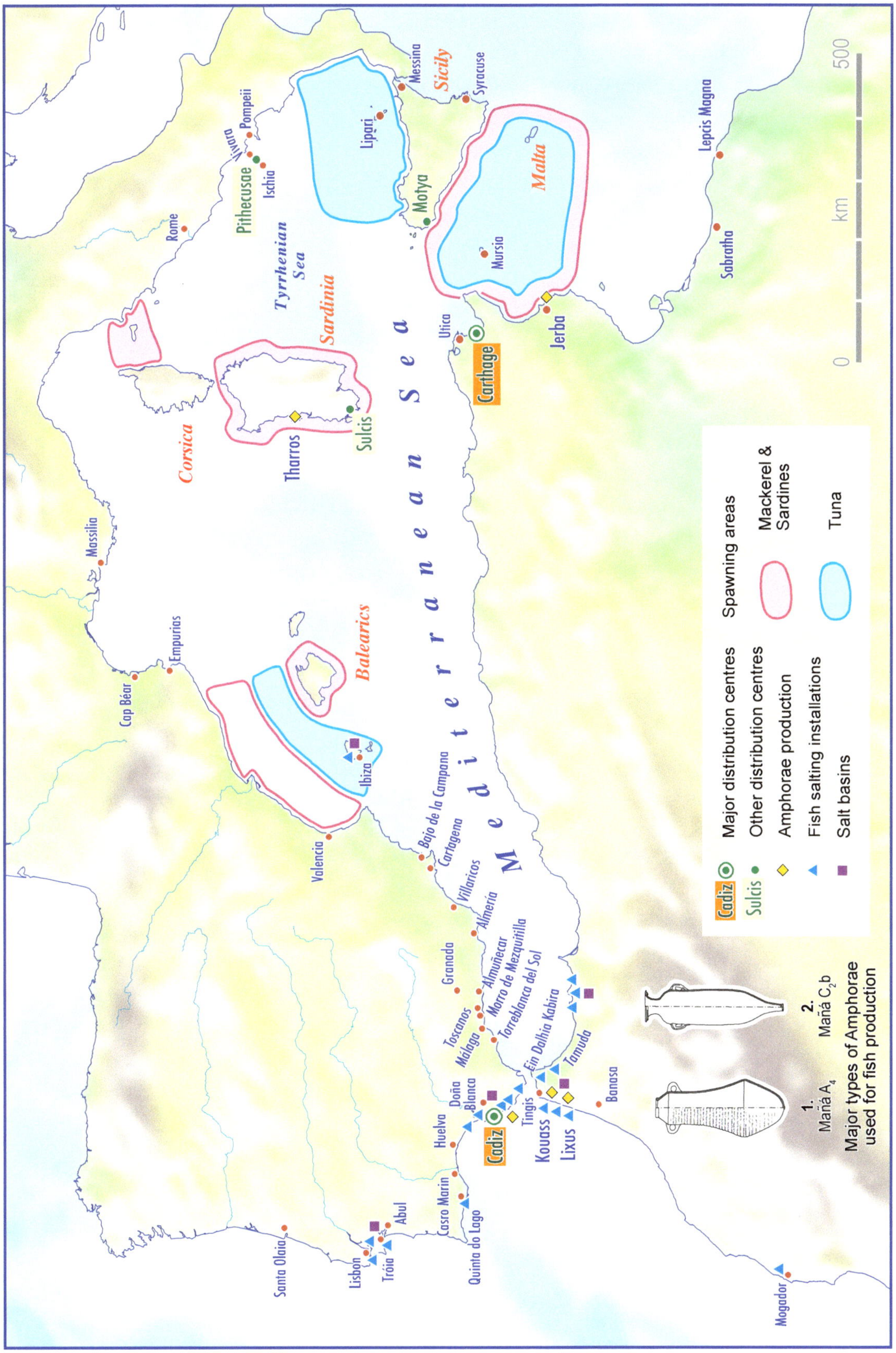

Map 4: The salted fish and fish sauce network

1984, fig. 8.3). Dated by Stern to the 5th-4th centuries BCE, this form is very close to fish amphorae from Phoenician sites in the area of Carthage (T7621), dated to the 2nd–1st centuries BCE (Ramón 1995: fig. 182.295). The Levantine forerunner has also been interpreted as a fish amphora. An example found at sea just north of Akko and dated to the 6th or 5th centuries BCE has been interpreted as an import from Egypt or North Africa. The ware of the amphora, however, is local (Raban 1976: 50, fig. 5.9). At 'Atlit, a Phoenician harbor and industrial center with seawater basins south of the Carmel Ridge, similar amphorae, though perhaps from a somewhat earlier period, have been found. This site is dated from the 8th or 7th centuries to the 5th or 4th centuries BCE, and this amphora type, although not discussed in the publication, seems earlier than the type from the area of Samaria that has been dated to the 5th–4th centuries (Raban 1996, fig. 18.5). These finds point to a continuity of fish processing and trade by the Canaanite-Phoenicians, as well as the close connection between and influence of the fish industry of the Levant on that of the Phoenician west Mediterranean.

Support for this assumption is the fact that the earliest and most enduring Canaanite-Phoenician routes in the central and western Mediterranean were found exactly within the spawning grounds of tuna fish, both red and blue. Vivara, Sicily, Ibiza, and Carthage are all sites where Canaanite-Phoenician presence has been documented, from the Late Bronze Age in the cases of Vivara and Sicily and throughout the 1st millennium BCE at all of them. The area of Ibiza and the adjacent Iberian coast, Carthage, Malta, and Sardinia are also major spawning grounds of mackerel (*Scomber scombrus*) and sardines (*Sardina pilchardus*), although more spawning areas for this species are found in the Adriatic and north Aegean Seas for both types, and also along the eastern Mediterranean coast for sardines (Pilar Tugores *et al.* 2011; Giannoulaki *et al.* 2017: fig. 3). Other areas rich in fish that have been harvested since ancient times until today are the Iberian western coast area and the islands west and south of Iberia: the Azore Islands, Madeira, and the Canary Islands (ICES-Advice 2018).

It should be noted that the names of the fish products, including the term *garum*, are only known from Greek and Roman sources from the 1st century BCE. Yet it remains unclear if *garum* was a type of fish sauce or not; fish sauce may actually have been called *liquamen* (Grainger 2018). For the time being, we have no evidence for the names of fish products in the Phoenician language or in local dialects in Spain, Sardinia, and Sicily, where fish processing took place. In later times, the Talmud contains lengthy discussions about if and when Jews could use *garum*, *garum* and vinegar (*oxygarum*), *tzir* (meaning broth), and *murias* (brine) (Babylonian Talmud, Avodah Zarah 39.2, and many other references). Residue analyses made on production vats and amphorae have revealed that fish sauce was made of mackerel, sardines, and also often mollusks, which explains the Talmudic reservation. It should also be noted that from the Bronze Age and onward, most of the fish remains found in excavations in Israel, which did not include tuna, were not caught along the Levantine coast but, rather, originated in the Sinai and Egypt.[6]

The Salted Fish Network

Fish Production

Salt was such a precious commodity that in many locations, such as ancient Egypt, its production and distribution was a royal monopoly, at least until the Roman period (Adams 2013: 272–5). Access to salt was essential for the production of salted fish, and it is thus best to locate this industry next to salt mines or beds. It is not coincidental that salted-fish installations were founded in Iberia. The quality of the salt on the Balearic Islands of Ibiza and Formentera and also at Cádiz Bay and Lisbon Bay has been celebrated since ancient times (Strab. 3.11). Of the 61 salteries (known as *cetariae* in the Roman period) counted in Iberia, 75% are located in the larger area of Cádiz and the Bay of Lisbon. Only three, however, date to the 5th–3rd centuries BCE: two in Cádiz and one at Almuñécar. Even though most of the world's salt comes from the New World and China today, Spain is still one of the largest salt producers in the world (Étienne and Mayet 2002: 18–19, 61–2, 65, fig. 12).

Salt basins also exist at Lixus and Kuass in Morocco. Sites producing salted fish and fish sauce have common geographical and architectural features all around Iberia and Morocco. In addition to these known Phoenician sites, another 15 salt sources, including salt mines, were located in this area. Some of the salt sources were adjacent to salted-fish production centers (Trakadas 2015: 127, figs. 126–7).

In addition to salt, another major component of an industrial fish-salting operation is the fish themselves, in considerable quantities. Fish bones collected in northwestern sites of Africa reveal that the following fish species were fished and processed in this area during the 6th century BCE to the 7th century CE: primarily tuna, mackerel, and sardines, but also bream, mullet, dory, and even whales and sharks, in addition to shellfish of various types (Trakadas 2015: 127, figs. 11–13).

Tuna (bluefin) is still widespread and a major source of protein in many parts of the world. Several studies that have followed the migration and reproduction patterns of tuna have revealed that, due to the specific conditions of temperature and salt concentration in the Mediterranean water, one of the major reproduction sites for tuna fish is located on the western coasts of the Balearic Islands, facing the eastern Iberian coast. Other spawning and migration sites are the area from Carthage eastward near the African coast, the area between Sicily and Naples Bay, and the islands within (Karakulak and Yildiz 2016: 320–2, fig. 2; Carruthers *et al.* 2018, figs. 4–8). Tuna fish was so important in the Phoenician sites of the West to their economy and their social organization (as attested by the fish industry associations in Cádiz area) that they also appear on coins (Di Natale 2014).

Salted fish installations were typically located at points where the spawning grounds and migratory routes of various fish types were closest to the coast, usually at river mouths, where the fresh water needed for this industry was available. In addition, at least along the western coast of Iberia, the land was not suitable for agriculture. Thus, people there had to turn to the sea for a livelihood. As this was barren land, it may have been uninhabited or thinly populated when the Phoenicians arrived there and chose to establish fish-salting factories in the area (Étienne, Mayet, and Taveres da Silva 2000; Trakadas 2005: 51, 69–70; Souter 2008: 275–6).

Remains of installations used to salt fish in western Iberia include rectangular preservation tanks and square, sealed vats dug into the ground. Some examples of rounded vats have also been found that were perhaps used to manufacture salted fish or meat, while the square and rectangular vats may have been used to produce *garum*. The vats were located close to the sea for the convenient offloading of the daily catch from the fishing boats. They were made in different sizes at each site and often surrounded a courtyard. In southern Spain, the installations were located outside the city, distant from the settlements, because of the smell they produced. In eastern Iberia, however, where most of the salteries were founded by the Romans, the factories were associated with villas. Close to 30 fish factories have been identified in the Bay of Cádiz, dated from the late 6th to the 1st centuries BCE, often associated with kilns and fish dumps (Bernal Casasola and Sáez Romero 2008: 107–9).

Almost 30 fish-salting sites have been identified thus far in northwestern Africa, dating from the late 6th century BCE to the 7th century CE, although production reduced dramatically in the 3rd century CE. These sites were associated, at least in their early phases, with a Phoenician presence. Some were adjacent to salt sources and some to amphorae production sites dating from the 6th century BCE to the 1st century CE (Trakadas 2015: 127, 136–7, figs. 124–5). In North Africa, some of the production sites were associated with villas while others, like those at Kuass and Lixus, were located outside the cities. This pattern seems to be the greatest change introduced to this industry by the Romans; while Phoenician cities were integrated into the social and economic fabric of Iberia and promoted it, the Romans had no interest in settling in or integrating into the land. Instead, the Romans founded fish-salting factories, complete with an owner's villa, in Iberia, North Africa, and the Black Sea during the 1st–5th centuries CE.

Until recently, it has been assumed that most of the production sites that have been excavated date to the Roman period. Even if that were the case, it certainly does not indicate that the phenomenon originated during the Roman period or was introduced into the western Mediterranean by the Romans. In fact, Roman installations were built on top of earlier Phoenician installations, many of which were probably damaged during the Second Punic War and the Roman takeover of Iberia from the Phoenicians (Trakadas 2005: 49, 52–7, 66; Souter 2008: 277). This is not the only case in which the Romans annexed a preceding Phoenician industry; they did the same for the metal trade. The trade and exploitation of metal sources, especially silver and tin, in Iberia and elsewhere in the Mediterranean, was predominantly in Phoenician hands until the 3rd century BCE, as reflected in the variety of metals used at Carthage. Until the same date, the Romans had very limited access to metal sources in the Mediterranean, and none to those in Iberia. However, the decline of available sources in Carthage is contemporaneous with an increase in Roman access to Mediterranean mines, especially the silver mines of Iberia (Kaufman *et al.* 2019: 4098).

Salting installations are unknown archaeologically in Italy before the 1st century BCE, and the earliest literary evidence mentions such factories in southern Italy only from the 4th century BCE. The Romans operated fish-salting installations in Iberia, North Africa, Sicily, and Gaul, following the Canaanite-Phoenician footprints in all aspects of production and distribution (Curtis 2001: 404, 411). As such, the location of Roman salted-fish factories may indicate not only that Iberia had been a major production center in the 1st millennium BCE but that North Africa and, on a smaller scale, Sicily and Gaul, were as well. Gaul, however, probably had not been part of the Phoenician trade network.

In addition to the salteries in the western Mediterranean, other Roman installations were operated in the Black Sea region, where they also would have built upon earlier, non-Phoenician factories. A 1st-century-CE, Roman-era factory with installations for fish-salting, similar to those found in Iberia, was found in 2019 about 2 km northwest of the ancient Canaanite-Phoenician city of Ashkelon.[7] This factory may point to the existence of fish-salting facilities in other Phoenician Levantine cities that predate the Roman period. At the very least, this find points to the implementation of Phoenician proficiency in fish-salting and the foundation of such an industry in an area populated by Phoenicians. The area of Ashkelon was a major Phoenician industrial hub which also produced wine during the Roman and Late Roman periods, attested by amphorae kilns found on site (Regev 2020: 43–50).

Although the Romans were following earlier footprints, mainly with regard to production centers, their economy was entirely different from Phoenician commercial orientation, goals, and needs. While the latter revolved around the shipment and distribution of goods in a trade network designed for the prosperity and profit of all parties and locations involved, the Roman economy focused on the need to feed the Roman army and enrich the Romans. The needs and benefit of local populations was never considered.

Fish Products Manufacturing in Iberia. Another possible marker of the location of sites involved in the ancient salted-fish industry may be the presence of large quantities of murex shells used in the dyeing industry. The two industries seem to have been connected and may have used the same installations. Such heaps of murex shells have been found in Almuñécar, where salted-fish installation also are known, as well as at Toscanos, Morro de Mezquitilla, Barcelona, and Torreblanca del Sol (Lowe 2004: 46).

At the site of San Fernando at Cádiz, the industrial stage of salting fish began no later than the last quarter of the 6th century BCE. This stage was preceded by an earlier period that lasted a century (i.e. from the late 7th to the late 6th century BCE), during which the local Phoenician residents salted fish for domestic use and did not accumulate surpluses for commercial purposes (Muñoz Vicente and De Frutos Reyes 2009: 83). Tagomago on Ibiza was an important center of production, the products from which were distributed in the central Mediterranean in the 5th century BCE (Sáez Romero 2017: 243). Phoenician salting installations dating between the 6th and 2nd centuries BCE have been found in the Cádiz area along with Phoenician amphorae of the types Mañá A4, and Mañá C and D, which contained fish remains. The same amphora type has been found at Corinth in the mid-5th century BCE. Salted fish was being produced in the Cádiz area sometime before the 6th century BCE, perhaps already starting in the 9th–8th centuries BCE (Curtis 2001: 319–20; Zimmerman Munn 2003: 200; Trakadas 2005: 48; Bernal Casasola and Sáez Romero 2008).

In the Hellenistic period, Cyprus, Samos, Kos, Egypt, Sicily, and Iberia were fish-production centers. The Zenon archive from the 3rd century BCE (P.Col. 3.2; P.Lond. 7.2141; P.Cair.Zen. 59682; 59012; 59013) and Diodorus Siculus (Diod. Sic. 1.36.1) in the 1st century BCE provide literary evidence of salted-fish production and distribution during the Hellenistic period. Notably, their lists do not include Iberia and North Africa, where fish products are known to have been processed from the Iron Age until the Hellenistic period. The production of salted fish in Phoenician installations in Iberia was interrupted ca. 200 BCE, after Carthage had lost its control over this area following the second Punic War. It was not resumed for about a century, when the Romans built new installations (Curtis 2001: 321; Trakadas 2005: 49).

Fish Products Manufacturing in North Africa. The salted-fish installations of North Africa stretched from the Mediterranean near Gibraltar to the Atlantic coast, primarily near Gibraltar but also as far south as the islands of Mogador (Essaouira). All were areas rich in fish. Large quantities of murex shells have been found in Sabratha and on the island of Mogador. However, salting installations in North Africa have been dated only to the Roman period and later. This is the case even at Kuass, where a kiln producing fish amphorae that is dated to the late 6th century BCE onwards has been found on site and associated with the salted-fish industry. Evidence that fish-filled amphorae were shipped from this site to Corinth in the 5th century BCE is provided by the excavation of such jars in that port city (Curtis 2001: 319; Lowe 2004: 46; Trakadas 2005: 64, 73).

Packaging Production: Amphorae

Dried, salted fish was packaged in non-traceable, perishable containers, but salted fish and fish sauce were packed and transported in sealed amphorae that can be traced. Evidence from the Roman period shows that fresh fish also were traded in fish tanks carried by boats, but these vessels have not been traced archaeologically. Obviously, we have very little evidence regarding the packaging of perishable materials. By necessity, then, most of the discussion has to be based on the amphorae used for fish products (Mazzorin 2000: 162).

It is commonly assumed that most amphora types contained only one type of commodity. The amphorae used for fish products were uniform and identifiable, as clearly seen in the amphorae produced on the Iberian Peninsula that contained fish products from the 6th century BCE onwards. Other amphora types used to package fish in other locations and from earlier times remain under-studied, although two amphora types from Cádiz dated to the 8th to mid-6th centuries BCE has been suggested to have served as fish amphorae (Bernal Casasola and Sáez Romero 2008: 109).

Garum amphorae of the 1st century CE had an average of 27.9 liters per unit; while this information is not necessarily comparable to earlier times, it should be noted that contemporary wine amphorae contained an average of 29 liters per unit and oil amphorae contained an average of 65.5 liters per unit (Ejstrud 2005: 177, table 3; Lund and Gabrielsen 2005: 162–3). If this ratio had also been characteristic of earlier times, we should expect the salted-fish amphorae to have been somewhat smaller than wine amphorae and less than half the size of oil amphorae. These proportions make sense, based on the nature and use of the products. Olive oil, used in cooking and for various cosmetic purposes, would have been consumed in larger volumes than wine and definitely in larger quantities than salted fish, which would have been used in small amounts at a time.

Archaeological evidence from the Roman period shows that, although salted fish products were produced in huge quantities on the Atlantic shores of Iberia, as they also had been during the Archaic to Hellenistic periods (8th–2nd centuries BCE), amphorae produced in this area were not distributed outside of it, southeastward into the Mediterranean. As such an enormous amount of salted fish could not have been locally consumed, this phenomenon has led to the inevitable conclusion that, during the Roman period, salted-fish products from western Iberia were shipped to Cádiz, where they were packed (or repacked) in identifiable fish amphorae. All salted-fish products that had been shipped from Iberia and North Africa to Cádiz for distribution were labeled "Gaditanian." This organizational scheme explains the lack of any textual reference to the production of salted fish in North Africa but the extensive reference to the salted fish of Gades/Cádiz.

Since the Romans used both the production centers and the distribution routes of earlier periods, it is reasonable to assume that, during the era when Phoenicians operated the salted-fish trade network, the products of west Iberian salteries were, likewise, shipped to Cádiz and packed for distribution at that location. Similarly, the existence of the *garum sociorum*, the organization that shipped salted-fish products under a brand name throughout the Roman Empire, could be used to suggest analogously that, during the earlier period, a single organization working for the Phoenician trade network had coordinated the entire salted-fish network (Trakadas 2005: 75; Teichner and Pons Pujol 2008: 304–5).

Such a sophisticated modus operandi was probably not restricted to western Iberia and the distribution center of Cádiz; it might also have represented the protocol used between Cádiz and Lixus and other production centers on the Atlantic shore of Africa. If so, centralized pottery workshops would have been set up and operated in coastal locations at river mouths, where water, clay, and wood were plentiful. And, indeed, as of 2008, 29 kiln sites producing amphorae from the 6th to 2nd centuries BCE had been counted in the Cádiz bay area. This number almost doubled during the Roman period, in the 1st century BCE to 5th century CE, and reflects the massive growth of markets and production of salted-fish products (Bernal Casasola and Sáez Romero 2008: 106, 109–11). The same protocol was probably characteristic of other Phoenician trade-nets, especially the one involving perfumed oils and medicinal preparations, which had also been packed in identifiable bottles (Teichner and Pons Pujol 2008: 305–8).

Amphorae Production in North Africa for Fish Products. Evidence from the Roman period shows that some of the main production centers of salted-fish products were located in northwestern Africa, mainly on the Atlantic. Thus far, kilns producing amphorae for fish products, dating from the 6th century BCE to the 1st century CE, have been found at 15 sites. Some of the kilns were in fish-salting sites, and some were located at a distance (Trakadas 2015: 127, figs. 128–9). At Kuass, fish amphorae were produced in local kilns that have been dated from the late 6th–1st centuries BCE. They include types Mañá A4, C and an earlier type, Kuass I (Pardo 1990). The type known variously as Mañá D, Cintas 315, and Ramón T-4.2.1.2 and 4.2.1.5 was a hole-mouthed, long and narrow amphora produced in Kuass from the 5th/4th century BCE perhaps until the 2nd century BCE. It was widely distributed in the western Mediterranean and North Africa and probably contained salted fish, although this is not certain. This Punic amphora was also produced at Tharros in Sardinia from the late 4th–early 3rd centuries BCE. Filled jars produced in Tharros have been found on the northeastern side of the island at Olbia containing fish remains (Cavaliere 2000; Delussu and Wilkens 2000: 53–5, fig. 1).

Africana types I and II were manufactured in North Africa and started to dominate the Roman import market in the 3rd century CE. Both types may have contained fish products. Africana I may have been used for olive oil, but Africana IIA was not (Panella 1968: 101–4; Bonifay 2004: 107, 111; Trakadas 2005: 74).

Amphora Types Produced in Both North Africa and Spain. Production in the Iron Age Period. At least one type, Ramon's T-10.1.2.1, and perhaps also T-10.1.1.1, dated to the 8th–mid-6th centuries BCE, has been identified as a fish amphora in the area of Cádiz and dated there to the 7th century BCE (Bernal Casasola and Sáez Romero 2008: 53–5). This type is very common in the Phoenician west and may provide additional evidence of an early fish trade network.

Production in the Classical Period. The main type found at Corinth is Mañá A3–4 (Mañá-Pascual A4), which has an average capacity of 45 liters. In Carthage, this hole-mouth, neckless, narrow fish amphora from southern Spain is dated approximately to the last third of the 5th century BCE and continued in use into the early 4th century BCE. Punic amphorae were manufactured in southern Iberia, North Africa, and Sardinia. This type was produced from the 6th or 5th to the early 4th centuries BCE on both sides of the Straits of Gibraltar, along the Atlantic coast of Morocco, and in Spain. The same type was produced at Kuass from the 5th–3rd centuries BCE in two variants: one with rounded shoulders and one with carinated shoulders (Pardo 1990: 13–15, figs. 1.II, 2.III; Ramón 1995: 233–7; Trakadas 2005: 78; Bechtold 2008: 16, 52, fig. 5.49–51, 53).

Production in the Hellenistic Period. A type known as Mañá C2/Ramon 7.3.0.0/Cintas 312/313 (Van der Werff 1), with two sub-types, was produced in the Hellenistic period starting in the 3rd century BCE at Banasa, on the bank of the Sebou river in northwest Morocco. In the 2nd century BCE, it was also produced at Kuass (Trakadas 2015: 128–30). Type C2a was typical of central North Africa. It is the characteristic amphora found in the destruction levels of Carthage in the mid-2nd century BCE and was produced between 175 and 125 BCE. Type C2b (Dressel 18), of similar dates, was produced in the kilns of Tamuda in northwest Africa. This type was considered to have originated only in North Africa at Carthage and Kuass but is now known also from Cádiz.

Some seals on the amphora type Dressel 1C were written in Punic script and some in Latin; they date from the late 2nd to the late 1st centuries BCE, a period when Iberia was already under Roman control. Some bear a stamp reading SOC or SOCI, which refers to the *societas cetariorum*, the association of producers of fish products. Others bear the stamp SCG, an abbreviation for either *socii cetarii Gaditani* or for *societas cetariorum Gaditanorum*. The term *cetarius* referred to a person who worked with tuna and other fish and their salted fish and derivatives, whether a fisherman, producer or vendor, while *cetarium* designated the container in which fish was packaged and *cetaria* the fish factory. Thus, the abbreviation SCG would refer both to the owners of the facilities located in the Baelo district and to the owners of the traps set along the adjoining coasts (Barrios 2014: 98, 104). An amphora of this type was found with an inscription indicating it contained *garum* fish sauce (*hallex*), and other amphorae of this type found at Cerro del Mar and Belo (Málaga) contained fish bones (Carre 1995: 253; Étienne and Mayet 2002: 110–13, fig. 26).

Mañá C2 was also produced on the island of Jerba from the early 2nd–1st centuries BCE during the island's Late Punic period (250–50 BCE). Jerba was already inhabited by Phoenicians in the 6th century BCE and exhibited Phoenician/Punic culture until the mid-1st century BCE and the Roman conquest. Nonetheless, the use of this amphora in Jerba to contain fish products has been rejected, due to the distance of the kilns from the coast and the non-existence of salteries on Jerba. They have been considered containers for oil and wine instead. Nonetheless, these amphorae could easily have been exported from Jerba to the Tunisian coast, where salteries did exist. Amphorae of this type have been found at Delos in a house used for the production of perfumes in a context dating to the late 2nd or early 1st century BCE (Brun 1999: 113, fig. 22.40–1; Fentress 2001: 253–68; Fentress *et al.* 2009: 35; Fontana *et al.* 2009: 271–7).

Mañá C1b/Van der Werff 3 was produced in the area of Carthage, Tripolitania, and perhaps also at Byzacene on Jerba. Its period of manufacture ran from the first half of the 3rd century until the early 2nd century BCE (Carre 1995: 251, fig. 75.545).

Mañá C1/2 is dated to the last quarter of the 3rd to the early/mid-2nd century BCE. An example of this type was found in Bolsena, Italy with a round stamp on the shoulder depicting a cluster of grapes. As these amphorae were known for their fish content, the grapes may indicate that this amphora contained fish preserved in wine. Residue analysis has indicated that, during the Roman period, fish was also preserved in vinegar. This vessel type, as well as the Mañá C2 type, was usually stamped with a Baal-Tinnit sign or with Punic or Greek letters (Carre 1995: 252, fig. 75.546; García Vargas and Bernal Casasola 2009: 147).

Amphora Types Produced in the Iberian Peninsula. Iberian-Punic amphorae in general were produced in Iberia from the 6th–2nd centuries BCE. Some contained wine. Workshops producing amphorae to contain salted fish were located mainly around Cádiz, but many other workshops were scattered along the coasts of southern Spain and Portugal. A few others were located on the northern part of the eastern coast. The sites date to the Roman period, and most of them produced Dressel 7–11 amphorae, which were characteristic of Iberia in the Early Roman period. Of the 75 workshops noted, 11 also produced Dressel 18/Mañá C2b amphorae that belonged to the Punic tradition and dated to the late Hellenistic period. All 11 workshops were located in Cádiz. Dozens of shipwrecks have been found in the western Mediterranean from Cádiz to Rome with such Roman amphorae on board, providing reliable testimony for the vast popularity of Iberian salted fish and *garum*. Large quantities of these vessels were found near Marseille and many also between Corsica, Sardinia, and the Etruscan shore (Étienne and Mayet 2002: 159–77, figs. 49, 61). This distribution, although revealing for the location of Roman legions and other Roman population foci, cannot help much in determining earlier destinations of Phoenician salted fish amphorae.

Production in the Iron Age. It seems that amphorae production in Iberia, either for salted fish or other products, did not begin before the 8th century BCE. The amphorae used in this industry at the beginning stages were probably local imitations of Phoenician amphorae: for example, the T-10.1.2.1 type mentioned above (Bernal Casasola and Sáez Romero 2008, fig. 2.1–2).

Production in the Classical Period. Information has already been given above on Mañá A3–4 (Mañá-Pascual A4) in the subsection "Amphora Types Produced in Both North Africa and Spain".

Production in the Hellenistic Period. Information on the type known as Dressel 18/Mañá C2b has been presented above in the subsection, "Amphora Types Produced in Both North Africa and Spain". Another type, Dressel 12, also originated from Iberia. A few examples from a shipwreck dated to the 1st century BCE near Cap Béar, a little south of Perpignan on the eastern Mediterranean coast of France, were found with fish remains. The condition of the fish bones in these amphorae indicates they contained conserved fish slices, not fish sauce (Desse and Desse-Berset 2000: 79–80, 93).

Production in the Roman Period. Dressel type 1C/12 has been dated to the second half of the 1st century BCE. It was sometimes marked SCG (*socii cetarii Gaditani* or *societas cetariorum Gaditanorum*), a stamp already introduced in the 2nd century BCE, which confirms its association with the salted-fish industry at Cádiz (Étienne and Mayet 2002: 113–18, figs. 27–8). Dressel type 21/22, dated from the second half of the 1st century BCE to the 1st century CE, was also produced in the area of Cádiz (Étienne and Mayet 2002: 120–2, fig. 30), as were Dressel types 7–11. The production of types 7–10 all began at the end of the 1st century BCE but they had varying termination dates for their manufacture in the 1st century CE. Dressel 7 is thought to have ceased production in the mid-1st century CE, Dressel 8 in the early 1st century CE, Dressel 9 in the last quarter of the 1st century CE, and Dressel 10 in the mid-1st century CE or somewhat later. Dressel 11 is the latest and shortest-lived of this series. It is dated to the second half of the 1st century CE (Étienne and Mayet 2002: 122–6, figs. 31–2).

Amphorae of Dressel types 7 and 9 were recovered with fish remains from a shipwreck near Sud Perduto off the southern coast of Corsica. They contained bones that were consistent with their having held conserved fish slices again, like the Dressel 12 jars from the wreck near Cap Béar, not *garum* fish sauce (Étienne and Mayet 2002: 75–9, 93). Beltrán type II was also typical of the production in the vicinity of the Bay of Cádiz. It might have been manufactured at Gibraltar. It is dated from 25 CE to ca. 150 CE (Étienne and Mayet 2002: 126–30, figs. 33–5).

Dressel type 14 was produced in both Spain and Portugal. Type 14A was manufactured initially in the area of Málaga but also later around Cádiz. Its dates of production are thought to have run from the first quarter of the 1st century to the end of the 2nd century CE. Type14B was manufactured around Lusitania from the end of the 1st to the mid-2nd centuries CE. One site of production has been identified at Tróia, next to the *garum* tanks, but other sites would have existed as well (Étienne and Mayet 2002: 81, 133–5, fig. 37; Souter 2008: 276–7, table 3). Dressel type 17 was produced in many workshops in southern Spain. It has been dated primarily to the second half of the 1st century CE (Étienne and Mayet 2002: 135–6, fig. 38).

Finally, in the Late Roman period, centers in Spain and Portugal produced a range of amphora types: Almagro 50 and 50A in south Spain, 50B in Portugal, 50C at Quinta do Lago in the Algarve region of Portugal next to *garum* tanks, Beltrán 27, Almagro 51c, Almagro 51a–b, Sado 1, and Sado 2 in one or the other region. All are dated to the 3rd–5th centuries CE (Étienne and Mayet 2002: 137–51, figs. 39–46; Souter 2008: 277, table 3).

Distribution Area and the Centers of Cádiz and Corinth

The salted-fish and fish-sauce products manufactured in the western Mediterranean could not have been packed and distributed eastward via a private or semi-private enterprise. These operations required capital as well as mercantile and organizational skills considerably greater than those possessed by the local Iberian and North African societies (Bekker-Nielsen 2002: 34). The necessary requirements were fulfilled by the Phoenician salted-fish network. Like its other industrial networks, it used major distribution centers from which products were shipped to smaller distribution centers. The main distribution centers of this salted-fish and fish-sauce network were Corinth and Cádiz.

During the Classical period, Corinth functioned as the major distribution center in the eastern Mediterranean for the Phoenician salted-fish network operating from Carthage. As a major distribution center of the Aegean, Corinth was also the destination center of salted fish shipped from the Black Sea (Möller 2007: 365). With the fall of Corinth and Carthage in 146 BCE, the Phoenician salted-fish network was taken over by the Romans.

Corinth provides evidence for the existence of a well-organized network for both the production and distribution of preserved fish in the 5th century BCE. About 40% of the amphorae found in the excavated Corinthian warehouse are Punic. Many contain the remains of preserved fish cut into small pieces inside. The containers for the preserved fish were manufactured at Phoenician bases in Kuass and Lixus in modern Morocco and then shipped empty to Cádiz in Spain, where the fish industry centers were located. There they were filled with their edible products and sent eastwards. The trade route extended from Cádiz to Emporias and from Ibiza to Sardinia. There, it divided in two, with one branch heading directly to Italy and the other heading via Sicily to Greece, where Corinth served as the main port of entry for this product. Greek literature of the 5th–4th centuries BCE confirms that salted fish from Cádiz was exported to Greece (Eupolis 310, fr. 186; Nikostratos 220, fr.4; Antiphanes 43, fr. 77) (Cabrera 1998: 201; Curtis 2001: 318–19; Zimmerman Munn 2003: 200–9; Trakadas 2005: 48).

After the publication of the excavation results from the Corinthian warehouse for amphorae, the identity of the traders remains debated. Both Greeks and Punic-Phoenicians have been proposed as logical candidates (Zimmerman Munn 2003). Given the elaborate network that involved several known Phoenician bases at Kuass, Lixus, and Cádiz, it was more likely to have been operated by Phoenicians than Greeks in the Classical period. It also seems that the salted-fish network was held by Phoenicians at least during part of the Hellenistic period, when Carthage, the coordinator between all three above-mentioned Phoenician bases, still existed. The proposal made by Morris and Papadopoulos regarding a Phoenician presence in Corinth beginning in the Archaic period (800–480 BCE) should be highlighted again. They maintain that Phoenicians not only were stationed in Corinth but that they initiated the local pottery industry there and operated trade in salted-fish and fish-sauce products around the Mediterranean during the Archaic period. Support for their view is provided by an inscription naming the Phoenician deity Ashtart on a sherd of pottery found during excavations at Corinth and dated to the late 5th century BCE (Morris and Papadopoulos 1998; SEG, 36: 316). It seems, then, that the Phoenician presence in Corinth was far more substantial than hitherto believed.

As attested by Phoenician finds and literary evidence of a Phoenician diaspora in some of these locations, other distribution centers of this network in the Geometric/Archaic/Iron Age period included Pithecusae, Rhodes, and somewhere in Egypt. During the Classical/Persian and the Hellenistic periods, the distribution centers were still Corinth and Rhodes, as well as Memphis or Naukratis and, later, Alexandria. The Etruscan distribution center at Pithecusae was replaced in the 6th century BCE by one or more centers in Sicily, and probably also new distribution centers on Sardinia and Malta. In addition to its role as a consumer and coordinator of the entire trade network, Carthage served as the major distribution center for salted fish for the routes leading north to Sicily, Italy, and Sardinia and east to Crete, Egypt, and the Levant. In the Levant, the distribution centers were Ashkelon and Akko in the south, Tyre and/or Sidon, Beirut or Arwad, and Al-Mina (later replaced by cities in Alexandretta Bay) in the north. All were Canaanite-Phoenician cities. Salted fish and fish sauce were shipped throughout the entire Mediterranean.

Organization

Based on current archaeological data, the fish factories were located primarily in Iberia but also in North Africa, in the Gibraltar Circle area. However, based on the location of fish-spawning areas, salt basins, and Phoenician fish-amphorae production sites, fish factories were probably also located in the Balearic Islands, Sardinia, Sicily, Malta, and on the coast between Carthage and the Bay of Jerba. All Iberian fish products were sent to Cádiz, where they were packed in the trademark amphorae produced around that local area. Details of the types have been covered in earlier subsections. From Cádiz, the fish amphorae were shipped for consumption in some instances directly to locations along the trade routes but mostly to secondary distribution centers, like Corinth in the 5th century BCE. A part of the Iberian production was intended for local consumption, but the majority of the product was destined for Carthage and other Phoenician/Punic settlements and trading posts on the central Mediterranean islands.

The Iberian factories flourished during the 5th–4th centuries BCE and until the Hellenistic era. Production reduced in volume during the Hellenistic period and ceased after the Second Punic War (218–202 BCE), which ended Carthaginian-Phoenician control in Spain. These facts show that Carthage was a major player in the salted-fish network, acting as the organizer and synchronizer of the entire network. While the Mediterranean was dominated by Phoenician and Punic fleets, the network operated at full capacity. When Greek rule over the eastern Mediterranean cut or disabled much of the trade between the Phoenicians of the East and those of the West, the salted-fish network experienced reduced activity. When Iberia was no longer under Carthaginian rule, the production and distribution of salted fish from Iberia ceased until the entire network was taken over by Rome. Meanwhile, other Phoenician bases started to produce salted fish in Sicily, Cyprus, Samos, and Kos. The Egyptian production of Nile salted fish increased during the Hellenistic period. As for the fish production taking place in North Africa, the data here are more complicated. Fish processing was carried out in northwestern Africa, mainly on the Atlantic shores of modern Morocco. Lixus and Kuass were the production centers on the Atlantic shores of Africa, producing salted fish and probably also amphorae. Production centers north of Lixus would have forwarded their products either north to Cádiz or south to Lixus to be packed in amphorae (Curtis 2001: 319–21).

Other, smaller, production areas (the Balearic, Sardinia, Sicily, and Malta) sent their products to Carthage, to be repacked and distributed. These areas are the richest in fish within the Mediterranean, and Sardinia produced its own fish amphorae. Other fish amphorae were produced in Jerba south of Carthage, which was also adjacent to one of the richest fishing zones. It is reasonable to assume, then, that an operation for fish products, similar to that of the Gibraltar Circle with Cádiz as its center, was based in Carthage during the same period.

The trade network of fish products was an extensive and lucrative operation at least from the 6th–5th centuries BCE onward, much before its products became the famous, staple food of every Roman household in the Roman Empire (Trentacoste, Nicholson, and Mylona 2018). The Phoenician trade network spread over vast areas in the Mediterranean and the west Atlantic Ocean, and it was probably Greeks who operated a smaller fish-products network between the Aegean and the Black Sea. The Phoenician network was operated by many people along the chain, from fishermen to workers in fish factories, potters producing amphorae, workers in packaging and distributing, seamen on boats transporting the products, and merchants in distribution centers. Some of the network products were extremely expensive, depending on the origin and prestige of the factory, which sealed its goods with a trademark, i.e. a specific amphora. It is no wonder, then, that the Romans used the famous Phoenician factories with their specific products, in their specific amphorae, to continue production and benefit from their fame and price long after the entire network was no longer in Phoenician hands.

—7—

Conclusions

Known in external sources of the Late Bronze Age as Canaanites, in those of the Iron Age as Phoenicians, and in those of the Classical, Hellenistic and Roman periods as both Phoenicians and Carthaginians, all Phoenicians were Canaanites, as ancient DNA tests have shown. In their internal sources, however, the Canaanite-Phoenicians call themselves either by their city name, i.e. Tyrians, Sidonians, Arwadians, etc., or by their collective name, Canaanites. Carthaginians, the western Phoenicians, were also known as Punes. The designation "Phoenician" comes from the Egyptian word *fnhw*, which means a shipbuilder or carpenter. As a term related to people from Syria and the Levant, it is first attested in the Old Kingdom period in Egypt in the middle of the 3rd millennium BCE.

The Canaanite-Phoenicians lived in Canaan-Phoenicia, a term that is synonymous with the Levant and which designates the entire eastern Mediterranean coast and some adjacent hinterland, from Alexandretta Bay in the north to Rhinokorura (El-'Arish) in the south. Similarities in pottery, architecture, metal vessels, figurines, and religious symbols from the Late Bronze Age into the Iron Age demonstrate that the Iron Age Phoenicians were the direct successors of the Bronze Age Canaanites. By the Late Bronze Age, the Canaanite-Phoenician culture was a fusion of Canaanite, Egyptian, Hittite, and Mesopotamian cultures. The new combination merged into a familiar Phoenician style which spread throughout the Mediterranean. The Canaanite-Phoenician ethnic, political, and religious identity terminated with the rise of Islam and the conquest of their homeland in the Levant.

Phoenician trade networks are best characterized using Abner Cohen's concept of a trade diaspora, and by accepting that a few mechanisms of trade and exchange coexisted in developed societies, like that of the Canaanite-Phoenicians society. In their civilization, the city-state, through its palace and temple institutions, was both the motivator and administrator of Canaanite-Phoenician trade. In addition, franchises were given to elite members who served as financiers, investors, traders, and directors of trading posts in remote nodes on the trade network. When resident in foreign lands, Phoenician merchants created associations called *mrzht* (plural; singular: *mrzh*) which were used to reinforce the affiliation between its members. Made up mainly of merchants, sailors, settlers, artisans, and craftsmen, the Phoenician trade diaspora did not act as, nor consider itself to be, a colonial power. Rather, *migration* and *diaspora* are terms believed to be more appropriate to a current understanding of Mediterranean mobility (Donnellan and Nizzo 2016).

Two examples of documented diasporas have been presented to demonstrate how trade diasporas have operated from the Middle Bronze Age to the modern era, using similar mechanisms and practices. These are: the Mesopotamian trade network known from the Karum Kanesh texts; and the Jewish trade network known from the Cairo Geniza. Although the same type of textual evidence is lacking for the earlier Canaanite-Phoenician trade diaspora, material remains relating to the production and distribution of certain goods indicate that it, too, shared the same modus operandi. These networks shared a solidarity based on ethnic identity, language, and religion; the use of distribution centers; the introduction of religion, rituals and social organizations at the new host location; the restricted participation by a few elite families in the trade; the longevity of the trade network and its nodes; the migration of artisans; and the use of merchants' representatives.

Canaanite-Phoenician trade and networks were sophisticated complex systems that operated for millennia. Only some of the networks have been presented in this book, and much work remains to be done on these, as well as others that have not yet been tackled. The main intention of this study has been to provide an outline of some traceable Canaanite-Phoenician trade networks and to present known details of their operation: the wine network, the network for scented oils and medicines, the network for salted fish and fish sauce, and the network for pottery. The discussion of each trade network includes the geographical scale of the operation, the likely sources of the raw materials required, the production sites of the vessels in which the product was distributed, the locations where packaging for the product were situated, and the location of likely distribution centers for the finished goods. The last two elements were often the same place, but not always.

Each of the networks discussed here operated on a somewhat different level of complexity, involving different particularities, geographical spheres, and spans of time. All, however, were based on a diaspora trade-net, a vital element without which the network could not operate or have control over all parts of the operation, from collecting the raw materials to the production of the finished product in trademarked packaging. All the networks were orchestrated by the Canaanite-Phoenician city-states. We cannot say yet which city-state operated which trade network, or if any network was operated by a single city at all; a few cities could have collaborated in the operation of one, some, or all of the networks.

That being said, we know as a fact from ancient written sources that the main operators were Tyre, Sidon, and Carthage. The Levantine centers controlled the networks for wine, pottery, and scent and medicinal oils and compounds. The fish-products network, however, was controlled from Carthage and Cádiz. This is not surprising, given their proximity to the production centers. Nonetheless, not all the Canaanite-Phoenician trade networks manufactured their products or artifacts near the raw materials. For example, the network for luxury objects, not discussed in this study, spread around the Mediterranean and the Near East, mainly in the early 1st millennium BCE. This network used metals from Iberia, Sardinia, Anatolia, the Levant, and probably other sources as well, and shipped the metals to the production centers which exhibited artisan work of the highest quality in the Levant. The final product was then shipped, along with other Levantine products, as far east as Assyria and as far west as the Straits of Gibraltar in the Mediterranean.

In general, we can divide the Canaanite-Phoenician products into three categories:

a. Merchandise produced in the Levant and adjacent production centers (for example, in Cyprus and Rhodes), the distribution of which to the entire Mediterranean was done by Canaanite-Phoenicians. Most of these goods were manufactured or processed in the Levant, but not all. These included Aegyptiaca of all types (imported from Egypt and artifacts produced in the Levant), ornamented objects, metal and glass bars, wood, dyed fabric and cloth, jewelry, ritual objects, as well as wine and oil.
b. Merchandise that was originally produced in the Levant and distributed to all sites with a Canaanite-Phoenician connection. This Levantine produce was quickly replaced by local versions in various locations, each with its own interpretation of the original product. This category includes mainly pottery.
c. Merchandise produced outside the Levant by Canaanite-Phoenicians, close to the location of raw materials, especially those that needed to be processed fresh. This group includes fish products and some of the perfumed oils.

Category (a) was comprised of finished objects and products manufactured in the Levantine Canaanite-Phoenician centers and distributed from there along overland and sea trade routes. Categories (b) and (c) were comprised of goods produced by Canaanite-Phoenician artisans and other experts at non-Levantine sites of production. It is not surprising, therefore, to see that, during the 2nd millennium BCE, most of the Canaanite-Phoenician products we find in the Mediterranean and in the Near East (Anatolia, Mesopotamia, and Egypt) are products that belong to category (a), while categories (b) and (c) appear in the 1st millennium BCE. Nonetheless, the products in category (a) still constituted the bulk of the volume of Canaanite-Phoenician merchandise distributed both in the Mediterranean and the Near East during the 1st millennium BCE.

During the Bronze and Iron Ages, the Canaanite-Phoenician trade networks were dendritic in nature, but later, once production centers became diffused, some became reticulated, like the perfumed-oil and salted-fish networks. This is not the only perceptible change during the long time the Canaanite-Phoenician trade-net endured; in some periods, products were very widely distributed, like the Late Bronze Age, Iron II, and late Hellenistic periods, while in other eras the extent of distribution was limited. When limited, it was usually restricted to the eastern Mediterranean.

The trade network with Egypt is the earliest Canaanite-Phoenician network, operated continuously from the 4th millennium BCE to the Byzantine period. Many structures that were used in later Canaanite-Phoenician trade networks were first designed and implemented here and had a significant impact on the development of a recognizable and enduring Canaanite-Phoenician style and corpora. Beginning in the Middle Bronze Age, the Canaanite-Phoenicians became the mediators of Egyptian culture, as Byblos traded scarabs to Minoan Crete. During the Late Bronze Age, Ugarit dominated the international trade, distributing Egyptian goods as well as other products sourced from around the Mediterranean, and during the Iron Age it was Tyre and Sidon. This trade network involved the exchange of Aegyptiaca, papyri, linen, and raw materials from Egypt, for wine, olive oil, timber, copper, boats, and luxury items from the city-states of the Levant.

Another early Canaanite-Phoenician trade network dated to the Late Bronze and Early Iron Age was with Hatti and was based primarily on the metal trafficking of copper from Faynan and Timna. The Canaanite-Phoenicians controlled the extraction and smelting processes at both sites and transported them to Anatolia. Details of the Arabian–Levantine–Syrian–Anatolian overland route and some of its branches have been traced, using the distribution of Hittite-inspired small jars in burials. Metal trade and its control played a major part in Anatolian and especially Hittite policy and economy in the Late Bronze Age. Other routes, including one along the Danube that connected to the mines in the Carpathian Mountains and another Anatolian–Greek route, were operated by local agents in those areas. It seems that the Hittites operated an elaborate network for exploiting metals stretching south, northwest, and southwest of Hatti. Along each branch, metal ores were extracted, processed into bars, and shipped to the Hittite Kingdom. It was a lucrative operation all around, which involved the introduction of new Hittite techniques, forms, and ideas along these routes, including cremation and the use of small jars of a specific form in tombs.

During the Late Bronze Age, the eastern Mediterranean from Hatti to Egypt was joined in international trade conducted by palatial economies. An International Style evolved, comprised of decorative styles, artifacts, and other goods that dominated the elite markets of the entire Mediterranean, including the Levant, Egypt, Cyprus, the Aegean, and Asia Minor. Items made of glass, ivory, and metal in Canaanite-Phoenician style, with characteristic motifs influenced by Egyptian and Mesopotamian art, are still too often considered to belong to Eastern, Syrian, or North Syrian styles.

The Canaanite-Phoenicians shipped and distributed Aegyptiaca around the Mediterranean and verified it as a marker of Phoenician presence. Most Phoenician burials and Phoenician-inspired burials found throughout the Mediterranean Basin include Aegyptiaca, along with Phoenician pottery, Cypriot and Greek pottery, and Etruscan and Sardinian objects. The commonest element comprising Aegyptiaca were scarabs, but it also included faience amulets, vessels, beads, stone vessels, bronze vessels, mirrors, ivory and bone statuettes, and decorated ostrich eggs and shells. Most of these items related to death and the afterworld. However, Aegyptiaca also included sacred pools.

In addition to Aegyptiaca, the Phoenicians traded various corpora. Items could include, over time: pottery; raw materials like metal bars, ivory, alum, and glass; luxury objects made of these materials; wine; perfumed oils and medicines; and fish products. These groups have been discussed along with some special items of Egyptian origin that now need to be included in the Canaanite-Phoenician corpus, like monkey imagery and phalli. The ivory duck boxes, however, have been assumed to have originated in Egypt, but this symbol is, in fact, Canaanite-Phoenician and has nothing to do with Egyptian symbolism.

Near Eastern finds in Greece from the 10th–9th centuries BCE have been recovered primarily from tombs belonging to elites, while the majority that date to the 8th–7th centuries BCE have been found in sanctuaries. The sanctuaries were located at major nodes on the maritime trade routes in Greece and the Aegean, nodes that were also on the Phoenician trade networks in the eastern Mediterranean.

They include Eretria (Eoboea), Athens, Corinth, Perachora, and the islands of Rhodes, Samos, and Delos. These nodes were the entrance portals for Phoenician religious ideas and symbolism into Greece. After absorption into Greek culture, certain aspects of Phoenician religion and beliefs were distributed via the religious centers of Delphi and Olympia. This process shows, at least to some degree, the gradual adaptation of Near Eastern religion and beliefs into Greek religion. The same process is also traceable in Etruria. It indicates that the influence of all aspects of Phoenician culture on Greek culture is much greater than has been acknowledged. The magnitude of Phoenician culture in Greece has been underestimated, and assemblages from old and new excavations should now be re-examined.

Canaanite-Phoenician networks can be divided into four geographical zones: the eastern Mediterranean, the western Mediterranean, North Africa and the central Mediterranean islands, and, finally, the Near East, Arabia, India, and the Persian Gulf. The history of each sphere's connections with Canaanite-Phoenicians and the main nodes of their trade network have been detailed based on current available data. Some of the locations were more significant to Canaanite-Phoenician trade than others. In addition to the major production and distribution centers, some areas or cities had an outstanding and different position in the Canaanite-Phoenician trade networks. First and foremost was Cyprus, which I have designated *Magna Phoenicia* because it functioned as the industrial area of Canaan-Phoenicia from the Late Bronze Age onward.

The four Phoenician industrial networks of wine, perfumed oil and medicines, salted fish, and Sigillata fine ware pottery, are examples of the Canaanite-Phoenician approach to trade. The global picture that emerges from the details presented in this study is one of Canaanite-Phoenician domination over Mediterranean maritime trade, at least from the Late Bronze Age to the Hellenistic period. The networks that were established in the Mediterranean and the Near East by the Canaanite-Phoenicians throughout the 2nd and 1st millennia BCE were later taken over in the 1st millennium CE by the Romans and then by the Muslims. The Canaanite-Phoenician trade network, then, had a profound impact on Mediterranean connectivity and communities, significantly beyond and past the destruction of the Canaanite-Phoenician homeland and culture. The Phoenicians provide a valuable historical lesson about how empires need not conquer locals and suppress and control them to be effective, and how cooperation led to the advance and enrichment of the host culture and Phoenician culture through the exchange of ideas and development of local industries.

Endnotes

1 I thank Ioram Melcer for reading and interpreting these Egyptian terms.

2 I thank Robert Kerr for the reference to Makomades and its original Phoenician roots, and to Robert Hoyland for notes on the original Arabic text. I also thank Hassan Janazreh for his help.

3 I thank Ada Yardeni, may she rest in peace, for her helpful notes and clarifications on this document.

4 Chemical spot tests, infrared spectroscopy (IR), high-performance liquid chromatography (HPLC), isotopic analysis of resins, the Fiegl spot test, Fourier transform/infrared spectroscopy (FT/IR), gas chromatography–mass spectrometry (GC-MS), high-performance liquid chromatography–tandem mass spectrometry (HPLC-MS-MS), and light stable isotopic (dD, d13C and d18O) values for bulk resins.

5 I thank Mark Nesbit for this observation.

6 I thank Omri Lernau for this information, June 2019.

7 I thank Tali Erickson-Gini for this information.

Bibliography

Abulafia, D. 2005. "Mediterraneans." In *Rethinking the Mediterranean*, edited by William Vernon Harris, 64–93. Oxford: Oxford University Press on Demand.

Abusch, Zvi. 1999. "Ishtar." In *Dictionary of Deities and Demons in the Bible*, edited by Karel Van der Toorn, Bob Becking, and Pieter Willem Van Der Horst, 452–6. Leiden: Brill.

Ackerman, Susan. 2013. "The Mother of Eshmunazor, Priest of Astarte: A Study of her Cultic Role." *Die Welt des Orients* 43 (2): 158–78.

Adams, Colin. 2013. "Natural Resources in Roman Egypt Extraction, Transport, and Administration." *The Bulletin of the American Society of Papyrologists* 50: 265–81.

Agelarakis, Anagnostis P. 2016. *A Dignified Passage through the Gates Of Hades: The Burial Custom of Cremation and the Warrior Order of Ancient Eleutherna*. Oxford: Archaeopress Publishing Ltd.

Agranat-Tamir, Lily, Shamam Waldman, Mario A. S. Martin, David Gokhman, Nadav Mishol, Tzilla Eshel, Olivia Cheronet, Nadin Rohland, Swapan Mallick, Nicole Adamski, Ann Marie Lawson, Matthew Mah, Megan Michel, Jonas Oppenheimer, Kristin Stewardson, Francesca Candilio, Denise Keating, Beatriz Gamarra, Shay Tzur, Mario Novak, Rachel Kalisher, Shlomit Bechar, 17 Vered Eshed, Douglas J. Kennett, Marina Faerman, Naama Yahalom-Mack, Janet M. Monge, Yehuda Govrin, Yigal Erel, Benjamin Yakir, Ron Pinhasi, Shai Carmi, Israel Finkelstein, Liran Carmel, and David Reich. 2020. "The Genomic History of the Bronze Age Southern Levant." *Cell* 181: 1146–57.

Ahituv, Shmuel. 2014. "Notes on the Kuntillet 'Ajrud inscriptions." In *"See, I will bring a scroll recounting what befell me" (Ps 40: 8). Epigraphy and Daily Life from the Bible to the Talmud. Dedicated to the Memory of Professor Hanan Eshel*. Göttingen: Vandenhoeck & Ruprecht

Ahrens, Alexander. 2015. "The Early 18th Dynasty in the Northern Levant: New Finds and a Reassessment of the Sources." In *There and Back Again: The Crossroads II. Proceedings of an International Conference Held in Prague, September 15–18, 2014*, edited by Jana Mynářová, Pavel Onderka, and Peter Pavúk, 353–71. Charles University in Prague.

Akurgal, Ekrem. 1981. "Aramean and Phoenician Stylistic and Iconographic Elements in Neo-Hittite Art." In *Temples and High Places in Biblical Times: Proceedings of the Colloquium in Honor of the Centennial of Hebrew Union College—Jewish Institute of Religion, Jerusalem 1977*, edited by A. Biran and I. Pommerantz, 131–41. Jerusalem.

Alberti, G. 2005. "The Earliest Contacts between Southeastern Sicily and Cyprus in the Late Bronze Age." In *Emporia: Aegeans in the Central and Eastern Mediterranean. Proceedings of the 10th International Aegean Conference, Athens,*

Italian School of Archaeology, April 2004, edited by Robert Laffineur and E. Greco, 343–51. Université de Liège, Belgium.

Albright, William Foxwell. 1949. *The Archaeology of Palestine: A Survey of the Ancient Peoples and Cultures of the Holy Land*, rev. ed. Harmondsworth: Penguin Books.

Alcock, Susan E. 1993a. "Surveying the Peripheries of the Hellenistic World." In *Centre and Periphery in the Hellenistic World*, edited by P. Bilde, T. Engberg-Pedersen, L Hannestad, J. Zahl, and K. Randsborg, 162–75. Aarhus: Aarhus University Press.

———. 1993b. *Graecia Capta: The Landscapes of Roman Greece*. Cambridge: Cambridge University Press.

Alexandridou, Alexandra. 2016. "Funerary Variability in Late Eighth-Century BCE Attica (Late Geometric II)." *American Journal of Archaeology* 120 (3): 333.

Alfaro Giner, C., and B. Costa Ribas. 2008. "Methodological Aspects of Purple Dye Production on Ibiza: The New Site of Cala Olivera." In *Vestidos Textiles y Tintes. Estudios sobre la producción de bienes de consumo en la Antigüedad: Actas del II Symposium Internacional sobre Textiles y Tintes del Mediterráneo en el Mundo Antiguo (Atenas, 24 al 26 de noviembre, 2005)*, edited by C. Alfaro Giner and L. Karali, 195–208. València: Universitat de València.

Algrain, Isabelle. 2014. "L'alabastre attique: Origine, forme et usages." *Études d'archéologie* 7: 121–7.

Allen, Mitchell. 1992. "The Mechanisms of Underdevelopment: An Ancient Mesopotamian Example." *Review (Fernand Braudel Center)* 15: 453–76.

Allon, Niv. 2007. "Seth is Baal: Evidence from the Egyptian Script." *Egypt and Levant* 17: 15–22.

Almagro Gorbea, Martin. 2004. "A Phoenician Bowl from Nubia and the Phoenician Trade in the Periphery of the Old World." *Complutum* 15: 7–32.

——— and Fernando Fontes. 1997. "The Introduction of Wheel-made Pottery in the Iberian Peninsula: Mycenaeans or Pre-orientalizing Contacts?" *Oxford Journal of Archaeology* 16 (3): 345–61.

———, Ester López Rosendo, Alfredo Mederos Martín, and Mariano Torres Ortiz. 2010. "Los sarcófagos antropoides de la necrópolis de Cádiz." *Mainake* 32: 357–94.

Álvarez Martí-Aguilar, Manuel. 2018. "The Network of Melqart: Tyre, Gadir, Carthage, and the Founding God." In *War, Warlords, and Interstate Relations in the Ancient Mediterranean*, edited by Toni Ñaco del Hoyo and Fernando López Sánchez, 113–50. Leiden and Boston: Brill.

Álvarez-Sanchís, J. R. 2000. "The Iron Age in Western Spain (800 BC–AD 50)." *OJA* 19: 65–89.

Amadasi Guzzo, Maria Giulia. 2000. "Quelques tessons inscrits du sanctuaire d'Astarté à Tas Silg." In *Actas del IV Congreso Internacional de Estudios Fenicios y Punicos, Cádiz 2–6.10.1995*, 181–196.

———. 2017. "The Idalion Archive, 2, The Phoenician Inscriptions." In *Archea Cyprus. Πρόσφατες εξελίξεις στην αρχαιολογία της ανατολικής Μεσογείου*, edited by N. Papadimitriou and M. Toli, 275–84. Athens: Cycladic Art Foundation.

Amadori, M. L., Carla Del Vais, P. Fermo, and P. Pallante. 2016. "Archaeometric Researches on the Provenance of Mediterranean Archaic Phoenician and Punic Pottery." *Environmental Science and Pollution Research* 24 (16): 13,921–49.

Ameling, W. 1990. "Koinon ton Sidonon." *ZPE* 81: 189–99.

Andersson, Ann. 2014. "Beads, Pendants and other Ornaments from Late 3rd–2nd Millennium BC Occupation on Failaka, Kuwait." *Polish Archaeology in the Mediterranean* 23: 209–23.

Angelini, Ivana, Bernard Gratuze, and Gilberto Artioli. 2019. "Glass and Other Vitreous Materials through History." *EMU Notes Mineral* 20: 87–150.

Antoniadis, Vyron. 2012. "Early Iron Age Cemeteries at Knossos: The Appreciation of Oriental Imports and their Imitations by Knossian Society." PhD, Universitat Pompeu Fabra.

Aranegui, Carmen, Mireia López-Bertran, and Jaime Vives-Ferrándiz. 2011. "The Strait and Beyond: Local Communities in Phoenician Lixus (Larache, Morocco)." In *Ceramics of the Phoenician-Punic World: Collected Essays*, edited by Claudia Sagona, 297–326. Leuven, Paris, and Walpole, MA: Peeters.

Arnaud, Pascal. 2005. *Les routes de la navigation antique: Itinéraires en Méditerranée*. Arles: Editions Errance.

———. 2016. "Conclusion." In *The Sea in History: The Ancient World*, edited by Pascal Arnaud and Philip de Souza, 617–42. Woodbridge: The Boydell Press.

Arruda, Ana Margarida. 2009. "Phoenician Colonization on the Atlantic Coast of the Iberian Peninsula." In *Colonial Encounters in Ancient Iberia, Phoenicians, Greeks and Indigenous Relations*, edited by M. Dietler and Carolina López-Ruiz, 113–30. Chicago: University of Chicago Press.

Artzy, Michal. 1980. "The Origin of the Palestinian Bichrome Ware." PhD thesis, Brandeis University, 1972.

———. 1990. "Pomegranate Scepters and Incense Stand with Pomegranates Found in Priest's Grave." *Biblical Archaeology Review* 16 (1): 48–51.

———. 1994. "Incense, Camels and Collared Rim Jars: Desert Trade Routes and Maritime Outlets in the Second Millennium." *OJA* 13: 121–47.

———. 2006a. "The Carmel Coast during the Second Part of the Late Bronze Age: A Center for Eastern Mediterranean Transshipping." *BASOR* 343: 45–64.

———. 2006b. *The Jatt Metal Hoard in the Northern Canaanite/Phoenician and Cypriot Context*. Cuadernos de Arqueología Mediterránea, Vol. 14. Barcelona: Universidad Pompeu Fabra de Barcelona.

Asheri, David, Alan Lloyd, and Aldo Corcella. 2007. *A Commentary on Herodotus*: Oxford: Oxford University Press.

Åström, P. 1991. "Canaanite Jars from Hala Sultan Tekke." In *Bronze Age Trade in the Mediterranean: Papers Presented at the Conference at Rewley House, Oxford 1989*, edited by N. H. Gale, 149–51. Jonsered: Åström.

———. 1992. "Continuity, Discontinuity, Catastrophe, Nucleation: Some Remarks on Terminology." In *The Crisis Years: The 12th Century BC: From Beyond to the Danube to the Tigris*, edited by W. A. Ward and M. S. Joukowsky, 27–30. Dubuque, IO: Kendall Hunt.

Aubet, Maria Eugenia. 1993. *The Phoenicians and the West: Politics, Colonies, and Trade*. Cambridge: Cambridge University Press.

———. 1996. "Notas sobre Arqueologia fineraria fenicia en Andalucia." In *Alle soglie della classicità il mediterraneo tra tradizione e innovazione: Studi in onore di Sabatino Moscati. 2. Archeologia e arte*, edited by E. Acquaro, 495–508. Pisa and Rome: Istituti editoriali e poligrafici internazionali.

———. 2001. *The Phoenicians and the West: Politics, Colonies, and Trade*, 2nd ed. Cambridge: Cambridge University Press.

———. 2007. "East Greek and Etruscan Pottery in a Phoenician Context." In *"Up to the Gates of Ekron": Essays on the Archaeology and History of the Eastern Mediterranean in Honor of Seymour Gitin*, edited by Sidnie White Crawford, 447–60. Jerusalem: The W. F. Albright Institute of Archaeological Research and the Israel Exploration Society.

———. 2008. "Political and Economic Implications of the New Phoenician Chronologies." In *Beyond the Homeland: Markers in Phoenician Chronology*, edited by C. Sagona, 247–59. Leuven: Peeters.

———. 2010. "The Phoenician Cemetery of Tyre." *Near Eastern Archaeology* 73 (2–3): 144–55.

Ávila, Javier Jiménez, ed. 2015. *Phoenician Bronzes in Mediterranean*. Madrid: Real Academia de la Historia Madrid.

Avner, Uzi. 2014. "Egyptian Timna: Reconsidered." In *Unearthing the Wilderness: Studies on the History and Archaeology of the Negev and Edom in the Iron Age*, edited by J. Tebes, 103–62. Leuven: Peeters.

Bacci, Giovanna Maria. 1998. "Zancle: Un aggioranamento." In *Euboica: l'Eubea e la presenza euboica in Calcidica e in occidente: Atti del convegno internazionale di Napoli, 13-16 novembre 1996*, edited by Michel Bats and Bruno D'Agostino, 387–92. Naples: Centre Jean Bérand.

——. 2005. "Zancle-Messana." In *Lo Stretto di Messina nell'antichità*, edited by F. Ghedini, J. Bonetto, A. R. Ghiotto, and F. Rinaldi, 253–73. Rome.

———. 2008. "Il deposito vovito di S. Raineri 'verso la punta della Zancle'." In *Archeologia a Messina. Studi su materiali preistorici, arcaici, hellenistici e romani del museo*, edited by M. A. Mastelloni, 31–86. Sicily.

———, Gabriella Tigano, Maria Ravesi, and Giusi Zavettieri. 2012. "L'area sacra dell'isolato Z a Messina e la ktisis di Zancle." In *Alle origini della Magna Grecia: Mobilità, migrazioni, fondazioni. Atti del cinquantesimo convegno di studi sulla Magna Grecia, Taranto, 1-4 ottobre 2010*, edited by Giovanna Maria Bacci and Mario Lombardo, 927–45. Taranto: Istituto per la storia e l'archeologia della Magna Grecia.

Bagnall, Roger S. 2005. "Egypt and the Concept of the Mediterranean." In *Rethinking the Mediterranean*, edited by W. V. Harris, 339–47. Oxford: Oxford University Press.

Barako, T. J. 2007. *Tel Mor: The Moshe Dothan Excavations, 1959–1960*. IAA Reports 32. Jerusalem: IAA.

Barnett, R. D. 1982. *Ancient Ivories in the Middle East*. Qedem 14. Jerusalem.

Barrachina Sánchez, Jorge, and Andrés María Adroher. 2018. "Las cáscaras de huevo de avestruz del depósito votivo ibérico de Iliberri (Granada)." *CuPAUAM* 44: 145–58.

Barrios, Lázaro Gabriel Lagóstena. 2014. "Nuevas consideraciones sobre la 'Societas Cetariorvm Gaditarorvm'." *Baetica Renascens* 1: 93–108.

Bartoloni, P. 1989. *Monte Sirai. Sardegna Archeologica: Guide e Itinerari 10*. Sassari: Carlo Delfino editore.

———. 2008. "Nuovi dati sulla cronologia di Sulky." *L'Africa romana Atti dell'XVII Convegno di studio "L'Africa Romana" (Sevilla, 2006)* 17: 1595–606.

Bass, George F. 1991. "Evidence of Trade from Bronze Age Shipwrecks." In *Bronze Age Trade in the Mediterranean: Studies in Mediterranean Archaeology XC*, edited by N. H. Gale, 69–82. Sweden.

Batmaz, Atilla. 2015. "Concept of a Culture: An Examination of the Urartian Identity." In *Changing Archaeology: Proceedings of the 1st TAG (Theoretical Archaeology Group) Turkey Meeting, 2013*, edited by Çiler Çilingiroğlu and N. Pınar Özgüner, 209–21. Ege Yayınları İzmir.

Bechtold, Babette. 2008. *Observations on the Amphora Repertoire of Middle Punic Carthage*. Ghent: Ghent University, Department of Archaeology and Ancient History of Europe.

———. 2012. "The Pottery Production of Punic Carthage." *FACEM* (version 06/06/2012).

Bedford, Peter. 2007. "The Persian Near East." In *The Cambridge Economic History of the Greco-Roman World*, edited by W. Scheidel, I. Morris, and R. Saller, 302–29. Cambridge: Cambridge University Press.

Bedigian, Dorothea, and Jack Harlan. 1986. "Evidence for Cultivation of Sesame in the Ancient World." *Economic Botany* 40 (2): 137–54.

Begley, Vimala. 1983. "Arikamedu Reconsidered." *American Journal of Archaeology* 87: 461–81.

Begley, V., and R. Tomber. 1999. "Indian Pottery Sherds." In *Berenike 1997: Report on the 1997 Excavations at Berenike and the Survey of the Eastern Desert, Including Excavations at Shenshef*, edited by S. E. Sidebotham and W. Z. Wendrich, 161–82. Leiden: Research School of Asian, African, and Amerindian Studies (CNWS).

Beitzel, Barry J. 2010. "Was There a Joint Nautical Venture on the Mediterranean Sea by Tyrian Phoenicians and Early Israelites?" *Bulletin of the American Schools of Oriental Research* 360 (1): 37–66.

Bekker-Nielsen, Tønnes. 1993. "Centres and Road Networks in Cyprus." In *Centre and Periphery in the Hellenistic World: Studies in Hellenistic Civilization IV*, edited by P. Bilde, 176–91. Aarhus: Aarhus University Press.

———. 2002. "Fish in the Ancient Economy." In *Ancient History Matters: Studies Presented to J. E. Skydsgaard on his Seventieth Birthday*, edited by K. Ascani, 29–37. Rome: Danish Institute in Rome.

Belardelli, C., M. A. Castagna, I. Damiani, A. De Guio, A. Di Renzoni, S. T. Levi, R. Peroni, A. Schiappelli, and A. Vanzetti. 2005. "L'impatto miceneo sulle coste dello Jonio e dell'Adriatico e l''alta congiuntura' del Bronzo recente italiano." In *Emporia: Aegeans in the Central and Eastern Mediterranean. Proceedings of the 10th International Aegean Conference, Athens, Italian School of Archaeology, April 2004*, edited by R. Laffineur and E. Greco, 507–18. Université de Liège, Belgium.

Belgiorno, Maria Rosaria. 2017. "Cosmetics." In *Archaeometry and Aphrodite Proceedings of the Seminar 13th June 2013 CNR Rome*, edited by Maria Rosaria Belgiorno. Nicosia: De Strobel.

Ben-Tor, Amnon. 1991. "New Light on the Relations between Egypt and Southern Palestine During the Early Bronze Age." *BASOR* 281: 3–10.

———, Anat Cohen-Weinberger, and Mark Weeden. 2017. "A Cooking-pot from Hazor with Neo-Hittite (Luwian) Seal Impressions." In *Rethinking Israel: Studies in the History and Archaeology of Ancient Israel in Honor of Israel Finkelstein*, edited by O. Lipschits, Y. Gadot, and Matthew J. Adams, 29–45. Winona Lake, IN: Eisenbrauns.

Ben-Tor, Daphna. 2006. "Chronological and Historical Implications of the Early Egyptian Scarabs on Crete." In *Timelines: Studies in Honour of Manfred Bietak*, edited by E. Czerny, 77–86. Leuven, Paris, and Dudley: Peeters.

———. 2018. "Scarabs." In *Rishon le-Zion. I. The Middle Bronze Age II Cemeteries*, Vol. I, No. 2, *Finds and Conclusions*, edited by Yosi Levy and Raz Kletter, 557–620. Münster: Zaphon.

Ben-Yosef, Erez. 2012. "Environmental Constraints on Ancient Copper Production in the Aravah Valley: Implications of the Newly Discovered Site of Khirbet Mana'iyah in Southern Jordan." *Tel Aviv* 39 (2): 58–74.

Ben Shlomo, D., Eleni Nodarou, and Jeremy B. Rutter. 2011. "Transport Stirrup Jars from the Southern Levant: New Light on Commodity Exchange in the Eastern Mediterranean." *American Journal of Archaeology* 115 (3): 329–53.

Bennet, John. 2008. "Palace™: Speculations on Palatial Production in Mycenaean Greece with (Some) Reference to Glass." In *Vitreous Materials in the Late Bronze Age Aegean*, edited by C. M. Jackson and E. C. Wager, 151–72 Oxford: Oxbow Books.

Berkin, Jon M. 2003. *The Orientalizing Bucchero from the Lower Building at Poggio Civitate (Murlo)*. Archaeological Institute of America Monographs New Series 6. Philadelphia: AIA.

Bernal Casasola, Dario, and A. Sáez Romero. 2008. "Fish-Salting Plants and Amphora Production in the Bay of Cádiz (Baetica, Hispania): Patterns of Settlement from the Punic Era to Late Antiquity." In *Thinking about Space: The Potential of Surface Survey and Contextual Archaeology in the Definition of Space in Roman Times*, edited by H. Vanhaverbeke, 45–113. Brepols: Turnhout.

Bernardini, P. 2013. "Organised Settlements and Cult Places in the Phoenician Western Expansion between the 9th and 7th Centuries BCE: A Reflection on the Tophet." In *The Tophet in the Phoenician Mediterranean*, edited by P. Xella, 1–22. Essedue.

Bertsch, Julia. 2018. "Preliminary Remarks on the Technical and Iconographical Aspects of the Middle Bronze Age Wall Paintings from Tell el-Burak (Lebanon) in Relation to the Aegean and Egypt." In *Tracing Technoscapes: The Production of Bronze Age Wall Paintings in the Eastern Mediterranean*, edited by J. Becker, J. Jungfleisch, and C. Von Rüden. Leiden: Sidestone Press.

Betancourt, P. P. 2005. "Egyptian Connections at Hagios Charalambos." In *Emporia: Aegeans in the Central and Eastern Mediterranean. Proceedings of the 10th International Aegean Conference, Athens April 2004*, edited by R. Laffineur and E. Greco, 449–53. Université de Liège, Belgium.

Betlyon, John Wilson. 2004. "Egypt and Phoenicia in the Persian Period: Patterns in Trade and Rebellion." In *Egypt, Israel, and the Ancient Mediterranean World: Studies in honor of D. B. Redford*, edited by G. N. Knoppers and A. Hirsch, 455–77. Leiden and Boston: Brill.

Bey, Osman Hamdi, Théodore Reinach, and Ernest Chantre. 1892. *Une nécropole royale à Sidon: Fouilles de Hamdy Bey*. Paris: E. Leroux.

Bieńkowski, P. A. 1982. "Some Remarks on the Practice of Cremation in the Levant." *Levant* 14: 80–9.

Bietak, Manfred. 1991. "Egypt and Canaan during the Middle Bronze Age." *BASOR* 281: 27–72.

———. 1997. "The Center of Hyksos Rule: Avaris (Tell el-Dab'a)." In *The Hyksos: New Historical and Archaeological Perspectives*, edited by E. Oren, 87–139. Pennsylvania: The University Museum.

———. 2007. "Bronze Age Paintings in the Levant: Chronological and Cultural Considerations." In *The Synchronisation of Civilisations in the Eastern Mediterranean in the Second Millennium B.C. III*, edited by Manfred Bietak and Ernst Czerny, 269–300. Vienna: Verlag der Österreichischen Akademie der Wissenschaften.

Bikai, Patricia Maynor. 1990. "Black Athena and the Phoenicians." *Journal of Mediterranean Archaeology* 3 (1): 67–75.

Bisi, Anna Maria. 1967. *Le stele puniche*, Vol. 27. Istituto di studi del vicino Oriente, Università.

Blouin, Katherine. 2014. *Triangular Landscapes: Environment, Society, and the State in the Nile Delta under Roman Rule*. Oxford: Oxford University Press.

Boardman, John. 1987. "Scarabs and Seals: Greek, Punic and Related Types." In *Tharros: A Catalogue of the Material in the British Museum from Phoenician and other Tombs at Tharros, Sardinia*, edited by R. D. Barnett and C. Mendelson, 98–105. London: British Museum Publications.

———. 2001. *The History of Greek Vases: Potters, Painters and Pictures*. London: Thames & Hudson.

———, I. E. S. Edwards, N. G. L. Hammond, and E. Sollberger. 1982. *The Cambridge Ancient History*. Vol. 3 Part 3. *Tenth to Eighth Centuries BC*. Cambridge: Cambridge University Press.

Böck, Barbara. 2014. *The Healing Goddess Gula: Towards an Understanding of Ancient Babylonian Medicine*. Leiden: Koninklijke Brill NV.

Boffa, Giovanni. 2013. "Il santuario di Apollo ad Eretria: Osservazioni sulla documentazione epigrafica di età geometrica." In *Archeologia dei luoghi e delle pratiche di culto: Atti del convegno (Cavallino, 26–27 gennaio 2012)*, edited by Liliana Giardino and Gianluca Tagliamonte, 31–43. Bari: Edipuglia.

Bohak, Gideon. 2008. "Egypt and Phoenicia Religions in the Classical Literature." In *Ancient Gods: Polytheism in Eretz Israel and Neighboring Countries from the Second Millennium BCE to the Islamic Period*, edited by M. Kister, J. Geiger, and N. Naaman, 102–28. Jerusalem: Eisenbrauns.

Bonadies, Luisa, and Lionel Marti. 2019. "Ce qu'ils disent de nous: Le monde phénicien vu par les Égyptiens et les Assyriens." In *Les Phéniciens, les Puniques et les autres: Échanges et identités en Méditerranée ancienne*, edited by Luisa Bonadies, Iva Chirpanlieva, and Élodie Guillon, 19–41. Paris: De Boccard

Bonfante, Larissa. 2006. "Etruscan Inscriptions and Etruscan Religion." In *The Religion of the Etruscans*, edited by N. Thomson de Grummond and E. Simon, 9–26. Austin: University of Texas Press.

Bonifay, M. 2004. "Observations préliminaires sur la céramique de la nécropole de Pupput." In *La nécropole romaine de Pupput*, edited by A. Ben Abed and M. Griescheimer, 21–57. Rome: École française de Rome.

Bonnet, C. 2007. "Melqart." In *Iconography of Deities and Demons*. A Research Project of the History of Religions Chair of the University of Zurich, Switzerland, in cooperation with Brill Academic Publishers, Leiden, Netherlands. http://www.religionswissenschaft.uzh.ch/idd/prepublication_4.php

Boozer, Anna Lucille. 2015. "The Social Impact of Trade and Migration: The Western Desert in Pharaonic and Post-Pharaonic Egypt." In *Oxford Handbooks Online*, 1–32. Oxford: Oxford University Press.

Borgard, Philippe. 2005. "Les amphores à alun (Ier siècle avant J.-C.–IVe siècle après J.-C.)." In *L'alun de Méditerranée, colloque international juin 2003*, edited by P. Borgard, J.-P. Brun and M. Picon, 157–70. Naples, Aix-en-Provence.

Borowski, Oded. 1995. "The Pomegranate Bowl from Tell Halif." *Israel Exploration Journal* 45: 150–4.

Boucharlat, R. 1991. "From the Iron Age to the 'Hellenistic' Period: Some Evidence from Mleiha (United Arab Emirates)." In *Internationale Archäologie*, Vol. 6, *Gölf Archäologie: Mesopotamien, Iran, Kuwait, Bahrein, Vereinigte Arabische Emirate und Oman*, edited by K. Schippmann, A. Herling, and J.-F. Salles, 289–300. Munich: Universität Göttingen and Maison de l'Orient Méditerranéen.

Boucharlat, Remy, and P Lombard. 1991. "Datations absolues de Rumeilah et chronologie de l'Age du Fer dans la péninsule d'Oman." In *Internationale Archäologie*, Vol. 6, *Gölf Archäologie: Mesopotamien, Iran, Kuwait, Bahrein, Vereinigte Arabische Emirate und Oman*, edited by K. Schippmann, A. Herling, and J.-F. Salles, 301–14. Munich: Universität Göttingen and Maison de l'Orient Méditerranéen.

——— and Michel Mouton. 1993. "Importations occidentales et influence de l'hellénisme dans la péninsule d'Oman." In *Arabia Antiqua: Hellenistic Centres Around Arabia*, edited by A. Invernizzi and J.-F. Salles, 275–89. Rome: Istituto italiano per il Medio ed Estremo Oriente.

Bourogiannis, Giorgos. 2013. "Who Hides Behind the Pots? A Reassessment of the Phoenician Presence in Early Iron Age Cos and Rhodes." *ANES* 50: 139–89.

———. 2014. "Rhodes et les parfums." In *Rhodes: Une île grecque aux portes de l'Orient XV–V siècle avant J.-C.*, edited by A. Coulié and M. Filimonos-Tsopotou. Paris.

———. 2018. "The Phoenician Presence in the Aegean during the Early Iron Age: Trade, Settlement and Cultural Interaction." *Rivista di Studi Fenici* 46: 43–88.

———. 2019. "Between Scripts and Languages: Inscribed Intricacies from Geometric and Archaic Greek Contexts." In *Understanding Relations between Scripts*, Vol. II, *Early Alphabets*, edited by Philippa M Steele and Philip J Boyes, 151–80. Oxford: Oxbow Books.

Bourriau, J. 2001. "The Provenance of Canaanite Amphorae Found at Memphis and Amarna in the New Kingdom." In *The Social Context of Technological Change; Egypt and the Near East, 1650–1550 BC*, edited by A. J. Shortland, 113–46. Oxford: Oxbow Books.

Bouzek, Jan. 1997. *Greece, Anatolia and Europe: Cultural Interrelations during the Early Iron Age*. Jonsered: Åström.

———. 2000. "Ceylon and the West: From Hellenistic Period to the 1st century AD." In *Les civilisations du Bassin Méditerranéen*, 341–4.

Bower, B. 2018. "A Bronze Age Tomb in Israel Reveals the Earliest Known Use of Vanilla." *Science News* 149 (12) (December 22): 10.

Bradbury, Louise. 1996. "Kpn-boats, Punt Trade, and a Lost Emporium." *Journal of the American Research Center in Egypt* 33: 37–60.

Brandl, Baruch. 2003. "The Cape Gelidonya Shipwreck Scarabs Reconsidered." In *The Synchronisation of Civilisations in the Eastern Mediterranean in the Second Millennium BC*, Vol. II, edited by M. Bietak, 249–61. Vienna: Austrian Academy of Sciences Press.

———. 2007. "Glyptics." In *Tel Mor: The Moshe Dothan Excavations, 1959-1960*, edited by T. J. Barako, 191–210. Jerusalem: IAA.

Braudel, Fernand. 2002. *The Mediterranean in the Ancient World*. Translated by S. Reynolds. London: Penguin.

Braun, Eliot L., and Edwin C. M. van den Brink. 2008. "Appraising South Levantine-Egyptian Interaction: Recent Discoveries from Israel and Egypt." In *Egypt at its Origins 2. International Conference. Origin of the State: Predynastic and Early Dynastic Egypt, Toulouse, France 2005*, 643–88. Leuven: Peeters.

Braun, T. 1995. "Barley Cakes And Emmer Bread." In *Food in Antiquity*, edited by J. Wilkins, D. Harvey, and M. Dobson, 25–37. Exeter: Short Run Press.

Bresson, Alain. 2005. "Ecology and Beyond: The Mediterranean Paradigm." In *Rethinking the Mediterranean*, edited by W. V. Harris, 94–114. Oxford: Oxford University Press.

Breton, J.-F. 1998. "Les temples de Ma'in et du Jawf (Yémen): État de la question." *Syria* 75 (1): 61–80.

Bretschneider, Joachim, Greta Jans, Anne-Sophie Van Vyve, Hendrik Hameeuw, and Klaas Vansteenhuyse. 2019. "Tell Tweini: A Long Story Short." In *About Tell Tweini (Syria): Artefacts, Ecofacts and Landscape Research Results of the Belgian Mission*, edited by Joachim Bretschneider and Greta Jans, 1–30. Leuven: Peeters.

Briant, Pierre. 1990. "The Seleucid Kingdom, the Achaemenid Empire and the History of the Near East in the First Millennium BC." In *Religion and Religious Practice in the Seleucid Kingdom*, edited by P. Bilde, 40–65. Aarhus: Aarhus University Press.

———. 2002. *From Cyrus to Alexander: A History of the Persian Empire*. Winona Lake, IN: Eisenbrauns.

——— and Raymond Descat. 1998. "Un registre douanier de la satrapie d'Égypte à l'époque achéménide." In *Le Commerce en Égypte ancienne*, edited by Nicolas Grimal and Bernadette Menu, 59–104. Cairo: Institut français d'archéologie orientale.

Brody, A. J. 1998. *"Each Man Cried Out to his God": The Specialized Religion of Canaanite and Phoenician Seafarers*. Harvard Semitic Museum Publications. Atlanta, Georgia: Scholars Press.

———. 2002. "From the Hills of Adonis through the Pillars of Hercules: Recent Advances in the Archaeology of Canaan and Phoenicia." *Near Eastern Archaeology* 65: 69–80.

Brogan, Olwen Phillis Frances, and R. J. A. Wilson. 2016a. *Lepcis Magna*. Oxford: Oxford University Press.

——— and R. J. A. Wilson. 2016b. *Sabratha*. Oxford: Oxford University Press.

Broodbank, C. 2013. *The Making of the Middle Sea: An Archaeological History of the Mediterranean from the Beginning to the Formation of the Classical World*. London: Thames & Hudson.

Bruins, Hendrik J, Albert J Nijboer, and Johannes van der Plicht. 2011. "Iron Age Mediterranean Chronology: A Reply." *Radiocarbon* 53 (1): 199–220.

Brun, Jean-Pierre. 1999. "Laudatissimum fuit antiquitus in Delo insula: La maison IB du Quartier du stade et la production des parfums a Delos." *Bulletin de Correspondance Hellénique* 123: 87–155.

———. 2000. "The Production of Perfumes in Antiquity: The Cases Of Delos and Paestum." *American Journal of Archaeology* 104: 277–308.

Bryce, Trevor. 2006. "The 'Eternal Treaty' from the Hittite Perspective." *British Museum Studies in Ancient Egypt and Sudan* 6: 1–11.

Brysbaert, Ann. 2013. "The Chicken or the Egg? Interregional Contacts Viewed through a Technological Lens at Late Bronze Age Tiryns, Greece." *Oxford Journal of Archaeology* 32: 233–56.

Buchner, Giorgio. 1982. "Die Beziehungen zwischen der euböischen Kolonie Pithekoussai auf der Insel Ischia und dem nordwestsemitischen Mittelmeerraum in der zweiten Hälfte des 8. Jhs. v. Chr." In *Phönizier im Westen: Die Beiträge des Internationalen Symposiums über die phönizische Expansion im westlichen Mittelmeerraum*, edited by H. G. Niemeyer, 277–306. Mainz: Verlag Philipp von Zabern.

Buhl, Marie-Louise. 1959. *The Late Egyptian Anthropoid Stone Sarcophagi*. Copenhagen: Nationalmuseet Copenhagen.

Bühler, B., and Andrea Pülz. 2008. "Die Goldfunde aus dem Artemision von Ephesos und ihre Herstellung." In *Die Archäologie der ephesischen Artemis: Gestalt und Ritual eines Heiligtums*, edited bu U. Muss, 167–72. Vienna: Phoibos Verlag

Burkert, Walter. 1997. *The Orientalizing Revolution. Near Eastern Influence on Greek Culture in the Early Archaic Age*. Cambridge, MA: Harvard University Press.

Burkhalter, Fabienne, and Anna Philippa-Touchais. 2003. "Fouilles et découvertes archéologiques en Grèce en 2001 et 2002." *Bulletin de correspondance hellénique* 127 (2): 683–1133.

Burstein, S. 1992. "Hecataeos of Abdera's History of Egypt." In *Life in a Multi-Cultural Society: Egypt from Cambyses to Constantine and Beyond*, edited by Janet H. Johnson, 45–9. Chicago: Oriental Institute, University of Chicago.

Buxó, Ramon. 2009. "The Agricultural Consequences of Colonial Contacts on the Iberian Peninsula in the First Millennium BC." In *Colonial Encounters in Ancient Iberia: Phoenicians, Greeks and Indigenous Relations*, edited by M. Dietler and Carolina López-Ruiz, 155–68. Chicago: Chicago University Press.

Cabrera, Paloma. 1998. "Greek Trade in Iberia: The Extent of Interaction." *Oxford Journal of Archaeology* 17 (2): 191–206.

Calvet, Yves. 1991. "Un bâtiment de l'Age du Bronze à Failaka (Koweït)." In *Internationale Archäologie*, Vol. 6, *Gölf Archäologie: Mesopotamien, Iran, Kuwait, Bahrein, Vereinigte Arabische Emirate und Oman*, edited by K. Schippmann, A. Herling, and J.-F. Salles, 133–44. Munich: Universität Göttingen and Maison de l'Orient Méditerranéen.

Cancik, Hubert. 2003. "Standardization and Ranking of Texts in Greek and Roman Institutions." In *Homer, the Bible, and Beyond: Literary and Religious Canons in the Ancient World*, edited by Margalit Finkelberg and Guy Stroumsa. Leiden: Brill.

Carannante, Alfredo. 2010. "Archaeomalacological Data from the Bronze Age Industrial Complex of Pyrgos-Mavroraki (Cyprus): A Non-dietary Mollusc Exploitation Case." *Munibe* 31: 157–67.

———. 2014. "Archaeomalacology and Purple-Dye. State of the Art and New Prospects of Research." In *Moluscos y púrpura en contextos arqueológicos atlántico-mediterráneos: Nuevos datos y reflexiones en clave de proceso histórico*, edited by Juan Jesús Cantillo, Darío Bernal, and José Ramos, 273–82. Servicio de Publicaciones de la Universidad de Cádiz.

Carpino, Alexandra. 2008. "Reflections from the Tomb: Mirrors as Grave Goods in Late Classical and Hellenistic Tarquinia." *Etruscan Studies* 11 (1): 1–34.

Carre, M.-B. 1995. "Les amphores de transport." In *Bolsena VII: Fouilles de l'École Française de Rome à Bolsena (Poggio Moscini). La citerne 5 et son mobilier: Production, importations et consommation. IIIe siècle/début Ier siècle av. J.-C. et deuxième tiers du Ier siècle ap. J.-C.*, edited by Marie-Hélène Santrot and Jacques Santrot, 251–65. Rome: École française de Rome.

Carruthers, T., A. Di Natale, M. Lauretta, A. Pagá García, and S. Tensek. 2018. "Migratory Behaviour of Atlantic Bluefin Tuna Entering the Mediterranean." *Collect. Vol. Sci. Pap. ICCAT* 74 (6): 3082–99.

Casson, Lionel. 1989. *The Periplus Maris Erythraei: Text with Introduction, Translation, and Commentary*: Princeton, NJ: Princeton University Press.

Catalán, Manuel Pellicer. 2007. *La necrópolis Laurita (Almuñécar, Granada) en el contexto de la colonización fenicia*. Cuadernos de Arqueología Mediterránea 15. Barcelona: Universitat Pompeu Fabra, Laboratorio de Arqueologia.

Catling, Hector W. 1964. *Cypriot Bronzework in the Mycenaean World*. Oxford Monographs on Classical Archaeology. Oxford: Clarendon Press.

Catling, R. 2005. "Emborio and Kambos: Two Archaic sites on Melos." In *Architecture and Archaeology in the Cyclades: Papers in Honour of J. J. Coulton*. BAR International Series 1455, edited by M. Yeroulanou and M. Stamatopoulou, 69–77. Oxford: BAR Publishing.
Caubet, Annie. 1983. "Les œufs d'autruche au Proche Orient Ancien." *Report of the Department of Antiquities Cyprus*: 193–8.
———. 1992. "Reoccupation of the Syrian Coast after the Destruction of the 'Crisis Years'." In *The Crisis Years: The 12th Century BC: From beyond the Danube to the Tigris*, edited by W. A. Ward and M. S. Joukowsky, 123–31. Dubuque, IO: Kendall Hunt.
———. 2014. "Tridacna Shell." In *Assyria to Iberia at the Dawn of the Classical Age*, edited by Joan Aruz, Sarah Graff, and Yelena Rakic, 163–6. New York: Metropolitan Museum of Art.
——— and M. Yon. 2006. "Ougarit et l'Égypte." In *Timelines: Studies in Honour of Manfred Bietak*, edited by E. Czerny, 87–95. Leuven, Paris, and Dudley: Peeters.
Cavaliere, Paola. 2000. "Anfore puniche utilizzate come contenitori di pesce: Un esempio olbiese." *Mélanges de l'École française de Rome: Antiquité* 112 (1): 67–72.
Cecchini, Serena Maria, Stefania Mazzoni, and Elena Scigliuzzo. 2009. *Syrian and Phoenician Ivories of the Early First Millennium BCE: Chronology, Regional Styles and Iconographic Repertories, Patterns of Inter-regional Distribution*. Pisa: Edizioni ETS.
Ceram, C. W. 1956. *Narrow Pass, Black Mountain: The Discovery of the Hittite Empire*. London: Gollancz in association with Sidgwick & Jackson.
Chaniotis, Angelos. 1999. "Milking the Mountains: Economic Activities on the Cretan Uplands in the Classical and Hellenistic Period." In *Minoan Farmers to Roman Traders: Sidelights on the Economy of Ancient Crete*, edited by Angelos Chaniotis, 181–220. Stuttgart: Franz Steiner Verlag.
Christian, Mark A. 2014. "Mediterranean Grottos and the Umm El-Amed: Coastal Shrines and Regional Inland Temples." *Phéniciens d'Orient et d'Occident: Mélanges Josette Elayi* 2: 373–92.
Cintas, P. 1950. *Céramique punique*. Publications de l'Institut des hautes études de Tunis 3. Paris: C. Klincksieck.
———. 1970. *Manuel d'archéologie punique*, Vol. I. *Histoire et archéologie comparées: Chronologie des temps archaïques de Carthage et des villes phéniciennes de l'ouest*. Edited by A. Picard and J. Picard. Paris.
Cline, Eric H. 1991. "Monkey Business in the Bronze Age Aegean: The Amenhotep II Faience Figurines at Mycenae and Tiryns." *ABSA* 86: 29–42.
———. 1999. "Coals to Newcastle, Wallbrackets to Tiryns: Irrationality, Gift Exchange, and Distance Value." *Aegaeum* 20: 119–23.
Cohen, Abner. 1971. "Cultural Strategies in the Organization of Trading Diasporas." In *The Development of Indigenous Trade and Markets in West Africa*, edited by C. Meillassoux, 266–81. London: Oxford University Press for the International African Institute.
Cohen, Robin. 2008. *Global Diasporas: An Introduction*, 2nd ed. London: Routledge.
Cohen, Susan L. 2002. *Canaanites, Chronologies, and Connections: The Relationship of Middle Bronze IIA Canaan to Middle Kingdom Egypt*. Winona Lake, IN: Eisenbrauns.
Cohen-Weinberger, Anat. 2007. "Petrography of Middle Bronze 2 Age Pottery: Implications to Understanding Egypto-Canaanite Relations." PhD, Tel-Aviv University.
Coldstream, John Nicolas. 1982. "Greeks and Phoenicians in the Aegean." In *Phönizier im Westen: Die Beiträge des Internationalen Symposiums über die phönizische Expansion im westlichen Mittelmeerraum*, edited by H. G. Niemeyer, 261–72. Mainz: Verlag Philipp von Zabern.
——— 1998a. "Crete and the Dodecanese: Alternative Eastern Approaches to the Greek World during the Geometric Period." In *Eastern Mediterranean: Cyprus-Dodecanese-Crete 16th–6th cent. BC*, edited by V. Karageorghis and N Stampolidis, 255–63. Athens: University of Crete and the A. G. Leventis Foundation.
———. 1998b. "The First Exchanges between Euboeans and Phoenicians: Who Took the Initiative." In *Mediterranean Peoples in Transition: Thirteenth to Early Tenth Centuries BCE*, edited by G. Gitin, A. Mazar, and E. Stern, 353–60. Jerusalem: Israel Exploration Society.

———. 1998c. "Minos Redivivus: Some Nostalgic Knossians of the Ninth Century BC (A Summary)." British School at Athens Studies, Vol. 2, Post-Minoan Crete: Proceedings of the First Colloquium on Post-Minoan Crete held by the British School at Athens and the Institute of Archaeology, University College London, 10–11 November 1995, 58–61.

———. 2003. *Geometric Greece: 900–700 BC*: London: Routledge.

———. 2008. "Early Greek Exports to Phoenicia and the East Mediterranean." In *Networking Patterns of the Bronze and Iron Age Levant: The Lebanon and its Mediterranean Connections*, edited by C. Doumet-Serhal, 167–88. Beirut: Lebanese British Friends of the National Museum.

——— and Hector W. Catling. 1996. *Knossos the North Cemetery: Early Greek Tombs*. London: The British School at Athens.

Coleman, John E. 1997. "Ancient Greek Ethnocentrism." In *Greeks and Barbarians: Essays on the Interactions between Greeks and Non-Greeks in Antiquity and the Consequences for Eurocentrism*, edited by J. E. Coleman and C. A. Walz, 175–220. Baltimore: Eisenbrauns.

Collins, B. J. 2008. *The Hittites and Their World*. Boston and Leiden: Brill.

Colonna, Giovanni. 2006. "Sacred Architecture and the Religion of the Etruscans." In *The Religion of the Etruscans*, edited by N. Thomson de Grummond and E. Simon, 132–68. Austin: University of Texas Press.

Comfort, Howard. 1958. "Imported Pottery and Glass from Timna." In *Archaeological Discoveries in South Arabia*, edited by R. Bowen and F. B. Albright, 199–207. Baltimore: The Johns Hopkins Press.

Cornelius, Izak. 2004. *The Many Faces of the Goddess: The Iconography of the Syro-Palestinian Goddesses Anat, Astarte, Qedeshet, and Asherah c. 1500–1000 BCE*. Orbis Biblicus et Orientalis, Vol. 204: Fribourg and Göttingen: Academic Press/Vandenhoeck & Ruprecht.

Costa, Benjamí, and Jordi H. Fernandez. 2003. "El Rostro de la Muerte: Representaciones de Gorgoneia en la Necrópolis del Puig des Molins (Eivissa)." In *Misceláneas de arqueología ebusitana, II. El Puig des Molins (Eivissa): Un siglo de investigaciones*, edited by Benjamí Costa and Jordi H. Fernandez, 197–250. Eivissa: Museo Arqueológico de Ibiza.

Coulié, Anne, Dominique Frère, Nicolas Garnier, and Andras Marton. 2017. "Le tombeau A de Camiros: Les vases archaïques et leurs contenus. L'apport de l'étude chronologique et des analyses chimiques des résidus." *Bulletin de correspondance hellénique* 141 (2): 553–621.

Counsell, David J. 2008. "Intoxicants in Ancient Egypt? Opium, Nymphea, Coca, and Tobacco." *Egyptian Mummies and Modern Science*: 195–215.

Craigie, Peter C. 1983. "Ugarit, Canaan, and Israel." *Tyndale Bulletin* 34: 145–67.

Crielaard, J.-P. 2015. "Powerful Things in Motion: A Biographical Approach to Eastern Elite Goods in Greek Sanctuaries." In *Sanctuaries and the Power of Consumption: Networking and the Formation of Elites in the Archaic Western Mediterranean World. Proceedings of the International Conference in Innsbruck, 20th–23rd March 2012*, edited by Erich Kistler, Birgit Öhlinger, Martin Mohr, and Matthias Hoernes, 351–72. Wiesbaden: Harrassowitz Verlag.

———. 2018. "Hybrid Go-betweens: The Role of Individuals with Multiple Identities in Cross-cultural Contacts in the Late Bronze Age and Iron Age Central and Eastern Mediterranean." In *Change, Continuity and Connectivity: North-Eastern Mediterranean at the Turn of the Bronze Age and in the Early Iron Age*, edited by Ł. Niesiołowski-Spanò and Marek Węcowski, 196–220. Wiesbaden: Harrassowitz Verlag.

Csapo, Eric, Alan W. Johnston, and Daniel Geagan. 2000. "The Iron Age Inscriptions." In *Kommos IV: The Greek Sanctuary*, edited by J. W. Shaw and M. C. Shaw, 101–34. Princeton, NJ: Princeton University Press.

Culican, William. 1966. *The First Merchant Venturers: The Ancient Levant in History and Commerce*. London: Thames & Hudson.

———. 1975. "Sidonian Bottles." *Levant* 7: 145–50.

——— and J. E. Curtis. 1974. "The Punic Wreck in Sicily: The Pottery from the Ship." *International Journal of Nautical Archaeology* 3 (1): 43–54.

Cunliffe, Barry. 1993. "Core–Periphery Relationships: Iberia and the Mediterranean." In *Centre and Periphery in the Hellenistic World*, edited by P. Bilde, 53–85. Aarhus: Aarhus University Press.

Curtin, Philip D. 1984. *Cross-cultural Trade in World History*: Cambridge: Cambridge University Press.

Curtis, Adrian. 2009. *Oxford Bible Atlas*: Oxford: Oxford University Press.

Curtis, R. I. 2001. *Ancient Food Technology*. Leiden, Boston, and Cologne: Brill.

D'Andrea, Bruno. 2014a. *I tofet del Nord Africa dall'età arcaica all'età romana (VIII sec. a. C.-II sec. d. C.): Studi Archeologici*. Pisa and Rome: Fabrizio Serra Editore.

———. 2014b. "Nuove stele dal tofet di Mozia." *Vicino Oriente* 18: 123–44.

———. 2014c. "Cartagine." In *I tofet del Nord Africa dall'età arcaica all'età romana (VIII sec. a. C.-II sec. d. C.): Studi Archeologici*, edited by Bruno D'Andrea. Pisa and Rome: Fabrizio Serra Editore.

——— and Sara Giardino. 2013. "Il tofet dove e perché: L'identità fenicia, il circolo di Cartagine e la fase tardo punica." *Bollettino di Archeologia Online* 1: 1–29.

Dafni, Amots, and Barbara Böck. 2019. "Medicinal Plants of the Bible—Revisited." *Journal of Ethnobiology and Ethnomedicine* 15 (1): 57.

Dandamayev, Muhammad A. 1989. *A Political History of the Achaemenid Empire*. Leiden: Brill.

———. 2004. "Twin Towns and Ethnic Minorities in First-Millennium Babylonia." In *Commerce and Monetary Systems in the Ancient World: Means of Transmission and Cultural Interaction. Proceedings of the Fifth Annual Symposium of the Assyrian and Babylonian Intellectual Heritage Project, Innsbruck 2002*, edited by R. Rollinger and C. Ulf, 135–51. Wiesbaden: Franz Steiner Verlag.

Dasen, Véronique. 2011. "Magic and Medicine: Gems and the Power of Seals." In *Gems of Heaven: Recent Research on Engraved Gemstones in Late Antiquity, C. AD 200–600*, edited by Christopher Entwistle and Noël Adams, 69–74. London: British Museum Press.

Daviau, Paulette Maria Michele. 1996. "The Fifth Season of Excavations at Tall Jawa (1994): A Preliminary Report." *Annual of the Department of Antiquities of Jordan* 40: 83–99.

———. 2001. "Family Religion: Evidence for the Paraphernalia of the Domestic Cult." In *The World of the Aramaeans*, Vol. 2, *Studies in History and Archaeology in Honour of P.-E. Dion*, edited by M. P. M. Daviau, J. W. Wevers and M. Weigl, 199–229. Sheffield: Sheffield Academic Press.

——— and Stanley Klassen. 2014. "Conspicuous Consumption and Tribute: Assyrian Glazed Ceramic Bottles at Khirbat al-Mudayna ath-Thamad." *BASOR* 372: 99–122.

David, Nicholas, and Carol Kramer. 2001. *Ethnoarchaeology in Action*: Cambridge: Cambridge University Press.

Day, Peter M., and Louise Joyner. 2005. "Coarseware Stirrup Jars from Cannatello, Sicily: New Evidence from Petrographic Analysis." *Studi Micenei ed Egeo-Anatolici* 45: 309–14.

Dayagi-Mendels, M. 2002. *The Akhziv Cemeteries: The Ben-Dor Excavations, 1941–1944*. IAA Reports 15. Jerusalem: Israel Antiquities Authority.

Dayton, J. 1984. "Herodotus, Phoenicia, the Persian Gulf and India in the First Millennium BC." In *Arabie orientale, Mésopotamie et Iran méridional de l'Age du Fer au début de la période islamique*, edited by R. Boucharlat and J.-F. Salles, 363–72. Paris: Éditions Recherche sur les Civilisations.

De Angelis, Franco. 2003. "Equations of Culture: The Meeting of Natives and Greeks in Sicily (ca. 750–450 BC)." *Ancient West and East* 2 (1): 19–50.

De Blois, Lukas, and R. J. van der Spek. 2019. *An Introduction to the Ancient World*, 3rd ed. London: Routledge.

De Vartavan, Christian, and Victoria Asensi Amorós. 1997. *Codex of Ancient Egyptian Plant Remains*. Triade Exploration's Opus Magnum Series: Egyptology 1. London: Triade Exploration.

Del Freo, M. 2005. "L'expression ka-ko na-wi-jo de la Tablette Jn 829 de Pylos." In *Emporia: Aegeans in the Central and Eastern Mediterranean. Proceedings of the 10th International Aegean Conference, Athens, Italian School of Archaeology, 2004*, edited by Robert Laffineur and E. Greco, 793–803. Université de Liège, Belgium.

Delgado, Ana, and Meritxell Ferrer. 2007. "Cultural Contacts in Colonial Settings: The Construction of New Identities in Phoenician Settlements of the Western Mediterranean." *Stanford Journal of Archaeology* 5: 18–42.

——— and Meritxell Ferrer. 2011. "Representing Communities in Heterogeneous Worlds: Staple Foods and Ritual Practices in the Phoenician Diaspora." In *Guess Who's Coming to Dinner: Feasting Rituals in the Prehistoric Societies of Europe and the Near East*, edited by Gonzalo Aranda Jiménez, Sandra Montón-Subías, and Margarita Sánchez Romero, 184–203. Oxford: Oxbow Books.

Delussu, Fabrizio, and Barbara Wilkens. 2000. "Le conserve di pesce: Alcuni dati da contesti italiani." *Mélanges de l'École française de Rome* 112 (1): 53–65.

Demakopoulou, Katie, Nicoletta Divari-Valakou, and Gisela Walberg. 1994. "Excavations and Restoration Work in Midea 1990–1992." *Opuscula Atheniensia* 20: 19–41.

Demesticha, Stella. 2009. "Questions on Trade: The Case of the Mazotos Shipwreck." *Centre d'Études Chypriotes* 39: 387–402.

Demetriou, Andreas. 2001. "Phoenicians in Cyprus and their Hellenisation: The Case of Kition." *Archaeologia Cypria* 4: 135–44.

Denton, Branwen E. 1999. "More Pottery, Seals and a 'Face-Pendant' from Cemeteries on Bahrain." *Arabian Archaeology and Epigraphy* 10 (2): 134–60.

Dercksen, J. G. 2016. "Kaspam lašqul 'Let Me Weigh Out the Silver': Mesopotamian and Anatolian Weights during the Old Assyrian Colony Period." In *Silver, Money and Credit: A Tribute to Robartus J. van der Spek on the Occasion of his 65th Birthday*, edited by K. Kleber and R. Pirngruber, 11–22. Leiden: Nederlands Instituut voor het Nabije Oosten.

Descoeudres, Jean-Paul. 2006. "Euboean Pottery Overseas (10th to 7th centuries BC)." *Mediterranean Archaeology* 19/20: 3–24.

Desse, Jean, and Nathalie Desse-Berset. 2000. "Salaisons de poissons marins aux marges orientales du monde gréco-romain: Contributions de l'archéozoologie." *Mélanges de l'École française de Rome* 112: 119–34.

Dever, William G., and H. Darrell Lance. 1986. *Gezer IV: The 1969–71 Seasons in Field VI. The "Acropolis"*. Annual of the Nelson Glueck School of Biblical Archaeology 4. Jerusalem: Hebrew Union College.

Dewan, Rachel. 2015. "Bronze Age Flower Power: The Minoan Use and Social Significance of Saffron and Crocus Flowers." *Chronika* 5: 42–55.

Di Natale, A. 2014. "The Ancient Distribution of Bluefin Tuna Fishery: How Coins Can Improve Our Knowledge." *Collect. Vol. Sci. Pap. ICCAT* 70: 2828–44.

Dickinson, Oliver Thomas Pilkington Kirwan. 1994. *The Aegean Bronze Age*. Cambridge: Cambridge University Press.

Dils, Peter. 1993. "Wine for Pouring and Purification in Ancient Egypt." In *Ritual and Sacrifice in the Ancient Near East*, edited by J. Quaegebeur, 107–23. Leuven: Peeters.

Docter, Roald, and Janien Sonneveld. 2009. "Punic Glass from Carthaginian Settlement Contexts." *Carthage Studies* 3: 125–45.

———, Fehti Chelbi, Boutheina Maraoui Telmini, Babette Bechtold, Hans Koens, Karin Schmidt, and W. Van Neer. 2003. "Carthage Bir Massouda: Preliminary Report on the First Bilateral Excavations of Ghent University and the Institut National du Patrimoine (2002–2003)." *BABesch* 78: 43–70.

———, B. Maraoui Telmini, Hans van der Plicht, Karin Mansel, F. Chelbi, A. J. Nijboer, Wim Van Neer, and S. Garsallah. 2008. "New Radiocarbon Dates from Carthage: Bridging the Gap between History and Archaeology?" In *Beyond the Homeland: Markers in Phoenician Chronology*, edited by C. Sagona, 378–422. Leuven, Paris, and Dudley, MA: Peeters.

Donnellan, Lieve. 2016. "'Greek Colonisation' and Mediterranean Networks: Patterns of Mobility and Interaction at Pithekoussai." *Journal of Greek Archaeology* 1: 109–48.

——— and Valentino Nizzo. 2016. "Conceptualising Early Greek Colonisation: Introduction to the Volume." In *Conceptualising Early Colonisation*, edited by Lieve Donnellan, Valentino Nizzo, and Gert Jan Burgers, 9–20. Brussels and Rome: Belgisch Historisch Instituut te Rome.

Donner, Fred. 1986. "Xenophon's Arabia." *Iraq* 48: 1–14.

Donner, Herbert, and Wolfgang Roellig. 2002. *Kanaanäische und aramäische Inschriften*, 2nd. rev. and enlarged ed. Wiesbaden: Harrassowitz Verlag.

Dothan, Trude. 2008. *Deir el-Balah: Uncovering an Egyptian Outpost in Canaan from the Time of the Exodus*. Jerusalem: Israel Museum.

——— and David Ben-Shlomo. 2007. "Ceramic Pomegranates and their Relationship to Iron Age Cult." In *Up to the Gates of Ekron: Essays on the Archaeology and History of the Eastern Mediterranean in Honor of Seymour Gitin*, edited by Sidnie White Crawford, 3–16. Jerusalem: Albright Institute of Archaeological Research.

——— and Baruch Brandl. 2010. *Deir el-Balah: Excavations in 1977–1982 in the Cemetery and Settlement, Qedem*. Jerusalem: Hebrew University, Jerusalem, Institute of Archaeology.

——— and Dalit Regev. 2011. "An Inscribed Baboon Statuette from Tel Miqne-Ekron." *Egypt & Levant* 21: 211–29.

——— and Dalit Regev. 2016a. "An Inscribed Thoth Baboon Statuette from Iron Age I Contexts." In *Miqne-Ekron 9/1. Field IV Lower: The Iron Age I Early Philistine City*, edited by Trude Dothan, Yosef Garfinkel and Seymour Gitin, 463–6. Winona Lake, IN: Eisenbrauns.

——— and Dalit Regev. 2016b. "An Iron Age I Limestone Phallus." In *Miqne-Ekron 9/1. Field IV Lower: The Iron Age I Early Philistine City*, edited by Yosef Garfinkel and Seymour Gitin Trude Dothan, 469–70. Winona Lake, IN: Eisenbrauns.

Doumet-Serhal, Claude. 2008. "The Kingdom of Sidon and its Mediterranean Connections." In *Networking Patterns of the Bronze and Iron Age Levant: The Lebanon and it Mediterranean Connections*, edited by C. Doumet-Serhal, 1–70. Beirut: Lebanese British Friends of the National Museum.

Drews, Robert. 1973. *The Greek Accounts of Eastern History*. Cambridge, MA: Center for Hellenic Studies, Harvard University Press.

Dunham, Dows. 1950. *El Kurru*. Edited by Boston Museum of Fine Arts. Vol. I of *The Royal Cemeteries of Kush*. Cambridge, MA: Harvard University Press.

Durand, Caroline. 2019. "Alula: at the Crossroads of the Ancient Arabian Trade Routes." In *Alula: Wonder of Arabia*. Paris: Gallimar.

Edelman, Diana Vikander. 1991. *King Saul in the Historiography of Judah*, Vol. 121: London: A&C Black.

———. 2016. "Iconography on Double-Shekel Sidonian Coinage in the Persian Period: Is It a God or a King in the Chariot?" In *Religion in the Achaemenid Persian Empire: Emerging Judaisms and Trends*, edited by D. V. Edelman, A. Fitzpatrick-McKinley, and P. Guillaume, 228–86. Tübingen: Mohr Siebeck.

Ejstrud, Bo. 2005. "Size Matters: Estimating Trade of Wine, Oil and Fish-Sauce from Amphorae in the First Century AD." In *Ancient Fishing and Fish Processing in the Black Sea Region*, edited by T. Bekker-Nielsen, 171–81. Aarhus: Aarhus University Press.

El-Bekri, A. O. 1911–13. *Description de l'Afrique septentrionale*. Trans. M. G. De Slane, 2nd ed. Paris: Joudan.

———. 2003. *Book of the Roads and Kingdoms (Kitāb al-masālik wa'l-mamālik)*. Beirut: Al-Kotob Al-ilmiyah.

Elayi, Josette. 2009. *Byblos, cité sacrée (8e-4e s. av. J.-C.)*. Transeuphratene Supplements 15. Paris: Gabalda.

Elgavish, Joseph. 1994. *Shiqmona: On the Seacoast of Mount Carmel*. Tel Aviv: IES and Hakibutz Hameuhad.

Emanuel, Jeffrey P. 2019. "Seafaring and Shipwreck Archaeology." In *The Oxford Handbook of the Phoenician and Punic Mediterranean*, edited by Brian R. Doak and Carolina López-Ruiz, 423–33. Oxford: Oxford University Press.

Eph'al, Israel, and Joseph Naveh. 1989. "Hazael's Booty Inscriptions." *Israel Exploration Journal* 39: 192–200.

Epstein, Claire. 1966. *Palestinian Bichrome Ware*. Leiden: Brill.

Erard-Cerceau, I. 1990. "Végétaux, parfums et parfumeurs a l'époque Mycénienne." *Studi Micenei ed Egeo-Anatolici* 28: 251–85.

Ercolani, Andrea. 2015. "Phoinikes: Storia di un etnonimo." In *Transformations and Crisis in the Mediterranean: "Identity" and Interculturality in the Levant and Phoenician West during the 12th-8th Centuries BCE*, edited by Giuseppe Garbati and Tatiana Pedrazzi, 170–82. Pisa and Rome: Fabrizio Serra Editore.

Eremin, Katherine, Patrick Degryse, Nathaniel Erb-Satullo, Monica Ganio, Joseph Greene, Andrew Shortland, Marc Walton, and Lawrence Stager. 2012. "Iron Age Glass Beads from Carthage." In *Historical Technology, Materials, and Conservation: SEM and Microanalysis*, edited by N. D. Meeks, A. Meek, A. Mongiatti, and C. Cartwright, 30–5. London: Archetype Publications and the British Museum.

Escacena Carrasco, Jose Luis. 2008. "Tartessos." In *El Río Guadalquivir*, edited by Javier Rubiales-Torrejón, 185–95. Seville: Junta de Andalucía, Consejería de Obras Públicas y Transportes.

Étienne, Robert, and Françoise Mayet. 2002. *Salaisons et sauces de poisson hispaniques: Trois clés de l'économie de l'Hispanie romaine*. Mission arch. française au Portugal, Musée monographique de Conimbriga.

———, Françoise Mayet, and Carlos Taveres da Silva. 2000. "Chronologie des usines de salaisons de Lusitanie." *Mélanges de l'École française de Rome* 112 (1): 99–117.

Fajardo, Federico Molina, and Josep Padró Parcerisa. 1983–84. "Nuevos materiales procedentes de la necrópolis del Cerro de San Cristóbal (Almuñécar, Granada)." *Empúries: Revista de món clàssic i antiguitat tardana* 45–46: 284–93.

Fales, Frederick Mario. 2017. "Phoenicia in the Neo-Assyrian Period: An Updated Overview." *State Arch. Assyria Bull.* 23: 181–295.

Faulkner, R. O. 1962. *A Concise Dictionary of Middle Egyptian*. Oxford: Griffith Institute, Ashmolean Museum.

Fedoseev, Nikolay Fyodorovitch. 2007. "The Necropolis of Kul Oba." *Bar International Series* 1675 (2): 979.

Feldman, Marian H. 2006. *Diplomacy by Design: Luxury Arts and an International Style in the Ancient Near East, 1400–1200 BCE*. Chicago: University of Chicago Press.

Fentress, Elizabeth. 2001. "Villas, Wine and Kilns: The Landscape of Jerba in the Late Hellenistic Period." *Journal of Roman Archaeology* 14: 249–68.

———, Ali Drine, Renata Holod, and Ali Aït Kaci. 2009. *An Island through Time*. Jerba Studies 1.

Fernández, Jordi H., María José López Grande, and Ana Mezquida Orti. 2009. *Amuletos Púnicos de Hueso Hallados en Ibiza*. Trabajos del Museo Arqueológico de Ibiza 62. Eivissa: Museu Arqueologic d'Eivissa i Formentera.

Ferrence, Susan C., and Gordon Bendersky. 2004. "Therapy with Saffron and the Goddess at Thera." *Perspectives in Biology and Medicine* 47 (2): 199–226.

Figueras, Pau. 2000. *From Gaza to Pelusium: Materials for the Historical Geography of North Sinai and Southwestern Palestine (332 BCE–640 CE)*. Beer Sheva 14. Beer Sheva: Ben-Gurion University of the Negev Press.

Finkelberg, Margalit. 2003. "Homer as a Foundation Text." In *Homer and Early Greek Epic: Collected Essays*, edited by Margalit Finkelberg, 318–30. Berlin: De Gruyter

Finkelstein, Israel. 1995. *Living on the Fringe: The Archaeology and History of the Negev, Sinai and Neighbouring Regions in the Bronze and Iron Ages*. Monographs in Mediterranean Archaeology 6. Sheffield: Sheffield Academic Press.

Finley, Moses I. 1999. *The Ancient Economy*. Berkley, Los Angeles, and London: University of California Press.

Firmin, Laurence, Didier Courtois, Vincent Pétiard, Charles Ehret, and Konrad Lerch. 1998. "Evaluation of the Natural Variability in Iron Content and Selection of Iris sp. for Perfume Production." *HortScience* 33 (6): 1046–47.

Fischer, Peter M. 1999. "Chocolate-on-White Ware: Typology, Chronology, and Provenance. The Evidence from Tell Abu al-Kharaz, Jordan Valley." *BASOR* 313: 1–29.

———. 2003. "The Preliminary Chronology of Tell el-'Ajjul: Results of the Renewed Excavations in 1999 and 2000." In *The Synchronisation of Civilisations in the Eastern Mediterranean in the Second Millennium BC*, Vol. II, edited by M. Bietak, 263–94. Vienna: Verlag der Österreichischen Akademie der Wissenschaften.

———. 2004. "Coast contra Inland: Tell el-Ajjul and Tell Abu al-Kharaz during the Late Middle and Late Bronze Ages." *Egypt & Levant* 14: 249–63.

———, ed. 2006. *The Chronology of the Jordan Valley during the Middle and Late Bronze Ages: Pella, Tell al-Kharaz, and Tell Deir 'Alla*. Denkschriften der Gesamtakademie. Vienna: Verlag der Österreichischen Akademie der Wissenschaften.

———. 2008. "A Middle Bronze Age III Jug from the Lebanese Coast at Tell Abu Al-Kharaz, Jordan Valley." In *The Bronze Age in the Lebanon: Studies on the Archaeology and Chronology of Lebanon, Syria and Egypt*, edited by M. Bietak and E. Czerny, 87–91. Vienna: Verlag der Österreichischen Akademie der Wissenschaften.

Flammini, Roxana. 2010. "Elite Emulation and Patronage Relationships in the Middle Bronze: The Egyptianized Dynasty of Byblos." *Tel Aviv* 37: 154–68.

Fletcher, Richard Nathan. 2006. "The Cultural Biography of a Phoenician Mushroom-Lipped Jug." *Oxford Journal of Archaeology* 25 (2): 173–94.

Fontana, S., S. Ben Tahar, C. Capelli, A. Drine, and R. Holod. 2009. "La ceramica tra l'età punica e la tarda antichità." In *An Island through Time.* Jerba Studies 1, edited by Elizabeth Fentress, Ali Drine, Renata Holod, and Ali Aït Kaci, 241–327.

Foster, Karen Polinger. 2008. "Minoan Faience Revisited." In *Vitreous Materials in the Late Bronze Age Aegean*, edited by C. M. Jackson and E. C. Wager, 173–86.

Fourrier, Sabine. 2019. "Cyprus." In *The Oxford Handbook of the Phoenician and Punic Mediterranean*, edited by Brian R. Doak and Carolina López-Ruiz. Oxford: Oxford University Press.

Foxhall, Lin. 1998. "Cargoes of the Heart's Desire: The Character of Trade in the Archaic Mediterranean World." In *Archaic Greece: New Approaches and New Evidence*, edited by N. Fisher and H. Van Wees, 295–311. London: ISD LLC.

Frangie-Joly, Dina. 2016. "Perfumes, Aromatics, and Purple Dye: Phoenician Trade and Production in the Greco-Roman Period." *Journal of Eastern Mediterranean Archaeology and Heritage Studies* 4 (1): 36–56.

Frede, Simone. 2000. *Die phönizischen anthropoiden Sarkophage, 1, Fundgruppen und Bestattungskontexte.* Mainz: Verlag Philipp von Zabern.

Frendo, Anthony J. 1993. "Some Observations on the Investigation of the Phoenicians/Canaanites in the Ancient Mediterranean World." *Journal of Mediterranean Studies* 3 (2): 169–74.

———. 2018a. "Review: Crawley Quinn, In Search of the Phoenicians." *Ancient History Bulletin* 8: 74–8.

———. 2018b. "Multicultural Synthesis, Ethnic Identity, and the Case of Phoenician-Punic Malta." In *The Lure of the Antique: Essays on Malta and Mediterranean Archaeology in Honour of Anthony Bonanno*, edited by Nicholas C. Vella, Anthony J. Frendo, and Horatio C. R. Vella, 237–46. Leuven, Paris, and Bristol, CT: Peeters.

Frère, Dominique, Nicolas Garnier, and Dodinet Elisabeth. 2016. "Archéologie des huiles parfumées et médicinales en Méditerranée nord-occidentale préromaine (VIIIe–VIe s. av. J.-C.)." In *Le corps: Soins, rituels et symboles*, edited by C. Malet, 99–120. Paris: L'Harmattan.

Freumann, B. 2009. "Lumbermen and Shipwrights: Phoenicians on the Mediterranean Coast of Southern Spain." In *Colonial Encounters in Ancient Iberia: Phoenician, Greek, and Indigenous Relations*, edited by M. Dietler and C. López-Ruiz, 169–90. Chicago: University of Chicago Press.

Freyne, S. 2002. "Introduction: Studying the Jewish Diaspora in Antiquity." In *Jews in the Hellenistic and Roman Cities*, edited by John R. Bartlett, 1–5. London and New York: Routledge.

Frick, Frank S., Glenda Friend, and Khālid Nashīf. 2000. *Tell Taannek, 1963–1968.* American Schools of Oriental Research, Palestinian Institute of Archaeology, Birzeit University.

Frost, Honor. 1981. *Lylibaeum: Atti della Accademia nazionale dei Lincei, Supp.* Rome: Accademia nazionale dei Lincei.

Fulford, Michael. 1992. "Territorial Expansion and the Roman Empire." *World Archaeology* 23: 294–305.

Gachet-Bizollon, Jacqueline. 2007. *Les ivoires d'Ougarit: Et l'art des ivoiriers du Levant au Bronze récent.* Ras Shamra-Ougarit 16. Paris: Éditions Recherche sur les civilisations.

Gal, Zvi, and Karen Covello-Paran. 1996. "Excavations at 'Afula, 1989." *'Atiqot* 30: 25–67.

Gallis, Kostas J. 1983. "Evidence for Funerary Rituals at Cremation Burials since Early Neolithic in Thessaly (Greece)." In *Intellectual Expressions of Prehistoric Man: Art and Religion. Acts of the Valcamonica Symposium '79*, edited by Emmanuel Anati, Antonio Beltrán Martinez, and M. Abreu, 99–104. Bresica and Milan: Edizioni del Centro, Centro Camuno di Studi Preistorica, Editoriale Jaca Book Spa.

Garbini, Giovanni. 2003. *Myth and History in the Bible.* London: Sheffield Academic Press.

García Vargas, E., and D. Bernal Casasola. 2009. "Roma y la producción de garvum y 'salsamenta' en la costa meridional de Hispania: Estado actual de la investigación." In *Arqueología de la pesca en el Estrecho de Gibraltar: De la Prehistoria al fin del Mundo Antiguo*, edited by D. Bernal Casasola, 133–81. Servicio de Publicaciones de la Universidad de Cádiz.

Gates, Marie-Henriette Carre. 2001. "Potmarks at Kinet Höyük and the Hittite Ceramic Industry." In *La Cilice: Espaces et pouvoir locaux (2e millénaire av. J.-C.-4e siècle ap. J.-C.): Actes de la Table Ronde Internationale d'Istanbul, 2-5 novembre 1999*, edited by E. Jean, A. M. Dinçol and S. Durugönül, 137–57. Istanbul Persée.

Gentelli, Liesel, and AbdelRahman Medhat. 2017. "A Multi-analytical Approach for the Archaeometric Identification of a Roman Period Glass Furnace in the Central Nile Delta." *Journal of Archaeological Science: Reports* 11: 330–7.

Genz, Hermann. 2011. "Foreign Contacts of the Hittites." In *Insights into Hittite History and Archaeology*, edited by Hermann Genz and Dirk Paul Mielke, 301–33. Leuven, Paris, and Walpole, MA: Peeters.

———. 2017. "Hittite Gods Abroad: Evidence for Hittite Diplomatic Activities?" In *Questions, Approaches, and Dialogues in Eastern Mediterranean Archaeology: Studies in Honor of Marie-Henriette and Charles Gates*, edited by Ekin Kozal, Murat Akar, Yağmur Heffron, Çiler Çilingiroğlu, Tevfik Emre Şerifoğlu, Canan Çakirlar, Sinan Ünlüsoy, and Eric Jean, 243–25. Münster: Ugarit-Verlag.

Georgiou, Giorgos. 2009. "Three Stone Sarcophagi from a Cypro-Classical Tomb at Kition." *Centre d'Études Chypriotes* 39: 113–39.

Geva, Shulamit. 1980. "A Fragment of a Tridacna Shell from Shechem." *ZDPV* 96: 41–7.

Ghaki, Mansour. 2015. "Toponymie et onomastique libyques: L'apport de l'écriture punique/néopunique." In *La Lingua nella Vita e la Vita della Lingua: Itinerari e Percorsi degli Studi Berberi*, edited by Anna Maria Di Tolla, 65–71. Naples: UNIOR.

Giannoulaki, Marianna, Maria M. Pyrounaki, Jean-Hervé Bourdeix, Lotfi Ben Abdallah, Angelo Bonanno, Gualtiero Basilone, Magdalena Iglesias, Ana Ventero, Andrea De Felice, Iole Leonori, Vasilis D. Valavanis, Athanassios Machias, and Claire Saraux. 2017. "Habitat Suitability Modeling to Identify the Potential Nursery Grounds of the Atlantic Mackerel and its Relation to Oceanographic Conditions in the Mediterranean Sea." *Frontiers in Marine Science* 4 (230).

Giardino, Claudio. 2005. "Metallurgy in Italy between the Late Bronze Age and the Early Iron Age: The Coming of Iron." In *Papers in Italian Archaeology VI: Communities and Settlements from the Neolithic to the Early Medieval Period. Proceedings of the 6th Conference of Italian Archaeology held at the University of Groningen, Groningen Institute of Archaeology, The Netherlands, April 15-17, 2003*, edited by Peter A. J. Attema, A. J. Nijboer, and A. Zifferero, 491–505. Oxford: Archaeopress.

Gibson, John C. L. 1982. *Textbook of Syrian Semitic Inscriptions*, III, *Phoenician Inscriptions: Including Inscriptions in the Mixed Dialect of Arslan Tash*. Oxford: Clarendon Press.

Gil, Moshe. 2003. "The Jewish Merchants in the Light of Eleventh-Century Geniza Documents." *Journal of the Economic and Social History of the Orient* 46 (3): 273–319.

Gilboa, Ayelet, and Dvory Namdar. 2015. "On the Beginnings of South Asian Spice Trade with the Mediterranean Region: A Review." *Radiocarbon* 57 (2): 265–283.

Giner-Larza, Eva M., Salvador Máñez, Rosa M. Giner, M. Carmen Recio, José M. Prieto, Miguel Cerdá-Nicolás, and José Luis Ríos. 2002. "Anti-inflammatory Triterpenes from Pistacia Terebinthus Galls." *Planta Medica* 68 (04): 311–5.

Giumlia-Mair, Alessandra, Rosa Maria Albanese Procelli, and Fulvia Lo Schiavo. 2011. "The Metallurgy of the Sicilian Final Bronze Age/Early Iron Age Necropolis of Madonna del Piano (Catania, Sicily)." *Trabajos de Prehistoria* 67 (2): 469–88.

Gledhill, David. 2002. *The Names of Plants*: Cambridge: Cambridge University Press.

Goitein, Shelomo Dov. 1967. *A Mediterranean Society: The Jewish Communities of the Arab World as Portrayed in the Documents of the Cairo Geniza*, Vol. 1: Berkeley: University of California Press.

Goldberg, Jessica L. 2012. *Trade and Institutions in the Medieval Mediterranean: The Geniza Merchants and their Business World*. Cambridge: Cambridge University Press.

Gonen, Rivka. 1981. "Tell el 'Ajjul in the Late Bronze Age: City or Cemetery?" *Eretz Israel* 15: 69–78.

González de Canales Cerisola, Fernando, Leonardo Serrano, and Jorge Llompart Gómez. 2006. "Las evidencias más antiguas de la presencia fenicia en el sur de la Península." In *Tiempos de Púrpura: Málaga antigua y antigüedades hispanas*, I, edited by Manuel Corrales Aguilar, 105–28. Málaga: Servicio de Publicaciones.

González Ruibal, A. 2004. "An Askos from Eivissa (Balearic Islands) in Galicia: Some Remarks on the Character of the Punic trade in the NW of Iberia." *Complutum* 15: 33–43.

Gophna, R., and I. Milevski. 2003. "Feinan and the Mediterranean During the Early Bronze Age." *Tel-Aviv* 30: 222–31.

Goren, Y., R. E. Jones, and S. T. Levi. 2001. "Studio di analisi archeometriche delle ceramiche preistoriche di Vivara e Monte Grande (AG)." In *La ricerca archeologica a Vivara e le attività dei laboratori dell'Istituto Universitario Suor Orsola Benincasa*, edited by Carla Pepe, 67–76. Naples: Istituto Universitario Suor Orsola Benincasa.

Grainger, J. D. 1991. *Hellenistic Phoenicia*. Oxford: Oxford University Press.

Grainger, Sally. 2018. "Garum and Liquamen: What's in a Name?" *Journal of Maritime Archaeology* 13 (3): 247–61.

Grami, Bahram. 2013. "Perfumery Plant Materials as Reflected in Early Persian Poetry." *Journal of the Royal Asiatic Society* 23 (1): 39–52.

Grant, Michael. 1980. *The Etruscans*. New York: Scribner.

Grayson, Albert Kirk. 1991. *Assyrian Rulers of the Early First Millennium BC*: Toronto: University of Toronto Press.

——— and Jamie Novotny. 2012. *The Royal Inscriptions of Sennacherib, King of Assyria (704-681 BC)*, Vol. 3, No. 1. Winona Lake, IN: Eisenbrauns.

——— and Jamie Novotny. 2014. *The Royal Inscriptions of Sennacherib, King of Assyria (704-681 BC)*, Vol. 3, No. 2. Winona Lake, IN: Eisenbrauns.

Green, M. 1983. "The Syrian and Lebanese Topographical Data in the Story of Sinuhe." *Chronique d'Égypte* 58: 38–59.

Greenberg, Raphael, Liora Kolska-Horwitz, and Omri Lernau. 1998. "A Sounding at Tel Na'ama in the Hula Valley." *'Atiqot* 35: 9–35.

Greene, Joseph A. 1996. "The Beginnings of Grape Cultivation and Wine Production in Phoenician/Punic North Africa." *Origins and Ancient History of Wine Food and Nutrition in History and Anthropology Series* 11: 311–37.

Greenlaw, Cybelle. 2005. "How Monkeys Evolved in Egyptian and Minoan Art and Culture." In *Symposium on Mediterranean Archaeology 2003: Proceedings of the Seventh Meeting of Postgraduate Researchers at the Institute of Archaeology, University College London*, 71–4.

———. 2006. "Monkeying around the Mediterranean: A Fresh Perspective on Ancient Primates." In *SOMA 2004*, 63–8.

Gropp, Gerd. 1991. "Christian Maritime Trade of Sasanian Age in the Persian Gulf." In *Internationale Archäologie*, Vol. 6, *Gölf Archäologie: Mesopotamien, Iran, Kuwait, Bahrein, Vereinigte Arabische Emirate und Oman*, edited by K. Schippmann, A. Herling, and J.-F. Salles, 83–8. Munich: Universität Göttingen and Maison de l'Orient Méditerranéen.

Grose, David Frederick. 1989. *The Toledo Museum of Art: Early Ancient Glass*: Hudson Hills/Toledo Museum of Art.

Gübel, Eric. 1988. "Phoenician Seals in the Allard Pierson Museum, Amsterdam (CGPH3)." *Rivista di Studi Fenici* 16 (2): 145–63.

———. 2000. "Multicultural and Multimedial Aspects of Early Phoenician Art, c. 1200–675 BCE." In *Images as Media: Sources for the Cultural History of the Near East and Eastern Mediterranean (1st Millennium BCE)*, edited by C. Uehlinger, 185–214. Fribourg and Göttingen: University Press/Vandenhoeck & Ruprecht.

———. 2014. "On the Interaction between Ammon, Moab and Edom with the Phoenician Coast: Some Addenda and Afterthoughts." *Akkadica Supplementum*.

———. 2015. "Bronze Work in the Phoenician Homeland: A Preliminary Survey." In *Phoenician Bronzes in Mediterranean*, edited by Javier Jiménez Avila, 241–68. Madrid: Real Academia de la Historia.

Gunter, Ann C. 2013. "Orientalism and Orientalization in the Iron Age Mediterranean." In *Critical Approaches to Ancient Near Eastern Art*, edited by Brian A. Brown and Marian H. Feldman, 79–108. Berlin: De Gruyter.

Guzzo Amadasi, Maria Giulia, and Vassos Karageorghis. 1977. *Fouilles de Kition*, III, *Inscriptions phéniciennes*. Nicosia: Zavallis Pr.

Haber, Marc, Claude Doumet-Serhal, Christiana Scheib, Yali Xue, Petr Danecek, Massimo Mezzavilla, Sonia Youhanna, Rui Martiniano, Javier Prado-Martinez, Michał Szpak, E. A. Matisoo-Smith, Holger Schutkowski, Richard Mikulski, Pierre Zalloua, Toomas Kivisild, and Chris Tyler-Smith. 2017a. "Continuity and Admixture in the Last Five Millennia of Levantine History from Ancient Canaanite and Present-day Lebanese Genome Sequences." *American Journal of Human Genetics* 101 (2): 274–82.

———, Claude Doumet-Serhal, Christiana Scheib, Yali Xue, Petr Danecek, Massimo Mezzavilla, Sonia Youhanna, Rui Martiniano, Javier Prado-Martinez, Michał Szpak, E. A. Matisoo-Smith, Holger Schutkowski, Richard Mikulski, Pierre Zalloua, Toomas Kivisild, and Chris Tyler-Smith. 2017b. "Continuity and Admixture in the Last Five Millennia of Levantine History from Ancient Canaanite and Present-day Lebanese Genome Sequences." *bioRxiv*.

Hadjisavvas, Sophoklis. 1999. "Chronique des fouilles et découvertes archéologiques à Chypre en 1998." *Bulletin de correspondance hellénique* 123 (2): 599–633.

———. 2007. "The Phoenician Penetration in Cyprus as Documented in the Necropolis of Kition." *Cahiers du Centre d'Études Chypriotes* 37 (1): 185–95.

———. 2012. *The Phoenician Period Necropolis of Kition*, Vol. 1. Shelby White and Leon Levy Program for Archaeological Publications. Nicosia: Department of Antiquities, Cyprus.

——— and Angelos Chaniotis. 2012. "Wine and Olive Oil in Crete and Cyprus: Socio-economic Aspects." In *Parallel Lives: Ancient Island Societies in Crete and Cyprus*, edited by Gerald Cadogan, Maria Iacovou, Katerina Kopaka, and James Whitley, 157–73. British School at Athens.

Halayqa, Issam, and Charlotte Mary Yonge. 2010. "The Demise of Ugarit in the Light of its Connections with Ḫatti." *Ugarit-Forschungen* 42: 297–332.

Hall, Jonathan M. 2002. *Hellenicity: Between Ethnicity and Culture*. Chicago: University of Chicago Press.

Hannestad, Lise. 1984. "The Pottery from the Hellenistic Settlement on Failaka." In *Arabie orientale, Mésopotamie et Iran méridional de l'Age du Fer au début de la période islamique*, edited by R. Boucharlat and J.-F. Salles, 67–83. Paris: Éditions Recherche sur les Civilisations.

Hansen, Mogens Herman, and Thomas Heine Nielsen. 2004. *An Inventory of Archaic and Classical Poleis: An Investigation Conducted by the Copenhagen Polis Centre for the Danish National Research Foundation*. Oxford: Oxford University Press.

Hansen, Svend. 2013. "Innovative Metals: Copper, Gold and Silver in the Black Sea region and the Carpathian Basin during the 5th and 4th Millennium BC." In *Metal Matters: Innovative Technologies and Social Change in Prehistory and Antiquity*, edited by Stefan Burmeister, Svend Hansen, Michael Kunst, and Nils Müller-Scheeßel, 137–70. Verlag Marie Leidorf GmbH.

———. 2014. "The 4th Millennium: A Watershed in European Prehistory." *Western Anatolia before Troy: Proto-Urbanisation in the 4th Millennium BC? Proceedings of the International Symposium held at the Kunsthistorisches Museum Wien, Vienna, Austria, 21–24 November, 2012.*

Hanson, Ann Ellis. 1992. "Egyptians, Greeks, Romans, Arabes, and Ioudaioi, in the First Century AD: Tax Archive from Philadelphia. P. Michigan inv. 880 recto and P. Princ. III 152 Revisited." In *Life in a Multi-cultural Society: Egypt from Cambyses to Constantine and Beyond*, 133–47. Oriental Inst Pubns Sales.

Harden, D. 1962. *The Phoenicians*. London: Thames & Hudson.

Harrison, Thomas. 2003. "Upside Down and Back to Front: Herodotus and the Greek Experience." In *Ancient Perspectives on Egypt*, edited by Roger J. Matthews and Cornelia Roemer, 145–56. London: UCL Press.

Haseeb, Sohaib, Bryce Alexander, Ricardo Lopez Santi, Alvaro Sosa Liprandi, and Adrian Baranchuk. 2019. "What's in Wine? A Clinician's Perspective." *Trends in Cardiovascular Medicine* 29 (2): 97–106.

Haw, Stephen George. 2017. "Cinnamon, Cassia and Ancient Trade." *Journal of Ancient History and Archaeology* 4 (1): 5–18.

Hawkins, J. David. 2009. "Cilicia, the Amuq, and Aleppo: New Light in a Dark Age." *Near Eastern Archaeology* 72 (4): 164–73.

—— and A. Morpurgo Davies. 1978. "On the Problems of Karatepe: The Hieroglyphic Text." *Anatolian Studies* 28: 103–19.

Hayes, J. W. 1996. "The Pottery." In *Berenike 1995: Preliminary Report on the 1995 Excavations at Berenike (Egyptian Red Sea Coast) and the Survey of the Eastern Desert*, edited by S. E. Sidebotham and W. Z. Wendrich, 147–78. Leiden: Research School CNWS, Leiden University.

———. 2008. *Roman Pottery: Fine-Ware Imports. The Athenian Agora*. Princeton, NJ: American School of Classical Studies in Athens.

Heimpel, Wolfgang. 1982. "A Catalog of Near Eastern Venus Deities." *Syro-Mesopotamian Studies* 4 (3): 9–22.

Henderson, Julian. 2013. *Ancient Glass: An Interdisciplinary Exploration*: Cambridge: Cambridge University Press.

Hermary, Antoine. 1998. "Votive Offerings in the Sanctuaries of Cyprus, Rhodes and Crete during the Late Geometric and Archaic Periods." In *Eastern Mediterranean, Cyprus-Dodecanese-Crete 16th-6th Cent. BC: Proceedings of the International Symposium Held at Rethymno, Crete*, edited by Vassos Karageorghis and N. Stampolidis, 265–75. Athens: Leventis Foundation.

———. 1989. *Catalogue des antiquités de Chypre: Sculptures*. Edited by Orientales Musée du Louvre. Département des Antiquités. Paris: Réunion des Musées Nationaux.

Hernández, Carlos Martín. 2013. "Phoenician Trade of Raw Materials and Changes in Metal Production Patterns in SW Iberia during the Orientalizing Period." In *Network Analysis in Archaeology: New Approaches to Regional Interaction*, edited by C. Knappet, 17–24. Oxford: Oxford University Press.

Herr, L. G. 2015. "Iron Age IIA–B: Transjordan." In *The Ancient Pottery of Israel and Its Neighbors, from the Iron Age through the Hellenistic Period*, edited by Seymour Gitin, 281–99. Jerusalem: Israel Exploration Society.

Herrmann, Virginia R., and Philip A. Johnston. 2018. "Worked Bone, Beads, and Ostrich Eggshell Fragments." In *Ashkelon 6: The Middle Bronze Age Ramparts and Gates of the North Slope and Later Fortifications*, edited by Lawrence E. Stager, J. David Schloen, and Ross Joseph Voss, 433–44. University Park, PA: Eisenbrauns.

Herzog, Z. 1997. "The Phoenician Settlement at Tel Michal." *Michmanim* 11: 31–43.

Hess, Richard S. 1993. *Amarna Personal Names*. ASOR Dissertation Series 9. Winona Lake, IN: Eisenbrauns.

———. 2006. "Cultural Aspects of Onomastic Distribution throughout Southern Canaan in Light of New Evidence." *Ugarit-Forschungen* 38: 353–61.

Higueras-Milena Castellano, Aurora, and Antonio M. Sáez Romero. 2018. "The Phoenicians and the Ocean: Trade and Worship at La Caleta, Cádiz, Spain." *International Journal of Nautical Archaeology* 47 (1): 81–102.

Hirschfeld, Nicolle E. 2004. "Eastwards via Cyprus? The Marked Mycenaean Pottery of Enkomi, Ugarit and Tell Abu Hawam." In *Travaux de la Maison de l'Orient et de la Méditerranée*, Vol. 41, *La céramique mycénienne de l'Égée au levant: Hommage à Vronwy Hankey*, edited by J. Balensi, J.-Y. Monchambert, and S. M. Celka, 97–104. Lyon: Maison de l'Orient et de la Méditerranée–Jean Pouilloux.

———. 2007. "Appendix S: Trireme Warfare in Herodotus." In *The Landmark Herodotus: The Histories*, edited by R. B. Strassler, 824–34. New York: Pantheon Books.

Hodos, Tamar. 2009. "Colonial Engagements in the Global Mediterranean Iron Age." *Cambridge Archaeological Journal* 19 (2): 221–41.

Höflmayer, Felix. 2007. "Ägyptische skarabäen auf kreta und ihre Bedeutung für die absolute Chronologie der minoischen Altpalastzeit (MM IB–MM IIB)." *Ägypten und Levante/Egypt and the Levant* 17: 107–25.

Hölbl, Günther. 1986. "Egyptian Fertility Magic within Phoenician and Punic Culture." In *Archaeology and Fertility Cult in the Ancient Mediterranean: First International Conference on Archaeology of the Ancient Mediterranean. University of Malta, 2-5 September 1985*, edited by Anthony Bonanno, 197–203. Amsterdam: John Benjamins Publishing.

———. 1987. "Typology of Form and Material in Classifying Small Aegyptiaca in the Mediterranean during Archaic Times: With Special Reference to Faience Found on Rhodian Sites." In *Early Vitreous Materials*, edited by M. Bimson and I. Freestone, 115–26. London: British Museum.

———. 1989. *Ägyptisches Kulturgut auf den Inseln Malta und Gozo: Die Objekte im Archäologischen Museum von Valletta*. Studien zum ägyptischen Kulturgut im Mittelmeerraum. Vienna: Verlag der Österreichischen Akademie der Wissenschaften.

———. 1999. "Funde aus Milet VIII: Die Aegyptiaca vom Aphroditetempel auf dem Zeytintepe." *Archäologischer Anzeiger* 3: 345–71.

———. 2006. "Die Aegyptiaca vom Aphroditetempel auf Thera." *AM* 121: 73–103.

———. 2008. "Ägyptisches Kulturgut im archaischen Artemision." In *Die Archäologie der ephesischen Artemis: Gestalt und Ritual eines Heiligtums*, edited by Ulrike Muss, 209–21. Vienna: Phoibos Verlag.

———. 2019. "Aegyptiaca from the Mound at Chatal Höyük." In *Excavations in the Plain of Antioch III: Stratigraphy, Pottery and Small Finds from Chatal Höyük in the 'Amuq Plain*, edited by Marina Pucci, 305–18. The Oriental Institute of the University of Chicago.

Holladay, John S. 2001. "Toward a New Paradigmatic Understanding of Long-Distance Trade in the Ancient Near East: From the Middle Bronze II to the Early Iron II—A Sketch." In *The World of the Aramaeans*, Vol. II, *Studies in History and Archaeology in Honour of Paul-Eugène Dion*, edited by P. M. M. Daviau, J. W. Wevers, and M. Weigl, 136–98. Sheffield: Sheffield Academic Press.

———. 2004. "Judaeans (and Phoenicians) in Egypt in the Late Seventh to Sixth Centuries BC." In *Egypt, Israel, and the Ancient Mediterranean World: Studies in Honor of Donald B. Redford*, edited by G. N. Knoppers and A. Hirsch, 405–37. Leiden and Boston: Brill.

———. 2006. "Hezekiah's Tribute, Long-Distance Trade, and the Wealth of Nations ca. 1000–600 BC: A New Perspective." In *Confronting the Past: Archaeological and Historical Essays on Ancient Israel in Honor of William G. Dever*, edited by S. Gitin, J. E. Write, and J. P. Dessel, 309–31. Winona Lake, IN: Eisenbrauns.

Hood, Sinclair. 2005. "Dating the Knossos Frescoes." In *Aegean Wall Painting: A Tribute to Mark Cameron*, edited by Lyvia Morgan. British School at Athens.

Horden, Peregrine, and Nicholas Purcell. 2000. *The Corrupting Sea: A Study of Mediterranean History*: Oxford: Wiley-Blackwell.

——— and Nicholas Purcell. 2006. "The Mediterranean and 'the New Thalassology'." *The American Historical Review* 111 (3): 722–40.

Hornblower, Simon, and Antony Spawforth. 1999. *The Oxford Classical Dictionary*: Oxford: Oxford University Press.

Hoyos, Dexter. 2010. *The Carthaginians*: London: Routledge.

Hudson, Michael. 1992. "Did the Phoenicians Introduce the Idea of Interest to Greece and Italy? And if so, When?" In *Greece between East and West: 10th-8th Centuries BC: Papers of the Meeting at the Institute of Fine Arts, New York University, 1990*, edited by Günter Kopcke and Isabelle Tokumaru, 128–43. Mainz: Verlag Philipp von Zabern.

Iakovidis, Spyros E. 2003. "Late Mycenaean Perati and the Levant." In *The Synchronisation of Civilisations in the Eastern Mediterranean in the Second Millennium BC*, Vol. II, edited by M Bietak, 501–12. Vienna: Verlag der Österreichischen Akademie der Wissenschaften.

ICES-Advice. 2018. Bay of Biscay and the Iberian Coast Ecoregion: Ecosystem Overview. ICES Ecosystem Overviews. International Council for the Exploration of the Sea (ICES)/Conseil International pour l'Exploration de la Mer (CIEM).

Immerwahr, Sara Anderson. 1989. "The Pomegranate Vase: Its Origins and Continuity." *Hesperia* 58: 397–410.

Isaac, Benjamin H. 2004. *The Invention of Racism in Classical Antiquity*. Princeton, NJ: Princeton University Press.

Israeli, Yael. 2003. *Ancient Glass in the Israel Museum: The Eliahu Dobkin Collection and Other Gifts*. Jerusalem: Israel Museum.

Jackson, Caroline M., and Paul Thomas Nicholson. 2010. "The Provenance of Some Glass Ingots from the Uluburun Shipwreck." *Journal of Archaeological Science* 37 (2): 295–301.

Jacopi, G. 1929. *Scavi nella necropoli di Jalisso, 1924-1928. Clara Rhodos: Studi e materiali pubblicati a cura dell'Istituto storico-archeologico di Rodi 3*. Rhodes: Istituto storico-archeologico.

———. 1933. *Esplorazione archeologica di Camiro, 2, Clara Rhodos: Studi e materiali pubblicati a cura dell'Istituto storico-archeologico di Rodi 6-7*. Rhodes: Istituto storico-archeologico.

James, Matthew A., Nicole Reifarth, Anna J. Mukherjee, Matthew P. Crump, Paul J. Gates, Peter Sandor, Francesca Robertson, Peter Pfälzner, and Richard P. Evershed. 2009. "High Prestige Royal Purple Dyed Textiles from the Bronze Age Royal Tomb at Qatna, Syria." *Antiquity* 83: 1109–18.

James, Thomas Garnet Henry. 1986. *Egyptian Painting and Drawing in the British Museum*. London: British Museum.

Jarus, Owen. 2019. "Ancient Inscription Points to Lost Temple of Unknown God in Yemen." *Live Science*, March 19. https://www.livescience.com/65024-ancient-inscription-lost-temple-yemen.html

Jenkins, G. K. 1971. *Coins of Punic Sicily*, Part I. Bern: Schweizerische Numismatische Gesellschaft. 25–78.

Jigoulov, Vadim S. 2010. *The Social History of Achaemenid Phoenicia: Being a Phoenician, Negotiating Empires*. London: Equinox.

Johnson, Barbara L. 2008. "The Pottery." In *Archaeological Excavations at Caesarea Maritima Areas CC, KK and NN. Final Reports I: The Objects*, edited by Joseph Patrich, 13–206. Winona Lake, IN: Eisenbrauns.

Jones, R. E., and S. J. Vaughan. 1991. "Traders and Craftsmen in the Central Mediterranean: Archaeological Evidence and Archaeological Research." In *Bronze Age Trade in the Mediterranean*, edited by N. H. Gale, 127–47. Jonsered: Åström.

———, Sara T. Levi, and Marco Bettelli. 2005. "Mycenaean Pottery in the Central Mediterranean: Imports, Imitations and Derivatives." In *Emporia: Aegeans in the Central and Eastern Mediterranean. Proceedings of the 10th International Aegean Conference, Athens, Italian School of Archaeology, April 2004*, edited by R. Laffineur and E. Greco, 539–45. Université de Liège, Belgium.

Jongeling, Karel. 2008. *Handbook of Neo-Punic Inscriptions*: Tübingen: Mohr Siebeck.

——— and Robert M. Kerr. 2005. *Late Punic Epigraphy: An Introduction to the Study of Neo-Punic and Latino-Punic Inscriptions*: Tübingen: Mohr Siebeck.

Jung, Reinhard. 2018. "Push and Pull Factors of the Sea Peoples between Italy and the Levant." In *An Archaeology of Forced Migration: Crisis-Induced Mobility and the Collapse of the 13th c. BCE Eastern Mediterranean*, edited by Jan Driessen, 273–306. Louvain: Presses universitaires de Louvain.

Karageorghis, Vassos. 1997. "A Phoenician Type Funerary Cippus from Cyprus." *Cahiers du Centre d'Études Chypriotes* 27 (1): 121–6.

———. 2008. "Les Phéniciens à Chypre." In *Networking Patterns of the Bronze and Iron Age Levant: The Lebanon and its Mediterranean Connections*, edited by Claude Doumet-Serhal, 190–214. Beirut: Lebanese British Friends of the National Museum.

Karakulak, F. Saadet, and Taner Yildiz. 2016. "Atlantic Bluefin Tuna in the Mediterranean Sea: Fisheries, Farming, Management and Conservation." In *The Turkish Part of the Mediterranean Sea: Marine Biodiversity, Fisheries, Conservation and Governance*, edited by Cemal Turan, B. Salihoglu, Elif Özgür Özbek and Bayram Öztürk, 320–32. Istanbul: Turkish Marine Research Foundation (TUDAV).

Kashtan, Nadav. 1988. "Akko-Ptolemais: A Maritime Metropolis in Hellenistic and Early Roman Times, 332 BCE–70 CE, as Seen Through the Literary Sources." In *Mediterranean Cities: Historical Perspectives*, edited by I. Malkin and R. L. Hohlefelder, 37–53. London: Routledge.

Kassianidou, Vasiliki, and George Papasavvas, eds. 2012. *Eastern Mediterranean Metallurgy and Metalwork in the Second Millennium BC: A Conference in Honor of James D. Muhly, Nicosia October 2009*. Oxford and Oakville: Oxbow Books.

Katzenstein, H. Jacob 1979. "Tyre in the Early Persian Period (539–486 BCE)." *The Biblical Archaeologist* 42 (1): 23–34.

———. 1991. "Phoenician Deities Worshipped in Israel and Judah during the Time of the First Temple." *Studia Phoenicia XI: Phoenicia and the Bible*: 187–91.

Kaufman, Brett, Roald Docter, Christian Fischer, Fethi Chelbi, and Boutheina Maraoui Telmini. 2016. "Ferrous Metallurgy from the Bir Massouda Metallurgical Precinct at Phoenician and Punic Carthage and the Beginning of the North African Iron Age." *Journal of Archaeological Science* 71: 33–50.

———, R. Docter, D. A. Scott, F. Chelbi, and B. M. Telmini. 2019. "Differential Access to Metal Wealth from Colony to Capital to Collapse at Phoenician and Punic Carthage: Non-ferrous Alloys and Mineral Resources from the Bir Massouda Site." *Archaeological and Anthropological Sciences* 11 (8): 4075–4101.

Keel, Othmar, and Christoph Uehlinger. 1998. *Gods, Goddesses and Images of God in Ancient Israel*. Edinburgh: T&T Clark.

Kennedy, Hugh. 2007. *The Great Arab Conquests: How the Spread of Islam Changed the World We Live in.* Boston, MA: Da Capo Press.

Kenzelmann Pfyffer, Anne, Thierry Theurillat, and Samuel Verdan. 2005. "Graffiti d'époque géométrique provenant du sanctuaire d'Apollon Daphnéphoros à Erétrie." *Zeitschrift für Papyrologie und Epigraphik*: 51–83.

Kerr, Robert M. 2010. *Latino-Punic Epigraphy: A Descriptive Study of the Inscriptions*: Tübingen: Mohr Siebeck.

———. 2018. "New Punic Punditry." *Journal of American Oriental Society* 138 (2): 395–401.

Kessler, John. 2008. "Diaspora and Homeland in the Early Achaemenid Period: Community, Geography and Demography in Zechariah 1–8." In *Approaching Yehud: New Approaches to the Study of the Persian Period*, edited by J. L. Berquist, 137–66. Leiden and Boston: Brill.

Kiderlen, Moritz, Michael Bode, Andreas Hauptmann, and Yannis Bassiakos. 2016. "Tripod Cauldrons Produced at Olympia Give Evidence for Trade with Copper from Faynan (Jordan) to South West Greece, c. 950–750 BCE." *Journal of Archaeological Science: Reports* 8: 303–13.

———, Anno Hein, Hans Mommsen, and Noémi S Müller. 2017. "Production Sites of Early Iron Age Greek Bronze Tripod Cauldrons: First Evidence from Neutron Activation Analysis of Casting Ceramics." *Geoarchaeology* 32 (3): 321–42.

Kilian-Dirlmeier, Imma. 1985. "Fremde Weihungen in griechischen Heiligtümern vom 8. bis zum Beginn des 7. Jahrhunderts v. Chr." *Jahrbuch des römisch-germanischen Zentralmuseums Mainz* 32: 215–54.

Killen, John T. 1994. "Thebes Sealings, Knossos Tablets and Mycenaean State Banquets." *Bulletin of the Institute of Classical Studies* 39 (1): 67–84.

King, Philip J. 2006. "Gezer and Circumcision." In *Confronting the Past: Archaeological and Historical Essays on Ancient Israel in Honor of William G. Dever*, edited by G. Gitin, J. Edward Wright, and J. P Dessel. Winona Lake, IN: Eisenbrauns.

——— and L. E. Stager. 2001. *Life in Biblical Israel.* Louisville, KY and London: Westminster John Knox Press.

Kingsley, Sean A. 2004. *Shipwreck Archaeology of the Holy Land: Processes and Parameters.* Bristol: Classical Press.

Klebinder-Gauss, Gudrun. 2008. "Weihegaben aus Bronze." In *Die Archäologie der ephesischen Artemis: Gestalt und Ritual eines Heiligtums*, edited by Ulrike Muss, 149–55. Vienna: Phoibos Verlag.

——— and Andrea Puelz. 2008. "'Fremdes' in der materiellen Kultur im Artemision von Ephesos." In *Die Archäologie der ephesischen Artemis: Gestalt und Ritual eines Heiligtums*, edited by Ulrike Muss, 201–7. Vienna: Phoibos Verlag.

Knapp, Bernard A. 1993. "Thalassocracies in Bronze Age Eastern Mediterranean Trade: Making and Breaking a Myth." *World Archaeology* 24: 332–47.

———. 2001. "Archaeology and Ethnicity: A Dangerous Liaison." *Κυπριακή Αρχαιολογία (Archaeologia Cypria)* 4: 29–41.

Knappett, Carl. 2013. "Introduction: Why Networks." In *Network Analysis in Archaeology: New Approaches to Regional Interaction*, edited by Carl Knappett, 3–16. Oxford: Oxford University Press.

——, Vassilis Kilikoglou, Val Steele, and Ben Stern. 2005. "The Circulation and Consumption of Red Lustrous Wheelmade Ware: Petrographic, Chemical and Residue Analysis." *Anatolian Studies* 55: 25–59.

Kochavi, Moshe. 1992. "Some Connections between the Aegean and the Levant in the Second Millennium BC. A View from the East." In *Greece between East and West: 10th–8th Centuries BC. Papers of the Meeting at the Institute of Fine Arts, New York University, 1990*, edited by G. Kopcke and I. Tokumaru, 7–15. Mainz: Verlag Philipp von Zabern.

Koehler, Carolyn G. 1996. "Wine Amphoras in Ancient Greek Trade." *The Origins and Ancient History of Wine.* Food and Nutrition in History and Anthropology 11, edited by Patrick E. McGovern, Stuart J. Fleming, and Solomon H. Kat: 323–37. Abingdon: Routledge.

Koehler, Ludwig, Walter Baumgartner, Johann Jakob Stamm, and Mervyn Edwin John Richardson. 1994–2000. *The Hebrew and Aramaic Lexicon of the Old Testament.* Leiden: Brill.

Kopetzky, Karin. 2008. "The MB IIB-Corpus of the Hyksos Period at Tell el-Dab'a." In *The Bronze Age in the Lebanon; Studies on the Archaeology and Chronology of Lebanon, Syria and Egypt*, edited by M. Bietak and E. Czerny, 195–241. Vienna: Verlag der Österreichischen Akademie der Wissenschaften.

Kotitsa, Z., C.-I. Adudumalli, and M. Chiaradia. 2002. "Tin-Foiled Ceramics from Macedonia." In *Modern Trends in Scientific Studies on Ancient Ceramics: Papers presented at the 5th European Meeting on Ancient Ceramics, Athens 1999*, edited by V. Kilikoglou, A. Hein, and Y. Maniatis, 163–70. BAR International Series. Oxford: British Archaeological Reports.

Kottaridi, Angeliki. 2011. "Queens, Princesses and High Priestesses: The Role of Women at the Macedonian Court." *Heracles to Alexander the Great: Treasures from the Royal Capital of Macedon, a Hellenic Kingdom in the Age of Democracy*: 93–126. Oxford Ashmolean Museum Publications.

Kourayos, Y. 2005. "Despotiko Mandra: A Sanctuary Dedicated to Apollo." In *Architecture and Archaeology in the Cyclades: Papers in Honour of J. J. Coulton.* BAR International Series 1455, edited by M. Yeroulanou and M. Stamatopoulou, 105–33. Oxford: BAR Publishing.

Kourou, Nota, and Alexandra Karetsou. 1998. "An Enigmatic Stone from Knossos: A Reused Cippus?" *Karageorghis y Stampolidis*: 243–53.

Koutsouflakis, George V. 2017. "Ancient and Medieval Shipwrecks in the Sea of the Dodecanese." *Protection and Enhancement of Cultural Heritage: The Case of Transport Amphorae. Proceedings of the Scientific Conference Rhodes, 30 September 2017.*

Kouwatli, Ibrahim, Hans H. Curvers, Barbara Stuart, Yvette Sablerolles, Julian Henderson, and Paul Reynolds. 2008. "A Pottery and Glass Production Site in Beirut (BEY 015)." *BAAL* 10: 103–30.

Krahmalkov, Charles Richard. 2000. *Phoenician-Punic Dictionary*: Leuven: Peeters.

Krings, Veronique. 1995. *La civilisation phénicienne et punique: Manuel de recherche.* Leiden: Brill.

Krispijn, Theo J. H. 2016. "Early Silver: Thoughts about the Sign KU3 in the Earliest Documents from Uruk." In *Silver, Money and Credit. A Tribute to Robartus J. van der Spek on the Occasion of his 65th Birthday*, edited by K. Kleber and R. Pirngruber, 1–10. Leiden: Nederlands Instituut voor het Nabije Oosten.

Kroll, John H. 2008. "Early Iron Age Balance Weights at Lefkandi, Euboea." *Oxford Journal of Archaeology* 27 (1): 37–48.

Kron, Geoffry. 2016. "Classical Greek Trade in Comparative Perspective: Literary and Archaeological Evidence." In *The Ancient Greek Economy: Markets, Households and City-States*, edited by E. M. Harris, D. M. Lewis, and M. Woolmer, 356–80. Cambridge: Cambridge University Press.

Kruse, Thomas. 2007. "P. Heid. Inv. G 5166 und die Organisation des Alaunmonopols im kaiserzeitlichen Ägypten." In *Proceedings of the 24th International Congress of Papyrology Helsinki, 1st–7th of August 2004*, edited by Jaakko Frösén, Tiina Purola, and Erja Salmenkivi, 523–47. Helsinki: Societas Scientiarum Fennica.

Krzyszkowska, Olga, and Robert Morkot. 2000. "Ivory and Related Materials." In *Ancient Egyptian Materials and Technology*, edited by P. T. Nicholson and I. Shaw, 320–31. Cambridge: Cambridge University Press.

Kyrieleis, H. 1986. "Chios and Samos in the Archaic Period." In *Chios: A Conference at the Homereion in Chios, 1984*, edited by John Boardman and C. E. Vaphopoulou-Richardson, 187–204. Oxford: Clarendon Press.

La'da, Csaba A., ed. 2002. *Foreign Ethnics in Hellenistic Egypt.* Edited by W. Clarysse. Studia Hellenistica 38. *Prospographia Ptolemaica 10.* Leuven, Paris, and Dudley, MA: Peeters.

La Rosa, V. 2005. "Pour une réflexion sur le problème de la première présence égéenne en Sicile." In *Emporia: Aegeans in the Central and Eastern Mediterranean: Proceedings of the 10th International Aegean Conference, Athens, April 2004*, edited by R. Laffineur and E. Greco, 571–83. Université de Liège, Belgium.

Lamberg-Karlovsky, Carl C. 1996. *Beyond the Tigris and Euphrates: Bronze Age Civilizations.* Beer Sheva 9. Beer Sheva: Ben-Gurion University of the Negev Press.

Lancel, Serge. 1995. *Carthage: A History.* Oxford: Wiley-Blackwell.

——— and Jean-Paul Thuillier. 1982. "Les niveaux d'ateliers métallurgiques." In *Byrsa II. Rapports préliminaires sur les fouilles 1977–1978: Niveaux et vestiges puniques*, edited by Serge Lancel, Jean-Paul Morel, and Jean-Paul Thuillier, 217–60. Rome: Mission archéologique française à Carthage.

Lanfranchi, Giovanni B. 2007. "The Luwian-Phoenician bilinguals of Çineköy and Karatepe: An Ideological Dialogue." In *Getrennte Wege? Kommunikation, Raum und Wahrnehmung in der alten Welt*, edited by Robert Rollinger, Andreas Luther, and Josef Wiesehöfer, 179–217. Frankfurt am Main: Verlag Antike.

Langdon, Stephen Herbert. 1990. "From Monkey to Man: The Evolution of a Geometric Sculptural Type." *American Journal of Archaeology* 94: 407–24.

Langgut, Dafna, Rachid Cheddadi, Josè Sebastián Carrión, Mark Cavanagh, Daniele Colombaroli, Warren John Eastwood, Raphael Greenberg, Thomas Litt, Anna Maria Mercuri, and Andrea Miebach. 2019. "The Origin and Spread of Olive Cultivation in the Mediterranean Basin: The Fossil Pollen Evidence." *The Holocene* 29 (5): 902–22.

Larsen, Mogens Trolle. 1987. "Commercial Networks in the Ancient Near East." In *Centre and Periphery in the Ancient World*, edited by Mogens Trolle Larsen and K. Kristiansen, 47–56. Cambridge: Cambridge University Press.

———. 2015. *Ancient Kanesh: A Merchant Colony in Bronze Age Anatolia*: Cambridge: Cambridge University Press.

Leegaard, Lone. 2002. "The Mediterranean and Central Europe in the 6th and 5th Centuries BC: The Trade-Route through the Rhône Valley in the Light of Discoveries of Local Plain Wares." In *Pots for the Living, Pots for the Dead*, edited by A. Rathje, A. M. Nielsen, and B. Bundgaard Rasmussen, 145–68. Copenhagen: Museum Tusculanum Press.

Lehmann, Gunnar. 2001. "Phoenicians in Western Galilee: First Results of an Archaeological Survey in the Hinterland of Akko." In *Studies in the Archaeology of the Iron Age in Israel and Jordan*, edited by A. Mazar, 65–112. Sheffield: Sheffield Academic Press.

Leidwanger, Justin, Carl Knappett, Pascal Arnaud, Paul Arthur, Emma Blake, Cyprian Broodbank, Tom Brughmans, Tim Evans, Shawn Graham, and Elizabeth S Greene. 2014. "A Manifesto for the Study of Ancient Mediterranean Maritime Networks." *Antiquity* 342: 1–5.

Lemaire, André. 2005. "Inscription Phenico-Arameenne de Gözlükule-Tarse." In *Field Season 2001–2003 of the Tarsus-Gözlükule: Interdisciplinary Research Project*, edited by Aslı Özyar. Istanbul: Ege Yayınları.

———. 2010. "Solomon & Sheba, Inc.: New Inscription Confirms Trade Relations between Towns of Judah and South Arabia." *The Biblical Archaeology Review* 36 (1): 54–9.

Lemos, Irene S. 2005. "The Changing Relationship of the Euboeans and the East." In *The Greeks in the East*, edited by A. Villiang, 53–60. London: British Museum Research Publications.

Leonard, A. Jr. 1987. "The Significance of the Mycenaean Pottery found East of the Jordan River." *Studies in the History and Archaeology of Jordan* 3: 261–6.

———. 1996. "'Canaanite Jars' and Late Bronze Age Aegeo-Levantine Wine Trade." In *The Origins and Ancient History of Wine*, edited by P. E. McGovern, S. J. Fleming, and Solomon H. Katz, 233–54. Amsterdam: Gordon and Breach Publications.

Leone, Barbara. 2012. "A Trade Route between Euboea and the Northern Aegean." *Mediterranean Archaeology*: 229–41.

Leprohon, Ronald J. 2004. "What Wenamun Could Have Bought: The Value of His Stolen Goods." In *Egypt, Israel, and the Ancient Mediterranean World*, 167–8.

Levi, Doro. 1976. *Festòs e la civiltà Minoica*. Edited by Istituto per gli studi micenei ed egeo-anatolici. Rome: Edizioni dell'Ateneo.

Levy, Thomas Evan. 2009. "Pastoral Nomads and Iron Age Metal Production in Ancient Edom." In *Nomads, Tribes, and the State in the Ancient Near East: Cross-disciplinary Perspectives*, edited by Jeffrey Szuchman, 147–77. Chicago: Oriental Institute of the University of Chicago.

———, Erez Ben-Yosef, and Mohammad Najjar. 2018. "Intensive Surveys, Large-Scale Excavation Strategies and Iron Age Industrial Metallurgy in Faynan, Jordan: Fairy Tales Don't Come True." In *Mining for Ancient Copper: Essays in Memory of Beno Rothenberg*, edited by Erez Ben-Yosef, 245–58. Winona Lake, IN and Tel Aviv: Eisenbrauns/Emery and Claire Yass Publications in Archaeology.

Lilyquist, Christine. 2012. "Treasures from Tell Basta: Goddesses, Officials, and Artists in an International Age." *Metropolitan Museum Journal* 47 (1): 9–72.

Linder, E. 2003. "The Search for the Origin and Cultural Identity of the Ship." In *The Ma'agan Mikhael Ship: The Recovery of a 2400-Year-Old Merchantman. Final Report*, edited by Y. Kahanov and E. Linder, 147–50. Jerusalem: Israel Exploration Society.

Lipiński, Edward. 1991. *Phoenicia and the Bible: Proceedings of the Conference held at the University of Leuven, 15–16.3.1990.* Leuven: Peeters.

———. 1992. *Dictionnaire de la civilisation phénicienne et punique*. Brussels and Paris: Brepols.

———. 1995. *Dieux et déesses de l'univers phénicien et punique*. Studia Phoenicia 14. Orientalia Lovaniensia Analecta 64. Leuven: Peeters.

———. 2004. *Itineraria Phoenicia, Studia Phoenicia*. Leuven: Peeters.

Liverani, Mario. 1991. "The Trade Network of Tyre According to Ezek. 27." *Ah, Assyria: Studies in Assyrian History and Ancient Near Eastern Historiography Presented to Hayim Tadmor*, edited by M. Cogan and I. Eph'al, 65–79. Jerusalem: Magnes Press.

———. 1998. "L'immagine dei fenici nella storiografia occidentale." *Studi storici* 39 (1): 5–22.

Lloyd, Alan B. 1975. *Herodotus, Book II*. Études préliminaires aux religions orientales dans l'empire romain 43. Leiden: Brill.

Lo Schiavo, Fulvia, E. MacNamara, and L. Vagnetti. 1985. "Late Cypriot Imports to Italy and their Influence on Local Bronzework." *Papers of the British School at Rome* 53: 1–71.

———, R. Maddin, and J. D. Muhly. 1985. "Preliminary Research on Ancient Metallurgy in Sardinia: 1984." *American Journal of Archaeology* 89 (2): 316–8.

Lombard, Pierre. 1988. "The Salt Mine Site and the 'Hasaean' Period in Northeastern Arabia." *Araby the Blest: Studies in Arabian Archaeology* 7: 117–37.

London, Gloria. 1989. "A Comparison of Two Contemporaneous Lifestyles of the Late Second Millennium BC." *Bulletin of the American Schools of Oriental Research* 273: 37–55.

López Castro, José Luis. 2019. "The Iberian Peninsula." In *The Oxford Handbook of the Phoenician and Punic Mediterranean*, edited by Brian R. Doak and Carolina López-Ruiz. Oxford: Oxford University Press.

———, Ahmed Ferjaoui, Alfredo Mederos Martín, Víctor Martínez Hahnmüller, and Imed Ben Jerbania. 2016. "La colonización fenicia inicial en el Mediterráneo Central: Nuevas excavaciones arqueológicas en Utica (Túnez)." *Trabajos de Prehistoria* 73 (1): 68–89.

Lopez Pardo, Fernando, and Luis A. Ruiz Cabrero. 2006. "Marinos, comerciantes y metalúrgicos en Kerne (Mogador): La onomástica." In *Tiempos de Púrpura: Málaga antigua y antigüedades hispanas*, I, edited by Manuel Corrales Aguilar, 213–41. Málaga: Servicio de Publicaciones.

Lorber, Catharine C. 2018. *Coins of the Ptolemaic Empire*, Part I, *Ptolemy I through Ptolemy IV*. New York: American Numismatic Society.

Lorrio, Alberto José. 2014. *La necrópolis orientalizante de Boliche (Cuevas del Almanzora, Almería): La colección Siret del Museo Arqueológico Nacional*. Edited by María Paz De Miguel and Elena Grau, Publicaciones del Gabinete de Antigüedades. Bibliotheca Archaeologica Hispana 43. Madrid: Real Academia de la Historia.

Lowe, Benedict. 2004. "The Industrial Exploitation of Murex: Purple Dye Production in the Western Mediterranean." In *Colour in the Ancient Mediterranean World*, edited by Liza Cleland and Karen Stears, 46–9. Oxford: John and Erica Hedges.

———. 2016. "The Trade in Fish Sauce and Related Products in the Western Mediterranean." In *The Inland Seas: Towards an Ecohistory of the Mediterranean and the Black Sea*, edited by Tønnes Bekker-Nielsen and Ruth Gertwagen, 215–37. Stuttgart: Franz Steiner Verlag.

Luaces, Max. 2015. "La relation entre le temps et la rationalité économique dans les contextes archéologiques de Gadir/Gadès (VIe–Ier s. av. J.-C.)." *Pallas: Revue d'études antiques* (99): 245–65.

Luís Cardoso, João, José Luis López Castro, Ahmed Ferjaoui, Alfredo Mederos Martín, Víctor Martínez Hahnmüller, and Imed Ben Jerbania. 2016. "What the People of Utica (Tunisia) ate at a Banquet in the 9th Century BCE: Zooarchaeology of a North African Early Phoenician Settlement." *Journal of Archaeological Science: Reports* 8: 314–22.

Luke, Joanna. 2003. *Ports of Trade: Al Mina and Geometric Greek Pottery in the Levant*. BAR International series 1100. Oxford: Archaeopress.

Lund, John. 1988. "Prolegomena to a Study of the Phoenician/Punic Colonization of Tunisia." *Acta Hyperborea* 1: 44–57.

———. 1997. "The Distribution of Cypriot Sigillata as Evidence of Sea-Trade Involving Cyprus." In *Res Maritimae: Cyprus and the Eastern Mediterranean from Prehistory to Late Antiquity*, edited by Stuart Swiny, Robert L. Hohlfelder, and Helena Wylde Swiny, 201–15. Atlanta, GA: Scholars Press.

———. 2002. "The Ontogenesis of Cypriot Sigillata." *Acta Hyperborea* 9: 185–223.

———. 2003. "Eastern Sigillata B: A Ceramic Fine Ware Industry in the Political and Commercial Landscape of the Eastern Mediterranean." In *Les céramiques en Anatolie aux époques hellénistique et romaine: Actes de la Table Ronde d'Istanbul, May 1996*, edited by C. Abadie-Reynal, 125–36. Paris: Anatoliennes.

———. 2006. "An Economy of Consumption: The Eastern Sigillata A Industry in the Late Hellenistic Period." *Archeologia Classica* 57: 233–52.

——— and Vincent Gabrielsen. 2005. "A Fishy Business: Transport Amphorae of the Black Sea Region as a Source for the Trade in Fish and Fish Products in the Classical and Hellenistic Periods." In *Ancient Fishing and Fish Processing in the Black Sea Region*, edited by Tonnes Bekker-Nielsen, 161–9. Aarhus: Aarhus University Press.

Luukko, Mikko. 2012. "The Correspondence of Tiglath-pileser III and Sargon II from Calah." *Nimrud* (SAA 19). Helsinki.

Macadam, Henry Innes. 1993. "Phoenicians at Home, Phoenicians Abroad: John D. Grainger, Hellenistic Phoenicia, 1991." *Topoi* 3 (1): 321–44.

Mackie, Hilary Susan. 1996. *Talking Trojan: Speech and Community in the Iliad*: Lanham, MD: Rowman & Littlefield.

Madrid Fernandez, M., and J. Buxeda i Garrigos. 2002. "A Review of the Archaeometric Studies of Western Mediterranean Terra Sigillata from the First Century BC to the Second Century AD: State of Art, Limitations and Potential." In *Modern Trends in Scientific Studies on Ancient Ceramics: Papers Presented at the 5th European Meeting on Ancient Ceramics, Athens 1999*, edited by V. Kilikoglou, A. Hein and Y. Maniatis, 287–98. BAR International Series. Oxford: British Archaeological Reports.

Maeir, Aren M. 2000. "The Political and Economic Status of MB II Hazor and MB II Trade: An Inter- and Intra-Regional View." *Palestine Exploration Quarterly* 132: 37–58.

Malbran-Labat, Florence. 1999. "Nouvelles données épigraphiques sur Chypre et Ougarit." *Report of the Department of Antiquities, Cyprus* 1999: 121–3.

Malfitana, Daniele. 2009. "Roman Sicily Project ('Rsp'): Ceramics and Trade. A Multidisciplinary Approach to the Study of Material Culture Assemblages. First Overview: The Transport Amphorae Evidence." *Facta* 2: 127–92.

Malkin, Irad. 2005. *Mediterranean Paradigms and Classical Antiquity*. London: Routledge.

Manniche, Lise. 1989. *An Ancient Egyptian Herbal*: Austin: University of Texas Press.

Manning, Joseph G. 2011. "Networks, Hierarchies and Markets in the Ptolemaic Economy." *The Economies of Hellenistic Societies, Third to First Centuries BC*: 296–323.

Maran, Joseph. 2007. "Seaborne Contacts between the Aegean, the Balkans and the Central Mediterranean in the 3rd Millennium BC: The Unfolding of the Mediterranean World." In *Between the Aegean and Baltic Seas: Prehistory Across Borders*, edited by Ioanna Galanaki, H. Tomas, Y. Galanakis and R. Laffineur, 3–24. Université de Liège, Belgium.

———. 2011. "Evidence for Levantine Religious Practice in the Late Bronze Age Sanctuary of Phylakopi on Melos?" *Eretz-Israel* 30: 65*–73*.

Marazzi, M., and Sebastiano Tusa. 2005. "Egei in Occidente: Le più antiche vie marittime alla luce dei nuovi scavi sull'isola di Pantelleria." *Aegaeum* 25: 137–51.

Marcus, Ezra S. 2007. "Amenemhet II and the Sea: Maritime Aspects of the Mit Rahina (Memphis) Inscription." *Egypt and the Levant* 17.

Markoe, Glenn E. 1985. *Phoenician Bronze and Silver Bowls from Cyprus and the Mediterranean: Classical Studies.* Berkeley: University of California Press.

———. 2000a. "Mediterranean Glass Eye Beads in China." In *Actas del IV congreso internacional de estudios fenicios y púnicos, Cádiz 1995.*

———. 2000b. *Phoenicians: People of the Past.* London: British Museum Press.

Marquié, Sandrine. 2002. "La circulation des sigillées d'époque impériale au sud de Chypre." In *Céramiques hellénistiques et romaines: Productions et diffusion en Méditerranée orientale (Chypre, Égypte et côte syro-palestinienne)*, edited by F. Blondé, P. Ballet, and J.-F. Salles, 289–301. Lyon: Maison de l'Orient Méditerranéen-Jean Pouilloux.

Marriner, Nick. 2009. *Geoarchaeology of Lebanon's Ancient Harbours.* BAR International Series 1953. Oxford: Archaeopress.

Martin, Geoffrey Thorndike. 1974. *The Royal Tomb at el-'Amarna I: The Objects.* London: Egypt Exploration Society.

Martin Ruiz, Juan Antonio. 2007. *La crisis del siglo VI aC en los asentamientos fenicios de Andalucía.* Málaga: Diputación Provincial de Málaga, Centro de Ediciones de la Diputación de Málaga.

———. 2018. "The Phoenician Population in Málaga Bay (Spain)." In *De Huelva a Malaka: Los fenicios en Andalucía a la luz de los descubrimientos más recientes*, edited by Massimo Botto, 285–303. Rome: CNR—Istituto di Studi sul Mediterraneo Antico.

Masson, Olivier, and Maurice Sznycer. 1992. "Kourion, 1883–1884: Inscriptions phéniciennes et objets divers." In *Studies in Honor of Vassos Karageorghis*, edited by G. O. Ioannides, 237–240. Nicosia: Society of Cypriot Studies.

Matoïan, Valérie. 2008. "Un œuf d'autruche peint découvert lors du dégagement de la 'salle du trône' du Palais royal d'Ougarit." In *Ras Shamra—Ougarit XVII: Le mobilier du Palais royal d'Ougarit*, 101–16. Lyon: Maison de l'Orient et de la Méditerranée.

Matthäus, Hartmut. 1988. "Heirloom or Tradition? Bronze Stands of the Second and First Millennium BC in Cyprus, Greece and Italy." In *Problems in Greek Prehistory: Papers Presented at the Centenary Conference of the British School at Athens, Manchester, April 1986*, edited by E. B. French and K. A. Wardle, 285–300. Bristol: Bristol Classical Press.

Mavrogenis, Andreas, Theodosis Saranteas, Konstantinos Markatos, Antonia Kotsiou, and Christina Tesseromatis. 2019. "Pharmacies for Pain and Trauma in Ancient Greece." *International Orthopaedics (SICOT)* 43 (6): 1529–36.

Mazar, Benjamin. 1965. "The Phoenicians on the Eastern Mediterranean Shore" In *The Western Galilee and the Galilean Shore (Hebrew)*, 1–16. Jerusalem: Israel Exploration Society.

Mazarakis Ainian, A. J. 2005. "Inside the Adyton of a Greek Temple. Excavations on Kythnos (Cyclades)." In *Architecture and Archaeology in the Cyclades: Papers in Honour of J. J. Coulton.* BAR International Series 1455, edited by M. Yeroulanou and M. Stamatopoulou, 87–104. Oxford: BAR Publishing.

Mazzorin, Jacopo De Grossi. 2000. "État de nos connaissances concernant le traitement et la consommation du poisson dans l'Antiquité, à la lumière de l'archéologie: L'exemple de Rome." *Mélanges de l'École française de Rome* 112: 155–67.

McDowell, Andrea Griet. 1999. *Village Life in Ancient Egypt: Laundry Lists and Love Songs.* New York: Oxford University Press

McGeough, Kevin M. 2007. *Exchange Relationships at Ugarit.* Ancient Near Eastern Studies, Supp. 26. Leuven, Paris, and Dudley, MA: Peeters.

McGovern, Patrick E. 1986. *The Late Bronze and Early Iron Ages of Central Transjordan: The Baq'ah Valley Project, 1977–1981.* University Museum Monograph 65. Philadelphia: University of Pennsylvania.

———. 2003. *Ancient Wine: The Search for the Origins of Viniculture.* Princeton, NJ: Princeton University Press.

McGrail, S. 1991. "Bronze Age Seamanship in the Mediterranean: A View from NW." In *Bronze Age Trade in the Mediterranean*, edited by N. H. Gale, 83–91. Jonsered: Åström.

Meiggs, Russell. 1982. *Trees and Timber in the Ancient Mediterranean World*: Oxford: Oxford University Press.

Mendleson, Carole. 1987. "Scarabs and Seals: Egyptian and Egyptianising." In *Tharros: A Catalogue of Material in the British Museum from Phoenician and Other Tombs at Tharros, Sardinia*, edited by Richard David Barnett and Carole Mendleson, 96–7. London: British Museum Press.

Michailidou, Anna, and Katerina Voutsa. 2005. "Merchants and Merchandise: Humans as a Commodity in Aegean and Oriental Societies." In *Emporia: Aegeans in the Central and Eastern Mediterranean: Proceedings of the 10th International Aegean Conference, Athens, April 2004*, edited by R. Laffineur and E. Greco, 17–28. Université de Liège, Belgium.

Michelau, H. 2015. "Recovering a Lost Phoenician Cult Object." *BAAL Hors-Série* 10: 337–58.

Militello, Pietro. 2005. "Mycenaean Palaces and Western Trade: A Problematic Relationship." In *Emporia: Aegeans in the Central and Eastern Mediterranean: Proceedings of the 10th International Aegean Conference, Athens, April 2004*, edited by R. Laffineur and E. Greco, 585–97. Université de Liège, Belgium.

Millard, Alan. 2000. "The Phoenicians at Sea." In *The Sea in Antiquity*, edited by G. J. Oliver, 75–80. British Archaeological Reports International Series. Oxford: BAR Publishing.

Möller, Astrid. 2007. "Classical Greece: Distribution." In *The Cambridge Economic History of the Greco-Roman World*, edited by S. Scheidel, I. Morris, and R. Saller, 362–84. Cambridge: Cambridge University Press.

Mongo Soares, Rui, Lídia Baptista, Rui Pinheiro, Lourdes Oliveira, Zélia Rodrigues, and Vale Nelson. 2017. "A necrópole da I Idade do Ferro do Monte do Bolor 1–2 (São Brissos, Beja)." In *Sidereum Ana III: El río Guadiana y Tartessos*, 263–301.

Moore, Karl James, and David Charles Lewis. 2000. "Multinational Enterprise in Ancient Phoenicia." *Business History* 42 (2): 17–42.

Morgan, Catherine. 2003. *Early Greek States beyond the Polis*. London: Routledge.

Morley, Neville. 2007. *Trade in Classical Antiquity*: Cambridge: Cambridge University Press.

Morris, Ian. 2003. "Mediterraneanization." *Mediterranean Historical Review* 18 (2): 30–55.

Morris, Sarah P. 1992a. "Introduction." In *Greece between East and West: 10th–8th Centuries BC: Papers of the Meeting at the Institute of Fine Arts, New York University, 1990*, edited by Günter Kopcke and Isabelle Tokumaru, xiii–xviii. Mainz: Verlag Philipp von Zabern.

———. 1992b. *Daidalos and the Origins of Greek Civilisation*. Princeton, NJ: Princeton University Press.

——— and John K. Papadopoulos. 1998. "Phoenicians and the Corinthian Pottery Industry." In *Archäologische Studien in Kontaktzonen der antiken Welt*, edited by R. Rolle, K. Schmidt, and Roald Docter, 251–63. Hamburg: Veröffentlichungen der Joachim Jungius-Gesellschaft der Wissenschaften.

Moscati, Sabatino. 1968. *The World of the Phoenicians*. Translated by Alastair Hamilton. London: Weidenfeld & Nicolson.

———. 1988. *The Phoenicians*. Milan: Bompiani.

——— and Maria Luisa Uberti. 1981. *Scavi a Mozia: Le stele*. Pubblicazioni del Centro di Studio per la Civiltà fenicia e punica 23. Consiglio nazionale delle ricerche.

——— and Maria Luisa Uberti. 1985. *Scavi al tofet di Tharros: I monumenti lapidei*, Vol. 21. Consiglio nazionale delle ricerche.

Most, Glenn W. 2006. *Hesiod: Theogony, Works and Days. Testimonia*. Vol. 1. New Loeb Classical Library. Cambridge, MA and London: Harvard University Press.

Mueller, Katja. 2006. *Settlements of the Ptolemies: City Foundations and New Settlement in the Hellenistic World*. Studia Hellenistica, Vol. 43. Leuven, Paris, and Dudley, MA: Peeters.

Muhly, D. 1970. "Homer and the Phoenicians." *Berytus* 19: 19–64.

Muir, Arthur H., and Renée F. Friedman. 2011. "Analysis of Predynastic Ostrich Eggshells from Hierakonpolis and Beyond." In *Egypt at its Origins 3. Proceedings of the Third International Conference "Origin of the State: Predynastic and Early Dynastic Egypt", London, 27th July–1st August 2008*, edited by Renée F. Friedman and Peter N. Fiske. Leuven, Paris, and Walpole, MA: Uitgeverij Peeters en Departement Oosterse Studies.

Muller, Beatrice. 2005. "De Mari à l'Égée: La peinture proche-orientale au 2e Millénaire av." In *The Greeks in the East*, edited by Alexandra Villing, 37–46. London: British Museum Press.

Muñoz Vicente, A., and G. De Frutos Reyes. 2009. "La pesca y las conservas en la Bahía de Cádiz en época fenicio-púnica." In *Arqueología de la pesca en el Estrecho de Gibraltar: De la prehistoria al fin del mundo antiguo*, edited by D. Bernal, 81–131. Servicio de Publicaciones de la Universidad de Cádiz.

Murray, Mary Anne. 2000a. "Fruits, Vegetables, Pulses and Condiments." In *Ancient Egyptian Materials and Technology*, edited by P. T. Nicholson and Ian Shaw, 609–55. Cambridge: Cambridge University Press.

———. 2000b. "Viticulture and Wine Production." In *Ancient Egyptian Materials and Technology*, edited by P. T. Nicholson and Ian Shaw, 577–608. Cambridge: Cambridge University Press.

Muscarella, Oscar White. 2013. *Archaeology, Artifacts and Antiquities of the Ancient Near East: Sites, Cultures, and Proveniences*. Culture and History of the Ancient Near East 62. Leiden: Brill.

Muss, Ulrike. 2008a. "Elfenbein und Bein aus dem Artemision von Ephesos." In *Die Archäologie der ephesischen Artemis: Gestalt und Ritual eines Heiligtums*, edited by Ulrike Muss, 103–16. Vienna: Phoibos Verlag.

———. 2008b. "Kultbild und Statuetten: Göttinnen im Artemision." In *Die Archäologie der ephesischen Artemis: Gestalt und Ritual eines Heiligtums*, edited by Ulrike Muss, 63–6. Vienna: Phoibos Verlag.

Na'aman, Nadav. 1982. "Eretz Israel during the Bronze Age: The Middle Bronze Age and the Late Bronze Age (ca. 2000–1200 BCE)." In *The History of Eretz Israel*, Vol. 1, *The Early Periods*, edited by I. Ef'al, 129–35.

———. 1994. "The Canaanites and their Land: A Rejoinder." *Ugarit-Forschungen* 26: 397–419.

———. 1999. "Four Notes on the Size of Late Bronze Age Canaan." *BASOR* 313: 31–7.

———. 2007. "The Growth and Development of Judah and Jerusalem in the Eighth Century BCE and the Assumed 'Melting Pot' Policy Attributed to King Hezekiah: A Reply to Israel Finkelstein." *Zion* 72: 338–46.

Naeh, Liat. 2015. "In Search of Identity: The Contribution of Recent Finds to our Understanding of Iron Age Ivory Objects in the Material Culture of the Southern Levant." *Altorientalische Forschungen* 42 (1): 80–96.

Namdar, Dvory, Ayelet Gilboa, Ronny Neumann, Israel Finkelstein, and Steve Weiner. 2013. "Cinnamaldehyde in Early Iron Age Phoenician Flasks Raises the Possibility of Levantine Trade with South East Asia." *Mediterranean Archaeology and Archaeometry* 12: 1–19.

Naso, Alessandro. 2010. "The Origin of Tomb Painting in Etruria." *Ancient West & East* 9: 63–86.

Negev, Avrāhām. 1974. *The Nabatean Potter's Workshop at Oboda*. Bonn: Habelt.

———. 1986. *The Late Hellenistic and Early Roman Pottery of Nabatean Oboda*. Qedem 22. Jerusalem: Institute of Archaeology, Hebrew University of Jerusalem.

Nemati, Zahra, Dörte Harpke, Almila Gemicioglu, Helmut Kerndorff, and Frank R. Blattner. 2019. "Saffron (*Crocus sativus*) is an Autotriploid that Evolved in Attica (Greece) from Wild *Crocus cartwrightianus*." *bioRxiv*: 537–688.

Nibbi, Alessandra. 1985. *Ancient Byblos Reconsidered*. Oxford: DE Publications.

———. 1991. "The Canaan in Egypt." In *Atti del II congresso internazionale di studi Fenici e Punici, Rome 1987*. Vol. I, 169–78.

Nicholson, Paul Thomas. 2008. "Glass and Faience Production Sites in New Kingdom Egypt: A Review of the Evidence." In *Vitreous Materials in the Late Bronze Age Aegean*, edited by C. M. Jackson and E. C. Wager, 1–13. Oxford: Oxbow Books.

Nicolis, F. 2005. "Long Distance Cultural Links between Northern Italy, the Ionian Islands and the Peloponnese in the Last Centuries of the 3rd Millennium BC." In *Emporia: Aegeans in the Central and Eastern Mediterranean: Proceedings of the 10th International Aegean Conference, Athens, April 2004*, edited by R. Laffineur and E. Greco, 527–38. Université de Liège, Belgium.

Niemeier, Wolf-Dietrich. 2005. "Minoans, Mycenaeans, Hittites and Ionians in Western Asia Minor." In *The Greeks in the East*, edited by Alexandra Villing, 1–36. London: British Museum.

Niemeyer, Hans Georg. 2001. "Archaeological Evidence of Early Iron Technology at Carthage and Other Phoenician Settlements." *Mediterranean Archaeology* 14: 83–93.

———. 2006. "The Phoenicians in the Mediterranean. Between Expansion and Colonisation: A Non-Greek Model of Overseas Settlement and Presence." In *Greek Colonisation: An Account of Greek Colonies and Other Settlements Overseas*, Vol. 1, edited by G. R. Tsetskhladze, 143–68. Leiden and Boston: Brill.

Nightingale, Georg. 2007. "Lefkandi: An Important Node in the International Exchange Network of Jewellery and Personal Adornment." *Aegaeum* 27: 421–32.

———. 2008. "Tiny, Fragile, Common, Precious: Mycenaean Glass and Faience Beads and Other Objects." In *Vitreous Materials in the Late Bronze Age Aegean*, edited by C. M. Jackson and E. C. Wager, 64–104. Oxford: Oxbow Books.

———. 2009. "Glass and Faience Beads from Perati: The End of the Mycenaean Tradition, the Beginning of the New Tradition of the Early Iron Age in Greece." In *Dōron: Timētikos tomos gia ton kathēgētē Spyro Iakōbidē, Seira monographiōn*, edited by D. Daniilidou, 495–512. Kentron Ereunēs tēs Archaiotētos 6. Athens.

Nigro, Lorenzo. 2015. "Temples in Motya and their Levantine Prototypes: Phoenician Religious Architectural Tradition." *BAAL Hors-Série* 10: 83–108.

Nijboer, Albert J. 2008. "Italy and the Levant during the Late Bronze and Iron Age (1200–750/700 BC)." In *Beyond the Homeland: Markers in Phoenician Chronology*, edited by C. Sagona, 357–94. Leuven, Paris, and Dudley, MA: Peeters.

———. 2013. "Banquet, Marzeah, Symposion and Symposium during the Iron Age: Disparity and Mimicry." In *Regionalism and Globalism in Antiquity: Exploring Their Limits*, edited by Franco De Angelis, 95–125. Leuven, Paris, and Walpole, MA: Peeters.

——— and Hans van der Plicht. 2008. "The Iron Age In The Mediterranean: Recent Radiocarbon Research at The University Of Groningen." In *A New Dawn for the Dark Age? Shifting Paradigms in Mediterranean Iron Age Chronology. Proceedings of the XV World Congress (Lisbon, 2006)*, edited by Dirk Brandherm and Martin Trachsel, 103–18. Oxford BAR Publishing.

———, S. L. Willemsen, P. A. J Attema, and J. F. Seubers, eds. 2013. *Research into Pre-Roman Burial Grounds in Italy*. Caeculus: Papers on Mediterranean Archaeology and Greek and Roman Studies. Leuven: Peeters.

Nikita, Kalliopi, G. Nightingale, and Simon Chenery. 2017. "Mixed-Alkali Glass Beads from Elateia-Alonaki: Tracing the Routes of an Alien Glass Technology in the Periphery of Post-Palatial Mycenaean Greece." In *Hesperos: The Aegean Seen from the West*, edited by M. Fotiadis, R. Laffineur, Y. Lolos, and A. Vlachopoulos, 517–23. Leuven: Peeters.

Nissenbaum, Arie. 1999. "Ancient and Modern Medicinal Applications of Dead Sea Asphalt (Bitumen)." *Israel Journal of Earth Sciences* 48 (3–4): 301–8.

———, Jürgen Rullkötter, and Yoseph Yechieli. 2002. "Are the Curative Properties of 'Black Mud' from the Dead Sea due to the Presence of Bitumen (Asphalt) or Other Types of Organic Matter?" *Environmental Geochemistry and Health* 24 (4): 327–35.

Niveau de Villedary y Mariñas, A. M., and Antonio M. Sáez-Romero. 2016. "The Red Slip Tableware of Punic and Early Roman Gadir/Gades (4th–1st Cent. BC): An Update on the So-Called 'Kuass Ware'." *International Association for Research on Pottery of the Hellenistic Period (IARPotHP)* 1: 55-68.

Noonan, Benjamin J. 2011. "Did Nehemiah Own Tyrian Goods? Trade between Judea and Phoenicia during the Achaemenid Period." *Journal of Biblical Literature* 130 (2): 281–98.

Nosch, M.-L. 2004. "Red Coloured Textiles in the Linear B Inscriptions." In *Colours in the Ancient Mediterranean World*, edited by L. Cleland, K. Stears, and G. Davis, 32–9. Oxford: British Archaeological Reports.

Núñez, Francisco J. 2018. "The Impact of the Sea Peoples in Central Levant: A Revision." In *Change, Continuity, and Connectivity: North-eastern Mediterranean at the Turn of the Bronze Age and in the Early Iron Age*, edited by Łukasz Niesiołowski-Spanò and Marek Węcowski, 116–40. Wiesbaden: Harrassowitz Verlag.

O'Brien, Robert Viking. 1999. "Astarte in the Temple of Venus: An Allegory of Idolatry." *Studies in Philology* 96 (2): 144–58.

Oates, David, Joan Oates, and Helen McDonald. 1998. *Excavations at Tell Brak*, Vol. 1, *The Mitanni and Old Babylonian Periods*. Cambridge: McDonald Institute for Archaeological Research.

Olalde, Iñigo, and Cosimo Posth. 2020. "Latest Trends in Archaeogenetic Research of West Eurasians." *Current Opinion in Genetics & Development* 62: 36–43.

Orsingher, Adriano. 2016. "The Ceramic Repertoire of Motya: Origins and Development between the 8th and 6th Centuries BC." In *Karthago Dialoge: Karthago und der punische Mittelmeerraum. Kulturkontakte und Kulturtransfers im 1. Jahrtausend vor Christus*, edited by Frerich Schön and Hanni Töpfer, 283–312. Tübingen: Mohr.

———. 2010. "Le oil bottles fenicie: Analisi dei contesti e considerazioni crono-tipologiche." *Sardinia, Corsica et Baleares antiqvae* 8: 37–69.

Palmer, Ruth. 1996. "Wine and Viticulture in the Linear A and B Texts of the Bronze Age Aegean." In *The Origins and Ancient History of Wine*, edited by P. E. McGovern, S. J. Fleming, and S. H. Katz, 269–85. Amsterdam: Gordon & Breach.

Palmieri, Alessandro. 2003. "Una possibile nuova lettura dell'uovo di struzzo dipinto da Montalto di Castro." *Studi Etruschi* 69: 25–41.

Panella, Clementina. 1968. *Appunti su un gruppo di anfore della prima, media e tarda eta imperiale (secoli I–V d.C.)*. Rome: De Luca.

Panossian, Alexander, and Georg Wikman. 2009. "Evidence-Based Efficacy of Adaptogens in Fatigue, and Molecular Mechanisms Related to their Stress-Protective Activity." *Current Clinical Pharmacology* 4 (3): 198–219.

Papadopoulos, John K. 2007. "The Athenian Agora from the End of the Bronze Age through the Protoattic Period." *The Art of Antiquity: Piet de Jong and the Athenian Agora.* The American School of Classical Studies at Athens, Athens.

Papalexandrou, Nassos. 2008. "Boiotian Tripods: The Tenacity of a Panhellenic Symbol in a Regional Context." *Hesperia* 77: 251–82.

———. 2014. "From Lake Van to the Guadalquivir: Monsters and Vision in the Pre-Classical Mediterranean." In *Assyria to Iberia at the Dawn of the Classical Age*, edited by Joan Aruz, Sarah B. Graff, and Yelena Rakic, 263–72. New York: Metropolitan Museum of Art.

Paraskevaidou, H. A. 1991. "The Name of the Phoenicians: Some Considerations." In *Atti del II congresso internazionale di studi Fenici e Punici, Rome 1987.* Vol. I., 523–28.

Pardee, Dennis. 2000. *Les textes rituels: Ras Shamra-Ougarit 12.* Paris: Éditions recherche sur les civilisations.

———. 2002. *Ritual and Cult at Ugarit*: Leiden: Brill.

Pardo, Femando López. 1990. "Nota sobre las ánforas II y III de Kuass (Marruecos)." *Antiquités Africaines* 26 (1): 13–23.

Pare, Christopher, ed. 2000. *Metals Make the World Go Round: The Supply and Circulation of Metals in Bronze Age Europe. Proceedings of a Conference held at the University of Birmingham in June 1997*: Oxford: Oxbow Books.

Parpola, Simo, and Kazuko Watanabe. 1988. *Neo-Assyrian Treaties and Loyalty Oaths: State Archives of Assyria 2.* Helsinki: Helsinki University Press.

Pavan, A., and H. Schenk. 2012. "Crossing the Indian Ocean before the Periplus: A Comparison of Pottery Assemblages at the Sites of Sumhuram (Oman) and Tissamaharama (Sri Lanka)." *Arab. Archaeol. Epigr.* 23 (2): 191–202.

Payne, Henry. 1940. *Perachora: The Sanctuaries of Hera Akraia and Limenia. Excavations of the British School of Archaeology at Athens 1930–33: Architecture, Bronzes, Terracottas.* Oxford: Clarendon Press.

Pećanac, Marija, Zlata Janjić, Aleksandar Komarčević, Miloš Pajić, Dušanka Dobanovački, and Sanja Mišković-Skeledžija. 2013. "Burns Treatment in Ancient Times." *Medicinski pregled* 66 (5–6): 263–7.

Peckham, B. 1992. "The Phoenician Foundation of Cities and Towns in Sardinia." In *Sardinia in the Mediterranean: A Footprint in the Sea*, edited by R. H. Tykot and T. A. Andrews, 410–8. Sheffield: Sheffield Academic Press.

Petrie, William Matthews Flinders. 1931. *Ancient Gaza: Tell el Ajjul.* London: British School of Archaeology in Egypt.

Peyronel, Luca. 2015. "A Long-Barrel Carnelian Bead from Ebla: A New Evidence for Long-Distance Contacts between the Indus Valley and the Near East." *Studia Eblaitica: Studies on the Archaeology, History, and Philology of Ancient Syria* 1: 217–20.

Phillips, Jacke. 2000. "Ostrich Eggshells." In *Ancient Egyptian Materials and Technology*, edited by P. T. Nicholson and I. Shaw, 332–3. Cambridge: Cambridge University Press.

Phillips, Jacqueline. 2008. *Aegyptiaca on the Island of Crete in their Chronological Context: A Critical Review*. Vienna: Verlag der Österreichischen Akademie der Wissenschaften.

Pierrat-Bonnefois, Geneviève. 2010. "L'alabastre: Un vase à parfum d'origine égyptienne?" *Les dossiers d'archéologie* 337: 28–32.

Piga, G., M. Guirguis, P. Bartoloni, A. Malgosa, and S. Enzo. 2008. "A Funerary Rite Study of the Phoenician-Punic Necropolis of Mount Sirai (Sardinia, Italy)." *International Journal of Osteoarchaeology*.

Pilar Tugores, M., Marianna Giannoulaki, Magdalena Iglesias, Angelo Bonanno, Vjekoslav Tičina, Iole Leonori, A. Machias, Konstantinos Tsagarakis, Nuria Diaz, Ana Giráldez, Bernardo Patti, Andrea Felice, Gualtiero Basilone, and Vasilis Valavanis. 2011. "Habitat Suitability Modelling for Sardine *Sardina pilchardus* in a Highly Diverse Ecosystem: The Mediterranean Sea." *Marine Ecology Progress Series* 443: 181–205.

Pilkington, Nathan. 2013. *An Archaeological History of Carthaginian Imperialism*: New York: Columbia University.

Pinch, Geraldine. 1993. *Votive Offerings to Hathor*. Oxford: Griffith Institute.

———. 2002. *Egyptian Mythology: A Guide to the Gods, Goddesses, and Traditions of Ancient Egypt*. Oxford: Oxford University Press.

Pisano, Giovanna, and Alessia Travaglini. 2003. *Le iscrizioni fenicie e puniche dipinte*. Studia Punica 13. Università degli studi di Roma "Tor vergata".

Polzer, Mark. 2014. "The Bajo de la Campana Shipwreck and Colonial Trade in Phoenician Spain." In *Assyria to Iberia at the Dawn of the Classical Age*, edited by Joan Aruz, Sarah Graff, and Yelena Rakic, 230–42. New York: Metropolitan Museum of Art.

——— and J. Pinedo. 2011. "The Final Season of the Claude and Barbara Duthuit Expedition to Bajo de la Campana, Spain: Excavation of a Late Seventh-Century BCE Phoenician Shipwreck." *INA Annual* 5: 6–17.

Pommerening, Tanja, Elena Marinova, and Stan Hendrickx. 2010. "The Early Dynastic Origin of the Water-lily Motif." *Chronique d'Égypte* 85 (169–170): 14–40.

Ponsich, Michel. 1967. *Nécropoles phéniciennes de la région de Tanger*, Vol. 3. Rabat: Éditions marocaines et internationales.

Popham, Mervyn R., and Irene S. Lemos. 1995. "A Euboean Warrior Trader." *Oxford Journal of Archaeology* 14: 151–7.

———, L. Hugh Sackett, and Petros G. Themelis. 1980. *Lefkandi I. The Iron Age: The Settlement, the Cemeteries. Text*, Supplementary Volume (British School at Athens) 11. London: Thames & Hudson.

Porada, Edith. 1973. "Notes on the Sarcophagus of Ahiram." *Journal of the Ancient Near Eastern Society* 5 (1): 2166.

Potts, Daniel T. 1990. *The Arabian Gulf in Antiquity*, II, *From Alexander the Great to the Coming of Islam*. Oxford: Clarendon Press.

———. 1993. "Rethinking Some Aspects of Trade in the Arabian Gulf." *World Archaeology* 24 (3): 423–40.

———. 2001. "Ostrich Distribution and Exploitation in the Arabian Peninsula." *Antiquity* 75 (287): 182–90.

Prag, Kay. 1984. "Continuity and Migration in the South Levant in the Late Third Millennium: A Review of T. L. Thompson and Some Other Views." *Palestine Exploration Fund Quarterly* 116: 58–68.

Pritchard, James Bennett. 1971. "The Phoenicians in their Homeland." *Expedition* 14 (1): 14–23.

———. 1978. *Recovering Sarepta, a Phoenician City: Excavations at Sarafand, Lebanon, 1969-1974, by the University Museum of the University of Pennsylvania*. Princeton. NJ: Princeton University Press.

Puech, Émile. 1998. "Inscriptions araméennes du Golfe: Failaka, Qala'at al-Bahrein et Mulayha (EAU)." *Transeuphratene* 16: 31–55.

Pulak, Cemal M. 1997. "The Uluburun Shipwreck." In *Res Maritimae: Cyprus and the Eastern Mediterranean from Prehistory to Late Antiquity*, edited by S. Swiny, R. Hohlfelder, and H. Swiny, 223–62. Atlanta, GA: American Schools of Oriental Research.

Pulsinger, Birgit. 2008. "Perlen aus dem Artemision: Mittler zwischen Mensch und Gottheit." In *Die Archäologie der ephesischen Artemis: Gestalt und Ritual eines Heiligtums*, edited by Ulrike Muss, 85–93. Vienna: Phoibos Verlag.

Quinn, Josephine Crawley. 2013. "Tophets in the 'Punic World'." In *The Tophet in the Phoenician Mediterranean*, edited by P. Xella, 29–30. Essedue.

———. 2017. *In Search of the Phoenicians*: Princeton, NJ: Princeton University Press.

Raban, Avner. 1976. "The Phoenician Jars from a Wrecked Ship off Philadelphia Village." *Srfunim* 5: 43–52.

———. 1996. "The Phoenician Harbour and 'Fishing Village' at 'Atlit." *Eretz-Israel* 25: 490–508.

———. 1997. "Phoenician Harbours in the Levant." *Michmanim* 2: 7*–27*.

———. 2000. "Conceptual Technology of Phoenician Harbours in the Levant." In *Actas del IV congreso internacional de estudios fenicios y púnicos, Cádiz 1995*, 1095–1105.

———. 2009. *The Harbour of Sebastos (Caesarea Maritima) in its Roman Mediterranean Context*. BAR International Series 1930. Oxford: British Archaeological Reports.

Rainey, Anson F. 1996. "Who is a Canaanite? A Review of the Textual Evidence." *Bulletin of the American Schools of Oriental Research* 304 (1): 1–15.

Ramón, J. 1995. *Las ánforas fenicio-púnicas del Mediterráneo central y occidental*. Publicacions Universitat de Barcelona, Collecció 2.

Rathje, Annette. 1976. "A Group of 'Phoenician' Faience Anthropomorphic Perfume Flasks." *Levant* 8 (1): 96–106.

Redissi, Taofic. 1992–93. "À propos d'une amphore égyptienne en faïence." *Africa: Série Reppal* 7–8: 325–41.

———. 2004. "Les alabastrons égyptiens et égyptisants de Carthage." *Africa* 20: 177–218.

Reed, Charles M. 2003. *Maritime Traders in the Ancient Greek World*. Cambridge: Cambridge University Press.

Reese, David S. 1988. "A New Engraved Tridacna Shell from Kish." *Journal of Near Eastern Studies* 47 (1): 35–41.

———. 2010. "Shells from Sarepta (Lebanon) and East Mediterranean Purple-Dye Production." *Mediterranean Archaeology and Archaeometry* 10 (1): 113–41.

——— and Catherine Sease. 1993. "Some Previously Unpublished Engraved Tridacna Shells." *Journal of Near Eastern Studies* 52 (2): 109–28.

——— and Catherine Sease. 2004. "Additional Unpublished Engraved Tridacna and Anadara Shells." *Journal of Near Eastern Studies* 63 (1): 29–41.

Regev, Dalit. 2013. "Egyptian Stone Objects from Miqne-Ekron: Canaanite-Phoenician Trade in Egyptian Cult-Objects and their Mediterranean Distribution." In *SOMA 2012: Identity and Connectivity. Proceedings of the 16th Symposium on Mediterranean Archaeology, Florence 2012*, edited by L. Bombardini, A. D'Agostino, G. Guarducci, Valentian Orsi, and Stefano Valentini, 103–10. Oxford: Archaeopress.

———. 2020. *New Light on Canaanite-Phoenician Pottery*. Edited by Diana Vikander Edelman, Worlds of the Ancient near East and Mediterranean. Sheffield: Equinox.

———. forthcoming. "Sidonians at Marisa." *Acts of the Conference "Images in Transition," Bern University, November 23-25, 2017.*

Reich, Ronny, Eli Shukron, and Omri Lernau. 2007. "Recent Discoveries in the City of David, Jerusalem." *Israel Exploration Journal* 57 (2): 153–69.

Reiche, Ina, Katharina Müller, Marie Albéric, Oliver Scharf, Andrea Wähning, Aniouar Bjeoumikhov, Martin Radtke, and Rolf Simon. 2013. "Discovering Vanished Paints and Naturally Formed Gold Nanoparticles on 2800 Years Old Phoenician Ivories Using SR-FF-microXRF with the Color X-ray Camera." *Analytical Chemistry* 85 (12): 5857.

Rey-Coquais, J.-P. 2000. "Inscriptions inédites de Sidon." In *Epigrafai: Miscellanea epigrafica in onore di Lidio Gasperini*, edited by G. Paci, 799–832. Tipigraf S.N.C.

Richey, Madadh. 2019. "Inscriptions." In *The Oxford Handbook of the Phoenician and Punic Mediterranean*, edited by Brian R. Doak and Carolina López-Ruiz. Oxford: Oxford University Press.

Ridgway, David. 1992. *The First Western Greeks*. Cambridge: Cambridge University Press.

———. 1997. "Nestor's Cup and the Etruscans." *Oxford Journal of Archaeology* 16 (3): 325–44.

Ritner, Robert K. 2000. "Innovations and Adaptations in Ancient Egyptian Medicine." *Journal of Near Eastern Studies* 59 (2): 107–17.

Rizio, A. 2005. "Vivara: An 'International' Port in the Bronze Age." In *Emporia: Aegeans in the Central and Eastern Mediterranean: Proceedings of the 10th International Aegean Conference, Athens, April 2004*, edited by R. Laffineur and E. Greco, 623–7. Université de Liège, Belgium.

Roebuck, Carl. 1972. "Some Aspects of Urbanization in Corinth." *Hesperia* 41 (1): 96–127.

Rolley, Claude. 1999. "Delphes: Les bronzes." *Bulletin de Correspondance Hellénique* 123 (2): 465–7.

Röllig, Wolfgang. 1992. "Asia Minor as a Bridge between East and West: The Role of the Phoenicians and Aramaeans in the Transfer of Culture." In *Greece between East and West: 10th-8th Centuries BC, Papers of the meeting at the Institute of Fine Arts, NYU 1990*, edited by Günter Kopcke and Isabelle Tokumaru, 93–102. Mainz: Verlag Philipp von Zabern.

———. 1995. "Onomastic and Palaeographic Considerations on Early Phoenician Arrow-heads." In *Actes du IIIe congres international des études phéniciennes et puniques, Tunis 1991*, edited by M'hamed Hassine Fantar and Mansour Ghaki 348–55. Tunis: Institut National du Patrimoine.

Rothenberg, Beno. 1988. *The Egyptian Mining Temple at Timna.* London: Institute for Archaeo-Metallurgical Studies, Institute of Archaeology, University College London.

Rotroff, Susan I. 1997. *The Athenian Agora 29. Hellenistic Pottery: Athenian and Imported Wheelmade Table Ware and Related Material. Results of Excavations Conducted by the American School of Classical Studies at Athens.*

Rougemont, Françoise. 2008. "The Textile Production and the Mycenaean Sanctuaries." In *Crossing Borders: Proceedings of the 7th, 8th and 9th International Workshops, Athens 1997-1999*, edited by C. Gillis and B. Sjöberg, 287–303. Jonsered: Åström.

Rubio-Moraga, Angela, Raquel Castillo-López, Lourdes Gómez-Gómez, and Oussama Ahrazem. 2009. "Saffron is a Monomorphic Species as Revealed by RAPD, ISSR and Microsatellite Analyses." *BMC Research Notes* 2 (1): 189.

Russell, Anthony, and Arthur Bernard Knapp. 2017. "Sardinia and Cyprus: An Alternative View on Cypriotes in the Central Mediterranean." *Papers of the British School at Rome* 85: 1–35.

Rutter, Jeremy B. 2008. "The Anatolian Roots of Early Helladic III Drinking Behavior." In *The Aegean in the Neolithic, Chalcolithic and the Early Bronze Age, October 13th-19th 1997, Urla-İzmir (Turkey)*, edited by Hayat Erkanal, Harald Hauptmann, Vasıf Şahoğlu, and Rıza Tuncel. Ankara Üniversitesi Sualti Arkeolojik Arastirma ve Uygulama Merkezi.

Sáez Romero, Antonio M. 2017. "Contando la historia: Experiencias de cuantificación y análisis volumétrico en centros artesanales púnicos de la Bahía de Cádiz." *Archivo Español de Arqueología* 90: 219–46.

——— Max Luaces, and Elena Moreno. 2016. "Late Punic or Early Roman? A 2nd Century BC Ceramic Assemblage from Gadir/Gades (Cádiz Bay, Spain)." *Herom* 5: 26–77.

Saggs, Henry W. F. 1955. "The Nimrud Letters, 1952." *Iraq* 17: 21–56, 126–60.

Sagona, Claudia. 1980. "Middle Bronze Faience Vessels from Palestine." *Zeitschrift des Deutschen Palästina-Vereins* 96: 101–20.

———. 2014. "Phoenician Settlement: How it Unfolded in Malta." *CIPOA* 2: 351–72.

Sakellarakis, Jannis A. 1993. "Ivory Trade in the Aegean in the 8th Century BCE." In *Biblical Archaeology Today: Proceedings of the Second International Congress on Biblical Archaeology, Jerusalem 1990*, edited by A. Biran and Joseph Aviram, 345–66. Jerusalem: Israel Exploration Society.

———, Efi Sapouna-Sakellaraki, and Nakou Foundation. 1997. *Archanes: Minoan Crete in a New Light.* Athens: Ammos Publications.

Salles, Jean-François. 1993. "Hellénisme et traditions orientales à Failaka." In *Arabia Antiqua: Hellenistic Centres around Arabia*, edited by A. Invernizzi and J.-F. Salles, 223–55. Rome: Istituto italiano per il Medio ed Estremo Oriente.

———. 2002. "Adaptation culturelle des céramiques hellénistiques? Importations et imitations de produits occidentaux en Inde." In *Céramiques hellénistiques et romaines: Productions et diffusion en Méditerranée orientale (Chypre, Égypte et Côte syro-palestinienne)*, edited by F. Blondé, P. Ballet, and J.-F. Salles, 189–212. Lyon: Maison de l'Orient Méditerranéen-Jean Pouilloux.

———, Yves Calvet, and Dominique Beyer. 1986. *Failaka: Fouilles françaises 1984-1985.* Mission archéologique française à Koweit. Travaux de la Maison de l'Orient et de la Méditerranéen 12. Lyon: Maison de l'Orient Méditerranéen.

Salmon, John B. 1984. *Wealthy Corinth: A History of the City to 338 BC*: Oxford: Oxford University Press.

Sannibale, Maurizio. 2014. "Orientalizing Etruria." In *The Etruscan World*, edited by Jean M. Turfa, 147–81. London: Routledge.
Sass, Benjamin. 1991. *Studia Alphabetica: On the Origin and Early History of the Northwest Semitic, South Semitic and Greek Alphabetic*. Fribourg: Vandenhoeck & Ruprecht.
———. 2002. "Wenamun and his Levant: 1075 BC or 925 BC?" *Ägypten und Levante/Egypt and the Levant* 12: 247–55.
———. 2005. *The Alphabet at the Turn of the Millennium: The West Semitic Alphabet* ca. *1150–850 BCE*. The Antiquity of the Arabian, Greek and Phrygian Alphabets. Tel-Aviv: Tel-Aviv University, Institute of Archaeology, Emery and Claire Yass Publications in Archaeology.
Sasson, Jack M. 1966. "Canaanite Maritime Involvement in the Second Millennium." *Journal of the American Oriental Society* 86: 126–38.
———. 1968. "Instances of Mobility among Mari Artisans." *Bulletin of the American Schools of Oriental Research* 190: 46–54.
Sauvage, Caroline, and Dennis Pardee. 2015. "L'itinéraire maritime d'une reine d'Ougarit: Note sur le texte RS 94.2406." *Syria* 92: 239–54.
Scandone, G. 1984. "Testimonianze egiziane in Fenicia dal XII al IV sec. a. C." *Rivista di Studi Fenici Roma* 12 (2): 133–63.
Schauer, Peter. 1985. "Spuren orientalischen und ägäischen Einflusses im bronzezeitlichen Nordischen Kreis." *Jahrbuch des Römisch-Germanischen Zentralmuseums Mainz* 32: 123–95.
Schlosser, Štefan. 2011. "Distillation: From Bronze Age Till Today." 38th International Conference of Slovak Society of Chemical Engineering, Tatranské Matliare, Slovakia, May.
Schmitt, Rüdiger. 2013. "Astarte, Mistress of Horses, Lady of the Chariot: The Warrior Aspect of Astarte." *Die Welt des Orients* 43 (2): 213–25.
Schmitz, P. C. 2000. "Semitic Graffiti." In *Berenike 1997: Report on the 1998 Excavations at Berenike and the Survey of the Eastern Desert, Including Excavations in Wadi Kalalat*, edited by S. E. Sidebotham and W. Z. Wendrich, 183–9. Leiden: Research School of Asian, African, and Amerindian Studies (CNWS).
Schubart, Hermanfrid, and Gerta Maass-Lindemann. 2017. *Morro de Mezquitilla: Die phönizisch-punische Niederlassung an der Algarrobo-Mündung*. Madrider Beiträge, Vol. 33. Wiesbaden: Reichert.
Sconzo, Paola. 2016. "The Archaic Cremation Cemetery on the Island of Motya: A Case-Study for Tracing Early Colonial Phoenician Culture and Mortuary Traditions in the West Mediterranean." In *Karthago Dialoge: Karthago und der punische Mittelmeerraum. Kulturkontakte und Kulturtransfers im 1. Jahrtausend vor Christus*, edited by Frerich Schön and Hanni Töpfer, 315–28. Tübingen: Mohr.
Scott, John C. 2019. "Phoenicians: The Quickening of Western Civilization." *Comparative Civilizations Review* 81 (1): 5.
SEG. "Editorial Board, 'Proper Names', in: Supplementum Epigraphicum Graecum, Current editors: A. T. N. R. A. Chaniotis Corsten Papazarkadas Tybout. Consulted online on 22 March 2017." *Supplementum Epigraphicum Graecum*.
Seland, Eivind Heldaas. 2007. "Red Sea and Indian Ocean: Ports and their Hinterland." In *Natural Resources and Cultural Connections of the Red Sea*, edited by J. Starkey, P. Starkey, and T. Wilkinson, 211–8.
———. 2014. "Archaeology of Trade in the Western Indian Ocean, 300 BC–AD 700." *Journal of Archaeological Research* 22 (4): 367–402.
———. 2016. "The Periplus of the Erythraean Sea: A Network Approach." *Asian Review of World Histories* 4: 191–205.
Serpico, M. 1999. "New Kingdom Canaanite Amphorae Fragments from Buhen." In *Studies on Ancient Egypt in Honor of H. S. Smith*, edited by A. Leahy and J. Tait, 267–72. London.: Egypt Exploration Society
——— and R. White. 2000a. "Resins, Amber and Bitumen." In *Ancient Egyptian Materials and Technology*, edited by P. T. Nicholson and Ian Shaw, 430–74. Cambridge: Cambridge University Press.
——— and R. White. 2000b. "Oil, Fat and Wax." In *Ancient Egyptian Materials and Technology*, edited by P. T. Nicholson and Ian Shaw, 390–429. Cambridge: Cambridge University Press.

———, J. Bourriau, L. Smith, Y. Goren, B. Stern, and C. Heron. 2003. "Commodities and Containers: A Project to Study Canaanite Amphorae Imported Into Egypt during the New Kingdom." In *The Synchronisation of Civilisations in the Eastern Mediterranean in the Second Millennium BC*, edited by M. Bietak, 365–75. Vienna: Verlag der Österreichischen Akademie der Wissenschaften.

Sheikhi, Mahta. 2014. "Study of Mythical Creatures of Ziwiye Ivory Plaques in Sanandaj Museum and National Museum of Iran." In *Proceedings of the 8th International Congress on the Archaeology of the Ancient Near East, 30 April–4 May 2012, University of Warsaw*, Vol. 2, *Excavation and Progress Reports*, 743–55. Wiesbaden: Harrassowitz Verlag.

Shelmerdine, C. W. 1985. *The Perfume Industry of Mycenaean Pylos*. Göteborg: Åström.

Sherratt, A., and S. Sherratt. 1991. "From Luxuries to Commodities: The Nature of Mediterranean Bronze Age Systems." In *Bronze Age Trade in the Mediterranean*, edited by N. H. Gale, 351–386. Jonsered: Åström.

Sherratt, Susan, and Andrew Sherratt. 1993. "The Growth of the Mediterranean Economy in the Early First Millennium BC." In *Ancient Trade: New Perspectives. World Archaeology* 24.3, edited by J. Oates, 361–78.

Shipley, G. 1993. "Distance, Development, Decline? World-Systems Analysis and the 'Hellenistic" World'." In *Centre and Periphery in the Hellenistic World*, edited by P. Bilde, 271–84. Studies in Hellenistic Civilization IV. Aarhus: Aarhus University Press.

Silver, Minna. 2014. "Equid Burials in Archaeological Contexts in the Amorite, Hurrian and Hyksos Cultural Intercourse." *ARAM* 26: 335–55.

Simon, Erika. 2006. "Gods in Harmony." In *The Religion of the Etruscans*, edited by N. Thomson de Grummond and E. Simon, 45–65. Austin: University of Texas Press.

Singer-Avitz, Lily, and Yoram Eshel. 1999. "Beersheba: A Gateway Community in Southern Arabian Long-Distance Trade in the Eighth Century BCE." *Tel Aviv* 26: 3–74.

Singer, Itamar. 2002. "On a Hittite Burial." *Beer-Sheva* 15: 47*–58*.

———. 2006. "The Hittites and the Bible Revisited." In *"I Will Speak the Riddles of Ancient Times": Archaeological and Historical Studies in Honor of Amihai Mazar on the Occasion of his Sixtieth Birthday*, edited by Aren M. Maeir and Pierre de Miroschedji, 723–56. Winona Lake, IN: Eisenbrauns.

Skarpelis, Nikos, and Ariadne Argyraki. 2009. "Geology and Origin of Supergene Ore at the Lavrion Pb-Ag-Zn Deposit, Attica, Greece." *Resource Geology* 59 (1): 1–14.

Skon-Jedele, N. J. 1994. *Aigyptiaka: A Catalogue of Egyptian and Egyptianizing Objects Excavated from Greek Archaeological Sites, Ca. 1100–525 BC, with Historical Commentary*: Philadelphia: University of Pennsylvania.

Smith, Anthony D. 1986. *The Ethnic Origins of Nations*. Oxford: Wiley-Blackwell.

Smith, Christopher. 1998. "Traders and Artisans in Archaic Central Italy." In *Trade, Traders and the Ancient City*, edited by H. Parkins and Christopher Smith, 31–51. London and New York: Routledge.

Smith, J. 2008. "Cyprus, The Phoenicians and Kition." In *Beyond the Homeland: Markers in Phoenician Chronology*, edited by C. Sagona, 261–303. Leuven, Paris, and Dudley, MA: Peeters.

Smith, L. M. V., J. Bourriau, Y. Goren, M. J. Hughes, and M. Serpico. 2004. "The Provenance of Canaanite Amphorae Found at Memphis and Amarna in the New Kingdom: Results 2000–2002." In *Invention and Innovation: The Social Context of Technological Change 2: Egypt, the Aegean and the Near East, 1650–1150 BC*, edited by J. Bourriau and J. Phillips, 55–77. Oxford: Oxbow Books.

Sommer, Michael. 2007. "Networks of Commerce and Knowledge in the Iron Age: The Case of the Phoenicians." *Mediterranean Historical Review* 22 (1): 97–111.

Soriga, Elena. 2017. "Mari(ne) Purple: Western Textile Technology in the Middle Bronze Age Syria." *Treasures from the Sea: Sea-silk and Shell Purple Dye in Antiquity*, edited by Hedvig Landenius Enegren and Francesco Meo. Oxford: Oxbow Books.

Souckova-Siegelova, Jana. 2001. "Treatment and Usage of Iron in the Hittite Empire in the 2nd Millennium BC." *Mediterranean Archaeology* 14: 189–92.

Souter, A. P. 2008. "Garum Production in Lusitania." In *SOMA 2005: Proceedings of the IX Symposium on Mediterranean Archaeology, Chieti (Italy), 24–26 February 2005*, edited by O. Menozzi, M. L. Di Marzio, and D. Fossataro, 275–82.

Spaer, Maud. 2001. *Ancient Glass in the Israel Museum: Beads and Other Small Objects*. Jerusalem: Israel Museum. British Archaeological Reports International Series. Oxford: BAR Publishing.

Sparks, Rachael Thyrza. 1996. "Egyptian Stone Vessels in Syro-Palestine during the Second Millennium BC and their Impact on the Local Stone Vessel Industry." *Abr-Naharaim Sup.* 5: 51–66.

Stager, Lawrence E. 2003. "Phoenician Shipwrecks in the Deep Sea." In *Sea Routes: Interconnections in the Mediterranean 16th–6th c. BC. Proceedings of the International Symposium, Rethymnon 2002*, edited by N. Stampolidis and V. Karageorghis, 233–247. Athens: University of Crete and the A. G. Leventis Foundation.

Stampolidis, Nicolas Chr. 2004. *Eleutherna. Polis-Acropolis-Necropolis*. Athens: Museum of Cycladic Art.

——— and Antonios Kotsonas. 2006. "Phoenicians in Crete." In *Ancient Greece: From the Mycenaean Palaces to the Age of Homer*, edited by I. Lemos and S. Deger-Jalkotzy, 337–60. Edinburgh: Edinburgh University Press.

Steadman, Sharon R., and Jennifer C. Ross. 2010. *Agency and Identity in the Ancient Near East: New Paths Forward*. Sheffield: Equinox.

Steen, Eveline van der. 2010. "Judha, Masos and Hayl: The Importance of Ethnohistory and Oral Traditions." In *Historical Biblical Archaeology and the Future: The New Pragmatism*, edited by Thomas E Levy. Sheffield: Equinox.

Stein, Gil. 1999. *Rethinking World-Systems: Diasporas, Colonies, and Interaction in Uruk Mesopotamia*: Tucson: University of Arizona Press.

Stern, Ben, Carl Heron, Tory Tellefsen, and Margaret Serpico. 2008. "New Investigations into the Uluburun Resin Cargo." *Journal of Archaeological Science* 35 (8): 2188–2203.

Stern, Ephraim, and Yitzhak Magen. 1984. "A Pottery Group of the Persian Period from Qadum in Samaria." *Bulletin of the American Schools of Oriental Research* 253: 9–27.

Stieglitz, Robert R. 1994. "The Minoan Origin of Tyrian Purple." *The Biblical Archaeologist* 57 (1): 46–54.

Stos-Gale, Z. A., and N. H. Gale. 1982. "The Sources of Mycenaean Silver and Lead." *Journal of Field Archaeology* 9 (4): 67–485.

Strøm, Ingrid. 1992. "Evidence from the Sanctuaries." In *Greece between East and West: 10th-8th Centuries BC, Papers of the meeting at the Institute of Fine Arts, NYU 1990*, edited by Günter Kopcke and Isabelle Tokumaru, 46–60. Mainz: Verlag Philipp von Zabern.

Sugerman, M. 2009. "Trade and Power in Late Bronze Age Canaan." In *Exploring the Longue Durée: Essays in Honor of Lawrance E. Stager*, edited by D. J. Schloen, 439–48. Winona Lake, IN: Eisenbrauns.

Sukenik, Naama, D. Iluz, Zohar Amar, A. Varvak, and S. Bar. 2017a. "New Evidence of the Purple-Dye Industry at Tel Shiqmona, Israel." *Archaeometry* 59 (4): 775–85.

———, David Iluz, Zohar Amar, Alexander Varvak, Vanessa Workman, Orit Shamir, and Erez Ben-Yosef. 2017b. "Early Evidence (Late 2nd Millennium BCE) of Plant-Based Dyeing of Textiles from Timna, Israel." *PLOS ONE* 12 (6): e0179014.

Swiny, Stuart. 2006. "Cypriot Anthropomorphic Figurines of a Certain Type." In *Confronting the Past: Archaeological and Historical Essays on Ancient Israel in Honor of William G. Dever*, edited by G. Gitin, J. Edward Wright, and J. P. Dessel, 181–6. Winona Lake, IN: Eisenbrauns.

Taloni, Maria. 2015. "Phoenician Metal Jugs." In *Phoenician Bronzes in Mediterranean*, edited by F. Javier Jiménez Avila, 119–46. Madrid: Real Academia de la Historia Madrid.

Tanner, Jeremy J. 2003. "Finding the Egyptian in Early Greek Art." In *Ancient Perspectives on Egypt*, edited by Roger J. Matthews and Cornelia Roemer, 115–44. London: UCL Press.

Teba, Tarek, Dimitris Theodossopoulos, and James Crow. 2016. "Exposing the Sacred Monumentality in Ugarit: Remodelling the Temple of Baal." 10th International Conference on Structural Analysis of Historical Constructions: SAHC 2016.

Teichner, Felix, and Lluis Pons Pujol. 2008. "Roman Amphora Trade across the Straits of Gibraltar: An Ancient 'Anti-Economic Practice'?" *Oxford Journal of Archaeology* 27 (3): 303–14.

Teixidor, Javier. 1980. "L'assemblée législative en Phénicie d'après les inscriptions." *Syria*: 453–64.

Tekkök, B. 2004. "The Pottery Workshops at Eceabat in Northwest Anatolia: The Hellenistic and Roman Traditions Continue." In *Ethnoarchaeological Investigations in Rural Anatolia*, edited by T. Takaoğlu, 97–114. Istanbul: Ege Yayinlari.

Thomson de Grummond, Nancy. 1985. "The Etruscan Mirror." *Notes in the History of Art* 4 (2–3): 26–35.

Thuillier, Jean-Paul. 1985. "Nouvelles découvertes de bucchero à Carthage." In *Colloque sur la céramique antique: Carthage 1980. CEDAC*, 155–63. Carthage: Consiglio Nazionale delle Ricerche.

Tilly, Charles. 2005. *Trust and Rule*: Cambridge: Cambridge University Press.

———. 2010. "Cities, States, and Trust Networks: Chapter 1 of Cities and States in World History." In *Contention and Trust in Cities and States*, edited by Michael Hanagan and Chris Tilly, 1–16. New York: Springer.

Tite, Michel Stanley. 2008. "The Scientific Examination of Aegean Vitreous Materials: Problems and Potential." In *Vitreous Materials in the Late Bronze Age Aegean*, edited by C. M. Jackson and E. C. Wager, 105–25. Oxford: Oxbow Books

——— and Andrew Shortland. 2008. *Production Technology of Faience and Related Early Vitreous Materials*. Oxford University School of Archaeology: Monograph 72. Oxford: Oxford University Press.

Tomber, R. S., and V. Begley. 2000. "Indian Pottery Sherds." In *Berenike 1997: Report on the 1998 Excavations at Berenike and the Survey of the Eastern Desert, Including Excavations in Wadi Kalalat*, edited by S. E. Sidebotham and W. Z. Wendrich, 149–67. Leiden: Research School of Asian, African, and Amerindian Studies (CNWS).

Torres Ortiz, Mariano. 2014. "Taršiš, Tartessos, Turdetania." In *Iberia. Protohistory of the Far West of Europe: From Neolithic to Roman Conquest*, edited by Martín Almagro Gorbea, 251–83. Fundación Atapuerca, Universidad de Burgos, Servicio de Publicaciones e Imagen Institucional.

Touchais, Gilles, Sandrine Huber, Yannis Varalis, and Anna Philippa-Touchais. 1999. "Chronique des fouilles et découvertes archéologiques en Grèce en 1998." *Bulletin de Correspondance Hellénique* 123 (123): 635–848.

Tower Hollis, Susan. 2009. "Hathor and Isis in Byblos in the Second and First Millennia BCE." *Journal of Ancient Egyptian Interconnections* 1 (2): 1–8.

Trakadas, Athena. 2005. "The Archaeological Evidence for Fish Processing in the Western Mediterranean." In *Ancient Fishing and Fish Processing in the Black Sea Region*, edited by T. Bekker-Nielsen, 47–82. Aarhus: Aarhus University Press.

———. 2015. *Fish-salting in the Northwest Maghreb in Antiquity*: Oxford: Archaeopress.

Trentacoste, Angela, Rebecca Nicholson, and Dimitra Mylona. 2018. "The Bountiful Sea: Fish Processing and Consumption in Mediterranean Antiquity." *Journal of Maritime Archaeology* 13: 207–17.

Tripati, Sila. 2017. "Seafaring Archaeology of the East Coast of India and Southeast Asia during the Early Historical Period." *Ancient Asia* 8.

Tusa, Sebastiano, and Jeffrey Royal. 2012. "The Landscape of the Naval Battle at the Egadi Islands (241 BC)." *Journal of Roman Archaeology* 25: 7–48.

Tusa, Vincenzo. 1965. "La questione fenicio-punica in Sicilia." In *Western Galilee and the Coast of Galilee: The Nineteenth Archaeological Convention October 1963*, 30–41. Jerusalem: Israel Exploration Society.

———. 1983. "La Sicilia fenicio-punica." *Dialogues d'histoire ancienne* 9 (1): 237–85.

Tylecote, Ronald Frank. 1982. "Metallurgy in Punic and Roman Carthage." In *Mines et fonderies antiques de la Gaule. Table ronde du CNRS Toulouse 1980*, edited by Claude Domergue, 259–78. Paris: CNRS.

Van de Mieroop, Marc. 2005. "The Eastern Mediterranean in Early Antiquity." In *Rethinking the Mediterranean*, edited by W. V. Harris, 117–40. Oxford: Oxford University Press.

Van den Broek, Roelof. 1972. *The Myth of the Phoenix According to Classical and Early Christian Traditions*. Translated by I. Seeger. Études préliminaires aux religions orientales dans l'empire romain 24. Leiden: Brill.

Van der Meer, Bouke. 2016. "Elite ideology in Praeneste: On the Imagery of Pear-Shaped Mirrors and *Cistae*." *BABESCH* 91: 105–28.

Van der Toorn, Karel, Bob Becking, and Pieter Willem Van Der Horst. 1999. *Dictionary of Deities and Demons in the Bible*: Grand Rapids, MI: Wm. B. Eerdmans Publishing.

Van Dommelen, Peter, and Stefano Finocchi. 2008. "Sardinia: Divergent Landscapes." In *Rural Landscape of the Punic World*, edited by Peter van Dommelen and C. Gómez Bellard, 159–201. Sheffield: Equinox.

Van Horn, Mark. 2017. "Re-forging the Past: Interpreting Phoenician Iron Production at Tel Akko, Israel." MA, Pennsylvania State University.

Veldhuijzen, H. A. 2012. "Just a Few Rusty Bits: The Innovation of Iron in the Eastern Mediterranean in the 2nd and 1st Millennia BC." In *Eastern Mediterranean Metallurgy and Metalwork in the Second Millennium BC: A Conference in Honour of James D. Muhly, Nicosia, October 2009*, edited by Vasiliki Kassianidou and George Papasavvas, 237–20. Oxford: Oxbow Books.

Ventris, Michael, and John Chadwick. 1956. *Documents in Mycenaean Greek*. Cambridge: Cambridge University Press.

Vercoutter, Jean. 1945. *Les objets égyptiens et égyptisants du mobilier funéraire carthaginois*. Bibliothèque archéologique et historique 40. Paris: Geuthner.

Versluys, Miguel John. 2016. "Exploring Aegyptiaca and their Material Agency throughout Global History." In *The Routledge Handbook of Archaeology and Globalization*, edited by Tamar Hodos, Alexander Geurds, and Paul J. Lane, 74–89. London: Routledge.

Vianello, Andrea. 2005. *Late Bronze Age Mycenaean and Italic Products in the West Mediterranean: A Social and Economic Analysis*. BAR International Series 1439. Oxford: Archaeopress.

Vigo, Matteo. 2014. "The Use of (Perfumed) Oil in Hittite Rituals with Particular Emphasis on Funerary Practices." *Journal of Intercultural and Interdisciplinary Archaeology* 1: 25–37.

Villing, Alexandra, and Udo Schlotzhauer, eds. 2006. *Naukratis: Greek Diversity in Egypt. Studies on East Greek Pottery and Exchange in the Eastern Mediterranean*. British Museum Research Publication 162. London: British Museum.

Viviers, Didier. 1999. "Economy and Territorial Dynamics in Crete from the Archaic to the Hellenistic Period." In *From Minoan Farmers to Roman Traders: Sidelights on the Economy of Ancient Crete*, edited by Angelos Chaniotis, 221–33. Stuttgart: Steiner Verlag.

Vonhoff, C. 2015. "Phoenician Bronzes in Cyprus." In *Phoenician Bronzes in Mediterranean*, edited by F. Javier Jiménez Avila, 261–94. Madrid: Real Academia de la Historia.

Waarsenburg, D. J., R. F. Docter, and C. Briese. 1992–93. "Astarte and Monkey Representations in the Italian Orientalizing Period: The Amber Sculptures from Satricum." In *Die Akten des Internationalen Kolloquiums "Interactions in the Iron Age: Phoenicians, Greeks and the Indigenous Peoples of the Western Mediterranean," Amsterdam 1992*, 33–71. Mainz: Philipp von Zabern

Wachsmann, Shelley, Richard K. Dunn, John R. Hale, Robert L. Hohlfelder, Lawrence B. Conyers, Eileen G. Ernenwein, Payson Sheets, Maria Luisa Pienheiro Blot, Filipe Castro, and Dan Davis. 2009. "The Palaeo-Environmental Contexts of Three Possible Phoenician Anchorages in Portugal." *International Journal of Nautical Archaeology* 38 (2): 221–53.

Walbank, Michael B. 1985. "Athens, Carthage and Tyre (IG ii^2 342+)." *Zeitschrift für Papyrologie und Epigraphik* 59: 107–11.

Wallerstein, Immanuel. 1974. *The Modern World-System I: Capitalist Agriculture and the Origins of the European World-Economy in the Sixteenth Century*: New York: Academic Press.

Wallinga, H. T. 2005. *Xerxes' Greek Adventure: The Naval Perspective*. Mnemosyne, Bibliotheca Classica Batava. Supplementum. Leiden and Boston: Brill.

Ward, Cheryl. 2003. "Pomegranates in Eastern Mediterranean Contexts during the Late Bronze Age." *World Archaeology* 34 (3): 529–41.

Ward, William A. 1972. "The Shasu 'Bedouin': Notes on a Recent Publication." *Journal of the Economic and Social History of the Orient* 15 (1/2): 35.

Wasmuth, M., and B. Ögüt. 2010. "A Syro-Hittite Weather-God in Egypt?" In *Proceedings of the 6th International Congress of the Archaeology of the Ancient Near East, 2009, "Sapienza", Università di Roma*, Vol. 1, *Near Eastern Archaeology in the Past, Present and Future*, edited by P. Matthiae, F. Pinnock, L. Nigro, and N. Marchetti, 567–78. Wiesbaden: Verlag Harrassowitz.

Wasserman, Stanley, and Katherine Faust. 1994. *Social Network Analysis: Methods and Applications*: Cambridge: Cambridge University Press.

Wathelet, Paul. 1983. "Les Phéniciens et la tradition homérique." *Studia Phoenicia* 1–2: 235–43.

Watson, Wilfred G. E. 1999. "Wonderful Wine (KTU 1.22 i 17–20)." *Ugarit-Forschungen* 31: 777–84.

Webster, G. S. 1992. "Toward the Study of Colonial–Native Relations in Sardinia from c. 1000 BC–AD 456." In *Sardinia in the Mediterranean: A Footprint in The sea. Studies in Sardinian Archaeology Presented to Miriam S. Balmuth*, edited by M. Teglund, 448–73. Sheffield: Sheffield Academic Press.

Weingarten, Judith. 2005. "How Many Seals Make a Heap: Seals and Interconnections on Prepalatial Crete." *Aegaeum* 25: 759–66.

Weinstein, James M. 1981. "The Egyptian Empire in Palestine: A Reassessment." *BASOR* 241: 1–28.

Weisgerber, G. 2006. "The Mineral Wealth of Ancient Arabia and its Use I: Copper Mining and Smelting at Feinan and Timna. Comparison and Evaluation of Techniques, Production and Strategies." *Arabian Archaeology and Epigraphy* 17: 1–30.

Weissbein, Itamar, Yosef Garfinkel, Michael G. Hasel, Martin G. Klingbeil, Baruch Brandl, and Hadas Misgav. 2020. "The Level VI North-east Temple at Tel Lachish." *Levant* 51 (1): 76–104.

White Muscarella, Oscar 1980. *The Catalogue of Ivories from Hasanlu, Iran*. Philadelphia: University of Pennsylvania, University Museum.

Whitewright, Julian. 2007. "How Fast Is Fast? Technology, Trade and Speed under Sail in the Roman Red Sea." In *Natural Resources and Cultural Connections of the Red Sea*, edited by J. Starkey, P. Starkey, and T. Wilkinson, 77–87. BAR International Series 1661. Society of Arabian Studies Monographs 5. Oxford: Archaeopress.

Whitley, James. 2002. "Objects with Attitude: Biographical Facts and Fallacies in the Study of Late Bronze Age and Early Iron Age Warrior Graves." *Cambridge Archaeological Journal* 12: 217–32.

Wiener, Malcolm H. 2007. "Homer and History: Old Questions, New Evidence." *Aegaeum* 28: 3–34.

Will, Elizabeth Lyding. 2004. "Mediterranean Amphoras in India." In *Transport Amphorae and Trade in the Eastern Mediterranean*, edited by J. Lund and J. Eiring. The Danish Institute at Athens.

Willemsen, S. L. 2013. "A Changing Funerary Ritual at Crustumerium (ca. 625–500 BC)." In *Research into Pre-Roman Burial Grounds in Italy*, edited by A. J. Nijboer, P. A. J Attema, S. L. Willemsen, and J. F. Seubers, 35–50. Leuven: Peeters.

Wilson, Penelope. 1997. *A Ptolemaic Lexikon: A Lexicographical Study of the Texts in the Temple of Edfu*. OLA 78. Leuven: Peeters.

——— and Gregory Gilbert. 2007. "Sais and its Trading Relations with the Eastern Mediterranean." In *Moving across Borders: Foreign Relations, Religion and Cultural Interactions in the Ancient Mediterranean*, edited by P. Kousoulis and K. Magliveras, 251–65. Leuven: Peeters.

Winter, Irene J. 1976. "Phoenician and North Syrian Ivory Carving in Historical Context: Questions of Style and Distribution." *Iraq* 38 (1): 1–22.

———. 1981. "Is There a South Syrian Style of Ivory Carving in the Early First Millennium BC?" *Iraq* 43 (2): 101–30.

———. 1995. "Homer's Phoenicians: History, Ethnography, or Literary Trope? (A Perspective on early Orientalism)." In *The Ages of Homer: A Tribute to Emily Townsend Vermeule*, edited by J. B. Carter and S. P. Morris, 247–71. Austin: University of Texas Press.

———. 2009. "Phoenician and North Syrian Ivory Carving in Historical Context: Questions of Style and Distribution." In *On Art in the Ancient Near East*, 185–224. Leiden: Brill.

Wolfson, Elizabeth Graff. 2018. *Pictorial Representations of Monkeys and Simianesque Creatures in Greek Art*: Columbia, MO: University of Missouri-Columbia.

Wood, Jonathan Robert. 2019a. "Semi-refined Silver for the Silversmiths of the Iron Age Mediterranean: A Mechanism for the Elusiveness of Iberian Silver." *Trabajos de Prehistoria* 76: 272–85.

———. 2019b. "The Transmission of Silver and Silver Extraction Technology across the Mediterranean in Late Prehistory: An Archaeological Science Approach to Investigating the Westward Expansion of the Phoenicians." University College London.

———, Ignacio Montero-Ruiz, and Marcos Martinón-Torres. 2019. "From Iberia to the Southern Levant: The Movement of Silver across the Mediterranean in the Early Iron Age." *Journal of World Prehistory* 32: 1–31.

Woudhuizen, Fred. 2007. "On the Byblos Script." *Ugarit-Forschungen* 39: 689–756.

Xella, Paolo. 2013. "'Tophet': An Overall Interpretation." In *The Tophet in the Phoenician Mediterranean*, edited by P Xella, 259–81. Essedue.

———. 2019. "Religion." In *The Oxford Handbook of the Phoenician and Punic Mediterranean*, edited by Brian R. Doak and Carolina López-Ruiz. Oxford: Oxford University Press.

Yahalom-Mack, Naama, Yuval Gadot, Adi Eliyahu-Behar, Shlomit Bechar, Sana Shilstein, and Israel Finkelstein. 2014. "Metalworking at Hazor: A Long-Term Perspective." *Oxford Journal of Archaeology* 33 (1): 19–45.

Yardeni, Ada. 1994. "Maritime Trade and Royal Accountancy in an Erased Customs Account from 475 BCE on the Ahiqar Scroll from Elephantine." *BASOR 324*: 67–78.

Yener, Aslihan K. 2008. "Revisiting Kestel Mine and Göltepe: The Dynamics of Local Provisioning of Tin during the Early Bronze Age." In *Ancient Mining in Turkey and the Eastern Mediterranean*, edited by Ü. Yalçin, H. Özbal, and A. Günham Paşamehmetoğlu, 57–64. Ankara: Atılım University.

———. 2009. "Strategic Industries and Tin in the Ancient Near East: Anatolia Updated." *TÜBA-AR Turkish Academy of Sciences Journal of Archaeology* 12: 143–54.

Yon, Marguerite, and William A. P. Childs. 1997. "Kition in the Tenth to Fourth Centuries BC." *Bulletin of the American Schools of Oriental Research* 308 (1): 9–17.

Young, G. K. 2001. *Rome's Eastern Trade: International Commerce and Imperial Policy, 31 BC–AD 305*. London: Routledge.

Zaccagnini, Carlo. 1983. "Patterns of Mobility among Ancient Near Eastern Craftsmen." *Journal of Near Eastern Studies* 42 (4): 245–64.

Zadok, R. 1985. *Geographical Names According to New- and Late-Babylonian Texts*, Vol. 8, *Répertoire Géographique des Textes Cunéiformes: Tübinger Atlas des Vorderen Orients (Tavo)*. Wiesbaden: Dr Ludwig Reichert Verlag.

Zalloua, Pierre, Catherine J. Collins, Anna Gosling, Simone Andrea Biagini, Benjamí Costa, Olga Kardailsky, Lorenzo Nigro, Wissam Khalil, Francesc Calafell, and Elizabeth Matisoo-Smith. 2018. "Ancient DNA of Phoenician Remains Indicates Discontinuity in the Settlement History of Ibiza." *Scientific Reports* 8 (1): 1–15.

Zamora López, José Ángel 2015. "Bronze and Metallurgy in Phoenician Sources." In *Phoenician Bronzes in Mediterranean*, edited by Javier Jiménez Ávila, 29–45. Madrid: Real Academia de la Historia.

Zimmermann, Thomas. 2007. "Anatolia as a Bridge from North to South? Recent Research in the Hatti Heartland." *Anatolian Studies* 57: 65–75.

Zimmerman Munn, M. L. 2003. "Corinthian Trade with the Punic West in the Classical Period." In *Corinth: The Cemetery, 1896–1996*, edited by C. K. Williams II and N. Bookidis, 195–215. Princeton, NJ: Princeton University Press.

Zohar, Irit, and Michal Artzy. 2019. "The Role of Preserved Fish: Evidence of Fish Exploitation, Processing and Long-Term Preservation in the Eastern Mediterranean during the Late Bronze Age (14th–13th Century BCE)." *Journal of Archaeological Science: Reports* 23: 900–9.

Zucca, Raimondo. 1987. *Bronzi nuragici da Tharros*. Provincia di Cagliari, Assessorato alla Cultura.

Zuckerman, Daphna. 2011. "An Ostrich Egg Container in the Hecht Museum Collection." *Michmanim* 23: 7*–14*.

Index

H

I

J

K

L

M

N

O

P

Q

R

S

www.ingramcontent.com/pod-product-compliance
Ingram Content Group UK Ltd.
Pitfield, Milton Keynes, MK11 3LW, UK
UKHW061542051026
15625UKWH00011B/571

* 9 7 8 1 7 8 1 7 9 8 2 5 6 *